STRING TRIMMER
SERVICE MANUAL

(First Edition)

CONTAINS

- TROUBLESHOOTING

- MAINTENANCE

- OPERATING SAFETY

- SERVICE & REPAIR

Published by

INTERTEC PUBLISHING CORPORATION
P.O. Box 12901, Overland Park, Kansas 66212

©Copyright 1988 by Intertec Publishing Corp. Printed in the United States of America.
Library of Congress Catalog Card Number 87-81178

Cover photograph courtesy of
Hoffco, Inc.

CONTENTS

───── GENERAL MAINTENANCE, SERVICE AND REPAIR ─────

───── TRIMMER SERVICE SECTIONS ─────

───────────────ENGINE SERVICE SECTIONS───────────────

GENERAL MAINTENANCE AND REPAIR

TYPES

Line trimmers and brush cutters are manufactured for every use from the smallest home lawn to large scale commercial landscaping and grounds-care operation.

The drive may be electrical from rechargeable batteries, from 110 volt AC current delivered through an extension cable or by a two-stroke air-cooled gasoline engine.

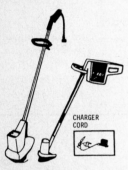

Battery powered trimmers are fine for light trimming, but can't handle heavy grass, weeds or brush. Most models must be recharged after about 45 minutes of operation. A full recharging may require 15 to 24 hours.

Electrical units operating on 110 volt AC current may have more power reserve than battery powered units, however, extension cord length should not exceed 100 feet even when using 14 gage or larger wire.

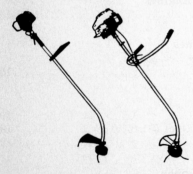

Gasoline engine powered trimmers may be used virtually anywhere that an operator can walk, but usually require more maintenance than a similar electrical unit.

Monofilament spin trimmers use spinning nylon line (or lines) which is 0.050 to 0.130 inches in diameter. It's not fishing line which requires high tensile strength compared with trimmer line which must resist bending against plants. Spinning monofilament line actually breaks plants off rather than cutting them, much like breaking a plant by striking the stem with a stick.

Depending on head design, trimmers may have one, two, three, or even four lines extended for cutting at the same time. As the line wears back or breaks off, more line may be extended manually or automatically. Manual models require trimmer engine to be stopped. Loosening a lock knob or screw and rotating a housing advances new line. On semi-automatic trimmer heads, line is advanced by tapping the trimmer head on the ground with engine running at full rpm while others require quick adjustment of throttle speed. A cutoff blade on the trimmer shield prevents automatic extenders from letting out too much line, which would then overload the trimmer and reduce cutting efficiency. The motor or engine must be stopped before line is manually extended on other trimmers.

Tall, tough weeds require a weed blade that can replace the monofilament head on some heavier gasoline-powered trimmers. Some of the strongest heavy-duty units can be equipped with brush or saw blade for cutting saplings, brush and low, small tree limbs. Only trimmers designed for such use should be equipped with weed or brush blades. To avoid trimmer damage and possibly serious accidents, only the recommended weed or brush blades should be used. A blade that is too large overloads the trimmer, and the speed of some trimmers is too fast for safe blade operation.

On some power trimmers, the cutting head is attached directly to the output shaft of the engine or motor that is mounted at the lower end of the machine. This eliminates the driveshaft, bearings, etc., required if the power source is attached at the upper end of the trimmer.

A lower engine location exposes the engine to more dust, dirt and debris than is found at the upper position. Placing the engine at the cutting head also shifts most of the weight to that position and operator must support the weight while cutting, increasing operator fatigue.

Trimmers with engine at the upper end expose the operator to more engine noise and heat, but weight of such trimmers is better balanced and the engine is easier to keep clean. Trimmers with a curved shaft drive the cutting head directly from the engine through a flexible shaft. This provides a simple, economical drive.

Straight shaft trimmers have a set of bevel gears in a case atop the cutting head which changes direction of power flow and can change head speed in rela-

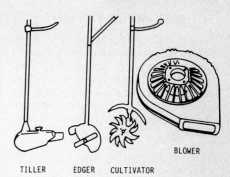

TILLER   EDGER   CULTIVATOR   BLOWER

tion to engine speed if desired. The lower, straight shaft makes it easier to trim farther under low tree limbs, fences and other obstacles.

On some trimmers, a centrifugal clutch (similar to those on chain saws) engages the trimmer head when the engine is accelerated and is disengaged when engine speed is reduced. This improves trimmer safety and makes it easier to start the engine by not having to spin the trimmer head or blade also.

A trimmer that "feels fine" in the store may feel very heavy after long use in the

hot sun. Both total weight and balance of a trimmer can affect how fast the operator becomes tired. For instance, some smaller gas trimmers weigh less than 8 pounds while bigger models weigh 25 pounds or more. (Electric models weigh approximately 2 to 10 pounds.)

Smaller trimmers may require more time to complete a given task, but operators with moderate strength may be able to use a smaller trimmer with fewer rest breaks and finish in about the same time as they would when using a trimmer that's too big.

Weed and brush blade should never be used without a shoulder harness on models fully supported by the operator. An approved shoulder harness will be designed to prevent the trimmer head from accidentally swinging back and possibly injuring the operator if the blade kicks against a solid object or if the operator slips. A correctly-adjusted shoulder harness also reduces fatigue and makes trimmer operation much easier.

The cutting head can be removed easily from some trimmers and replaced by other attachments. A blower attachment

can remove leaves and grass clippings from sidewalks, driveways, etc. A power edger provides a neat appearance between lawns and sidewalks, driveways or other paved areas. And, a power hoe can weed gardens or flower beds and loosen soil for better infiltration of moisture.

Such attachments eliminate the need to buy separate power units for each tool and, thus, can save considerable money. However, they are usually best for smaller lawns and gardens, particularly if two or more attachments must be used simultaneously.

OPERATING SAFETY

Edger and trimmers are cutting tools and must be operated with great care to reduce the chance of injury. Dangers include electrical shock, burning, muscle strain and being hit by projectile thrown by rotating unit. The operator should exercise caution and observe the following checklist.

Observe the following check list **in addition to STANDARD SAFETY PRACTICES.**

1. Remove debris from working area.
2. Keep people and animals well away from working area. (At least 20 feet from trimmer.)
3. Maintain proper balance and footing at all times. Don't overreach.
4. Be extremely careful of kick back, especially when using a hard blade cutter.
5. Cut only with discharge aimed at a safe direction, away from operator, windows, etc.
6. Use weed and brush blades only on edger/trimmers designed for their use. If the operator carries the full weight of the unit, an attached harness designed to prevent accidental injury to operator must be used.

If the edger/trimmer is powered by a gasoline engine, check fuel requirement

before filling tank. The engines of spin trimmers which are carried by the operator, are lubricated by oil which should be mixed with the gasoline before filling tank. Overheating, rapid wear and serious damage will result if tank of 2 stroke engines requiring gasoline and oil mix is filled with only gasoline. Recommended ratio of oil to fuel is often marked on cap of fuel tank, but operator's manual should be checked for recommended type and amount oil.

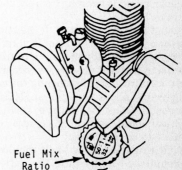

Fuel Mix Ratio

SETTING UP THE UNIT

Key to setting up and operating is the direction of rotation at the cutter. Cutting should only occur in the segment of the cutting plane that will discharge cuttings away from the operator or to the side. The cutter of some models rotates clockwise while the cutter of others turns counter-clockwise.

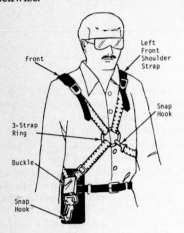

On models so equipped, put the shoulder harness on and adjust size to the user's body. Adjust position of hip guard so that suspension hook will be correct height for easy control of edger/trimmer. The harness plates on back and chest should be level. Make final adjustment so that pressure is even on both shoulders.

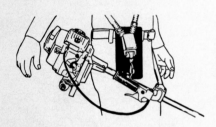

Trimmer should hang freely in front when operator stands squarely with feet about shoulder distance apart. Change balance by moving the hook eye on the drive shaft tube. When fuel tank is empty, trimmer head should float slightly above ground.

Adjust handle bar position for comfortable convenient operation while edger/trimmer is hanging from shoulder strap or harness.

Adjust for trim **mowing**, by positioning the cutting head horizontal, parallel to the ground. Adjust for **trimming** around trees, sidewalks, driveways, curbs, lawn furniture, etc., by turning the cutting head at about 30 degree angle from horizontal. Adjust for **edging** by positioning cutting head vertical (90 degrees from surface to be trimmed).

Adjusting the cutting angle should be accomplished by turning the cutting head or by relocating the handle. Forcibly holding the unit at an uncomfortable angle is only suggested if a change is for a very short time.

On gasoline powered models, fill fuel tank with correct type or mixture of fuel as specified by manufacturer.

Vibration, heat and noise of the operating unit may increase fatigue, decrease operator control and impair hearing. Nonslip gloves, properly adjusted shoulder strap (or harness), ear protection and appropriate protective clothing will help reduce the danger to the operator.

On all models, inspect area to cut and remove all debris that may clog or damage cutting head and all debris which could be damaged or thrown by cutter. Wire, string, rope, vines and cords can wrap around rotating head causing damage or possible injury. Rocks, cans, bottles, sticks and similar items can be thrown by cutter causing damage to property or injury to humans or animals.

STARTING ENGINE

DANGER: Before starting the edger/trimmer, make sure that all other people and animals are at least 20 feet away and that all parts are in place and tight.

On gasoline powered models, lay the edger/trimmer down on flat, clear area away from tall grass or brush. Operate primer or choke, move ignition switch to "ON" position; then, open fuel shut-off valve and open fuel tank cap vent. Squeeze and hold throttle trigger to ½ speed position, hold trimmer to ground as convenient and pull rewind starter

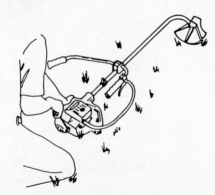

handle smartly. Do not let cord snap back because starter may be damaged.

On models with primer, it may be necessary to operate primer to keep engine running after first starting. On 2 stroke engines with choke, push choke in, then attempt to start after engine has tried to start.

On all models, engine should warm enough to idle smoothly without operating primer or with choke open soon after starting. If equipped with automatic

clutch, cutting head should not rotate at idle speed.

MOWING

Trim mowing is very much like having a very narrow rotary lawn mower for places where a regular mower is too wide. String trimmers are also used to mow areas too rough for a standard rotary mower, such as some rocky places.

Cut only in segment of the cutting plane that is away from the operator as indicated by the shaded area in the illustration. Discharge will then be away from operator. When mowing, the cutting head must be kept parallel to the ground. The cut height of the grass should be maintained as if cut with a regular mower. Smooth even cutting will be im-

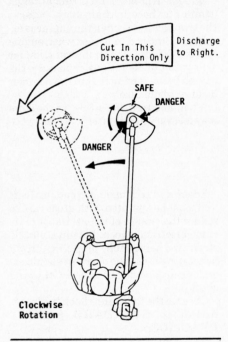

Cut In This Direction Only. Discharge to Right.

SAFE
DANGER
DANGER

Clockwise Rotation

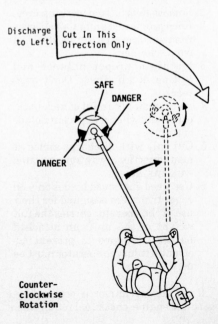

Discharge to Left. Cut In This Direction Only

SAFE
DANGER
DANGER

Counter-clockwise Rotation

possible if cutting head is angled while attempting to mow.

TRIMMING

The cutting head should be about 30 degrees to the horizontal when trimming around sidewalks, driveways, curbs, lawn furniture, etc. The lower edge should be next to the sidewalk, etc., and should taper upward to the regular cut height of the grass.

WARNING: Always cut so that discharge is away from operator. Never operate with discharge toward feet or legs.

It is possible to forcibly hold the trimmer at the 30 degree angle; however, operator fatigue is increased unnecessarily and safety is compromised. Handle, hook eye or cutting head angles are easily adjusted so that correct 30 degree angle is the natural, easy position of trimmer.

Adjust angle so that the cutting plane is higher on discharge side. Confine cutting to the segment of the cutting plane away from operator so that discharge will be away from operator.

CAUTION: Be careful when trimming around objects such as small pipes, rods or fencing. Trimmer string will wrap around small objects and damage end of trimmer string.

String that is frayed from use is more gentle for trimming around trees and plants than line that has been recently extended and cut. Be careful not to damage bark of trees while trimming.

SCALPING

It's sometimes desirable to remove all grass from certain areas. This scalping is accomplished in much the same way as trimming, except much closer.

Adjust the cutting head so that cutting plane is about 30 degrees from horizontal and discharge is away from operator. Adjust handle, hook eye or cutting head as required so that trimmer will easily assume the desired angle naturally.

Confine cutting to the segment of the cutting plane so that discharge will be away from operator.

Begin scalping area around object, by first cutting perimeter. After establish-

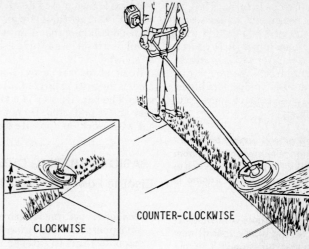

CLOCKWISE COUNTER-CLOCKWISE

ing outer limits, scalp inside by working in direction necessary to discharge grass toward perimeter.

When cutting next to trees or plants, frayed ends of trimmer string will be more gentle than if the line is recently extended and cut. Trees can be damaged or killed if bark is removed from circumference of tree.

CAUTION: Be careful when cutting around objects such as pipes or rods. Trimmer string may wrap around small objects which can't be moved and are too strong to be cut.

EDGING

The cutter head should be turned so that cutting plane is vertical, perpendicular to part being edged and so that discharge is toward front away from operator.

Counter-Clockwise Rotation

DANGER: Cut grass, dirt, stones, etc., will be discharged violently when edging, because of the position of the cutting head. Always wear protective glasses or goggles when operating edger. Be especially cautious of the discharge and make sure other people, animals, automobiles, etc., will not be affected by discharge.

Adjust position of handle, hook eye or cutting head angle so that edger is in a natural easy position for comfortable control.

WEED, BRUSH AND CLEARING BLADES

Some edgers and trimmers can be equipped with hard plastic or metal blades for cutting weeds, brush or small trees.

WARNING: Rigid blades should be used only on units supported by wheels or suspended from operator by a harness.

Monofilament string trimmers are designed for safe, easy operation while cutting light grass. Blades may be available to replace the string cutting head; however, make sure that replacement blade is for specific model and is recommended by the manufacturer.

DANGER: Be careful of kick back. Harnesses are designed to minimize danger of injury, but be extremely careful to maintain control at all times when using rigid blades.

Cutting blades that are hard are more dangerous to use than a monofilament string, even through general operation is similar. Blades may be metal or hard plastic, but the rigid design is used to force the cutting edge through the object to be cut. If the object can't be moved or cut by the blade, something else will happen, often with undesirable results.. Three results are: The blade breaks apart; The blade stops turning; The cutting head kicks back pushing blade away from object to be cut. Even when used properly, rigid blades impose heavy shock loads to the blade and drive. Stop engine and check condition of blade frequently. Never operate unit if condition of blade, any part of drive or control is cracked, broken or slipping.

DANGER: Always stop engine before inspecting condition or removing debris from around blade. NEVER depend upon clutch to keep blade from turning while engine is running.

Consult dealer for tools and instructions for sharpening blade. Install new blade if condition is questioned. The cost of a new blade is much less costly than injury.

Blades with 3 to 8 widely spaced large teeth or cutter bars are available for some models. This blade is designed for cutting larger grass/weeds and may be made of either ridged plastic or metal. Install blade with sharp cutting edge toward direction of rotation.

DANGER: Kick back is able to occur more easily with wide tooth spacing. Do not swing cutter into hard to cut areas. Check area to be cut carefully and remove or mark anything that would impair cutting or trip operator.

These blades are highly effective for cutting large unrestricted areas, but violent kick back is likely to occur if used near fences, walls or similar firm objects. Blades with more than three teeth are not recommended for use around objects which could cause kick back, but blade can sometimes be installed upside down to reduce kick back. Remove and install blade correctly, with sharp cutting edge toward direction of rotation as soon as practical.

Circular saw blades and clearing blades made especially for specific models can be used to cut brush, including small trees. This type of blade should be used only at ground level; never overhead.

Install blade with sharp cutting edge toward direction of rotation for normal cutting.

WARNING: Blade and drive parts will be damaged by hitting blade against trees, rocks or other solid objects.

Always cut by moving the cutting head, twisting your whole body opposite the rotation of the cutting head. Do not just swing the unit with your arms and hands. Do not cut during the return swing. Cuts should be a series of wedge shaped arcs as shown.

Work stops are provided on some models for cutting larger (but still small) trees. The heavier stop is usually at the rear and is preferred. Do not attempt to cut with work on opposite side of stop.

BASIC OPERATING CHECK LIST
Electric Powered Edger/Trimmers

Check for proper line length or blade for sharpness and condition before use. Stop, disconnect extension cord and check condition frequently during use.

Check cooling air filters for cleanliness and condition before using. Stop and clean cooling air filter frequently, especially when operating in dirty conditions.

Lubricate as recommended by manufacturer. Most use permanently lubricated bearings and require no lubrication; however some require periodic oiling.

Check for proper length extension cord to reach all areas without exceeding safe limit. Attach extension cord and check for operation.

Notice any irregularities during operation, especially vibration or speed. Check for blade or line damage and overheating.

Remove and clean cooling air filter at the end of each working day. Install new filter if damaged.

Clean all accumulated grass, dirt and other debris from motor and cutter.

Inspect cutting blade or line and service if required. Rigid blades can be sharpened. Consult dealer for sharpening tools and instruction.

Gasoline Powered Edger/Trimmers

Check for proper line length or blade for sharpness and condition before use. Stop engine and check condition frequently during use, especially if engine speed increases or unit begins to vibrate.

Check cooling air passages for cleanliness. Grass and dirt should have been cleaned after use, but regardless, don't start off with unit dirty. Also, birds or insects may have built nests in cooling passages since last use.

Check for sufficient amount of fuel to finish anticipated work that day. Be sure that fuel for models requiring gasoline and oil blend is mixed in proper ratio.

Clean around fuel filler cap before removing cap for filling.

Fill fuel tank with required type of gasoline and oil mix. Always leave some room for expansion in tank. Some manufacturers suggest ¾ full.

Start engine and check for proper engine operation. Accelerate and check operation of clutch (if so equipped) and cutter. If binding, overloading or vibration is evident, stop, and repair cause.

At the end of each working day, clean air passages, clean engine air filter and sharpen blade, if equipped with rigid blade.

Fill gear box with approved lubricant at end of each working day. Lithium grease is used for most models with gear box at lower end of drive shaft.

After each 20 hours of operation, remove, clean and lubricate drive shaft, then reinstall, reversing ends to equalize wear.

ROUTINE MAINTENANCE

Three key elements for good maintenance are:

Keep the electric motor or gasoline engine cool.

Keep dirt and trash out of the rotating parts, especially engine parts.

Keep parts lubricated.

Attention to these items will result in longer life and the comfortable feeling of knowing the equipment will run when you need it.

COOLING THE MOTOR OR ENGINE

Excess heat ruins both electric motors and gasoline engines. This destructive heat is produced when a motor or engine is overloaded or its cooling system is clogged with debris. Motors and engines which are located low, near the ground, will get dirty faster than if mounted high.

The electric motors used with edger/trimmers are equipped with a fan to circulate cool air around the motor. Since these motors are near the ground, a filter is necessary to stop dirt, grass and other trash from being drawn into the cooling passages. Usually the filter is an open cell foam pad that is easily accessible for removal and cleaning or replacement. Clean filter with mild soap and water only. Check condition of filter before reinstalling. Consult authorized dealer or parts distributor for proper replacement filter.

WARNING: Never operate electric edger/trimmer with filter pad missing. Overheating, especially with filter missing, can cause a fire. Be sure filter is dry before reinstalling.

Cooling air for gasoline powered edger/trimmers must flow freely through the engine fan and across the cooling fins. Grass, leaves and dust can build up and block the flow of cool air, making the engine overheat. Remove shrouds that cover the fan and other air passages at least once a year so that all debris can be removed. Edger/trimmers with low mounted engines should be cleaned much more often and all units should be cleaned when build up is noticed. Use a brush, compressed air and non-metallic scraper to remove grass, dirt, leaves and any crusty deposits from fan and fins.

CAUTION: Cover openings to carburetor, exhaust and fuel tank vent when cleaning the cooling passages. The dirt should not be cleaned from outside of engine only to fall inside.

Excessive heat can ruin gasoline engines by removing the thin layer of oil that should separate moving internal parts. If the internal parts touch, each part can wear the other. Heat can also cause parts such as seals that are designed to be flexible to become hard and brittle. Overheating is especially easy when caused by more than one problem such as cooling fins clogged with debris and overloading. Overheating in a small localized area is often as disastrous as general high temperature, because of the resulting distortion of the shape of the parts. Gasoline engines will sometimes seize because of overheating. Damage is not corrected by cooling. Prevent damage from occurring by using proper procedures to eliminate causes of overheating.

CAUTION: Never attempt to cool overheated part by plunging into water or by spraying water on overheated engine or part. Rapid cooling may cause parts to crack or become brittle. Uneven cooling may cause more distortion and damage parts even more.

OVERLOADING

Dirt or trash may wrap around the rotating parts causing drive system to be overloaded. String trimmers will also be overloaded if cutting line is too long. Dull metal or rigid plastic blades will overload drive as will attempting to cut trees or brush too large for blade design.

An overloaded motor or engine turns slower than normal, so its cooling fan moves less cooling air, even though more cooling is required. Electric motors will

begin to smoke and smell (from burned wires). Often wires or connections will be damaged by overheating, preventing normal operation even after cooling.

LUBRICATION

Dirt or other debris will damage motors and engine if permitted to enter the lubrication system. Internal parts can be damaged by the abrasive action of dirt and by overheating caused by overloading. The heat of overloading can thin the oil enough to result in improper lubrication. Insufficient amount of oil or incorrect type of oil can also result in parts operating without lubrication.

The 2 stroke engines used on lightweight gasoline edger/trimmers are lubricated by oil mixed with gasoline. This special oil lubricates, then is burned and exhausted with the fuel. Dirt can enter the lubrication system by falling into the fuel tank or by entering with air through the carburetor. Be sure to use the correct type and amount thoroughly mixed with the gasoline before filling tank. Don't let dirt or other debris fall into fuel while filling tank. Service air cleaner properly and often to keep dirt from entering the engine. Never reuse any air filter which is punctured or that allows dirt to pass around or through it. Consult authorized dealer or parts supplier for proper replacement filters.

STRING TRIMMER LINE

The string trimmer cutting head may be constructed in a wide variety of ways and procedure for disassembly will differ.

The monofilament line is extended from many self feeding heads by operating the unit, then tapping the center of the hub lightly on the grass. Cutting line is extended by a centrifugal force and if line is too short, line will probably require manual extension to about 3 inches. The protective shield is usually equipped with a sharp cutter to trim the line to the proper length. If line will not feed, stop gasoline engine or unplug electric cord and check the cutting head. Cutting line is extended by centrifugal force and if line is too short, line many require manual extension to approximately 3-4 inches for normal operation. Depress center of hub while pulling line. It is possible to pull only short lengths of line from hub at one time. Release pressure from center of hub and pull on line, then repeat procedure to withdraw another section of line as required. If line is not visible, all line may be gone or line may be broken inside hub. Disassembly will be required with either problem.

Cutting line is extended from some models by accelerating engine speed, slowing engine to idle then accelerating to high speed. Proper extension depends

upon size and weight of line extended from the cutting head, engine speed and the tension of springs located in the cutting head. If line will not feed, stop engine and check the cutting head. Cutting line depends upon centrifugal force to pull line from head and if line is too short it must be extended manually before it will work automatically. Remove cover, turn spool to extend line approximately 4 inches from eyelet in housing, then reassemble. If line is not visible, all line may be gone, line may be broken or tangled inside hub requiring further disassembly.

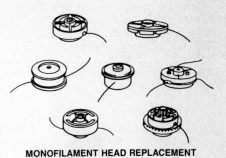

MONOFILAMENT HEAD REPLACEMENT

CAUTION: It is important to keep the cutting head clean and to use the correct type and size of monofilament line on all models. Consult authorized dealer for recommended line to use and for other servicing problems.

Spools for self feeding monofilament line can be refilled. Be sure to use the correct type and size of line and wind the line in the correct direction. Some common line diameters are 0.051 inch (1.3 mm), 0.065 inch (1.6 mm), 0.080 inch (2.0 mm), 0.095 inch (2.4 mm), and 0.130 inch (3.3 mm). Cutting heads may be designed with 1,2,3 or more lines extended. Shapes of the spools onto which line is stored in the cutting head seems to be unlimited. Be sure that correct spool is used. Most spools are marked with arrow indicating correct direction for winding new line.

The flexible drive shaft used on many models should be removed, cleaned, coated with grease, then reinstalled with ends reversed after every 20 hours of operation. Reversing ends will equalize load and wear so that cable will last longer. Cable can be pulled from either end of most models, but removal of the cutting head assembly from lower end of drive shaft housing is usually easier.

CAUTION: Be sure that both ends of cable engage the drive and driven parts. It is sometimes possible to assemble with end of flexible drive shaft along side of drive coupling. The shaft may be damaged but will not turn when either end is assembled incorrectly this way.

OTHER ADJUSTMENTS, SERVICES AND REPAIRS

ON-OFF IGNITION SWITCH

Electric Powered Trimmers

Electric powered trimmers are equipped with a spring loaded "trigger" type on-off switch. Trigger is located on trimmer handle (Fig. 10) of most models and is spring loaded as a safety feature. Trimmer motor will stop when trigger is released.

To renew trigger switch, first disconnect trimmer from power source. Remove screws retaining handle sections (Fig. 11). Separate handle sections carefully noting location of trigger switch (Fig. 12). Disconnect switch lead wires and remove switch.

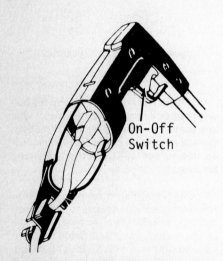

Fig. 10—View showing typical location for the spring loaded trigger type on-off switch used on electric trimmer models.

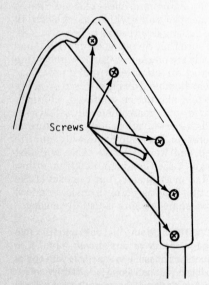

Fig. 11—Screws must be removed to separate handle for access to spring loaded trigger type switch used on many models.

Gasoline Powered Trimmers

Gasoline powered trimmers may be equipped with a simple spring loaded ignition grounding switch (Fig. 13), an "ON-OFF" toggle switch (Fig. 14) or a slider type switch (Fig. 15). Switch may be located on engine cover/handle assembly, on a bracket attached to engine or on drive shaft housing tube.

To renew switch located on engine cover/handle assembly, it will be necessary to separate engine cover or handle. Engine cover removal procedure of most models with full engine cover is outlined in the appropriate TRIMMER SERVICE section of this manual.

Switch located on bracket attached to engine is usually a toggle type and is secured to plate with nuts. To renew switch disconnect wires, remove nuts and remove switch.

Slider type switch may be located in engine cover/handle assembly or on drive shaft housing. Refer to the appropriate TRIMMER SERVICE section of this manual for engine cover removal and access to switch. Removal of switch located on drive shaft housing tube is obvious after examination.

ENGINE CHOKE/PRIMER

Gasoline Powered Trimmers

Gasoline powered trimmers may be equipped with a choke or primer mechanism to enrich fuel starting mixture.

Choke may be a simple plunger which when turned, closes off carburetor opening (Fig. 16) or a more complex system using a choke plate activated by pulling a choke lever. Choke plates are usually connected to choke lever by a wire control rod. Refer to the carbure-

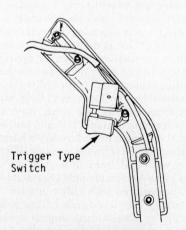

Fig. 12—Trigger assembly is trapped inside handle on many models.

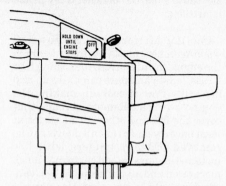

Fig. 13—A simple spring loaded grounding switch is used to stop engine on many models. Push spring down and hold switch lever until engine stops completely.

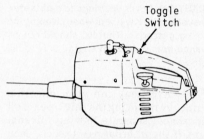

Fig. 14—A toggle switch is used for the ignition switch on many models.

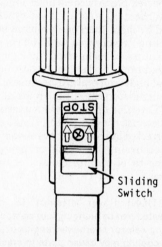

Fig. 15—Some models are equipped with a sliding type ignition switch.

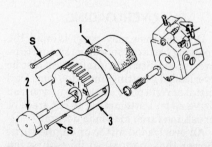

Fig. 16—Choke assembly on some models is a simple plunger(2) which rotates on a ramp and plugs carburetor opening.

tor paragraphs in the appropriate ENGINE SERVICE section of this manual for choke information.

Primer systems consist of a primer bulb (Fig. 18) located on carburetor or, on models with full engine cover, may be located at an external location and connected to the carburetor by a fuel tube. Primer bulb is compressed to provide a rich initial fuel charge for engine starting. Refer to the carburetor paragraphs in the appropriate ENGINE SERVICE section of this manual for primer information.

ENGINE THROTTLE

Gasoline Powered Trimmers

All gasoline powered trimmers are equipped with a spring loaded throttle trigger assembly. Throttle trigger is spring loaded to return carburetor throttle lever to idle position when trigger is released. Throttle trigger may be located in trimmer engine cover/handle assembly and be connected to carburetor throttle lever by a wire connecting rod or, throttle trigger may be located on drive shaft housing tube or a handle

attached to drive shaft housing tube and is connected to the carburetor throttle control lever by a throttle cable.

Throttle cable of models so equipped should be lubricated at 20 hour intervals. Apply SAE 30 oil to each end of inner wire. Throttle cable service and adjustment information for some specific models is located in TRIMMER SERVICE sections of this manual.

ENGINE REMOVAL

Gasoline Powered Trimmers

The engine can be separated from drive shaft housing tube of most models after loosening clamp bolt or bolts (Fig. 19). Drive shaft will separate from drive shaft adapter or clutch adapter as engine is removed. When reinstalling engine, make certain drive shaft engages adapters fully.

Some models are equipped with a threaded collar which screws onto engine adapter housing as shown in Fig. 20. Unscrew collar and separate engine from drive shaft housing tube. Drive shaft will separate from drive shaft

adapter or clutch adapter as engine is removed. When reinstalling engine, make certain drive shaft engages adapters fully.

On some models with a solid drive shaft, clutch drum is threaded onto drive shaft. On these models, separate engine at adapter/clutch housing by removing any bolts securing housing to engine (Fig. 21).

DRIVE SHAFT ADAPTER/CLUTCH

Gasoline Powered Trimmers

Direct drive models (models with no clutch) are equipped with a drive shaft adapter threaded onto crankshaft as shown in Fig. 22. Adapter may be an integral part of the flywheel nut. These models use a flexible drive shaft and adapter is machined to engage the squared drive shaft end. When installing drive shaft, make certain squared drive shaft end engages adapter fully to prevent drive shaft damage.

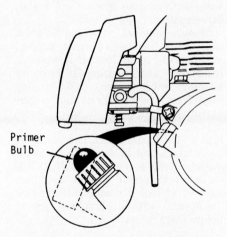

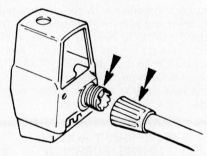

Fig. 20—Clutch housing or engine cover on some models are equipped with threads which engage a threaded collar on drive shaft housing tube to secure engine to drive shaft housing tube.

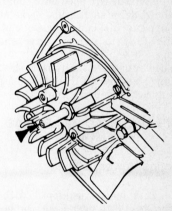

Fig. 22—Most direct drive models are equipped with a drive shaft adapter which also serves as the flywheel retaining nut.

Fig. 18—Some models are equipped with a primer bulb which, when squeezed, injects a measured amount of fuel into carburetor.

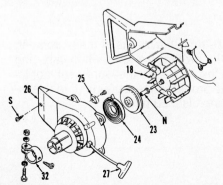

Fig. 21—On some models equipped with solid drive shaft which is threaded onto clutch drum, engine must be separated from clutch housing by removing clutch housing bolts.

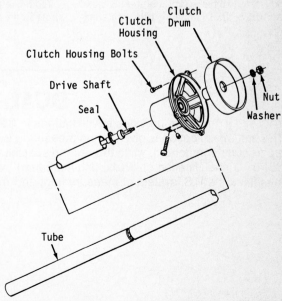

Fig. 19—A clamp (32) and bolt assembly secures engine to drive shaft housing tube on many models.

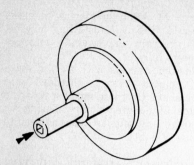

Fig. 23—Clutch drum on models equipped with a centrifugal clutch is equipped with a drive shaft adapter.

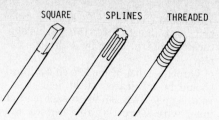

Fig. 24—Drive shaft ends may be square, equipped with splines or threaded.

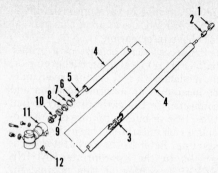

Fig. 26—Exploded view of a typical solid drive shaft and housing.

1. Adapter
2. Adapter
3. Bushing
4. Drive shaft housing
5. Drive shaft
6. Snap ring
7. Snap ring
8. Bearing
9. Bearing
10. Input shaft & gear
11. Gear head housing
12. Clamp shim

Models equipped with a clutch are equipped with drive shaft adapters connected to clutch drum (Fig. 23). Models with flexible drive shaft have adapters machined to engage the squared end of the flexible drive shaft and models with solid drive shaft may be machined to engage a splined drive shaft end or are threaded to screw onto the solid drive shaft (Fig. 24). When installing drive shaft on models equipped with squared or splined drive shaft ends, make certain drive shaft ends engage clutch adapter fully to prevent drive shaft damage. On models with clutch drum threaded onto drive shaft, use a thread locking compound on threads when installing clutch on drive shaft.

BEARING HEAD/GEAR HEAD REMOVAL

Gasoline Powered Trimmers

On most models equipped with a bearing head or a gear head, the head may be removed by removing the clamping bolt or bolts and locating screw (Fig. 25). Drive shaft will separate from drive shaft adapter as head and drive shaft housing tube are sepa-

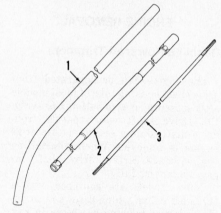

Fig. 25—Flexible drive shaft (3) on some models is supported in drive shaft housing tube (1) in a renewable liner (2).

rated. On models with clutch mounted at lower end of drive shaft tube, refer to the TRIMMER SERVICE section of this manual for the model being serviced. Refer to the TRIMMER SERVICE section for removal procedure of bearing head or gear head on specific models.

DRIVE SHAFT HOUSING LINERS/BUSHINGS

Gasoline Powered Trimmers

Models equipped with a flexible drive shaft in a curved drive shaft tube hous-

ing may be equipped with a drive shaft housing liner (2-Fig. 25). Liner may be renewed by separating drive shaft housing tube from bearing head and engine assemblies. Pull drive shaft (3) out of housing and liner. Mark location of liner (2) in housing (1) and pull liner out of housing. Install new liner at old liner location. Lubricate drive shaft with lithium base grease and install drive shaft.

Models equipped with a solid drive shaft may have drive shaft support bushings (3-Fig. 26) located at intervals inside drive shaft housing (4). To renew bushings, separate drive shaft housing tube from trimmer head and engine assembly. Mark locations of old bushings before removal. Install new bushings at old bushing locations. Bushing installation tool is available for some models. Refer to TRIMMER SERVICE section for specific models and part number of tool if available. Lubricate drive shaft with lithium base grease before installation.

DUAL DIMENSIONS

This service manual provides specifications in both the U.S. Customary and Metric (SI) systems of measurement. The first specification is given in the measuring system perceived by us to be the preferred system when servicing a particular component, while the second specification (given in parenthesis) is the converted measurement. For instance, a specification of "0.011 inch (0.28 mm)" would indicate that we feel the preferred measurement, in this instance, is the U.S. system of measurement and the metric equivalent of 0.011 inch is 0.28 mm.

ALPINA

GASOLINE POWERED
STRING TRIMMER

Model	Engine Manufacturer	Engine Model	Displacement
160	Tanaka	....	22.6 cc
180	Tanaka	....	30.5 cc
200	Tanaka	....	37.4 cc

ENGINE INFORMATION

All Models

Tanaka (TAS) two-stroke air-cooled gasoline engines are used on all listed Alpina line trimmers and brush cutters. Identify engine by engine displacement and refer to the TANAKA (TAS) ENGINE SERVICE section of this manual.

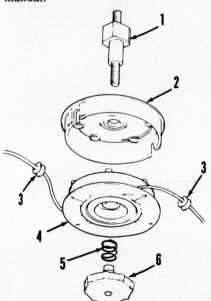

Fig. AL10—Exploded view of dual strand manual feed trimmer head available for most models.

1. Drive shaft adapter
2. Housing
3. Line guides
4. Spool
5. Spring
6. Lock knob

STRING TRIMMER

All Models

A dual strand manual feed trimmer head is available for most models (Fig. AL10). To extend line, loosen lock knob (6) until line may be pulled from housing. Pull line to desired length and tighten lock knob (6).

To renew line, remove lock knob (6), spring (5) and spool (4). Remove any remaining old line and install new line on spool. Wind line in direction indicated by arrow on spool and insert line ends through line guides (3). Install spool, spring and lock knob.

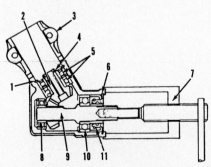

Fig. AL12—Cross-section view of gear head used on most models.

1. Snap ring
2. Input shaft & gear
3. Housing
4. Snap ring
5. Bearings
6. Snap ring
7. Puller
8. Bearing
9. Arbor shaft & gear
10. Bearing
11. Seal

BLADE

All Models

All models may be equipped with a four cutting edge grass, weed and brush blade, an eight cutting edge blade or a saw blade. Always make certain cup washer above blade and adapter plate below blade are centered and fit flat against surface of blade when installing blade.

All Models

All models are equipped with a solid drive shaft supported in a straight drive shaft housing tube. Drive shaft is supported in bushings located in drive shaft housing tube. Drive shaft requires no regular maintenance however, if drive shaft is removed, lubricate shaft with lithium base grease before reinstallation.

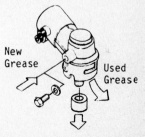

New Grease

Used Grease

Fig. AL13—A good quality lithium base grease should be pumped into gear head housing through filler opening until grease appears at arbor shaft seal. Refer to text.

GEAR HEAD

All Models

All models are equipped with a gear head similar to the one shown in Fig. AL12. Gear head should be lubricated

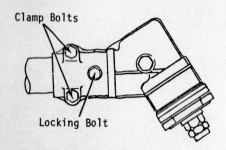

Fig. AL14—To separate gear head from drive shaft housing, remove clamp bolts and locking (head locating) bolt.

at 50 hour intervals of use. To lubricate, remove trimmer head or blade assembly. Remove grease plug from side of gear head housing. Pump lithium base grease into housing through plug opening until grease appears at bearing seal (Fig. AL13).

To disassemble gear head, remove clamp bolts and head locking bolt (Fig. AL14). Separate head from drive shaft and housing. Remove snap ring (6-Fig. AL12). Install suitable puller as illustrated in Fig. AL12 and remove oil seal, bearing and arbor shaft assembly. Remove gear (9) from housing. Remove snap ring (1). Insert suitable puller bolt through input shaft and thread a nut on bolt against input gear (Fig. AL15). Remove input shaft and bearing assembly. Remove snap ring (4-Fig. AL12) and press bearings from input shaft. To remove bearing (8), heat gear head

housing to 212° F (100° C) and tap housing against wooden block.

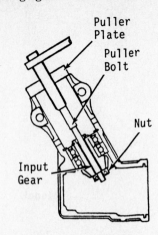

Fig. AL15—To remove input shaft, gear and bearing assembly, install puller as shown.

BLACK & DECKER
ELECTRIC STRING TRIMMERS

Model	Volts	Amps	Swath	Diameter	Cutting Line RPM
82205	120	1.4	9 in.	0.050 in.	10,500
82209	120	1.4	9 in.	0.050 in.	10,500
82210	120	1.5	10 in.	0.050 in.	9,500
82212	120	3.9	12 in.	0.065 in.	10,000
82214	120	4.3	14 in.	0.065 in.	8,500
82230	120	2.5	10 in.	0.050 in.	10,000
82232	120	3.2	12 in.	0.050 in.	9,500
82234	120	4.3	14 in.	0.050 in.	10,000

ELECTRICAL REQUIREMENTS

All models require electrical circuits with 120-volt alternating current. Extension cord length should not exceed 100 feet (30.5 m). Make certain all circuits and connections are properly grounded at all times.

STRING TRIMMER

Model 82205

Model 82205 is equipped with a manual advance line trimmer head designed to cut a 9 inch (229 mm) swath with 0.050 in. (1.3 mm) monofilament line. To extend line, disconnect power cord. Pull line up out of line slot (2-Fig. BD1) and pull line around spool in direction indicated by arrow and "UNWIND LINE" printed on spool. To renew line, push spool (8) in while turning in direction indicated by arrow and "REMOVE SPOOL" printed on spool. Remove spool, plastic line retainer (5) and any remaining old line. Insert one end of new line in hole in lower side of spool and wind new line onto spool in direction indicated by arrow on upper surface of spool. Insert line end through hole (4) in line retainer and install line retainer over spool. Install spool in housing and push spool in while turning spool to lock tabs (6) in housing (1).

Models 82209, 82210, 82212 And 82214

Models 82209, 82210, 82212 and 82214 are equipped with a single strand semi-automatic trimmer head shown in Fig. BD2. Models 82209 and 82210 are equipped with 0.050 inch (1.3 mm) line and Models 82212 and 82214 are equipped with 0.065 inch (1.6 mm) line. On all models, to extend line with trimmer motor off, push bump button (7) in while pulling on line end. Procedure may have to be repeated until desired line length has been obtained. To extend line with trimmer motor running, tap bump button (7) on the ground. Each time bump button is tapped on the ground a measured amount of new line will be advanced.

To renew line, disconnect power cord. Remove cover (8), button (7) and spool (6). Clean all parts thoroughly and remove any remaining old line from spool. Wind new line onto spool in direction indicated by arrow on spool. Insert line end through line guide opening in drum (1) and install spool, button and cover.

Models 82230, 82232 And 82234

Models 82230, 82232 and 82234 are equipped with a push button line feed system equipped with 0.050 inch (1.3 mm) line. Line is advanced by pushing button on secondary handle with trimmer motor running. Each time button is pushed, approximately 5/8 inch (16 mm) of line is advanced.

To renew line, disconnect power cord.

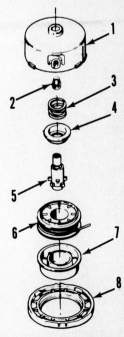

Fig. BD2—Exploded view of single strand semi-automatic head similar to the one used on Models 82209, 82210, 82212 and 82214.

1. Housing
2. Line guide
3. Spring
4. Spring adapter
5. Drive adapter
6. Spool
7. Bump button
8. Cover

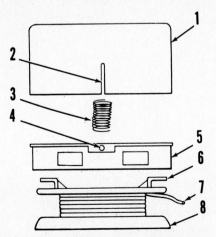

Fig. BD1—Exploded view of single strand manual trimmer head used on Model 82205.

1. Housing
2. Line slot
3. Spring
4. Line hole
5. Line retainer
6. Lock tabs
7. Line
8. Spool

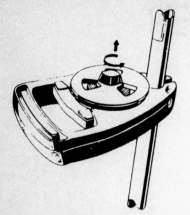

Fig. BD3—Turn spool nut in direction indicated to remove.

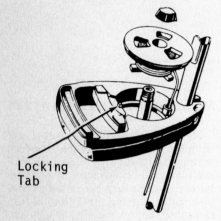

Locking Tab

Fig. BD4—Insert line end through line hole as shown and install spool in bail.

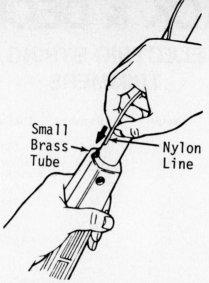

Small Brass Tube

Nylon Line

Fig. BD5—Insert line end through the brass line tube and work line down through tube until line is extending from line guide opening in trimmer head.

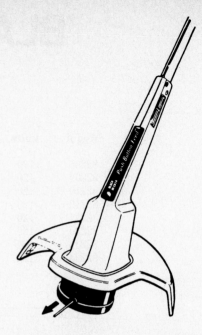

Fig. BD6—Line must extend from line guide opening in trimmer head after line installation.

Remove spool nut as shown in Fig. BD3. Lift spool out of handle assembly. Remove remaining old line and clean spool and bail assemblies. Wind new line onto spool leaving 3 feet (0.9 m) of line unwound from spool. Insert line end down through hole in bail handle assembly that is closest to handle tube (Fig. BD4). Install spool in bail assembly and install spool nut. Insert line end into line tube (Fig. BD5) and work entire length of free line through tube. At this point trimmer line should be extending from trimmer head line guide (Fig. BD6). If no line is at trimmer head, remove line spool and advance more free line before installing spool again.

BLACK & DECKER
GASOLINE POWERED STRING TRIMMER

Model	Engine Manufacturer	Engine Model	Displacement
8271-04	Kioritz	....	16.0 cc
8289-04	Kioritz	....	21.2 cc
82255	McCulloch	....	21.2 cc
82257	McCulloch	....	21.2 cc
82267	McCulloch	...	21.2 cc

ENGINE INFORMATION

All Models

Early models are equipped with Kioritz two-stroke air-cooled gasoline engines and later models are equipped with McCulloch two-stroke air-cooled gasoline engines. Identify engine model by engine manufacturer and engine displacement. Refer to KIORITZ ENGINE SERVICE or McCULLOCH ENGINE SERVICE section of this manual.

FUEL MIXTURE

All Models

Manufacturer recommends mixing regular grade gasoline (unleaded is an acceptable substitute) with a good quality two-stroke air-cooled engine oil at a 25:1 ratio. Do not use fuel containing alcohol.

STRING TRIMMER

Model 8271-04

Model 8271-04 is equipped with a single strand semi-automatic trimmer head shown in Fig. BD10. Line may be manually advanced with engine stopped by pushing in on housing (9) while pulling on line. Procedure may have to be repeated to obtain desired line length. To advance line with engine running, operate engine at full rpm and tap housing (9) on the ground. Each time housing is tapped on the ground, a measured amount of trimmer line will be advanced.

To renew trimmer line, remove cotter key (10) and twist housing (9) counterclockwise to remove housing. Remove

foam pad (6) and any remaining line on spool (3). Clean spool and inside of housing. Cut off approximately 25 feet (7.6 m) of 0.080 inch (2 mm) monofilament line and tape one end of line to spool (Fig. BD12). Wind line on spool in direction indicated by arrow on spool (Fig. BD14). Install foam pad with line

end protruding from between foam pad and spool as shown in Fig. BD14. Insert line end through line guide and install housing and spring assembly on spool.

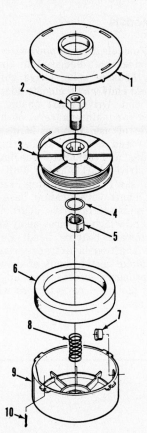

Fig. BD10—Exploded view of single strand semi-automatic trimmer head used on Model 8271-04.

1. Cover
2. Drive adapter
3. Spool
4. "O" ring
5. Drive adapter nut
6. Foam pad
7. Line guide
8. Spring
9. Housing
10. Cotter pin

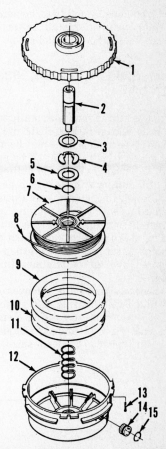

Fig. BD11—Exploded view of single strand semi-automatic trimmer head used on Models 8289-04, 82255, 82257 and 82267.

1. Cover
2. Drive adapter
3. Washer
4. Retainer
5. Washer
6. Retainer ring
7. Spool
8. Line
9. Foam pad
10. Foam pad
11. Spring
12. Housing
13. Cotter pin
14. Line guide
15. Retainer

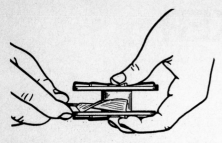

Fig. BD12—Tape one end of new line to center of spool as shown.

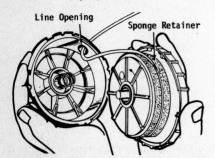

Fig. BD13—Install foam pads with line protruding from between pads. Wind line in direction indicated by arrow on spool.

Push in on housing and twist housing to lock into position. Install cotter key through hole in housing and cover.

Model 8289-04, 82255, 82257 And 82267

A single strand semi-automatic trimmer head shown in Fig. BD11 may be used on these models. Line may be manually advanced with engine off by pushing in on housing (12) while pulling on line. Procedure may have to be repeated until desired line length is obtained. To advance line with engine running, operate trimmer engine at full rpm and tap housing (12) on the ground. Each time housing is tapped on the ground, a measured amount of trimmer line is advanced.

To renew trimmer line, remove cotter pin (13). Twist housing (12) counterclockwise and remove housing. Remove foam pads (9 and 10) and any remaining line from spool (7). Clean spool and

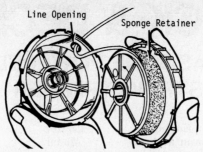

Fig. BD14—Install foam pad with line protruding between pad and spool as shown. Wind line in direction indicated by arrow on spool.

inner area of housing. Cut off approximately 25 feet (7.6 mm) of 0.080 inch (2 mm) monofilament line and tape one end of line to spool (Fig. BD12). Wind line on spool in direction indicated by arrow on spool (Fig. BD13). Install foam pads (9 and 10-Fig. BD11) so line is protruding from center of foam pads (Fig. BD13). Insert end of line through line guide and install spool, housing and spring. Push in on housing and twist housing in clockwise direction to lock in position and install cotter pin (13-Fig. BD11).

DRIVE SHAFT

All Models

All models are equipped with a flexible drive shaft enclosed in the drive shaft housing tube. Drive shaft has squared ends which engage adapters at each end. Drive shaft should be removed for maintenance at 50 hour intervals of use. Remove screw (4-Fig. BD15) and bolt (3) at bearing head housing and separate bearing head from drive shaft housing. Pull flexible drive shaft from housing. Lubricate drive shaft with lithium base grease and reinstall in drive shaft housing with end which was previously at clutch end toward bearing head. Reversing drive shaft ends extends drive shaft life. Make certain ends of drive shaft are properly located into upper and lower square drive adapters when installing.

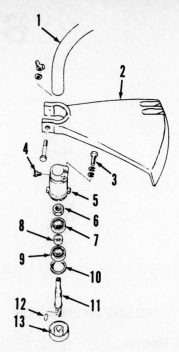

Fig. BD15—Exploded view of bearing head used on all models. Bearings (7 and 9) are sealed bearings and require no regular maintenance.

1. Drive shaft housing
2. Shield
3. Bolt
4. Screw
5. Housing
6. Nut
7. Bearing
8. Spacer
9. Bearing
10. Snap ring
11. Arbor (output) shaft
12. Pin
13. Cup washer

BEARING HEAD

All Models

All models are equipped with the bearing head shown in Fig. BD15. Bearing head is equipped with sealed bearings and requires no regular maintenance. To disassemble bearing head, remove trimmer head assembly and cup washer (13). Remove screw (4) and bolt (3) and separate bearing head from drive shaft housing tube. Remove snap ring (10) and use a suitable puller to remove arbor shaft (11) and bearing assembly. Remove nut (6) and press bearings (7 and 9) and spacer (8) from arbor shaft as required.

BUNTON

GASOLINE POWERED
STRING TRIMMER

Model	Engine Manufacturer	Engine Model	Displacement
LBF18K	Kawasaki	TD-18	18.4 cc
LBS24K	Kawasaki	TD-24	24.1 cc
LBS33K	Kawasaki	TD-33	33.3 cc

ENGINE INFORMATION

All Models

All models are equipped with a two-stroke air-cooled gasoline engine manufactured by Kawasaki. Refer to appropriate KAWASAKI ENGINE SERVICE section of this manual.

FUEL MIXTURE

All Models

Manufacturer recommends mixing a good quality two-stroke air-cooled engine oil with regular grade gasoline of at least 87 octane rating. Mix gasoline and oil at a 25:1 ratio. Unleaded regular gasoline is an acceptable substitute.

STRING TRIMMER

All Models

All models may be equipped with a dual strand manual trimmer head as shown in Fig. BT10. To install trimmer head, refer to Fig. BT10 for assembly sequence for Model LBF18K and to Fig. BT11 for assembly sequence for Models LBS24K and LBS33K. Note that trimmer head retaining nut on all models has left-hand threads. On all models, line may be extended (with engine stopped) by loosening lock knob on underside of trimmer head and rotating spool in direction which will advance line. Tighten lock knob.

To renew line, remove lock knob and spool. Remove any remaining old line and install new line on spool. Wind line in direction indicated by arrow on spool Insert line ends through line guide openings in housing and install spool and lock knob.

BLADE

All Models

All models may be equipped with an eight blade weed and grass blade. Blade is installed on Model LBF18K as shown in Fig. BT12. Blade is installed on Models LBS24K and LBS33K as shown in

Fig. BT10—Trimmer head parts assembly sequence for trimmer head installation on Model LBF18K.

1. Drive shaft housing   3. Cup washer
2. Spacer   4. Trimmer head

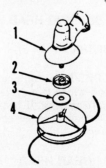

Fig. BT11—Trimmer head parts assembly sequence for trimmer head installation on Models LBS24K and LBS33K.

1. Gear head   3. Washer
2. Cup washer   4. Trimmer head

Fig. BT13. Make certain adapter plate (7) is centered and seated squarely on blade during installation.

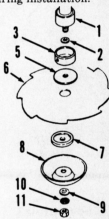

Fig. BT12—Parts assembly sequence for blade installation on Model LBF18K.

1. Drive shaft housing   7. Adapter plate
2. Spacer   8. Cover
3. Cup washer   9. Washer
4. Washer   10. Lock washer
5. ~
6. Blade   11. Nut (LH)

Fig. BT13—Parts assembly sequence for blade installation on Models LBS24K and LBS33K.

1. Gear head   8. Cover
5. Cup washer   9. Washer
6. Blade   10. Lock washer
7. Adapter plate   11. Nut (LH)

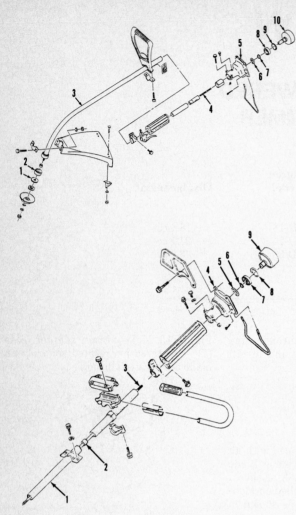

Fig. BT15—Exploded view of flexible drive shaft and housing on Model LBF18K.

1. Cup washer
2. Spacer
3. Drive shaft housing
4. Drive shaft
5. Clutch housing
6. Washer
7. Snap ring
8. Bearing
9. Snap ring
10. Clutch drum

Fig. BT16—Exploded view of drive shaft and housing used on Models LBS24K and LBS33K.

1. Drive shaft housing
2. Bushing
3. Drive shaft
4. Clutch housing
5. Washer
6. Snap ring
7. Bearing
8. Snap ring
9. Clutch drum

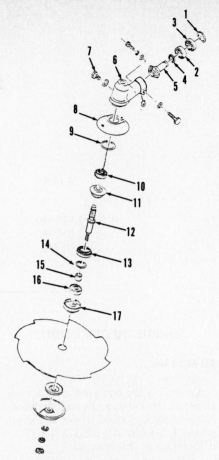

Fig. BT17—Exploded view of gear head assembly used on Models LBS24K and LBS33K.

1. Snap ring	
2. Bearing	
3. Bearing	10. Bearing
4. Snap ring	11. Gear
5. Input shaft	12. Arbor shaft
6. Housing	13. Bearing
7. Check plug	14. Snap ring
8. Anti-wrap cover	15. Spacer
9. Snap ring	16. Seal
	17. Cup washer

DRIVE SHAFT

Model LBF18K

Models LBF18K is equipped with a flexible drive shaft (Fig. BT15) enclosed in the tube housing (3). Drive shaft has squared ends which engage clutch drum (10) adapter at engine end and head adapter at head end. Drive shaft should be removed for maintenance at 30 hour intervals. Remove and clean drive shaft after marking end positions. Inspect for damage. Coat with lithium base grease and make certain drive shaft is installed with ends in opposite locations. Alternating drive shaft squared ends between clutch and trimmer head ends will extend drive shaft life.

Models LBS24K And LBS33K

Models LBS24K and LBS33K are equipped with a solid drive shaft (3-Fig. BT16) supported in drive shaft housing (1) in bushings (2) and at gear head and

clutch housing ends in sealed bearings. Drive shaft requires no regular maintenance however, if drive shaft is removed, lubricate drive shaft with lithium base grease before reinstallation. Drive shaft bushings (2) may be renewed. Mark locations of old bushings in drive shaft tube before removing. Install new bushings at old bushing locations in tube.

BEARING HEAD

Model LBF18K

Model LBF18K is equipped with a bearing head which is an integral part of drive shaft housing. If bearing head is worn or damaged, renew entire drive shaft housing.

GEAR HEAD

Models LBS24K And LBS33K

Models LBS24K and LBS33K are

equipped with the bearing head shown in Fig. BT17. At 30 hour intervals of use, remove trimmer head or blade assembly and install a grease fitting at check plug (7) opening. Pump lithium base grease into housing until new grease appears at seal (16) and spacer (15).

To disassemble gear head, remove trimmer head or blade assembly. Remove cup washer (17). Remove snap ring (1) and use a suitable puller to remove input shaft (5) and bearing assembly. Remove snap ring (4) and press bearings (2 and 3) from input shaft as required. Remove seal (16) and spacer (15). Remove snap ring (14) and use a suitable puller to remove arbor shaft (12) and bearing assembly as required. Press bearing (13) from arbor shaft. If bearing (10) stays in housing, heat housing to 140° F (60° C) and tap housing on wooden block to remove bearing.

JOHN DEERE

GASOLINE POWERED STRING TRIMMERS

Model	Engine Manufacturer	Engine Model	Displacement
82G	Poulan	. . . . .	26.2 cc
83G	Fuji	. . . . .	28.0 cc
90G	Kioritz	. . . . .	30.1 cc
100G	Kioritz	. . . . .	16.0 cc
200G	Kioritz	. . . . .	21.2 cc
250G	Kioritz	. . . . .	21.2 cc
350G	Kioritz	. . . . .	30.1 cc

ENGINE INFORMATION

All Models

John Deere gasoline powered string trimmers and brush cutters may be equipped with two-stroke engines manufactured by Fuji, Kioritz or Poulan. Refer to trimmer or brush cutter model number in the preceding identification chart to determine engine manufacturer. Engine model number and/or displacement is required to identify correct engine service section. Refer to the appropriate engine service section in this manual.

FUEL MIXTURE

All Models

John Deere recommends mixing a good quality two-stroke air-cooled engine oil with a BIA certification for TC-W service with regular grade gasoline of at least 87 octane. Do not use low-lead, unleaded premium gasoline, gasohol or other alcohol blended fuels. Models 82G and 83G should have fuel mixed at a 16:1 ratio. All other models should have fuel mixed at a 32:1 ratio.

STRING TRIMMER

Model 82G

Model 82G trimmer is equipped with a single strand, semi-automatic head with 40 feet (12.2 m) of 0.080 in. (2.03 mm) monofilament line. Early models are equipped with head shown in Fig. JD10. Later models are equipped with similar head which may be identified by noting top of drum (2) is smooth on early models and grooved on later models.

To adjust line length with engine STOPPED, depress release button (8) and pull line out until it stops. If more line is required, repeat procedure. To extend line with engine running, operate trimmer at full throttle and "tap" release button of cutting head firmly but quickly on the ground. Cutting spool will automatically extend approximately 1½ in. (3.8 cm) of line according to how full the spool is.

To renew line, STOP engine, depress latch (L—Fig. JD10) and rotate cover (9) counterclockwise to remove cover. Remove release button (8) and spool (6). Inspect teeth on inner cam (5) and spool (6). Excessive wear indicates unnecessary pressure on release button during operation. Remove any remaining old line and note direction of arrow on spool. Wind approximately 40 feet (12.2 m) of 0.080 inch (2.03 mm) diameter line in direction indicated by arrow on spool. Install spool in cover (2) with arrow side visible. Install

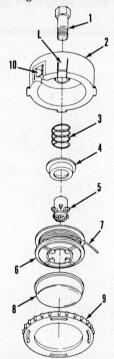

Fig. JD10—Exploded view of single strand semi-automatic trimmer head used on Model 82G.

1. Drive shaft adapter	6. Spool
2. Drum	7. Line
3. Spring	8. Button
4. Spring adapter	9. Cover
5. Drive cam	10. Line guide

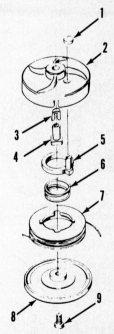

Fig. JD11—Exploded view of dual strand semi-automatic trimmer head used on Model 83G.

1. Cap	
2. Housing	6. Spring
3. Line guide	7. Spool
4. Drive shaft adapter	8. Cover
5. Lock ring	9. Screw

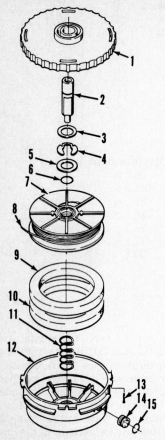

Fig. JD13—Exploded view of single strand semi-automatic trimmer head used on Models 90G, 100G and 200G.

1. Cover	
2. Drive shaft adapter	9. Foam pad
3. Washer	10. Foam pad
4. Retainer	11. Spring
5. Washer	12. Housing
6. Retainer	13. Cotter pin
7. Spool	14. Line guide
8. Line	15. Retainer

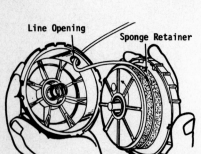

Fig. JD14—Install foam pads with line protruding from between pads. Wind line in direction indicated by arrow on spool.

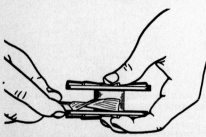

Fig. JD15—Tape end of new line to center of spool as shown.

release button and cover (9). Rotate cover in clockwise direction until it locks.

Model 83G

Model 83G trimmer is equipped with a dual strand trimmer head (Fig. JD11) which utilizes a double grooved spool wound with approximately 50 feet (12.2 m) of 0.080 inch (2.03 mm) diameter monofilament line.

To adjust line length depress release button and pull line out from both line openings in cutting head until line stops. Repeat procedure until at least 6 inches (15.2 cm) of line is extended from both openings. Each line must be 6 inches (15.2 cm) long measured from line opening. Clip line with line clippers. DO NOT operate trimmer with line extended beyond recommended length. To renew line, hold trimmer head and remove the 7/32 inch screw (9). Remove the cover (8), spring (6) and spool (7). Each side of double spool will hold approximately 25 feet (7.6 m) of 0.080 inch (2.03 mm) diameter monofilament line. To install new line on spool, insert ends of lines in holes located within spool and wind in direction indicated by arrows on the spool. Make certain line savers (3) are in position and place spool in housing (2). Spool is marked with "THIS SIDE IN". Install spring and replace cover. Tighten the 7/32 inch screw and cut line to proper length.

Models 90G, 100G And 200G

Models 90G, 100G and 200G are equipped with a single strand semi-automatic trimmer head shown in Fig. JD13. The

trimmer head will hold approximately 45 feet (13.7 m) of 0.080 inch (2.03 mm) diameter monofilament line. Line may be manually advanced with engine stopped by pushing in on housing (12) while pulling on line. Procedure may have to be repeated until desired line length is obtained. To advance line with engine running, operate trimmer engine at full rpm and tap housing (12) on the ground. Each time housing is tapped on the ground, a measured amount of trimmer line is advanced.

To renew trimmer line, remove cotter pin (13). Twist housing (12) counterclockwise and remove housing. Remove foam pads (9 and 10) and any remaining line from spool (7). Clean spool and inner area of housing. Tape one end of new line to spool (Fig. JD15). Wind line on spool in direction indicated by arrow on spool (Fig. JD14). Install foam pads so line is protruding from center of pads (Fig. JD14). Insert end of line through line guide and install spool, housing and spring. Push housing in and twist in clockwise direction to lock in position then install cotter pin (13—Fig. JD13).

Models 250G And 350G

Models 250G and 350G are equipped with a dual strand manual trimmer head. The trimmer head will hold two 0.095 inch (2.4 mm) lines approximately 12 feet (3.8 m) in length.

To extend line, stop trimmer engine and wait until all trimmer head rotation has stopped. Loosen lock knob on bottom of trimmer head until lines may be pulled out to desired length. Tighten lock knob.

To renew trimmer line, remove lock knob, cover, spring and spool. Remove any

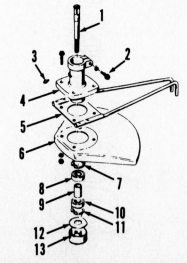

Fig. JD16—Exploded view of bearing head used on Model 82G.

1. Drive shaft adapter	
2. Clamp bolt	8. Bearing
3. Locating screw	9. Spacer
4. Housing	10. Bearing
5. Bracket (as equipped)	11. Snap ring
6. Shield	12. Washer
7. Snap ring	13. Drive disc

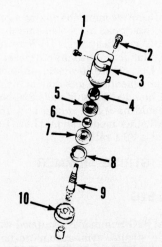

Fig. JD17—Exploded view of bearing head used on Models 100G and 200G.

1. Screw	6. Spacer
2. Clamp screw	7. Bearing
3. Housing	8. Snap ring
4. Nut	9. Shaft
5. Bearing	10. Adapter plate & key

remaining old line and clean spool and housing. Install ends of the new line into the locating holes on the back side of the spool allowing line ends to extend ¼ inch (6.4 mm) through locating holes. Hold lines tight and wind in a counter-clockwise direction onto spool making certain lines do not cross. Insert ends of each line into slots leaving 6 inches (15.2 cm) to extend. Install spool into housing. Insert line ends through line guides and pull tight. Install spring, cover and lock knob.

BLADE

Models 83G, 90G, 250G And 350G

Model 83G may be equipped with a four cutting edge blade or a saw blade. Models 90G, 250G and 350G may be equipped with an eight tooth weed blade or an 80 tooth saw blade. When installing blade make certain all adapter washers are centered and square with blade surface.

DRIVE SHAFT

Models 82G, 100G And 200G

Models 82G, 100G and 200G are equipped with a flexible drive shaft. Drive shaft should be removed from drive shaft housing, cleaned, lubricated with lithium base grease and installed with ends reversed at 10 hour intervals of use.

To remove drive shaft, separate drive shaft housing from clutch housing. Mark drive shaft end and pull drive shaft from housing. Clean and lubricate drive shaft then install with end which was at clutch end now at trimmer head end. Reversing drive shaft ends extends drive shaft life.

Models 83G, 90G, 250G And 350G

Models 83G, 90G, 250G and 350G are equipped with a solid drive shaft supported in drive shaft housing in bushings. Drive shaft requires no regular maintenance however, if drive shaft is removed it should be lubricated with lithium base grease before reinstallation.

Drive shaft bushings located in drive shaft housing may be renewed on some models. To renew bushings, mark old bushing locations and remove old bushings. Install new bushings at old bushing locations.

BEARING HEAD

Model 82G

Model 82G is equipped with the bearing head shown in Fig. JD16. Bearing head is equipped with sealed bearings and requires no regular maintenance.

To disassemble bearing head, remove

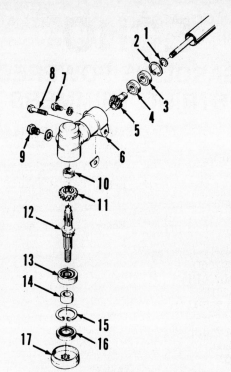

Fig. JD18—Exploded view of gear head used on Models 83G, 250G and 350G.

1. Snap ring	7. Clamp bolt	
2. Snap ring	8. Bolt	13. Bearing
3. Bearing	9. Check plug	14. Spacer
4. Bearing	10. Bearing	15. Snap ring
5. Input shaft	11. Gear	16. Seal
6. Housing	12. Arbor shaft	17. Cup washer

trimmer head. Remove clamp bolt (2) and locating screw (3). Separate bearing head assembly from drive shaft housing. Remove shield (6) and bracket (5) (as equipped). Remove cup washer (13) and washer (12). Carefully press drive shaft adapter (1) out of bearings. Remove snap rings (11 and 7). Press bearings (8 and 10) and spacer (9) out of housing.

Models 100G And 200G

Models 100G and 200G are equipped with the bearing head shown in Fig. JD17. Bearing head is equipped with sealed bearings and require no regular maintenance. To disassemble bearing head, remove screw (1) and clamp screw (2). Remove adapter plate (10) and snap ring (8). Use suitable puller to remove screw (2). Remove nut (4) and remove bearings and spacer as required.

GEAR HEAD

Models 83G, 90G, 250G And 350G

Models 83G, 90G, 250G and 350G are equipped with gear head shown in Fig. JD18. Check plug (9) should be removed and gear head lubricant checked at 10 hour intervals of use. Gear head housing should be kept ⅔ full of lithium base grease.

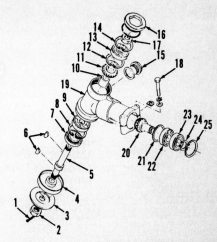

Fig. JD19—Exploded view of gear head used on Model 90G.

1. Cotter pin		
2. Nut		
3. Adapter plate		14. Snap ring
4. Adapter plate		15. Level check plug
5. Arbor shaft		16. Plug
6. Keys		17. Nut
7. Seal		18. Clamp bolt
8. Snap ring		19. Housing
9. Bearing		20. Gear
10. Spacer		21. Spacer
11. Gear		22. Bearing
12. Snap ring		23. Bearing
13. Bearing		24. Snap ring
		25. Snap ring

To disassemble gear head, remove trimmer head or blade assembly. Remove clamp bolt and head locating screw and separate gear head from drive shaft housing. Remove cup washer (17) and spacer (14). Remove snap ring (2) and use a suitable puller to remove input shaft (5) and bearing assembly. Remove snap ring (1) and press bearings (3 and 4) from input shaft as required. Remove seal (16) and snap ring (15). Use suitable puller to remove arbor shaft (12) and bearing assembly. Press bearing (13) and gear (11) from shaft as required. If bearing (10) remains in housing (6), heat housing to 140° F (60° C) and tap housing on wooden block to remove bearing.

Model 90G

Model 90G is equipped with gear head shown in Fig. JD19. Check plug (15) should be removed and gear head lubricant checked at 10 hour intervals of use. Gear head housing should be kept ⅔ full of lithium base grease.

To disassemble gear head, separate gear head from drive shaft housing tube. Remove cotter pin (1), nut (2), adapter plate (3), blade and adapter plate (4). Remove snap ring (25) and use suitable puller to remove input shaft and bearing assembly (20). Remove plug (16). Remove seal (7) and snap ring (8). Remove snap ring (14). Press arbor and bearing assembly from housing (19). Note (12) indicates snap ring position. Remove required snap rings and remove gears and bearings.

ECHO
GASOLINE POWERED
STRING TRIMMERS

Model	Engine Manufacturer	Engine Model	Displacement
SRM-140D, SRM-140DA, GT-140, GT-140A, GT-140B	Echo	. . . . .	13.8 cc
GT-160, GT-160A, GT-160AE	Echo	. . . . .	16.0 cc
SRM-200, SRM-200AE, SRM-200BE, SRM-200D, SRM-200DA, SRM-200DB, SRM-200E, SRM-201F, SRM-201FA, SRM-202D, SRM-202DA, SRM-202F, SRM-202FA, SRM-210E, SRM-210AE, GT-200, GT-200A, GT-200B, GT-200BE	Echo	. . . . .	21.2 cc
SRM-300, SRM-302ADX	Echo	. . . . .	30.1 cc
SRM-300E, SRM-300E/1, SRM-300AE, SRM-300AE/1	Echo	. . . . .	30.8 cc
SRM-400E, SRM-400AE, SRM-402DE	Echo	. . . . .	40.2 cc

ENGINE INFORMATION

All Echo trimmers and brush cutters are equipped with Echo two-stroke air-cooled gasoline engines. Refer to ECHO ENGINE SERVICE section of this manual.

FUEL MIXTURE

All Models

Manufacturer recommends mixing regular grade gasoline (unleaded is an acceptable substitute) with a good quality two-stroke air-cooled engine oil at a 25:1 ratio. Do not use fuel containing alcohol.

STRING TRIMMER

Refer to Figs. E1 through E17 for an exploded view of string trimmer heads used on Echo string trimmers. Not all heads will be covered in detail; however, the most widely used heads are covered. Service procedure for remaining heads is similar.

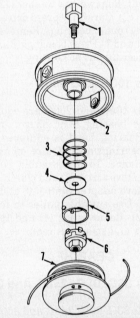

Fig. E1—Exploded view of dual strand semi-automatic trimmer head used on some SRM-200, SRM-201, SRM-202, SRM-300, SRM-302 and SRM-400 models.

1. Bolt
2. Drum
3. Spring
4. Washer
5. Outer drive
6. Inner cam
7. Spool

Semi-Automatic Dual Strand Trimmer Head

Models SRM-200, 200AE, 200BE, 200D, 200DA, 200DB, SRM-201F, 201FA, SRM-202D, 202DA, 202F, 202FA, SRM-300, 300AE, 300AE/1, 300E, 300E/1, SRM-302ADX, SRM-400AE, 400BE, and 400E may be equipped with dual strand semi-automatic trimmer head as shown in Fig. E1. To manually advance line with engine stopped, push in on button (7) and pull on each line. Procedure may have to be repeated to obtain desired line length. To extend line with engine running, operate trimmer at full operating rpm and tap button (7) on the ground. Line will automatically advance a measured amount.

To renew trimmer line, hold drum firmly and turn spool in direction shown in Fig. E2 to remove slack. Twist with a hard snap until plastic peg is between holes. Pull spool out of drum. Remove old line from spool. Spool will hold approximately 20 feet (6 m) of monofilament line. Insert one end of new line through hole on

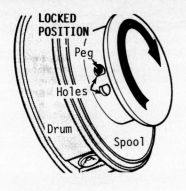

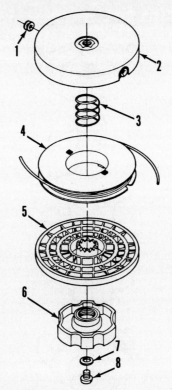

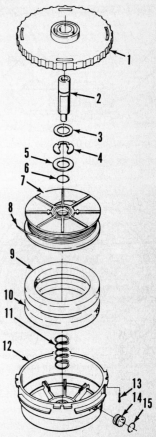

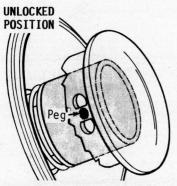

Fig. E2—To remove spool, hold drum firmly and turn spool in direction shown to take up slack, then twist with a sudden snap until plastic peg is between holes as shown in lower view.

Fig. E5—Exploded view of manual trimmer head used on some SRM-200, SRM-201, SRM-202, SRM-300, SRM-302 and SRM-400 models. This head is no longer available.

1. Line guide
2. Hub
3. Spring
4. Spool
5. Cover
6. Ball lock
7. Washer
8. Screw

Fig. E6—Exploded view of semi-automatic trimmer head used on some GT-140, GT-160, GT-200 and GT-210 models.

1. Plate
2. Adapter
3. Washer
4. Retainer ring
5. Washer
6. Retainer ring
7. Spool
8. Line
9. Foam pad
10. Foam pad
11. Spring
12. Hub
13. Cotter pin
14. Line guide
15. Retainer

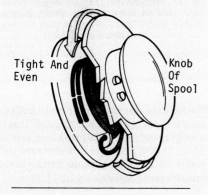

Fig. E3—End of line must be inserted through hole on spool as shown in lower view. Wind line tightly in direction indicated by arrow on spool.

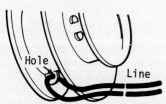

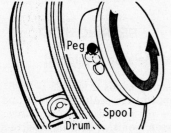

Fig. E4—Hold drum firmly and twist suddenly to lock spool in position.

spool (Fig. E3) and pull line through until line is the same length on both sides of hole. Wind both ends of line at the same time in direction indicated by arrow marked "cc" on edge of spool. Wind tightly and evenly from side to side and do not twist line. Insert ends of line through line guide openings, align pegs on drum with slots in spool and push spool into drum. Hold drum firmly, twist spool suddenly in direction shown in Fig. E4 until peg enters hole with a click and locks spool in position. Trim extending lines to desired lengths.

Manual Advance Dual Strand Trimmer Head

Models SRM-200, 200AE, 200BE, 200D, 200DA, 200DB, SRM-201F, 201FA, SRM-202D, 202DA, 202F, 202FA, SRM-300, 300AE, 300AE/1, 300E, 300E/1, SRM-302ADX, SRM-400AE and 400E may be equipped with manual advance dual strand trimmer head shown in Fig. E5. To extend line, stop engine and wait until all head rotation has stopped. Loosen lock knob (6) approximately one turn. Pull out the line on each side until line lengths are 6 inches (152 mm).

To renew line, remove slotted screw (8) and washer (7). Unscrew ball lock (6),

remove cover (5) and spring (3). Remove spool (4). Cut two 12 foot (4 m) lengths of 0.095 inch (2.4 mm) monofilament line. Insert one end of each line through the slot and into the locating hole on bottom side of spool. Line ends should extend approximately ¼ inch (6.4 mm) through locating holes. Hold lines tight and wind in a counterclockwise direction using care not to cross the lines. Insert the end of each line into each slot leaving approximately 6 inches (152 mm) of line extending from spool. Place spool into drum and feed one line through each of the line guides. Install spring, cover, ball lock, washer and screw.

Semi-Automatic Single Strand Trimmer Head

Models GT-140B, GT-160, 160A, 160AE, GT-200A, 200B, 200BE, 200CE, SRM-210AE and 210E may be equipped with a semi-automatic single strand trimmer head shown in Fig. E6. Line may be manually advanced with engine stopped by depressing "bump" button and pulling line out as required.

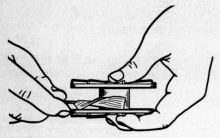

Fig. E7—Tape one end of line to center of spool.

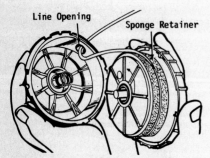

Fig. E9—Foam pads are installed on spool with trimmer line between them.

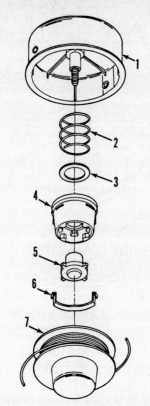

Fig. E11—Exploded view of semi-automatic trimmer head used on some SRM-140D and SRM-140DA models.

1. Hub	
2. Spring	5. Inner cam
3. Washer	6. Clip
4. Outer drive	7. Spool

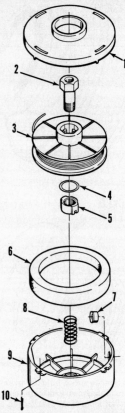

Fig. E12—Exploded view of semi-automatic trimmer head used on some GT-140B, GT-160, GT-160A, GT-200A, GT-200B and SRM-210E models. This head is no longer available.

1. Plate	6. Foam pad
2. Drive adapter	7. Line guide
3. Spool	8. Spring
4. "O" ring	9. Hub
5. Drive adapter nut	10. Cotter pin

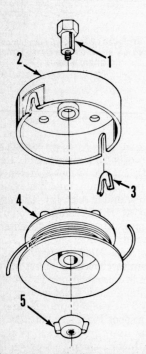

Fig. E10—Exploded view of manual trimmer head used on some GTL-140 and SRM-140 models. This head has also been used on light duty SRM-200, SRM-201 and SRM-202 models. Bolt (1) may be right or left hand thread according to model.

1. Bolt	
2. Drum	4. Spool
3. Line guide	5. Wing nut

To renew line, remove cotter pin (13). Rotate housing (12) counterclockwise and remove housing and line spool (7). Remove foam pads (9 and 10) and any remaining old line. Clean spool and inner surface of outer housing (12). Check indexing teeth on spool and in housing. Cut off approximately 25 feet (7.6 mm) of 0.080 inch (2 mm) monofilament line and tape one end of line to spool (Fig. E7). Wind line on spool in direction indicated by arrow on spool (Fig. E9). Install foam pads (9 and 10—Fig. E6) with line between pads as shown in Fig. E9. Insert line end through line guide (14-Fig. E6) opening then install spool and housing. Push housing in and rotate clockwise to lock in position. Install cotter pin (13).

Maxicut Trimmer Head

The "Maxicut" trimmer head (Fig. E17) is equipped with three plastic blades (2) attached to a plastic mounting disc (3) and is available as an after-market item. Note that nut (6) may be left or right-hand thread depending upon model being serviced.

BLADE

All Models So Equipped

An eight tooth weed and grass blade (A-Fig. E18) and an eighty tooth saw blade are available for some models. To install either blade, rotate the drive shaft until the holes in upper adapter plate and the gear or bearing head are aligned. Insert a locking rod (Fig. E19) into holes. Install blade making certain it is centered correctly on the adapter plate. Install lower adapter plate and locking nut. Install cotter pin.

To sharpen the eight tooth weed and grass blade, round the tooth bottom 1-2 mm (0.04-0.08 in.) (Fig. E20) to prevent blade cracking. Length of cutting edge must be about 10 mm (0.4 in.) from the base of the tooth, but the rounded 2 mm part is not to be sharpened. Sharpen each blade equally to retain balance.

To sharpen the eighty tooth saw blade, setting can be done by using a circular saw setter. Sharpen blade as shown in Fig. E21.

BEARING HEAD

All Models So Equipped

Bearing heads (Fig. E22 or E23) are equipped with sealed bearings and require no periodic maintenance. To disassemble either bearing head, remove screw (1) and clamp screw (2). Remove adapter plate (10) and snap ring (8). Use

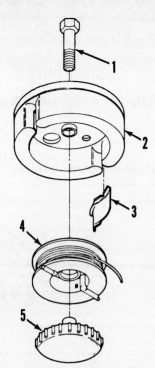

Fig. E13—Exploded view of manual trimmer head used on some GT-140B, GT-160, GT-160A, GT-160AE, GT-200A, GT-200B, GT-200CE, SRM-210E and SRM-210AE models.

1. Bolt
2. Drum
3. Line guide
4. Spool
5. Ball lock

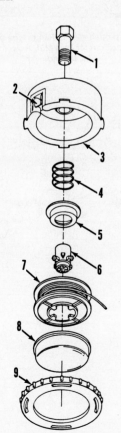

Fig. E14—Exploded view of semi-automatic trimmer head used on GT-200 model. This head is no longer available.

1. Bolt
2. Line guide
3. Drum
4. Spring
5. Spring adapter
6. Inner cam
7. Spool
8. Button
9. Cover

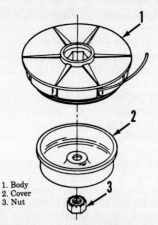

1. Body
2. Cover
3. Nut

Fig. E15—Exploded view of manual trimmer head used on some GT-140, GT-140A and GT-200 models. Nut (3) is right hand thread for GT-140A and GT-200 models but is left hand thread for GT-140 model.

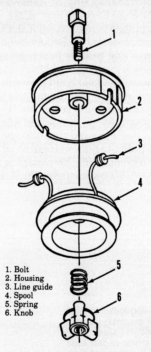

1. Bolt
2. Housing
3. Line guide
4. Spool
5. Spring
6. Knob

Fig. E16—Exploded view of heavy duty manual trimmer head used on some SRM-200, SRM-201, SRM-202, SRM-250, SRM-300, SRM-302 and SRM-400 models.

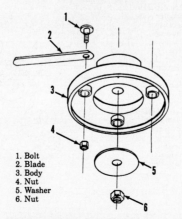

1. Bolt
2. Blade
3. Body
4. Nut
5. Washer
6. Nut

Fig. E17—Exploded view of "Maxicut" head which is available for all GT and SRM trimmers. Nut (6) may have left or right hand threads depending upon model.

Fig. E18—Weed and grass blade (A) and brush blade (B) are available for some models.

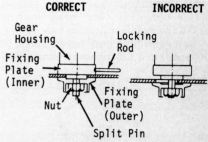

Fig. E19—Make certain blade is centered on adapter plate (fixing plate) during installation.

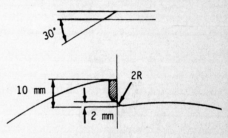

Fig. E20—The eight tooth weed and grass blade may be sharpened as shown.

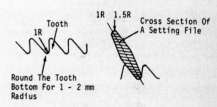

Fig. E21—The eighty tooth brush blade may be sharpened as shown.

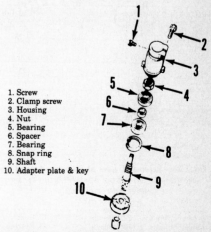

1. Screw
2. Clamp screw
3. Housing
4. Nut
5. Bearing
6. Spacer
7. Bearing
8. Snap ring
9. Shaft
10. Adapter plate & key

Fig. E22—Exploded view of bearing head used on some models.

suitable puller to remove bearing and arbor assemblies. Remove nut (4) and remove bearings and spacer as required.

GEAR HEAD

All Models So Equipped

Gear heads (Figs. E24, E25, E26 and E27) should have gear lubricant checked at 50 hour intervals. To check, remove check plug (15). Gear head housing should be ⅔ full of lithium base grease.

To disassemble gear heads shown in Figs. E24 and E25, remove trimmer head

or blade assembly. Remove screw (14) and clamp bolt (16). Remove seal (5) from housing (13) and remove snap ring (7). Remove bushing (6) as equipped. Remove snap ring (20). Use suitable puller to remove input shaft and gear (17). Use suitable puller to remove arbor shaft (9). Remove required snap rings and remove bearings and gears.

Gear heads shown in Figs. E26 and E27 are similarly constructed. Spacers (17 and 18-Fig. E27) may also be used in gear head shown in Fig. E26. Remove trimmer head or blade assembly. Remove screw (13-Fig. E26 or E27) and clamp bolt (14). Separate gear head from drive shaft housing tube. Remove snap ring (5), seal (6) and bushing (7). On gear head shown in Fig. E26, seal (6) must be removed to gain access to snap ring (5). Remove snap ring (21-Fig. E26 or Fig. E27). Use suitable pullers to remove input shaft and arbor shaft assemblies. Remove required snap rings and remove bearings, gears and spacers.

To disassemble gear head shown in Fig. E28, separate gear head from drive shaft housing tube. Remove cotter pin (1), nut (2), adapter plate (3), blade and adapter plate (4). Remove snap ring (25) and use suitable puller to remove input shaft and bearing assembly (20). Remove plug (16). Remove seal (7) and snap ring (8). Remove

snap ring (14). Press arbor and bearing assembly from housing (19).

DRIVE SHAFT

All Models With Flexible Drive Shaft

Flexible drive shaft should be removed, cleaned and lubricated with lithium base grease at 18 hour intervals of use. To remove, separate drive shaft housing tube from engine assembly. Mark posi-

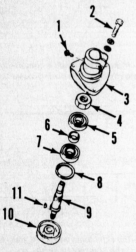

Fig. E23—Exploded view of bearing head used on some models.

1. Screw	5. Bearing	
2. Clamp screw	6. Spacer	9. Shaft
3. Housing	7. Bearing	10. Adapter
4. Nut	8. Snap ring	11. Key

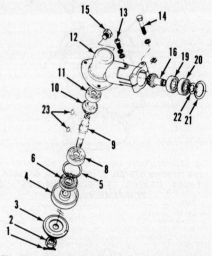

Fig. E26—Exploded view of flange type gear head with arbor shaft cut for keys (23). Refer to Fig. E27 for legend.

Fig. E25—Exploded view of gear head assembly used on many models. Gear head shown is similar to gear head shown in Fig. E24 except arbor shaft has splines instead of keys.

1. Cotter pin
2. Nut
3. Adapter plate
4. Adapter plate
5. Seal
6. Bushing
7. Snap ring
8. Bearing
9. Arbor shaft
10. Snap ring
11. Gear
12. Bearing
13. Housing
14. Screw
15. Level check plug
16. Clamp bolt
17. Gear
18. Bearing
19. Bearing
20. Snap ring
21. Snap ring

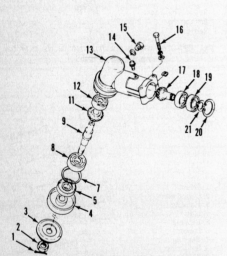

Fig. E24—Exploded view of gear head used on many models. Note arbor shaft (9) is cut for keys. Refer also to Fig. E25.

1. Cotter pin	9. Arbor shaft	
2. Nut	11. Gear	
3. Adapter plate	12. Bearing	17. Gear
4. Adapter plate	13. Housing	18. Bearing
5. Seal	14. Screw	19. Bearing
7. Snap ring	15. Level check plug	20. Snap ring
8. Bearing	16. Clamp bolt	21. Snap ring

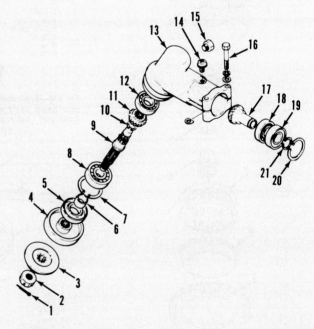

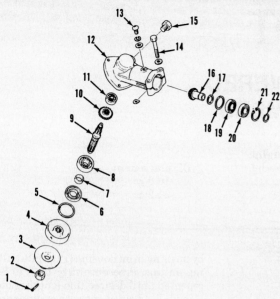

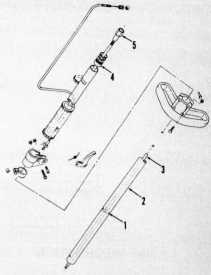

Fig. E27—Exploded view of gear head which is equipped with splined arbor shaft (9). Refer to Fig. E26.

1. Cotter pin
2. Nut
3. Adapter plate
4. Adapter plate
5. Snap ring
6. Seal
7. Bushing
8. Bearing
9. Arbor shaft
10. Gear
11. Bearing
12. Housing
13. Screw
14. Clamp bolt
15. Level check plug
16. Gear
17. Spacer
18. Spacer
19. Bearing
20. Bearing
21. Snap ring
22. Snap ring

Fig. E29—Exploded view of housing and solid drive shaft.
1. Internal drive shaft bearing
2. Drive shaft housing
3. Solid steel drive shaft
4. Drive shaft bearing
5. Drive shaft adapter

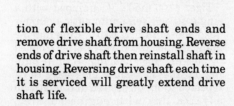

Fig. E28—Exploded view of gear head used on SRM-302ADX models.

1. Cotter pin	10. Spacer
2. Nut	11. Gear
3. Adapter plate	12. Snap ring	19. Housing
4. Adapter plate	13. Bearing	20. Gear
5. Arbor shaft	14. Snap ring	21. Spacer
6. Keys	15. Level check plug	22. Bearing
7. Seal	16. Plug	23. Bearing
8. Snap ring	17. Nut	24. Snap ring
9. Bearing	18. Clamp bolt	25. Snap ring

All Models With Solid Drive Shaft

A solid steel drive shaft is used on heavy duty models which may be equipped with grass and weed or saw blade. Drive shaft runs through housing and is supported in bushings in drive shaft housing tube (Fig. E29). No regular maintenance is required; however, if drive shaft is removed, lubricate with lithium base grease before reinstallation.

tion of flexible drive shaft ends and remove drive shaft from housing. Reverse ends of drive shaft then reinstall shaft in housing. Reversing drive shaft each time it is serviced will greatly extend drive shaft life.

ELLIOT

GASOLINE POWERED STRING TRIMMERS

Model	Engine Manufacturer	Engine Model	Displacement
Tiger 4100	Kioritz	. . . . .	16.0 cc
Tiger 4200	Kioritz	. . . . .	21.2 cc

ENGINE INFORMATION

All Models

All Elliot trimmer models listed are equipped with Kioritz two-stroke air-cooled gasoline engines. Identify engine model by trimmer model or engine displacement. Refer to KIORITZ ENGINE SERVICE section of this manual.

FUEL MIXTURE

All Models

Manufacturer recommends mixing regular grade gasoline (unleaded is an acceptable substitute) with a good quality two-stroke air-cooled engine oil at a 25:1 ratio. Do not use fuel containing alcohol.

STRING TRIMMER

Tiger 4100 Model

Tiger 4100 model is equipped with a single strand semi-automatic trimmer head shown in Fig. EL10. Line may be manually advanced with engine stopped by pushing in on housing (9) while pulling on line. Procedure may have to be repeated to obtain desired line length. To advance line with engine running, operate engine at full rpm and tap housing (9) on the ground. Each time housing is tapped on the ground, a measured amount of trimmer line will be advanced.

To renew trimmer line, remove cotter key (10) and twist housing (9) counterclockwise to remove housing. Remove foam pad (6) and any remaining line on spool (3). Clean spool and inside of housing. Cut off approximately 25 feet (7.6 m) of 0.080 inch (2 mm) monofilament line and tape one end of line to spool (Fig. EL12). Wind line on spool in direction indicated by arrow on spool (Fig. EL14). Install foam pad with line end protruding from between foam pad and spool as shown in Fig. EL14. Insert line end through line guide and install housing and spring assembly on spool. Push in on housing and twist housing in a clockwise direction to lock into position. Install cotter key through hole in housing and cover.

Tiger 4200 Model

Tiger 4200 model is equipped with a single strand semi-automatic trimmer head shown in Fig. EL11. Line may be manually advanced with engine stopped

by pushing in on housing (12) while pulling on line. Procedure may have to be repeated until desired line length is obtained. To advance line with engine running, operate trimmer engine at full rpm and tap housing (12) on the ground. Each time housing is tapped on the ground, a measured amount of trimmer line is advanced.

Fig. EL10—Exploded view of single strand semi-automatic trimmer head used on Tiger 4100 model.

1. Cover	6. Foam pad
2. Drive adapter	7. Line guide
3. Spool	8. Spring
4. "O" ring	9. Housing
5. Drive adapter nut	10. Cotter pin

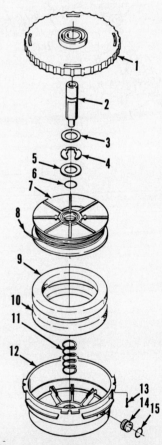

Fig. EL11—Exploded view of single strand semi-automatic trimmer head used on Tiger 4200 model.

1. Cover	6. Retainer ring	11. Spring
2. Drive adapter	7. Spool	12. Housing
3. Washer	8. Line	13. Cotter pin
4. Retainer	9. Foam pad	14. Line guide
5. Washer	10. Foam pad	15. Retainer

To renew trimmer line, remove cotter pin (13). Twist housing (12) counter-clockwise and remove housing. Remove foam pads (9 and 10) and any remaining line from spool (7). Clean spool and inner area of housing. Cut off approximately 25 feet (7.6 mm) of 0.080 inch (2 mm) monofilament line and tape one end of line to spool (Fig. EL12). Wind line on spool in direction indicated by arrow on spool (Fig. EL13). Install foam pads (9 and 10—Fig. EL11) so line is protruding from center of foam pads (Fig. EL13). Insert end of line through line guide and install spool, housing and spring. Push in on housing and twist housing in a clockwise direction to lock in position and install cotter pin (13-Fig. EL11).

DRIVE SHAFT

All Models

All models are equipped with a flexible drive shaft enclosed in the drive shaft housing tube. Drive shaft has squared ends which engage adapters at each end. Drive shaft should be removed for maintenance at 50 hour intervals of use. Remove screw (4-Fig. EL15) and bolt (3) at bearing head housing and separate bearing head from drive shaft housing. Pull flexible drive shaft from housing.

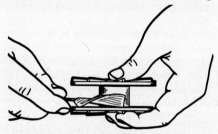

Fig. EL12—Tape one end of new line to center of spool as shown.

Lubricate drive shaft with lithium base grease and reinstall in housing with end which was previously at clutch end at bearing head end. Reversing drive shaft ends extends drive shaft life. Make certain ends of drive shaft properly engage upper and lower square drive adapters when installing.

BEARING HEAD

All Models

All models are equipped with the bearing head shown in Fig. EL15. Bearing head is equipped with sealed bearings

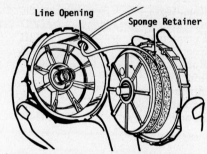

Fig. EL13—Install foam pads with line protruding from between pads. Wind line in direction indicated by arrow on spool.

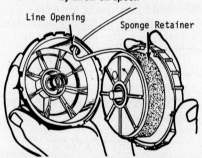

Fig. EL14—Install foam pad with line protruding between pad and spool as shown. Wind line in direction indicated by arrow on spool.

and requires no regular maintenance. To disassemble bearing head, remove trimmer head assembly and cup washer (13). Remove screw (4) and bolt (3) and separate bearing head from drive shaft housing tube. Remove trimmer head assembly and cup washer (13). Remove snap ring (10) and use a suitable puller to remove arbor shaft (11) and bearing assembly. Remove nut (6) and press bearings (7 and 9) and spacer (8) from arbor shaft as required.

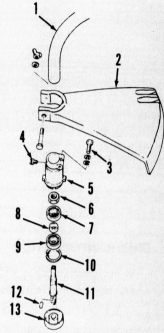

Fig. EL15—Exploded view of bearing head used on all models. Bearings (7 and 9) are sealed bearings and require no regular maintenance.

1. Drive shaft housing
2. Shield
3. Bolt
4. Screw
5. Housing
6. Nut
7. Bearing
8. Spacer
9. Bearing
10. Snap ring
11. Arbor (output) shaft
12. Pin
13. Cup washer

GREEN MACHINE
GASOLINE POWERED STRING TRIMMERS

Model	Engine Manufacturer	Engine Model	Displacement
1600	PPP	99E	31.0 cc
1730	Komatsu	G2E	25.4 cc
1800	PPP	99E	31.0 cc
2200	Komatsu	G2E	25.4 cc
2230	PPP	99E	31.0 cc
2340	Komatsu	G2E	25.4 cc
2500LP	Komatsu	G2D	22.5 cc
2510LP	Komatsu	G2D	22.5 cc
2540LP	Komatsu	G2D	22.5 cc
3000LP	Komatsu	G2E	25.4 cc
3000SS	Shindaiwa	...	24.1 cc
3540	Shindaiwa	...	24.1 cc
4000LP	Komatsu	G4K	41.5 cc
4500LP	Komatsu	G4K	41.5 cc

ENGINE INFORMATION

Green Machine trimmers and brush cutters may be equipped with Piston Powered Products (PPP), Komatsu or Mitsubishi two-stroke air-cooled gasoline engines. Identify engine by manufacturer, engine model number or engine displacement. Refer to the appropriate PISTON POWERED PRODUCT ENGINE SERVICE, KOMATSU ENGINE SERVICE or MITSUBISHI ENGINE SERVICE section of this manual.

FUEL MIXTURE

All Models

Models 1600, 1800 and 2230 require a fuel/oil mixture ratio of 20:1 which is 6.4 ounces (187.6 mL) of oil to 1 gallon (3.8 L) of gasoline. All other models require a fuel/oil mixture ratio of 25:1 which is 5.12 ounces (150 mL) of oil to 1 gallon (3.8 L) of gasoline. Manufacturer recommends mixing regular grade gasoline of at least 87 octane rating, with good quality two-stroke air cooled engine oil. Do not use fuel containing alcohol.

STRING TRIMMER

Models 1600, 1730, 1800, 2230, 2340, 2500LP, 2510LP, 2540, 3540, 4000LP And 4500LP

Dual strand semi-automatic (Tap-For-Cord) trimmer head shown in Figs. GM10 and GM11 are standard equipment for most models. To extend line on trimmer head shown in Fig. GM10 or GM11 with trimmer engine stopped, push in on spool button and pull line ends out to desired length. To extend line with trimmer engine running, operate trimmer engine at full rpm and tap spool button on the ground. Each time spool button is tapped on the ground, a measured amount of line will be advanced.

To renew trimmer line, refer to Fig. GM10. Push in on the two lock tabs on cap (10) and remove cap and spool. Remove any remaining line on spool. Clean spool, cap and inner cavity of housing. Note that Models 1600, 1730, 1800 and 2230 require 16 feet (4.9 m) of

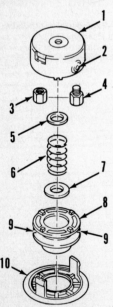

Fig. GM10—Exploded view of the dual strand semi-automatic (Tap-For-Cord) trimmer head used on Models 1600, 1730, 1800, 2230, 2340, 2500LP, 2510LP, 2540, 3540, 4000LP and 4500LP. Note only one adapter (3) or (4) will be used according to model. Refer also to Fig. GM11.

1. Housing
2. Line guides
3. Adapter
4. Adapter
5. Washer
6. Spring
7. Washer
8. Spool
9. Line notch
10. Cap

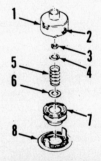

Fig. GM11—Exploded view of trimmer head used on some models which is similar to head shown in Fig. GM10. Note differences in housing (1-Fig. GM11) and lack of adapter (3 or 4-Fig. GM10).

1. Housing
2. Line guides
3. Pal nut
4. Washer
5. Spring
6. Washer
7. Spool
8. Cap

0.080 inch (2 mm) line, Models 2340, 2540 and 3540 require 30 feet (12.6 m) of 0.080 inch (2 mm) line and Models 2500LP, 2510LP, 4000LP and 4500LP require 50 feet (21.8 m) of 0.105 inch (2.6 mm) line. On all models, loop one end of new line through the two holes in spool (Fig. GM12) and rotate spool so line is wound tightly and neatly in direction indicated by arrow on spool (Fig. GM16). Slip lines into notches in spool (8-Fig. GM10), insert line ends through line guides (2) and install spool in housing. Align locking tabs of trimmer head cap (10) with notches in housing (1) and snap cap onto housing. Advance line manually to make certain line is free.

Model 2200

Model 2200 is equipped with a dual strand semi-automatic trimmer head shown in Fig. GM13. To extend line with trimmer engine stopped, pull on lines while pushing in on button (cap) (8). To extend line with engine running, operate trimmer engine at full rpm and tap button (8) on the ground. Each time button is tapped on the ground, a measured amount of new line will be advanced.

To renew line, unsnap cap (8) from screw (7). Note screw (7) has left-hand

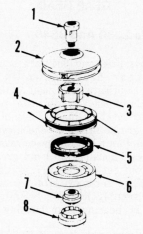

Fig. GM12—Rotate spool to wind line in direction indicated by arrow on spool.

Fig. GM13—Exploded view of dual strand semi-automatic trimmer head used on Model 2200.
1. Adapter
2. Upper housing
3. Cam
4. Spool
5. Foam pad
6. Lower housing
7. Screw (LH)
8. Cap

threads. Remove screw (7), cover (6) and spool (4). Remove any remaining line from spool. Clean spool, cover and housing (2). Cut two 14 foot (4.4 m) of 0.080 inch (2 mm) monofilament line. Insert one end of each line into each of the two holes in spool. Rotate spool to wind line evenly in direction indicated by arrow on spool (Fig. GM14). Install foam pad (5-Fig. GM13). Insert line ends through line guides and reinstall spool into housing. Spool is installed so side of spool with arrow will be toward the ground. Install cover, screw and snap button onto screw.

Model 3000SS

Model 3000SS may be equipped with trimmer head shown in Fig. GM15. Trimmer head may be a manual line feed or a semi-automatic (Tap-For-Cord) line feed according to model. To extend line on manual models, stop trimmer engine and wait for all head rotation to stop. Loosen lock knob (12) and pull line ends out of housing until desired line length is obtained. To extend line on semi-automatic trimmer head, push in on lock knob (12) while pulling lines from housing. Procedure may have to be repeated until desired line length has been obtained. To extend line with engine running, operate trimmer engine at full rpm and tap lock knob on the ground. Each time lock knob is tapped on the ground a measured amount of new line will be advanced.

To renew line on either model, note lock knob has left-hand threads and remove lock knob (12), cover (11) and spool (9). Remove any remaining line from spool. Clean spool, cover and inner cavity of housing (1). Cut two 20 foot (8.7 mm) lengths of 0.095 inch (2.4 mm) monofilament line. Insert one end of each line into each of the two holes in inside wall of spool. Rotate spool to wind lines in direction indicated by arrow on spool. Insert line ends through line guides and install spool into upper housing with notched side

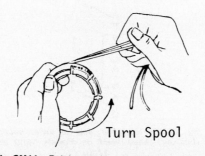

Fig. GM14—Rotate spool to wind line in direction indicated by arrow on spool.

toward housing. Install cover and lock knob.

BLADE

All Models So Equipped

All models except Models 1600 and 1730 may be equipped with one of the blades shown in Fig. GM17. To install

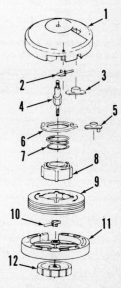

Fig. GM15—Exploded view of trimmer head used on Model 3000SS. Trimmer head may be manual line feed or semi-automatic line feed according to parts installed. Note parts designated (TFC) are for semi-automatic line feed heads and parts designated (M) are for manual line feed heads.
1. Upper housing
2. Line saver
3. Button (M)
4. Arbor
5. Button (TFC)
6. Lock ring (M)
7. Spring
8. Cam
9. Spool
10. Line saver
11. Lower housing
12. Lock knob

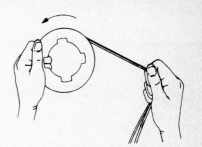

Fig. GM16—Rotate spool to wind line in direction indicated by arrow on spool.

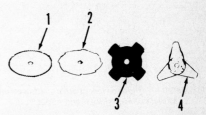

Fig. GM17—A variety of blades are offered for some models.
1. Saw blade
2. Eight edge blade
3. Four edge blade
4. Three edge blade

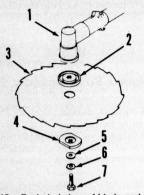

Fig. GM18—Exploded view of blade and attaching parts. Refer to text.

1. Gear head
2. Upper cup washer
3. Blade
4. Lower cup washer
5. Flat washer
6. Lock washer
7. Bolt (LH)

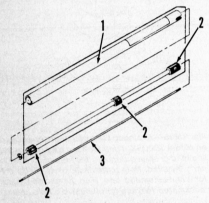

Fig. GM19—Exploded view of drive shaft used on Models 2200, 2230, 2340, 2500LP, 2510LP, 2540LP, 3000LP and 3000SS.

1. Drive shaft housing
2. Bushings
3. Drive shaft

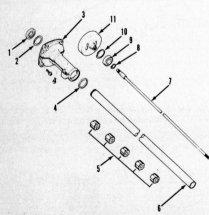

Fig. GM20—Exploded view of drive shaft used on Models 3540, 4000LP and 4500LP.

1. Seal
2. Snap ring
3. Housing
4. Seal
5. Bushings
6. Drive shaft housing
7. Drive shaft
8. Snap ring
9. Bearing
10. Snap ring
11. Clutch drum

blade, assemble parts in sequence shown in Fig. GM18. Note bolt (7) has left-hand threads. Make certain splines in cup washers (2 and 4) are aligned with splines on arbor shaft and cup washer (4) must be squarely seated.

DRIVE SHAFT

Models 1600, 1730 And 1800

Models 1600, 1730 and 1800 are direct drive trimmers (no clutch assembly) equipped with a flexible drive shaft. Drive shaft on all models should be removed, cleaned and lubricated with lithium base grease at 10 hour intervals of use. Make certain flexible drive shaft cable IS NOT reversed during reassembly. Drive shaft cable may be wound for rotation in one direction only.

Models 2200, 2230, 2340, 2500LP, 2510LP, 2540LP, 3000LP And 3000SS

Models 2200, 2230, 2340, 2500LP, 2510LP, 2540LP, 3000LP and 3000SS are equipped with solid steel drive shaft mounted in bushings installed in drive shaft housing. Drive shaft requires no regular maintenance. Bushings may be renewed using bushing removal and installation tool number 309727. Bushing removal and installation tool is marked for installation of bushings in correct locations. If bushing tool is not available, mark locations of old bushings in drive shaft housing before bushing removal. Install new bushings in the same positions from which old bushings were removed. Lubricate drive shaft with lithium base grease prior to installation.

Models 3540, 4000LP And 4500LP

Models 3540, 4000LP and 4500LP are equipped with a solid steel drive shaft mounted in bushings in drive shaft housing. Drive shaft requires no regular maintenance. Bushings (5-Fig. GM20)

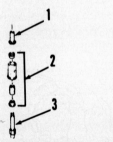

Fig. GM21—Exploded view of lower bearing (bushing) head used on Models 1600 and 1730.

1. Arbor
2. Bushing kit
3. Arbor

may be removed using bushing removal and installation tool number 400337. Bushing removal and installation tool is marked for installation of bushings in correct locations. If bushing tool is not available, mark locations of old bushings in drive shaft housing before bushing removal. Install new bushings in the same positions from which old bushings were removed. Lubricate drive shaft with lithium base grease prior to installation.

BEARING HEAD

Models 1600 And 1730

Models 1600 and 1730 are equipped with a bearing head shown in Fig. GM21. Bearing head requires no regular maintenance. A bearing kit (part number 160305) is available for bearing head repair.

BEARING HEAD/LOWER CLUTCH

Model 1800

Model 1800 is equipped with a bearing head incorporated in the lower clutch unit (Fig. GM22). Bearing head is equipped with sealed bearings and requires no regular maintenance.

To renew bearings or remove clutch assembly, remove trimmer head and cup washer (15). Remove the three bolts retaining bearing plate (11) to housing (4). Separate housing from bearing plate. Remove clutch shoe assembly (6) as required. Remove clutch drum (7) and shield (5). Press arbor shaft (8) from bearings. Remove snap rings (9 and 14). Remove bearings (10 and 13) and spacer (12).

GEAR HEAD

Models 2230 And 3540

Models 2230 and 3540 are equipped with gear head shown in Fig. GM23. Lubricate gear head at 10 hour intervals of use. To lubricate, remove trimmer head or blade assembly. Install a grease fitting at check plug (1) location. Pump lithium base grease into gear head housing until old grease is forced out between seal (7) and spacer (8). Failure to remove trimmer head or blade assembly prior to lubrication will result in bearing/gear housing damage.

To disassemble gear head, remove trimmer head or blade assembly and separate gear head from drive shaft housing. Remove all bolts (19) and separate gear housing halves (2 and 18).

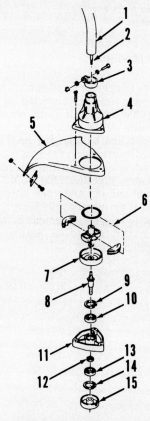

Fig. GM22—Exploded view of lower clutch and bearing head unit used on Model 1800.

1. Drive shaft housing	
2. Drive shaft	
3. Clamp	9. Snap ring
4. Housing	10. Bearing
5. Shield	11. Bearing plate
6. Clutch assembly	12. Spacer
7. Clutch drum	13. Bearing
8. Arbor	14. Snap ring
	15. Upper cup washer

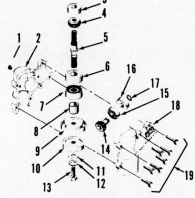

Fig. GM23—Exploded view of gear head used on Models 2230 and 3540.

1. Check plug	
2. Housing	11. Flat washer
3. Bearing	12. Lock washer
4. Gear	13. Bolt (LH)
5. Arbor (output) shaft	14. Input shaft
6. Bearing	15. Bearing
7. Seal	16. Bearing
8. Spacer	17. Snap ring
9. Upper cup washer	18. Housing
10. Lower cup washer	19. Bolts

Remove shaft, bearing and gear assemblies. Press bearings and gears from input shaft (14) and arbor shaft (5) as required. Lubricate parts during reassembly and pack housing with lithium base grease prior to reassembly.

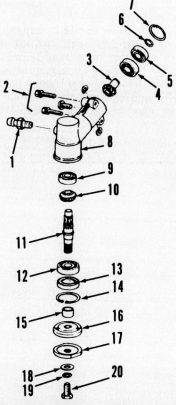

Fig. GM24—Exploded view of gear head used on Models 2200, 2500LP, 2540LP, 3000LP, 3000SS, 4000LP and 4500LP.

1. Grease fitting	11. Arbor (output) shaft
2. Bolts	12. Bearing
3. Input shaft	13. Seal
4. Bearing	14. Snap ring
5. Bearing	15. Spacer
6. Snap ring	16. Upper cup washer
7. Snap ring	17. Lower cup washer
8. Housing	18. Flat washer
9. Bearing	19. Lock washer
10. Gear	20. Bolt (LH)

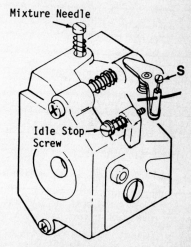

Fig. GM25—Shaft puller is available from Green Machine to pull arbor shaft and input shaft.

1. Washer	3. Bolt
2. Nut	4. Puller body

Models 2200, 2500LP, 2540LP, 3000LP, 3000SS, 4000LP And 4500LP

Models 2200, 2500LP, 2540LP, 3000LP, 3000SS, 4000LP and 4500LP are equipped with gear head shown in Fig. GM24. Lubricate gear head at 30 hour intervals of use. To lubricate gear head, remove trimmer head or blade assembly. Pump lithium base grease into grease fitting (1) until grease appears at seal (13) pushing spacer (15) out. Make certain spacer (15) is pushed back into position and reinstall trimmer head or blade assembly. Failure to remove trimmer head or blade assembly prior to lubrication may result in bearing, or housing damage.

To disassemble gear head, remove trimmer head or blade assembly. Sepa-

Fig. GM26—Loosen set screw (S) and move throttle cable to provide 0.02-0.04 inch (0.5-1.0 mm) trigger movement before carburetor throttle lever begins to move.

Fig. GM27—Exploded view of throttle cable junction.

1. Inner throttle cable	3. Jam nut
2. Throttle cable housing	4. Adjustment nut

rate gear head from drive shaft housing. Remove snap ring (7). Insert screwdriver or suitable wedge into gear head housing split and carefully expand housing. Remove input shaft (3) and bearing assembly. Remove snap ring (6) and press bearings (4 and 5) from input shaft as required. Remove spacer (15) and snap ring (14). Use a suitable puller (Fig. GM25) to remove arbor (output) shaft (11-Fig. GM24) and bearing assembly. If bearing (9) stays in housing (8), heat housing to 140°F (60°C) and tap housing on wooden block to remove bearing (9). Press bearing (12) and gear (10) from arbor shaft as required. Lubricate all parts during assembly. Fill housing (8) with lithium base grease prior to shaft installations.

THROTTLE TRIGGER AND CABLE

Models 1600, 1800 And 2230

Throttle trigger located on drive shaft housing tube controls engine rpm. Throttle cable should be lubricated at each end by applying SAE 30 oil to inner throttle cable wire. Lubricate throttle cable at 20 hour intervals of use.

Throttle cable should be adjusted to provide 0.02-0.04 inch (0.5-1.0 mm) throttle trigger movement before carburetor throttle lever begins to move. Adjust by loosening set screw (S-Fig. GM26) and moving cable housing and inner wire to provide specified free

play. Tighten set screw (S) to maintain adjustment.

All Other Models

Throttle trigger located on drive shaft housing tube is connected to a throttle cable for controlling engine rpm. Throttle cable should be lubricated at each end by applying SAE 30 oil to inner throttle wire. Throttle cable should be adjusted at adjustment nut at throttle cable junction (Fig. GM27). Loosen jam nut (3) and turn adjustment nut (4) to provide 0.06 inch (1.6 mm) throttle trigger movement before carburetor throttle valve begins to move. Tighten jam nut.

HOFFCO
GASOLINE POWERED STRING TRIMMERS

Model	Engine Manufacturer	Engine Model	Displacement
P-9, P-10, P-10A, P-85, P-850, WW 76, WW 77, WW 85, WW 850	Tecumseh	AV520-670	85 cc
JP420D, JP420, WT320H, GT320	Tecumseh	TC200	32.8 cc
GT256SPL, WT250HT, JP300	Fuji	ECO2-F	25.6 cc
JP390	Fuji	ECO3-F	30.5 cc
PC22, PC22A, PC225, PC380, WT230HT, GT22, GT22A, GT225, GT225SPL, HOFFIE 22, GTX, GTX-R, WC22, JP660, JP225, JP320	Fuji	ECO2-R	22.5 cc
GT160TL, GT160B, GT160T, WT160H, WT160HT, LIL WHIZ 1600	Fuji	ECO1-R	15.4 cc
WC215H-T, GT215B-H-T, JP215, WT215HB, JP270	Kioritz	H1-AH	21.2 cc
GT14-B-T, WT14H, LIL WHIZ 600	Kioritz	G1-AH	13.8 cc

ENGINE INFORMATION

All Models

Hoffco gasoline powered string trimmers and brush cutters may be equipped with two-stroke engines manufactured by Tecumseh, Fuji or Kioritz. Refer to trimmer or brush cutter model number in the preceding identification chart to determine engine manufacturer, then refer to the appropriate engine service section in this manual. Engines may be identified by manufacturer, model number or engine displacement.

FUEL MIXTURE

All Models

Hoffco recommends a fuel/oil mixture of 24:1. Mix regular grade gasoline with a good quality oil recommended for two-stroke air cooled engines.

STRING TRIMMER

Single Strand Trimmer Head

EARLY MODEL. Refer to Fig. HF10 for exploded view of semi-automatic single strand trimmer head used on early models. To manually advance line with engine stopped, push hub assembly toward drive tube while pulling line out. Procedure may have to be repeated to provide adequate line length. To advance line with engine running, tap hub assembly on the ground with engine at full operating rpm. Line will automatically advance a measured amount.

To disassemble trimmer head, remove cotter pin (13) and twist hub (12) counterclockwise. Remove hub and spool (7). Remove foam pads (9 and 10) and remaining old line. Clean all internal parts of hub, spool and cover. To renew line, cut off approximately 25 feet (7.6 m) of 0.080 inch (2 mm) monofilament line. Tape one end to center of spool (Fig. HF11) and carefully wind line in direction indicated by arrow on

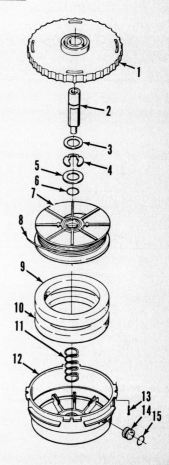

Fig. HF10—Exploded view of early type semi-automatic single strand trimmer head.

1. Plate	
2. Adapter	9. Foam pad
3. Washer	10. Foam pad
4. Retainer ring	11. Spring
5. Washer	12. Hub
6. Retainer ring	13. Cotter pin
7. Spool	14. Line guide
8. Line	15. Retainer

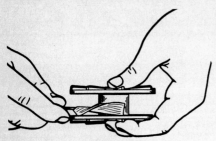

Fig. HF11—Tape line to spool center when renewing line.

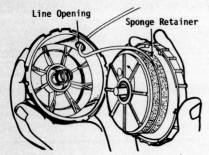

Fig. HF13—After line is wound on spool, install foam pads with line protruding as shown.

spool (Fig. HF13). Leave a short length of line extending from spool and install foam pads (9 and 10-Fig. HF10) so that line is between pads after installation (Fig. HF13). One side of spool is marked "motor" and the other side is marked "top". Side marked "motor" is installed toward cover (1-Fig. HF10). Side marked "top" is toward hub (12). Slip extended line end through line guide (14) in hub (12) and install spool in hub. Install hub and spool assembly on cover (1). Push in on hub against spring tension and rotate in a clockwise direction to engage lock tabs. Install cotter pin (13).

LATE MODEL. Refer to Fig. HF14 for an exploded view of semi-automatic single strand line trimmer head used on later models. To manually advance line with engine stopped, push button (7) toward trimmer tube and pull on line. Procedure may have to be repeated until desired line length has been obtained. To extend line with engine running, operate trimmer at full rpm and tap button (7) on the ground. Line will advance a measured amount each time button is tapped on the ground.

To renew line, remove cover (8), button (7) and spool (5). Clean all parts thoroughly and remove any remaining old line from spool. Wind approximately 30 feet (9 m) of 0.080 inch (2 mm) monofilament line onto spool in direction indicated by arrow on spool. Insert line end through line guide opening in drum (1) and install spool, button and cover.

Semi-Automatic Dual Strand Trimmer Head

Refer to Fig. HF15 for an exploded view of dual strand trimmer head used on some models. To manually advance line with engine stopped, push in on button (7) and pull on each line. Procedure may have to be repeated to obtain desired line length. To extend line with engine running, operate trimmer at full operating rpm and tap button (7) on the ground. Line will automatically advance a measured amount.

To renew trimmer line, hold drum firmly and turn spool in direction shown in Fig. HF16 to remove slack. Twist with a hard snap until plastic peg is between holes. Pull spool out of drum. Remove old line from spool. Spool will hold aproximately 20 feet (6 m) of 0.095 inch (2.4 mm) monofilament line. Insert end of new line through hole on spool (Fig. HF17) and pull line through until line is the same length on both sides of hole. Wind both ends of line at the same time in direction indicated by arrow on end of spool. Wind tightly and evenly from side to side and do not twist line.

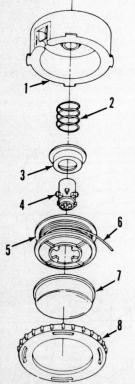

Fig. HF14—Exploded view of late style semi-automatic single line trimmer head.

1. Drum
2. Spring
3. Spring adapter
4. Inner cam
5. Spool
6. Line
7. Button
8. Cover

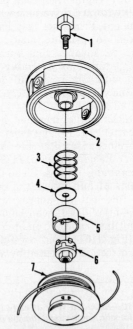

Fig. HF15—Exploded view of semi-automatic dual line trimmer head.

1. Adapter
2. Drum
3. Spring
4. Washer
5. Outer cam
6. Inner cam
7. Spool

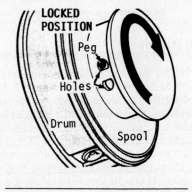

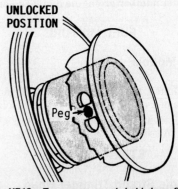

Fig. HF16—To remove spool, hold drum firmly and turn spool in direction shown to take up slack, then twist with a sudden snap until plastic peg is between holes as shown in lower view.

Insert ends of line through line openings, align pegs on drum with slots in spool and push spool into drum. Hold drum firmly, twist spool suddenly in direction shown in Fig. HF18 until peg enters hole with a click and locks spool in position.

Triple Strand Trimmer Head

Refer to Fig. HF19 for an exploded view of triple strand trimmer head used on some models.

To renew trimmer line, align hole in cup washer with hole in bearing head or gear housing. Insert a 5/32 inch Allen wrench or similar tool into holes in cup washer and head to prevent drive shaft from turning. Turn tri-line head counterclockwise to remove head. Unscrew bolt (6) and remove cover (5). Clean inside of rotary head. Wind new monofilament line on spools as shown in Fig. HF20. Place spools (3-Fig. HF19) back in upper body (1), install springs (4) and install cover (5).

TRI-KUT BLADE

The following list indicates Hoffco models which may be equipped with a "TRI-KUT" blade (Fig. HF24) for heavier weeds and grasses.

P-10	JP-320
P-85	JP-420
P-850	JP-660
WW-76	PC-22
WW-77	PC-225
WW-85	PC-380
WW-850	WT-14

JP-215	WT-160
JP-225	WT-215
JP-270	WT-320

Models JP-215, JP-225, JP-270, JP-320, JP-420, WT-14, WT-160, WT-215 and WT-320 may be equipped with an 8 inch "TRI-KUT" blade drilled for a 20 mm arbor. Blade part number is 208559.

Models PC-22, PC-225 and PC-380 may be equipped with an 8 inch "TRI-KUT" blade drilled for a 5/8 inch arbor. Blade part number is 205706.

Models P-10, P-85, P-850, WW-76, WW-77, WW-85, WW-850 and JP-660 may be equipped with an 11 inch "TRI-KUT" blade drilled for a 5/8 inch arbor. Blade part number is 10625.

To install "TRI-KUT" blade, note rotation is clockwise as viewed from the engine end looking down the shaft towards the lower head. Make certain blade is centered on arbor and seated against the face of cup washer (3-Fig. HF25). Assemble the blade, arbor washer and anti-vibration lock nut in sequence shown in Fig. HF25. Insert the blade of a screwdriver or similar tool into the aligned notches of the lower head casting and the cup washer and hold them together. Make certain cup washer remains in place flush against the lower head casting. This will allow nut, washer and blade to be tightened into position.

BRUSH BLADE

Models P-10, P-85, P-850, WW-76, WW-77, WW-85, WW-850 and JP-660 may be equipped with a 9 inch brush blade (Fig. HF24). Blade part number is 10624.

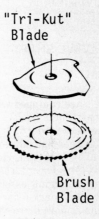

Fig. HF24—A "TRI-KUT" weed and grass blade and a brush blade are available for some models.

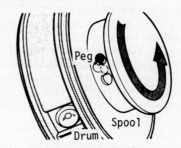

Fig. HF18—Hold drum firmly and twist suddenly to lock spool in position.

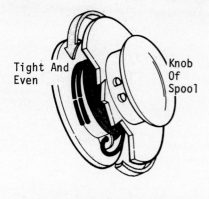

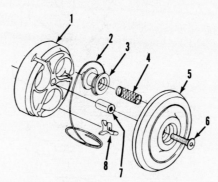

Fig. HF19—Exploded view of "Tri-Line" trimmer head used on some models.

1. Body
2. Line
3. Spool (3)
4. Spring
5. Cover
6. Bolt
7. Retainer
8. Line retainer

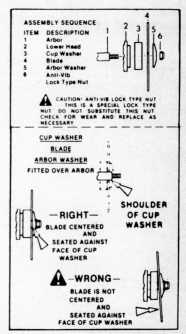

Fig. HF25—Follow assembly sequence shown to install blade.

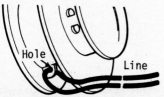

Fig. HF17—End of line must be inserted through hole on spool as shown in lower view. Wind line tightly in direction indicated by arrow on spool.

Fig. HF20—Line is wound on spools and routed as shown.

Models PC-22, PC-225 and PC-380 may be equipped with a 9 inch brush blade (Fig. HF24). Blade part number is 205707.

Brush blade installation is similar to installation procedure outlined for "TRI-KUT" blade.

To sharpen brush blade, refer to Fig. HF26. Hoffco file template (part number 208984) is available. Teeth angled toward the rear provide poor self-feed and saw feels dull. Forward angled teeth increase binding and kick-back.

If the blade has hit a stone or solid object, the entire damaged section must be filed off as shown in Fig. HF26. Make certain all teeth are of the same length. Template provides correct filing height for front edge angle (90°), side angle (20°) and correct clearance depth of 0.9 mm (0.04 in.).

DRIVE SHAFT

All Models

All models are equipped with a flexible drive shaft. Some models are equipped with a grease fitting at upper end of drive shaft housing; however, drive shaft should be removed, cleaned and inspected at 20 hour intervals. To remove, separate engine assembly from drive shaft tube. Mark drive shaft end locations and remove drive shaft. Clean and inspect drive shaft for wear or damage. If drive shaft is damaged, both drive shaft and tube (housing) must be renewed. Lubricate drive shaft with a good quality high temperature wheel bearing grease and install drive shaft. Exchange drive shaft ends (clutch end at trimmer head end) each time drive shaft is serviced to extend drive shaft life. Make certain squared drive shaft ends engage clutch adapter and trimmer head adapters during installation to prevent drive shaft damage.

BEARING HEAD

Integrated Drive Shaft Housing/ Bearing Head. Light duty models are equipped with an integrated drive shaft housing/bearing head assembly (Fig. HF27). Bearings consist of 2 powder metal type bushings at upper end of housing and 2 prelubricated, precision ball bearings packed between double seals. If bearing failure occurs, entire housing assembly must be renewed.

Kick Stand Type Bearing Head. Refer to Fig. HF28 for an exploded view of kick stand type bearing head. To service, remove clamping screw (3) and set screw (7). Slip head off trimmer tube. Remove trimmer head or blade assembly. Remove snap ring (11). Secure head assembly in a vise. Place a 1-3/8 inch wooden dowel with a 3/4 inch hole drilled through center to over arbor shaft, against the square coupling end. Tap wooden dowel with a mallet. Bearings and arbor assembly will slip from lower head. Disassemble bearings, coupling and arbor assembly as necessary.

To reassemble, place coupling (4) and washer (5) on arbor (12). Press one bearing onto arbor. Install assembly into housing. Install spacer (9) and press remaining bearing onto arbor and into housing. Install snap ring.

Flange Type Bearing Head. Refer to Fig. HF29 for an exploded view of flange type bearing head used on some

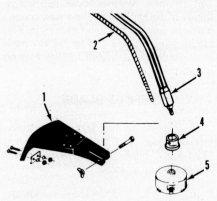

Fig. HF27—Exploded view of drive shaft housing and trimmer head.

1. Shield
2. Flexible drive shaft
3. Housing
4. Adapter
5. Trimmer head

Fig. HF26—Sharpen brush blade to dimensions shown. Refer to text.

Fig. HF28—Exploded view of kick stand type bearing head.

1. Kick stand
2. Screw
3. Screw
4. Adapter
5. Washer
6. Housing
7. Screw
8. Bearing
9. Spacer
10. Bearing
11. Snap ring
12. Arbor
13. Cup washer

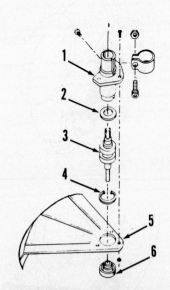

Fig. HF29—Exploded view of flange type bearing head used on some models.

1. Housing
2. Washer
3. Arbor & bearing assy.
4. Snap ring
5. Shield
6. Cup washer

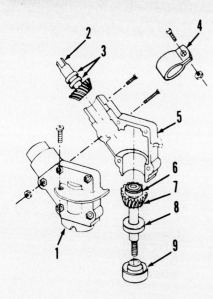

models. To service, remove shield (5). Remove clamp and screw securing head to drive shaft tube. Separate head from drive shaft tube (housing). Remove trimmer head and cup washer (6). Remove snap ring (4) and press bearing and arbor assembly (3) from housing (1). Remove washer (2).

Fig. HF30—Exploded view of gear head assembly. Housing style may vary slightly.

1. Housing (half)	
2. Input gear	
3. Bearings	6. Bearing
4. Clamp	7. Output gear & arbor
5. Housing (half)	8. Bearing
	9. Cup washer

GEAR HEAD ASSEMBLY

All Models So Equipped

Refer to Fig. HF30 for an exploded view of gear head assembly. Gear head assembly is equipped with sealed ball bearings and needs no periodic maintenance. To service, remove trimmer head or blade assembly. Separate gear head from drive shaft tube (housing). Remove retaining bolts and separate housing halves. Lift input shaft (2) and bearing assembly from housing. Lift output shaft (7) and bearing assembly from housing. Renew bearings as required.

HOMELITE

ELECTRIC STRING TRIMMERS

Model	Volts	Amps	Cutting Swath	Line Diameter
ST-20	120	2.2	10 in.	0.065 in.
ST-40	120	3.3	14 in.	0.065 in.
ST-60	120	4.0	16 in.	0.065 in.

ELECTRICAL REQUIREMENTS

Model ST-20, ST-40 and ST-60 string trimmers are designed to be used on electrical circuits with 120-volt alternating current. All models are double-insulated and do not require a ground wire. A two-wire extension cord is recommended and wire gage should be matched to cord length to prevent power loss. Use no more than 100 feet (30.5 m) of #18 wire or no more than 150 feet (45.7 m) of #16 wire.

All models are equipped with an automatic string advance system. The string trimmer will automatically feed out string by cycling the trimmer motor from on to off. The string spool must stop completely to advance the string, and if sufficiently short, it may be necessary to cycle the trimmer on and off several times. Operation is similar to that described in OPERATING SAFETY section in this manual.

If string will not advance on ST-40 or ST-60 models, it may be necessary to remove the high speed slider spring (the larger of the two springs) and compress the spring several times. This will reduce spring tension and allow the high speed slider to cock at a lower rpm. If a new high speed slider spring is being installed, it should also be compressed a couple of times before installation.

NOTE
All wiring must be routed exactly as shown in wiring diagram.

NOTE
All wiring must be routed exactly as shown in wiring diagram.
CAUTION
Make sure that the wire terminals do not touch after assembly of the motor housing

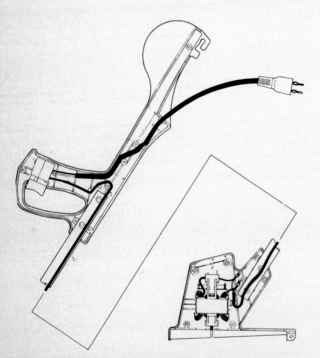

Fig. HL27-1—Wiring diagram showing correct routing of wire on Model ST-20.

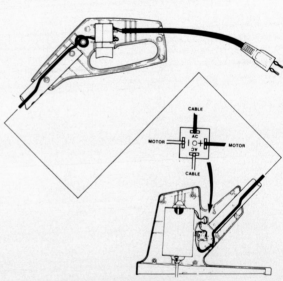

Fig. HL27-2—Wiring diagram showing correct routing of wire on Models ST-40 and ST-60.

Illustrations Courtesy Homelite Div. of Textron, ©1987

HOMELITE

GASOLINE STRING TRIMMERS

Model	Engine Make	Displ.
ST-80	Homelite	26.2 cc
ST-100	Homelite	26.2 cc
ST-120	Homelite	26.2 cc
ST-160	Homelite	26.2 cc
ST-160A	Homelite	26.2 cc
ST-165	Homelite	26.2 cc
ST-180	Homelite	26.2 cc
ST-200	Homelite	31.2 cc
ST-210	Homelite	31.2 cc
ST-260	Homelite	26.2 cc
ST-310	Homelite	31.2 cc

ENGINE INFORMATION

All models are equipped with a Homelite engine. Refer to appropriate HOMELITE ENGINE SERVICE section of this manual.

STRING TRIMMER

All Models Except ST-160A, ST-165, ST-260 And ST-310.

These models are equipped with an automatic string advance system (Model ST-210 is a brushcutter in a standard configuration but may be optionally equipped as a string trimmer). The string trimmer will automatically feed out string by cycling the engine throttle from full speed to idle speed. String head (17—Fig. HL29-1, HL29-3 and HL29-4) encases two slider and spring pairs for high speed and low speed engagements of string spool (18). Heavy spring (13) is used with high speed slider (14) and light spring (16) is used with low speed slider (15). Note position of lugs in Fig. HL29-2 to identify sliders. When string length is at desired cutting length engine speed is approximately 6500 rpm and high speed slider lug drives the string spool. As the string is shortened, engine speed will increase so that centrifugal force disengages the high speed slider lug from the string spool lug. The low speed slider lug picks up a string spool lug which allows the high speed slider to cock behind a string spool lug.

When the engine is slowed to idle speed, the low speed slider will disengage and the high speed slider will engage the next string spool lug thereby allowing the string spool to rotate 1/6 turn and feed out string. The amount of string ad-

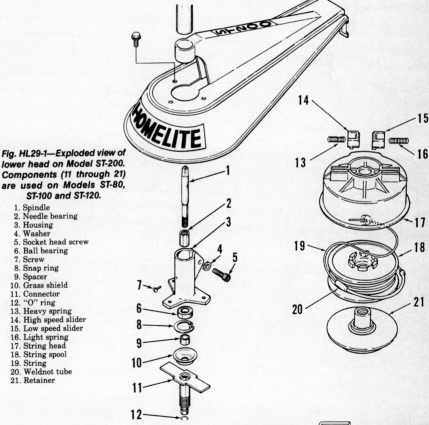

Fig. HL29-1—Exploded view of lower head on Model ST-200. Components (11 through 21) are used on Models ST-80, ST-100 and ST-120.

1. Spindle
2. Needle bearing
3. Housing
4. Washer
5. Socket head screw
6. Ball bearing
7. Screw
8. Snap ring
9. Spacer
10. Grass shield
11. Connector
12. "O" ring
13. Heavy spring
14. High speed slider
15. Low speed slider
16. Light spring
17. String head
18. String spool
19. String
20. Weldnot tube
21. Retainer

vanced automatically is determined by the amount of string on the spool. Approximately 2¼ inches (57 mm) of string will be advanced from a full spool, and about ¾ inch (19 mm) from a nearly empty spool.

If automatic string advance malfunctions, be sure proper string is used, string advance components move freely and engine is properly tuned and will run at

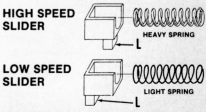

HIGH SPEED SLIDER HEAVY SPRING
L

LOW SPEED SLIDER LIGHT SPRING
L

Fig. HL29-2—Note position of lug (L) when identifying high and low speed sliders. Be sure correct spring is installed in slider.

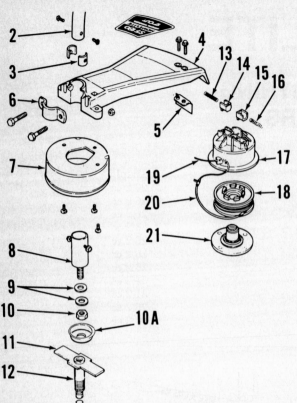

2. Drive tube
3. Inner clamp
4. Deflector
5. Cut-off blade
6. Clamp
7. Grass shield
8. Housing
9. Washer
10. Nut
10A. Shield
11. Connector
12. "O" Ring
13. Heavy spring
14. High speed slider
15. Low speed slider
16. Light spring
17. String head
18. String spool
19. String
20. Weldnot tube
21. Retainer

full speed of at least 7500 rpm. Engine must idle below 4200 rpm (refer to engine service section for carburetor adjustment).

Insufficient string length (less than 2 inches) will not allow automatic string advance. If string is less than 2 inches, remove string head and manually extract string until string length is 5 inches. Install Weldnot tube so large end is towards outer string end.

Spool retainer (21—Figs. HL29-1, HL29-3 and HL29-4) has left-hand threads and must be turned clockwise for removal. Connector (11) has left-hand threads.

Models ST-200 and ST-210, remove snap ring (8—Fig. HL29-1) and press bearings out of housing. When installing bearings, install needle bearing (2) with lettered end up and ball bearing (6) with sealed end out. Install snap ring (8) with square edge to outside.

Be sure connector (11—Figs. HL29-1, HL29-3 and HL29-4) is fully seated in recess of string head (17) to prevent slider ejection. Apply a light coat of multipurpose grease to bore of spool before installation.

Models ST-160A, ST-165, ST-260 And ST-310

Refer to Fig. HL29-6 for an exploded view of the string trimmer head assembly.

To remove string trimmer spool (13), unscrew retainer (14) — retainer has left-hand threads. When installing string, insert string end through holes in spool as shown in Fig. HL29-7. Wrap string around spool in direction of arrow on spool. Do not wrap more than 25 feet (7.6 mm) of string onto spool. Position string between lugs on spool before passing string through outlet of string head. To check string advance operation, alternately press down and release retainer (14) while pulling on string.

To separate lower drive shaft assembly (8) from string head (10), retaining ring (11) must be cut and removed. To gain access to the retaining ring press drive shaft assembly down into string head approximately ¼ inch (6.4 mm). Cut retaining ring, then remove and discard ring. DO NOT attempt to reuse retaining ring. Separate drive shaft assembly from string head. When installing drive shaft assembly and string head, install retaining ring so inner points are towards end of drive shaft.

BRUSHCUTTER

A brushcutter head is standard on Model ST-210 and optional on Model ST-200. Refer to Fig. HL29-5 for an exploded view. Blade retaining nut (15) has

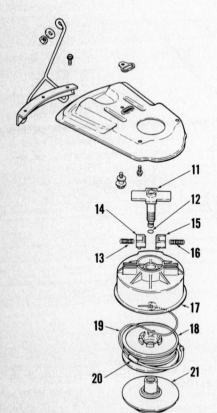

Fig. HL29-4—Exploded view of lower head on Model ST-80. Models ST-100 and ST-120 are similar.

11. Connector	
12. "O" ring	17. String head
13. Heavy spring	18. String spool
14. High speed slider	19. String
15. Low speed slider	20. Weldnot tube
16. Light spring	21. Retainer

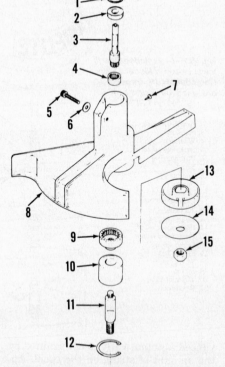

Fig. HL29-5—Exploded view of bruschcutter head which is standard on Model ST-210 and optional on Model ST-200.

1. Snap ring	
2. Ball bearing	9. Ring gear
3. Pinion shaft	10. Ball bearing
4. Needle bearing	11. Spindle
5. Clamp screw	12. Snap ring
6. Washer	13. Cup washer
7. Socket head screw	14. Shield
8. Head	15. Nut

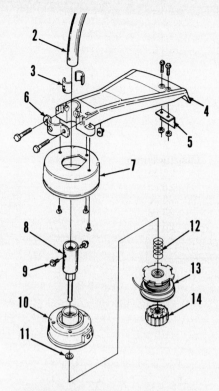

Fig. HL29-6—Exploded view of lower head on Models ST-160A, ST-165, ST-260 and ST-310.

2. Drive tube
3. Inner clamp
4. Deflector
5. Cut-off blade
6. Clamp
7. Grass shield
8. Lower drive shaft assy.
9. Screw
10. String head
11. Retaining ring
12. Spring
13. String spool
14. Retainer

left-hand threads and must be turned clockwise for removal. Head (8) is aligned with drive tube by screw (7) which aligns holes in head and drive tube. Loosen clamp screw (5) to remove head from drive tube. When assembling head, install bearing (2) with sealed side up.

Note that the brushcutter kit for early Model ST-200 uses ball bearing (2) and

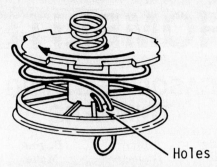

Fig. HL29-7—Insert string end through holes in spool as shown on Models ST-160A, ST-165, ST-260 and ST-310.

needle bearing (4) to support pinion shaft (3). Two ball bearings (2) are used to support the pinion shaft on later models.

DRIVE SHAFT

Models ST-160 and ST-180 are equipped with a flexible drive shaft which should be inspected and greased annually. Detach drive tube from engine housing and pull drive shaft from drive tube. Clean drive shaft. Swap drive shaft end-to-end before inserting in drive tube to prolong shaft service life. While inserting drive shaft into drive tube, apply molybdenum disulfide grease to shaft; do not apply excess grease. Reconnect drive tube to engine housing while being sure drive shaft is properly connected.

Models ST-200 and ST-210 are equipped with a flexible drive shaft between the engine and drive head. The flexible drive shaft should be removed, inspected and lubricated after every 25 hours of operation. To remove drive shaft, remove screw (7—Fig. HL29-1 or HL29-5) and loosen clamp screw (5). Slide head off drive tube and pull flexible shaft from tube. Clean and inspect shaft, then lubricate shaft with lithium grease. Insert shaft into

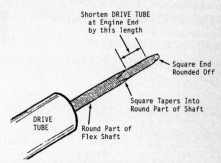

Fig. HL29-8—Shorten drive shaft as shown to prevent rounding off cable end.

drive tube (shaft ends are identical and shaft ends may be reversed to extend shaft life). Install head while turning head to engage shaft ends in engine and head. Align holes in front side of head and drive tube and install screw (7). Tighten clamp screw (5) so head will not turn.

For early Models ST-200 and ST-210, bushing kit number A-96064 is available to install a bushing in the lower end of the drive tube. There must be at least 1¼ inches from bottom of drive tube to bottom of flex shaft. New drive tubes are equipped with bushings.

Early production ST-200 and ST-210 models were produced with a drive shaft housing having a bump on the end which was designed to index with a notch in the engine housing. Service parts will supply a drive shaft housing, part number A-96205-1, without a bump which is designed to fit all early and late models.

Some ST-160 and ST-180 models may have a drive shaft housing that is too long to allow full engagement of the flexible drive shaft. When a failure occurs, the drive shaft will be rounded off at the end as shown in Fig. HL29-8. Measure the length of the square tapers on the drive shaft and shorten the drive shaft housing at the engine end the same amount.

HOMELITE

GASOLINE STRING
TRIMMERS

Model	Cutting Swath	Line Diameter	Engine Make	Displacement
ST-155	15 in.	0.080 in.	Homelite	25 cc
ST-175	17 in.	0.080 in.	Homelite	25 cc
ST-185	17 in.	0.080 in.	Homelite	25 cc
ST-285	17 in.	0.080 in.	Homelite	25 cc
ST-385	17 in.	0.105 in.	Homelite	25 cc

ENGINE INFORMATION

All models are equipped with a Homelite engine. Refer to appropriate HOMELITE ENGINE SERVICE section of this manual.

STRING TRIMMER

E-Z Line Advance. All models except the ST-385 are equipped with the Homelite E-Z Line string advance system. The ST-155 uses a single line system while the ST-175, ST-185 and ST-285 use dual line systems. String is advanced by tapping the spool retainer on the ground while the unit is running. Each time the retainer is tapped, the spring loaded spool rotates 1/6 turn feeding out string.

To replace or rewind the spool, remove spool retainer by turning counterclockwise (R.H. thread). Lift spool with compression spring from stringhead. Inspect spool lugs and shaft bore for wear. Replace as required. Replacement spools are only available prewound with 25 feet (7.6 m) of string.

To rewind string on spool for a single line system, insert one end of a 25 foot length of premium quality 0.080 inch (2.0 mm) diameter string through one of the two holes in the outer spool flange and then back through the other hole forming a small loop. Pull loop tight. For a dual line system, center the spool in the 25 foot (7.6 m) length of string before pulling the loop tight.

Wind string clockwise (when viewed from the bottom spool flange) in an even pattern. Be careful not to twist the strings when winding the spool on a dual line system.

To install the spool and string into the stringhead, capture the string(s) in the slotted lug(s) on the spool. Feed the string through the eyelets(s). Slide the spool onto the shaft. Push the spool into the string head until the string(s) are released from

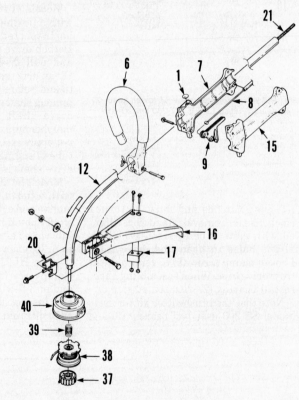

Fig. HL30-1—Exploded view of the string trimmer assembly used on ST-155 and ST-175 models. Refer to Fig. HL30-5 for legend except the following.
6. Front handle
20. Clamp

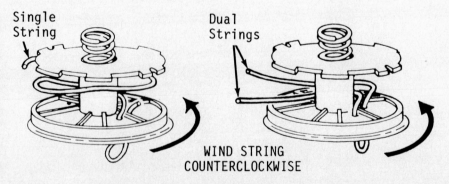

Fig. HL30-2—Wind string around spool in direction shown. Left view shows proper attachment of string to spool for single line models. Drawing on right shows correct attachment for dual string models.

Illustrations Courtesy Homelite Div. of Textron, ©1987

the lugs. Press down on the spool while installing the retainer by turning clockwise (R.H. thread).

To test the operation of the string advance, pull on the string while alternately pressing down on and releasing the retainer.

Manual Advance. The ST-385 is equipped with a manual advance string head assembly. Advancing the string is accomplished by turning the retainer nut clockwise (L.H. thread) to loosen. Loosen retainer enough to be able to pull spool about ¼ inch (6.4 mm) from string head. Pull down on spool and rotate to advance string. Each string should measure approximately 6½ inches (16.5 cm).

After advancing the string, rotate spool slightly in either direction to line up locating lugs on spool with locating holes in string head. Tighten retainer by turning counterclockwise (L.H. thread).

To replace or rewind the spool, remove retainer by turning clockwise (L.H. thread). Pull spool from string head. To rewind string on spool, insert one end of an 18 foot (5.5 m) length of premium quality 0.105 inch (2.7 mm) diameter string through one of the two holes in the spool and then back through the other hole. Center the spool in the 18 foot (5.5 m) length of string. Pull loop tight and wind both lengths of string in the same (either) direction around the spool taking care not to twist the string.

Install spool and string into string head. Feed 6½ inches (16.5 cm) of string through each eyelet. Tilt spool and place into string head taking care that the string does not slip under the spool flange. Rotate spool slightly in either direction to engage locating lugs on spool with locating holes in string head. Install retainer by turning counterclockwise (L.H. thread).

BRUSHCUTTER

Models ST-185 and ST-385 will accept either an 8 inch (20.3 cm) Tri-Arc blade for cutting heavy weeds and brush up to ½ inch (12.7 mm) thick or an 8 inch saw blade for saplings up to 3 inches (7.6 cm) thick. Blades can be installed after first

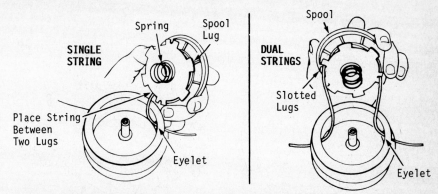

Fig. HL30-4—Automatic feed models with a single string should position the string between lugs as shown at left. Models with dual strings should have strings located in slotted lugs as shown at right.

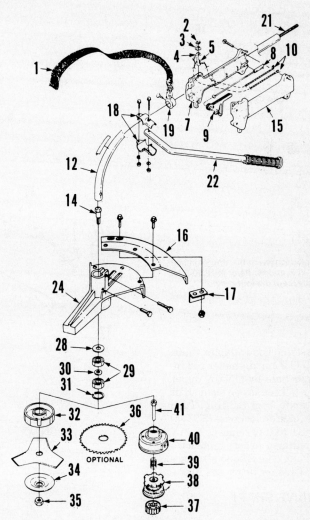

Fig. HL30-5—Exploded view of the string trimmer assembly, saw and Tri-Arc blade for ST-185 models.

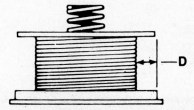

Fig. HL30-3—Line should be wound around spool until about ¼-inch (6.4 mm) from top as indicated by "D".

1. Harness	16. Grass deflector	31. Snap ring
2. Nut	17. Cut-off blade	32. Flange washer
3. Switch plate	18. Handle bar clamp	33. Tri-Arc blade
4. Grounding washer	19. Hanger bracket	34. Cupped washer
5. Stop switch	21. Flexible shaft	35. Locknut
7. Grip half	22. Handle bar	36. Saw blade
8. Throttle cable	24. Lower bearing	37. Spool retainer
9. Throttle trigger	housing	38. Spool & line
10. Stop switch lead wires	28. Thrust washer	39. Compression spring
12. Drive shaft housing	29. Ball bearings	40. Housing & eyelet
14. Spindle shaft	30. Bearing spacer	41. Drive connector
15. Grip half		

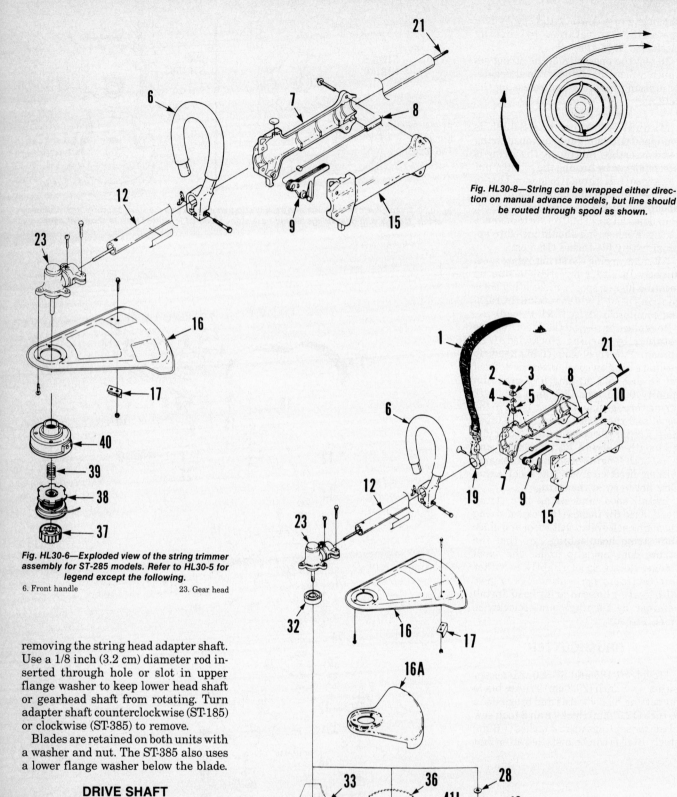

Fig. HL30-8—String can be wrapped either direction on manual advance models, but line should be routed through spool as shown.

Fig. HL30-6—Exploded view of the string trimmer assembly for ST-285 models. Refer to HL30-5 for legend except the following.

6. Front handle   23. Gear head

removing the string head adapter shaft. Use a 1/8 inch (3.2 cm) diameter rod inserted through hole or slot in upper flange washer to keep lower head shaft or gearhead shaft from rotating. Turn adapter shaft counterclockwise (ST-185) or clockwise (ST-385) to remove.

Blades are retained on both units with a washer and nut. The ST-385 also uses a lower flange washer below the blade.

DRIVE SHAFT

Models ST-155, ST-175, ST-185 and ST-285 are equipped with a flexible drive shaft which should be inspected and greased annually. Detach drive tube from engine housing or tube adapter and pull drive shaft from drive tube. Clean drive shaft. Swap drive shaft end-to-end before inserting in drive tube to prolong shaft service life. While inserting drive shaft

Fig. HL30-7—Exploded view of the string trimmer assembly, saw and Tri-Arc blade used on ST-385 models.

6. Front handle
16A. Saw guard
23. Gear head

35L. Nut (L.H. thread)
36L. Saw blade

37L. Spool retainer (L.H. thread)
41L. Drive connector (L.H. thread)

Illustrations Courtesy Homelite Div. of Textron,©1987

into drive tube, apply molybdenum disulfide grease to shaft.

Reconnect drive tube to engine housing

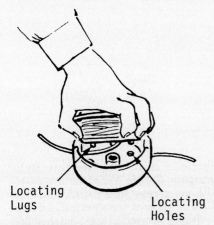

Locating Lugs

Locating Holes

Fig. HL30-9—Insert string through eyelets and insert spool as shown. Be sure lugs on spool engage holes.

or tube adapter making sure drive shaft is properly connected.

The Model ST-385 is equipped with a solid steel drive shaft which is square at the clutch end and splined at the gear head end.

CLUTCH DRUM AND TUBE ADAPTER

The clutch drum is supported in the tube adapter by a ball bearing. The bearing is pressed into the tube adapter and retained by an internal snap ring. The square adapter end of the clutch drum is pressed through the ball bearing and retained by an external snap ring.

LOWER BEARING HEAD (ST-185)

Removal of the lower bearing head assembly from the drive shaft housing is achieved by loosening the clamp screw and removing the locating screw on the side of the head. Remove the string head adapter shaft or the blade. Unscrew the flanged washer from the spindle shaft and remove the spindle shaft. Remove the internal snap ring from the bottom of the lower bearing head. Press the two ball bearings, spacer, and thrust washer from the lower head. Inspect bearings and replace as required.

GEAR HEAD ASSEMBLY (ST-285 and ST-385)

Removal of the gear head assembly is achieved by loosening the two clamp screws and removing the locating screw from the top of the gear head. Slide gear head assembly from the drive shaft housing. The gear head on both units is serviced as a complete assembly only. Do not attempt to disassemble the gear heads.

HOMELITE

BRUSHCUTTER

Model	**Engine Make**	**Displ.**
ST-400	Homelite	54 cc

ENGINE INFORMATION

Model ST-400 brushcutter is powered by a Homelite engine. Refer to appropriate HOMELITE ENGINE SERVICE section of this manual.

SAW BLADE

The saw blade may be removed after unscrewing retaining nut. Prevent shaft rotation by inserting a suitable pin through the grass shield. Note when installing a toothed saw blade that shaft rotation is clockwise as viewed from underside.

DRIVE SHAFT

The flexible drive shaft should be removed, inspected and lubricated after every 25 hours of operation. To remove drive shaft, loosen clamp screw and remove screw in front side of lower head (26—Fig. HL32-1). Slide head off drive tube (23) and pull flexible shaft (15) from tube. Clean and inspect shaft, then lubricate shaft with Homelite Multi-Purpose Grease 17237 or a suitable lithium grease. Insert shaft into drive tube (shaft ends are identical and shaft ends may be reversed to extend shaft life). With 3-5 inches (7.6-12.7 cm) of shaft extending from drive tube engage shaft in lower head. Then while turning lower head so upper end of shaft engages clutch drum, install lower head on drive tube. Align holes in front side of lower head and drive tube and install screw. Tighten clamp screw so lower head will not turn.

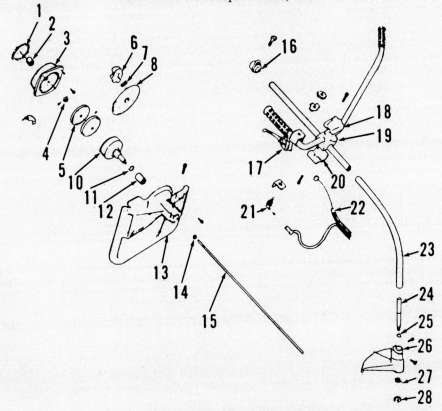

Fig. HL32-1—Exploded view of ST-400 brushcutter.

1. Gasket	11. Snap ring	20. Clamp
2. Bearing	12. Bearing	21. Ignition switch
3. Drivecase	13. Upper head	22. Throttle cable
4. Seal	14. Snap ring	23. Drive tube
5. Cover	15. Drive shaft	24. Spindle
6. Clutch shoe	16. Hanger	25. Snap ring
7. Spring	17. Throttle lever	26. Lower head
8. Clutch hub	18. Clamp	27. Bearing
10. Clutch drum	19. Block	28. Snap ring

HOMELITE

TRIMMER/BRUSHCUTTER

Model	Cutting Swath	Engine Make	Displacement
HK-18	14 in.	Homelite	18.4 cc
HK-24	16 in.	Homelite	24.1 cc
HK-33	18 in.	Homelite	33.3 cc

ENGINE INFORMATION

All models are equipped with a Homelite engine. Refer to appropriate HOMELITE ENGINE SERVICE section of this manual.

STRING TRIMMER

Model HK-18 is equipped with a string trimmer head while Models HK-24 and HK-33 may be equipped with a string trimmer head or brushcutting blade.

The string trimmer head may be removed after unscrewing retaining nut (L.H. threads). The string is advanced manually by unscrewing retaining nut, then pulling out spool so lugs disengage while rotating spool. String will be expelled from outlet holes if spool is rotated in proper direction. Push spool back into head while engaging lugs in holes of head. Reinstall retainer nut.

To install string on an empty spool, a length of string 15 feet should be inserted through the holes in the spool as shown in Fig. HL33-3. The spool should be centered between both ends of the string. Wrap both ends of string around spool in the same direction; wrapping may be done in either direction as long as both ends are wrapped in the same direction. Install the spool in the head while inserting string ends through the outlet holes in the head. Do not trap string between underside of spool and head. Complete assembly of trimmer head.

SAW BLADE

The saw blade may be removed after unscrewing retaining screw or nut. Note that screw or nut has left-hand threads. Prevent blade rotation by inserting shaft holder tool into lower flange (1—Fig. HL33-1 or 28—Fig. HL33-2). Install saw blade so blade cuts when turning clockwise as viewed from underside.

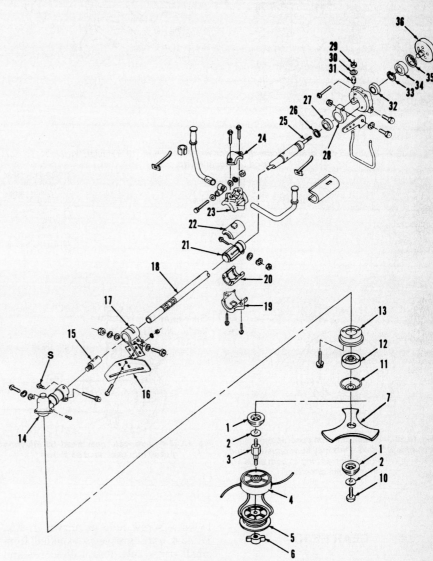

Fig. HL33-1—Exploded view of early Model HK-33. Early Model HK-24 is similar.

1. Lower flange	15. Connector	27. Collar
2. Wave washer	16. Guard blade	28. Clutch housing
3. Shaft bolt	17. Bracket	29. Locknut
4. Head	18. Drive shaft housing	30. Washer
5. Spool	19. Bracket	31. Screw
6. Nut (L.H.)	20. Isolator	32. Collar
7. Blade	21. Handle hoop	33. Snap ring
10. Screw (L.H.)	22. Isolator	34. Bearing
11. Cup	23. Bracket	35. Snap ring
12. Upper flange	24. Bracket	36. Clutch drum
13. Cover	25. Drive shaft	
14. Gear head	26. Snap ring	

Illustrations Courtesy Homelite Div. of Textron, ©1987

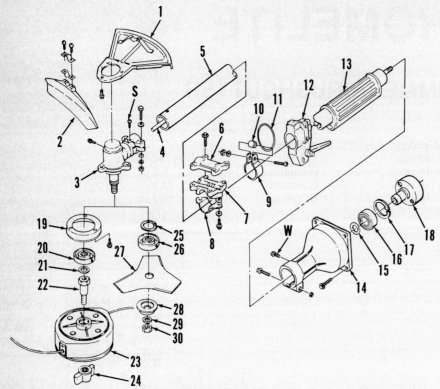

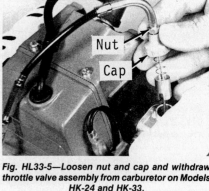

Fig. HL33-5—Loosen nut and cap and withdraw throttle valve assembly from carburetor on Models HK-24 and HK-33.

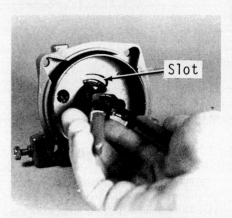

Fig. HL33-6—Snap ring is accessible through slot in clutch drum.

Fig. HL33-2—Exploded view of later Model HK-24 and HK-33. Model HK-18 is similar. Washer (21) is not used on Model HK-18.

1. Shield	11. Ring
2. Shield	12. Throttle assy.
3. Gear head	13. Grip
4. Drive shaft	14. Clutch housing
5. Drive shaft housing	15. Snap ring
6. Bracket	16. Bearing
7. Bracket	17. Snap ring
8. Bracket	18. Clutch drum
9. Hanger	19. Cover
10. Spacer	20. Upper flange

21. Special washer
22. Shaft bolt
23. Trimmer assy.
24. Nut (L.H.)
25. Snap ring
26. Upper flange
27. Blade
28. Lower flange
29. Special washer
30. Nut (L.H.)

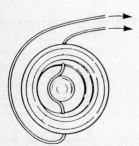

Fig. HL33-3—Install string on spool as shown and as outlined in text. Ends may be wrapped around spool in either direction as long as both ends are in the same direction.

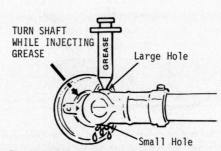

TURN SHAFT WHILE INJECTING GREASE

GREASE

Large Hole

Small Hole

Fig. HL33-4—Lubricate gear head by injecting grease into gear head as shown.

1/16 in. (1.6mm)

Fig. HL33-7—Throttle trigger end play should be 1/16 inch (1.6 mm) measured at end of lever.

GEAR HEAD

Gear head (14—Fig. HL33-1 or 3—Fig. HL33-2) is lubricated using Multi-purpose All-Temp Grease (part 17193). The gear head should be lubricated after every 50 hours of operation.

To lubricate gear head, remove large slotted screw and small Phillips head screw on sides of gear head. While rotating gear head shaft, inject grease into large screw hole as shown in Fig. HL33-4 until grease is expelled from small screw hole. Reinstall screws and clean off excess grease.

To remove shaft bolt (3—Fig. HL33-1) on early models, secure lower flange (1) using shaft holder tool and turn bolt clockwise (L.H. threads). To remove shaft bolt (22—Fig. HL33-2) on later models, prevent shaft rotation by inserting a 3/16 inch (4 mm) rod through cover (19) and into upper flange (20). Turn shaft bolt clockwise (L.H. threads) to remove.

To remove gear head, back out alignment screw (S—Fig. HL33-1 or HL33-2) approximately 1/8 inch (3.2 mm). Loosen clamp screw(s) and separate gear head from drive shaft housing. On early models, use a suitable tool to engage shaft connector (15—Fig. HL33-1) and unscrew connector from gear head shaft.

The gear head on all models must be serviced as a unit assembly. Individual components are not available.

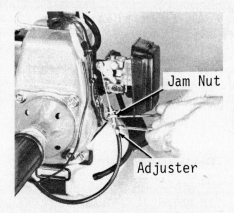

Jam Nut

Adjuster

Fig. HL33-8—Adjust throttle trigger end play on Model HK-18 by loosening locknut and turning cable adjuster.

Cable Adjuster

Fig. HL33-9—Adjust throttle trigger end play on Models HK-24 and HK-33 by loosening locknut and turning cable adjuster.

DRIVE SHAFT

The drive shaft does not normally require lubrication. If a new drive shaft is installed or the old drive shaft is removed, the drive shaft should be lubricated. Apply Homelite Multipurpose Grease 17237 or a suitable lithium base grease to the drive shaft. Do not apply an excessive amount of grease.

To remove drive shaft assembly, refer to preceding section and remove gear head. On Model HK-18, detach throttle cable bracket from engine fan housing, disconnect throttle cable and disconnect stop switch wire at connector adjacent to throttle cable bracket. On Models HK-24 and HK-33, loosen throttle cable guide nut (N—Fig. HL33-5), unscrew carburetor cap (C) and lift out throttle valve assembly (cover carburetor opening and be careful not to damage throttle valve components). Remove four screws securing clutch housing (28—Fig. HL33-1 or 14—Fig. HL33-2) to engine and detach clutch housing with drive shaft housing. On early Model HK-33, loosen locknuts (29—Fig. HL33-1) and back out locating screws (31). On later models, back out housing alignment screw (W—Fig. HL33-2). On all models, loosen clamp screw and withdraw drive shaft housing from clutch housing. Drive shaft will remain attached to clutch.

To detach the drive shaft from the clutch drum, proceed as follows: On early models, insert a suitable rod through the clutch housing and the holes in the clutch drum so the drum cannot rotate. Grasp the opposite end of the drive shaft with a wrench and unscrew the drive shaft from the clutch drum. On later models, grasp the drive shaft in a soft-jawed vise then use a suitable tool inserted in the two-holes in the clutch drum and unscrew the drum off the drive shaft.

Reassemble by reversing the disassembly procedure. Be sure throttle valve assembly is properly installed on Model HK-18.

CLUTCH

The clutch assembly is accessible after removing the clutch housing as outlined in the preceding DRIVE SHAFT section. Inspect components and renew any which are damaged or excessively worn.

To remove the clutch drum on early Model HK-33, remove the drive shaft as previously outlined. Working through the elongated slot in the clutch drum, detach snap ring (35—Fig. HL33-1) as shown in Fig. HL33-6. Using Homelite tool 94455 or a suitable equivalent, press clutch drum and bearing (34—Fig. HL33-1) out of clutch housing. Remove snap ring (33) and press clutch drum out of bearing. If necessary, remove rear collar (32), snap ring (26) and front collar (27).

To remove the clutch drum on Models HK-18, HK-24 and later Model HK-33, remove snap ring (33—Fig. HL33-1 or 15—Fig. HL33-2). Press clutch drum out of bearing. Remove snap ring (35—Fig. HL33-1 or 17—Fig. HL33-2). Using Homelite tool 94455 or a suitable equivalent, press bearing out of clutch housing.

Reassemble by reversing disassembly procedure.

THROTTLE TRIGGER

Throttle trigger end play must be properly adjusted to obtain desired engine operation and to allow clutch to disengage. Throttle trigger end play should be 1/16 inch (1.6 mm) measured at end of trigger lever. See Fig. HL33-7. Loosen locknut and rotate cable adjuster shown in Fig. HL33-8 or HL33-9 to adjust end play. Tighten locknut against adjuster after performing adjustment.

NOTE: Insufficient throttle trigger end play may not allow engine to reach idle speed and clutch may not disengage.

HUSQVARNA

GASOLINE POWERED CLEARING SAWS

Model	Engine Manufacturer	Engine Model	Displacement
36R	Husqvarna	.....	36.0 cc
140R	Husqvarna	.....	40.0 cc
244R	Husqvarna	.....	44.0 cc
244RX	Husqvarna	.....	44.0 cc
165R	Husqvarna	.....	65.0 cc
165RX	Husqvarna	.....	65.0 cc

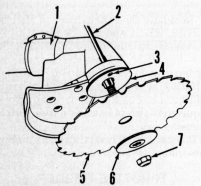

Fig. HQ3—View showing assembly sequence for blade installation on some models.

1. Gear head
2. Tool
3. Hole
4. Drive disc
5. Blade
6. Washer
7. Nut (LH)

ENGINE INFORMATION

All Models

Husqvarna clearing saws are equipped with Husqvarna two-stroke air-cooled gasoline engines. Identify engine by engine displacement. Refer to HUSQVARNA ENGINE SERVICE section of this manual.

FUEL MIXTURE

All Models

Manufacturer recommends mixing regular grade gasoline (unleaded is an acceptable substitute) with a good quality two-stroke air-cooled engine oil at a 25:1 ratio. Do not use fuel containing alcohol.

TRIMMER HEAD

All Models

All models may be equipped with a trimmer head as an option. To install trimmer head, insert a locking rod (2-Fig. HQ3) in hole in gear head and hole in drive disc (3). Some models have a slot at front of gear head housing instead of hole. Remove left-hand threaded nut (7), adapter washer (6) and blade (5) from all models. Some models may have a cover between nut (7) and adapter washer (6). Install trimmer head as shown in Fig. HQ4.

To renew line in trimmer head, align hole in trimmer housing and line guide opening and feed new line onto spool while winding lower plate (Fig. HQ5). Tighten trimmer head to 20 N·m (15 ft.-lbs.).

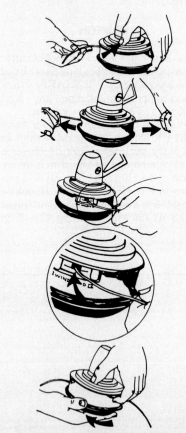

Fig. HQ4—Trimmer head may be installed on all models. Note trimmer head has left-hand threads and is tightened to 20 N·m (15 ft.-lbs.).

Fig. HQ5—To renew line in trimmer head, refer to text and follow sequence of illustration.

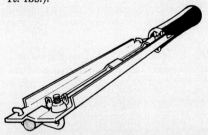

Fig. HQ6—To sharpen saw blade, use a 5.5 mm (7.32 in.) round file in holder (part number 501 58 02-01).

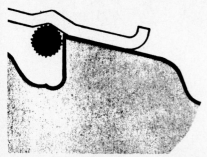

Fig. HQ7—Sharpen front edge of tooth only. Make certain file holder is held firmly against the edge of the tooth.

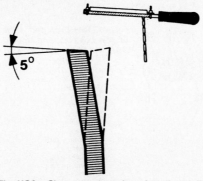

Fig. HQ9—Sharpen outer edge of tooth at a 5° angle.

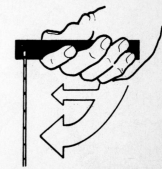

Fig. HQ12—Use set gage (part number 501 31 77-01) to adjust tooth set when teeth have been filed down approximately 50 percent.

BLADE

All Models

All models may be equipped with a saw blade, a four cutting edge blade (Fig. HQ14) or a three cutting edge blade (Fig. HQ15). To remove blade, carefully rotate blade until hole in upper driving disc is aligned with hole in gear head housing. Insert a 4.5 mm (0.16 in.) round rod into holes to prevent blade rotation. Nut retaining blade has left-hand threads and remove nut, cover, drive disc and blade. When installing blade, tighten left-hand thread nut to 35-50 N·m (26-30 ft.-lbs.).

To sharpen saw blade, use a 5.5 mm (7.32 in.) round file in file holder (part number 501 58 02-01) (Fig. HQ6). Follow filing sequence outlined in Figs. HQ7 through HQ13.

To sharpen the four cutting edge blade use a single cut flat file and blade guard part number 502 03 45-02 (Fig. HQ14).

To sharpen the three cutting edge blade use a single cut flat file and blade guard part number 502 09 58-01 (Fig. HQ15).

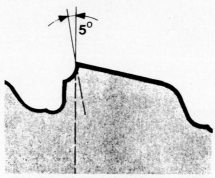

Fig. HQ10—Tooth front edge angle should be 5°. Hard wood and large trees may require a smaller angle.

Fig. HQ13—Tooth set should provide 1 mm (0.04 in.) distance between tooth tips.

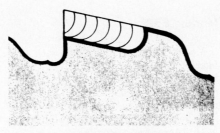

Fig. HQ11—Reduce tooth height evenly during repeated sharpenings.

DRIVE SHAFT

All Models

All models are equipped with a solid drive shaft supported in drive shaft housing tube. Drive shaft requires no regular maintenance; however, if drive shaft is removed, lubricate with lithium base grease before reinstallation.

GEAR HEAD

Models 36R, 140R, 244R And 244RX

Models 36R, 140R, 244R and 244RX are equipped with gear head shown in Fig. HQ16. Gear head lubricant level should be checked at 50 hour intervals of use. To check, remove check plug (11).

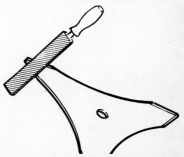

Fig. HQ14—Use a single cut flat file and blade guard (part number 502 03 45-02) to sharpen the four cutting edge blade.

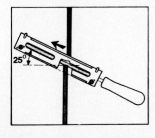 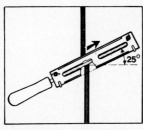

Fig. HQ8—Alternate filing one tooth to the right and the next tooth to the left. File at a 25° angle.

Fig. HQ15—Use a single cut flat file and blade guard (part number 502 09 58-01) to sharpen the three cutting edge blade.

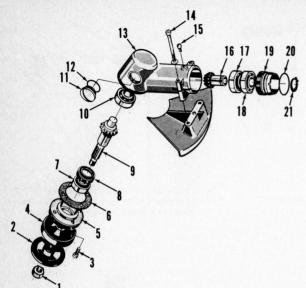

Fig. HQ16—Exploded view of gear head used on Models 36R, 140R, 244R and 244RX.

1. Nut (LH)
2. Adapter washer
3. Screw
4. Drive disc
5. Cover
6. Gasket
7. Bearing
8. Spacer
9. Arbor shaft
10. Bearing
11. Check plug
12. Sealing ring
13. Housing
14. Clamp bolt
15. Locating screw
16. Input shaft
17. Bearing
18. Bearing
19. Sleeve
20. "O" ring
21. Snap ring

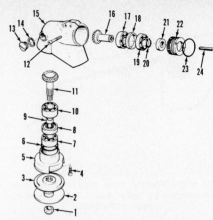

Fig. HQ18—Exploded view of gear head assembly used on Model 165RX.

1. Nut (LH)	13. Check plug
2. Adapter plate	14. Sealing washer
3. Drive disc	15. Housing
4. Screws	16. Input shaft
5. Cover	17. Bearing
6. "O" ring	18. Spacer
7. Bearing	19. Bearing
8. Spacer seal	20. Snap ring
9. Spacer	21. Seal
10. Bearing	22. Sleeve
11. Arbor shaft	23. "O" ring
12. Clamp screw	24. Drive shaft

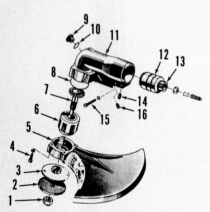

Fig. HQ17—Exploded view of gear head used on Model 165R.

1. Nut (LH)	8. "O" ring
2. Adapter washer	9. Check plug
3. Drive disc	10. Sealing ring
4. Screw	11. Housing
5. Shield & cover assy.	12. Bearing & spacer assy.
6. Bearing	13. Input shaft
7. Arbor shaft	

Gear head should be 3/4 full of lithium base grease.

To disassemble gear head, remove trimmer head or blade assembly. Remove the four screws (3) retaining cover (5) to housing and use puller (part number 502 50 09-01) to remove cover. Remove clamp bolts (14) and locating screw (15). Separate gear head assembly from drive shaft housing tube. Re-

move sleeve (19) using remover (part number 502 51 11-01). Heat housing (13) to 140° F (60° C) and remove input shaft (16) and bearing assembly and arbor shaft (9) and bearing assembly. If bearing (10) remains in housing, tap housing against a wooden block while housing is still hot to remove bearing. Remove snap ring (21) and press bearings (17 and 18) from input shaft as required. Remove bearing (7) and spacer (8) as required.

Model 165R

Model 165R is equipped with the bearing head shown in Fig. HQ17. Gear head lubricant level should be checked at 50 hour intervals of use. To check, remove check plug (9). Gear head housing should be kept 3/4 full of lithium base grease.

To disassemble gear head, remove trimmer head or blade assembly. Remove the five blade guard screws (4) and remove guard. Remove clamp bolts (15) and locating screw (14) and separate gear head from drive shaft housing tube. Heat housing (11) to 140° F (60° C) and use puller (part number 502 50 65-01) to remove arbor shaft (7) and

bearing assembly. Remove locking screw (16) and use puller (part number 502 50 63-01) to remove input shaft (13) and bearing assembly. Press bearings and spacer (12) from input shaft as required.

Model 165RX

Model 165RX is equipped with the bearing head shown in Fig. HQ18. Gear head lubricant level should be checked at 50 hour intervals of use. To check, remove check plug (13). Gear head housing should be 3/4 full of lithium base grease.

To disassemble gear head, remove trimmer head or blade assembly. Remove clamp screws (12) and separate gear head from drive shaft housing. Remove the four cover screws (4) and remove cover (5). Remove sleeve (22) using remover tool (part number 502 51 11-01). Use suitable puller to remove input shaft (16) and bearing assembly. Use suitable puller to remove arbor shaft (11) and bearing assembly. Remove bearings and spacers from arbor shaft and input shaft as required.

KAAZ

GASOLINE POWERED BRUSH CUTTERS

Model	Engine Manufacturer	Engine Model	Displacement
V20	Mitsubishi	T110PD	21.2 cc
V20	Kawasaki	TD18	18.4 cc
V25	Mitsubishi	T140PD	24.1 cc
V25	Kawasaki	TD24	24.1 cc
V35	Mitsubishi	T180PD	32.5 cc
V35	Kawasaki	TD33	33.3 cc
V40	Mitsubishi	T200PD	40.6 cc

ENGINE INFORMATION

All Models

Kaaz brush cutters are available in each model with Kawasaki or Mitsubishi two-stroke air-cooled gasoline engines. Engines may be identified by engine model number and engine displacement. Refer to KAWASAKI ENGINE SERVICE or MITSUBISHI ENGINE SERVICE sections of this manual.

FUEL MIXTURE

All Models

Manufacturer recommends mixing regular grade gasoline (unleaded is an acceptable substitute) with a good quality two-stroke air-cooled engine oil at a 25:1 ratio. Do not use fuel containing alcohol.

BLADE

All Models

All models may be equipped with a four cutting edge brush blade, an eight cutting edge blade or a sixty tooth saw blade. Make certain upper cup washer and lower adapter washer are centered and squarely seated on blade.

DRIVE SHAFT

All Models

All models are equipped with a solid steel drive shaft supported in bushings located in drive shaft housing tube. Drive shaft requires no regular mainte-

nance; however, if drive shaft has been removed, lubricate drive shaft with lithium base grease before reinstallation. Bushings (2-Fig. KZ10) in drive shaft housing tube (1) may be renewed. Mark locations of old bushings in drive shaft housing before removing bushings. Install new bushings at old bushing locations.

GEAR HEAD

All Models

Refer to Fig. KZ11 for an exploded view of the gear head used on all models. Gear head lubricant level should be checked at 30 hour intervals of use. To check, remove check plug (8). Gear head housing should be 2/3 full of lithium base grease.

To disassemble gear head, remove blade assembly. Remove clamp bolts (10) and locating screw (9) and separate gear head from drive shaft housing. Remove snap ring (16) and use a suitable puller to remove input shaft (12) and bearing assembly. Remove snap

ring (1) and use a suitable puller to remove arbor shaft (4) and bearing assembly. If bearing (6) stays in housing (7), heat housing to 140° F (60° C) and tap housing on wooden block to remove bearing. Note spacers (11) are installed at gear head housing clamp split to prevent housing damage from overtightening clamp bolts.

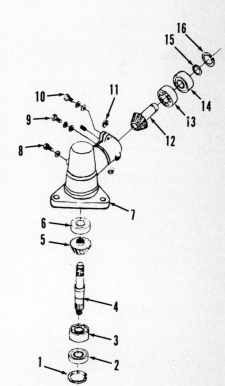

Fig. KZ11—Exploded view of gear head assembly used on all models.

1. Snap ring	9. Locating plug
2. Seal	10. Clamp bolts
3. Bearing	11. Shim (spacer)
4. Arbor shaft	12. Input shaft
5. Gear	13. Bearing
6. Bearing	14. Bearing
7. Housing	15. Snap ring
8. Check plug	16. Snap ring

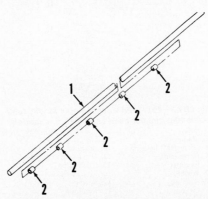

Fig. KZ10—Exploded view of drive shaft housing (1) and bushings (2) used on most models.

LAWN BOY
GASOLINE POWERED STRING TRIMMER

Model	Engine Manufacturer	Engine Model	Displacement
SSI	PPP	....	31.0 cc
SSII	PPP	....	31.0 cc
1100	PPP	....	31.0 cc
1150	PPP	....	31.0 cc
1400	PPP	....	31.0 cc
1480	PPP	....	31.0 cc

ENGINE INFORMATION

All Models

All models are equipped with a two-stroke engine manufactured by Piston Powered Products. Refer to PISTON POWERED PRODUCTS ENGINE SERVICE section of this manual. Trimmer model number decal is located on engine cover.

FUEL MIXTURE

All Models

Manufacturer recommends mixing 8 ounces (236.6 mL) of Lawn Boy 2 cycle oil with 2 gallons (7.5 L) of regular grade gasoline of at least 87 octane rating. Unleaded regular gasoline is an acceptable substitute.

STRING TRIMMER

Trimmer may be equipped with a single strand semi-automatic trimmer head or a dual strand semi-automatic trimmer head. Refer to appropriate paragraph for model being serviced.

Single Strand Trimmer Head

To extend line on single strand trimmer head (Fig. LB10) with engine off, push in on bump button (20) and pull on line until desired length is obtained. To extend line with engine running, operate trimmer engine at full rpm and bump the button (20) on the ground. Line will automatically advance a measured amount.

To renew trimmer line, hold drum (15) and unscrew bump button (20).

Remove spool (19). Clean inner surface of drum and spool. Check indexing teeth on spool and drum for wear. Insert one end of a 25 foot (7.6 m) length of 0.080 inch (2 mm) monofila-

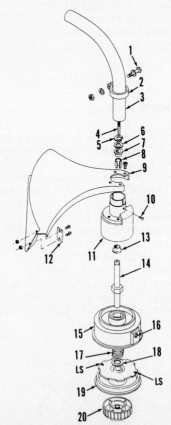

Fig. LB10—Exploded view of single strand semi-automatic trimmer head used on some models.

1. Bolt	
2. Clamp	12. Line cutter
3. Drive shaft housing	13. Bushing
4. Drive shaft	14. Drive shaft adapter
5. Retainer	15. Housing
6. Washer	16. Line guide
7. Bushing	17. Spring
8. Bushing	18. Retainer
9. Shield	19. Spool
10. Locating screw	20. Lock knob & bump button
11. Bushing housing	LS. Line slot

ment line into one of the holes in spool from the inside out, and back through the second hole to the inside. Wind line in direction indicated by arrow on spool until all but about 3 inches (76.2 mm), then clip line temporarily into one of the line lock slots (LS) on spool. Insert line end through line guide in drum and install spool and bump button. Pull line to release from line lock slot on spool after assembly is complete.

Dual Strand Trimmer Head

To extend line on the dual strand semi-automatic trimmer head (Fig. LB11) with engine off, push in on bump button (8) while pulling lines out. Procedure may have to be repeated until desired line length has been obtained. To extend line with engine running, operate trimmer engine at full operating rpm and bump the button (8) on the ground. Each time bump button is tapped on the ground, approximately 1 inch (25 mm) of new line will be advanced.

To renew line, hold drum (2) and unscrew bump button (8). Remove spool (7) and remove any remaining old line. Clean spool and inner surface of drum. Check indexing teeth in drum and on spool. Loop a 25 foot (7.6 m) length of 0.080 inch (2 mm) monofilament line into two equal lengths. Insert the two line ends into the two holes in spool from the bottom and pull line out until loop is against spool. Wind both strands of line around spool at the same time and in the direction indicated by arrow on spool. Wind in tight even layers until almost all line is wrapped around spool, then temporarily clip each line into one of the two line slots (6). Insert line ends through line guides (3) in housing (2), install spool and tighten lock knob and bump button (8). Pull line ends to free from line slots after assembly is complete.

BLADE

Model 1480

Models 1460 and 1480 may be equipped with the optional four point brush blade (Fig. LB13). To install blade, refer to Fig. LB13 for assembly sequence. Tighten nut (11) to 225-250 in.-lbs. (26-28 N·m).

DRIVE SHAFT

Models SSI, SSII, 1100, 1150 And 1400

Models SSI, SSII, 1100, 1150 and 1400 are equipped with a flexible drive shaft enclosed in the drive shaft housing tube. Models 1100 and 1150 are direct drive models with no clutch. All other models are equipped with a centrifugal clutch. Drive shaft has squared ends which engage clutch adapter at engine end and head adapter at trimmer head end. Drive shaft should be removed for maintenance at 10 hour intervals of continuous use. Remove drive shaft, mark end positions, then clean shaft and inspect for damage. Lubricate drive shaft with a good quality high temperature wheel bearing grease and make certain shaft is installed with ends in

opposite locations. Alternating drive shaft squared ends between clutch and trimmer head ends will extend life of the shaft.

Models 1480

Model 1480 is equipped with a solid steel drive shaft mounted in bushings in the drive shaft housing. Drive shaft requires no regular maintenance; however, if drive shaft has been removed, lubricate with lithium base grease before reinstallation.

LOWER DRIVE SHAFT BUSHINGS

Models SSI, 1100, 1150 And 1400

Models SSI, 1100, 1150 and 1400 are equipped with drive shaft support bushings located in bushing head as shown in Fig. LB14. Bushing head requires no regular maintenance. A bushing kit (2) is available for service.

BEARING HEAD/LOWER CLUTCH

Model SSII

Model SSII is equipped with a bearing head incorporated in the lower clutch unit (Fig. LB15). Bearing head is equipped with sealed bearings and requires no regular maintenance.

To renew bearings or remove clutch assembly, remove trimmer head and cup washer (15). Remove the three bolts retaining bearing plate (11) to housing (4). Separate housing from bearing plate. Remove clutch shoe assembly (6) as required. Remove clutch drum (7) and shield (5). Press arbor shaft (8) from bearings. Remove snap rings (9 and 14). Remove bearings (10 and 13) and spacer (12).

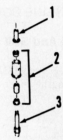

Fig. LB14—Exploded view of lower drive shaft support bushing assembly.

1. Adapter
2. Bushing kit
3. Drive shaft (head)

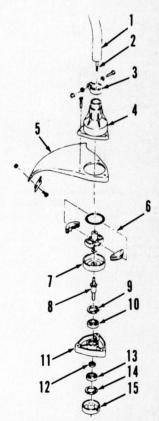

Fig. LB15—Exploded view of lower clutch and bearing head assembly used on Model SSII.

1. Drive shaft housing	
2. Drive shaft	9. Snap ring
3. Clamp	10. Bearing
4. Housing	11. Bearing plate
5. Shield	12. Spacer
6. Clutch assy.	13. Bearing
7. Clutch drum	14. Snap ring
8. Shaft	15. Cup washer

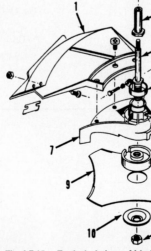

Fig. LB11—Exploded view of dual strand semi-automatic trimmer head used on most models.

1. Drive shaft adapter	5. Spring
2. Housing	6. Line slot
3. Line guide	7. Spool
4. Retainer	8. Lock knob & bump button

Fig. LB13—Exploded view of blade assembly.

1. Shield	
2. Drive shaft housing	7. Bearing housing
3. Sleeve	8. Cup washer
4. Drive shaft adapter	9. Blade
5. Drive shaft (head)	10. Adapter plate
6. Clamp	11. Nut

GEAR HEAD

Model 1480

Model 1480 is equipped with a gear head assembly. Check plug in gear head should be removed and lubricant level checked at 50 hour intervals of use. Gear head housing should be 2/3 full of lithium base grease. Service parts are not available from Lawn Boy. Gear head must be renewed as a complete unit.

ENGINE COVER

Models SSI And SSII

Models SSI and SSII are equipped with a full engine cover (Fig. LB17). To remove cover, remove all Phillips

screws around outer cover. Remove head adjustment screw (12). Remove

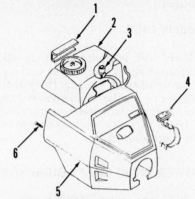

Fig. LB18—Exploded view of partial engine cover used on Models 1150, 1400 and 1480.

1. Fuel tank mount	4. Switch
2. Fuel tank	5. Engine cover
3. Fuel line assy.	6. Screw

the side of housing (7) opposite fuel tank filler cap (11). Covers are mounted in rubber grommets (1) also and may be slightly difficult to remove. Note locations of starter rope guide (2), throttle trigger (5), spring (6), switch (3) and fuel tank mounting before removing cover side (10). Fuel tank cap (11) must be removed to separate cover from fuel tank.

Models 1150, 1400 And 1480

Models 1150, 1400, and 1480 are equipped with a partial engine cover (Fig. LB18). To remove cover, disconnect spark plug lead and remove screw retaining cover extension stand (8-Fig. LB19). Remove cover extension stand. Disconnect the two wire leads at the ignition module. Remove the two inner engine cover retaining screws located just under fuel tank at each side (6-Fig. LB18). A long screwdriver is required to reach inner screws. Slide cover forward on tube as starter handle is worked through opening in engine cover.

Before reinstalling engine cover, make certain the two ignition module wire leads are secured in retainer slot.

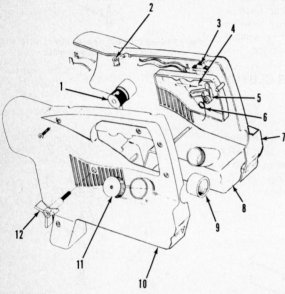

Fig. LB17—Exploded view of engine cover assembly used on SSI and SSII models.

1. Rubber grommet	7. Cover half
2. Rope guide	8. Fuel tank
3. Switch	9. Rubber sleeve
4. Throttle cable	10. Cover half
5. Throttle trigger	11. Fuel tank cap
6. Throttle spring	12. Tube clamp screw

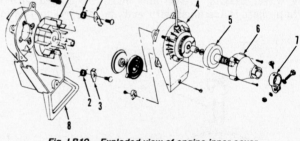

Fig. LB19—Exploded view of engine inner cover assembly.

1. Flywheel	5. Clutch drum
2. Spring	6. Clutch cover
3. Pawl	7. Clamp
4. Recoil housing	8. Stand

MARUYAMA

GASOLINE POWERED
STRING TRIMMERS

Model	Engine Manufacturer	Engine Model	Displacement
BC184	Kawasaki	KE18	18.4 cc
BC184C	Kawasaki	KE18	18.4 cc

ENGINE INFORMATION

All Models

Maruyama line trimmers and brush cutters are equipped with Kawasaki two-stroke air-cooled gasoline engines. Engines may be identified by manufacturer, engine model number and engine displacement. Refer to KAWASAKI ENGINE SERVICE section of this manual.

FUEL MIXTURE

All Models

Manufacturer recommends mixing regular grade gasoline (unleaded is an acceptable substitute) with a good quality two-stroke air-cooled engine oil at a 25:1 ratio. Do not use fuel containing alcohol.

STRING TRIMMER

All Models

Refer to Fig. MA10 for an exploded view of the dual strand manual trimmer head used on most models. To extend line, stop trimmer engine and wait until all head rotation has stopped. Loosen lock knob (6) (left-hand thread) until line ends may be pulled from housing. Pull lines until desired length has been obtained. Correct line length is 3.4-4.7 inches (10-12 cm).

To renew line, remove lock knob (6) and housing (5). Remove any remaining line on spool (2) and clean spool and housing. Install new line on spool. Wind line in direction indicated by arrow on spool. Diameter when new line is wound on spool must not exceed spool flange diameter. Insert line ends through line guides (4) then reinstall housing and lock knob.

BLADE

Model BC184

Model BC184 may be equipped with a 9 inch blade. Blade may be a four cutting edge blade, an eight cutting edge blade or a saw blade. To remove blade, rotate anti-wrap guard (1-Fig. MA11) until hole (H) in guard is aligned with hole (H) in cup washer (2). Insert a round tool into aligned holes to prevent blade rotation. Remove bolt (7) (left-hand thread), washer (6), cover (5) and adapter (4). Remove blade (3). When installing blade, tighten bolt (7) to 250 in.-lbs. (28 N·m).

DRIVE SHAFT

Model BC184

Model BC184 is equipped with a solid steel drive shaft supported in drive shaft housing tube. Drive shaft requires no regular maintenance; however, if drive shaft has been removed, lubricate drive shaft with lithium base grease before reinstallation.

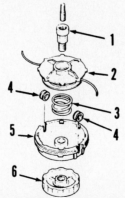

Fig. MA10—Exploded view of the dual strand manual trimmer head standard on most models.
1. Drive shaft adapter
2. Spool
3. Spring
4. Line guides
5. Housing
6. Lock knob

Model BC184C

Model BC184C is equipped with a flexible drive shaft enclosed in the drive shaft housing tube. Drive shaft has squared ends which engage adapters at each end. Drive shaft should be removed for maintenance at 20 hour intervals of use. To remove, separate drive shaft housing from engine. Mark locations of drive shaft ends and pull drive shaft out of housing. Clean drive shaft and lubricate with lithium base grease. Reinstall drive shaft in housing. Make certain drive shaft ends are installed at original location.

BEARING HEAD

Model BC184C

Model BC184C is equipped with sealed bearing housing (3-Fig. MA12). No regular maintenance is required and no service parts are available.

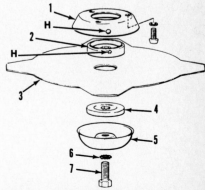

Fig. MA11—Exploded view of blade assembly on Model BC184.
1. Anti-wrap guard
2. Cup washer
3. Blade
4. Adapter plate
5. Cover
6. Washer
7. Bolt (LH)

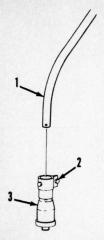

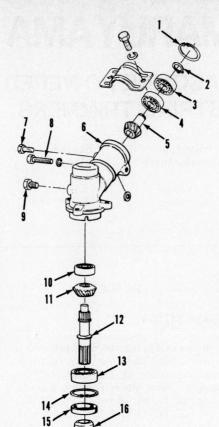

Fig. MA12—Bearing head assembly (3) is attached to drive shaft housing tube (1) by clamp (2). No service parts are available for bearing head.

Fig. MA13—Exploded view of gear head used on Model BC184.

1. Snap ring
2. Snap ring
3. Bearing
4. Bearing
5. Input shaft
6. Housing
7. Locating screw
8. Clamp bolt
9. Check plug
10. Bearing
11. Gear
12. Arbor (output) shaft
13. Bearing
14. Snap ring
15. Seal
16. Spacer

GEAR HEAD

Model BC184

Model BC184 is equipped with the gear head shown in Fig. MA13. Gear head lubricant level should be checked at 50 hour intervals of use by removing check plug (9). Gear head housing should be 2/3 full of lithium base grease. Do not use a pressure grease gun to install grease as bearing seal and housing damage will occur.

To disassemble gear head, remove trimmer head or blade assembly. Remove locating screw (7) and clamp bolt (8) then separate gear head from drive shaft housing. Remove snap ring (1). Insert a screwdriver into clamp split in gear head housing and carefully expand housing. Remove input shaft (5) and bearing assembly. Remove snap ring (2) and press bearings (3 and 4) as required. Remove spacer (16) and seal (15). Remove snap ring (14) and use a suitable puller to remove arbor shaft (12) and bearing assembly. If bearing (10) stays in housing, heat housing to 140° F (60° C) and tap housing on wooden block to remove bearing. Remove gear (11) from arbor shaft. Press bearing (13) from arbor shaft as required.

McCULLOCH
GASOLINE POWERED STRING TRIMMERS

Model	Engine Manufacturer	Engine Model	Displacement
MAC 60	Kioritz	...	13.8 cc
MAC 70	Kioritz	...	13.8 cc
MAC 80	Kioritz	...	21.2 cc
MAC 95	Kioritz	...	21.2 cc
MAC 60A	McCulloch	...	21.2 cc
MAC 80A	McCulloch	...	21.2 cc
MAC 85A	McCulloch	...	21.2 cc
MAC 90A	McCulloch	...	21.2 cc
MAC 95A	McCulloch	...	21.2 cc
MAC 100A	McCulloch	...	21.2 cc
SUPER MAC 90A	McCulloch	...	21.2 cc
SUPER MAC 95A	McCulloch	...	21.2 cc
PRO S I*	McCulloch	...	21.2 cc
PRO S II	McCulloch	...	21.2 cc
PRO S III	McCulloch	...	21.2 cc

* "PRO S" is the abbreviation for "PRO SCAPER" models.

ENGINE INFORMATION

All Models

Early model trimmers and brush cutters are equipped with engines manfactured by Kioritz. Late model trimmers and brush cutters are equipped with engine manufactured by McCulloch. Service procedure and specifications are similar. Identify engine by manufacturer and engine displacement. Refer to appropriate McCULLOCH ENGINE SERVICE or KIORITZ ENGINE SERVICE section of this manual.

FUEL MIXTURE

All Models

Manufacturer recommends mixing regular grade gasoline (unleaded is an acceptable substitute) with a good quality two-stroke air cooled engine oil at a 20:1 ratio. Do not use fuel containing alcohol.

STRING TRIMMER

All Models

Trimmer may be equipped with a single strand semi-automatic trimmer head or dual strand trimmer head. Two basic single strand trimmer heads have been used. An early model head (Fig. MC10) and a late model head (Fig. MC14). The dual strand semi-automatic trimmer head is shown in Fig. MC16.

Early Style Single Strand Trimmer Head

Early style single strand semi-automatic trimmer head is shown in Fig. MC10. Line may be manually advanced with engine stopped by pushing in on housing (9) while pulling on line. Procedure may have to be repeated to obtain desired line length. To advance line with engine running, operate engine at full rpm and tap housing (9) on the ground. Each time housing is tapped on the ground, a measured amount of trimmer line will be advanced.

To renew trimmer line, remove cotter key (10) and twist housing (9) counterclockwise to remove housing. Remove foam pad (6) and any remaining line on spool (3). Clean spool and inside of housing. Cut off approximately 25 feet (7.6 m) of 0.080 inch (2 mm) monofilament line and tape one end of line to spool (Fig. MC11). Wind line on spool in direction indicated by arrow on spool (Fig. MC12). Install foam pad with line end protruding from between foam pad and spool as shown in Fig. MC12. Insert end of line through line guide and install spool, housing and spring. Push housing in and twist in clockwise direc-

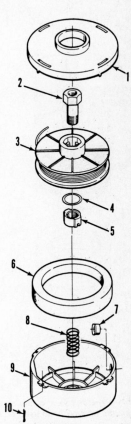

Fig. MC10—Exploded view of early style single strand semi-automatic trimmer head used on some models.

1. Cover
2. Drive shaft adapter
3. Spool
4. "O" ring
5. Drive adapter nut
6. Foam pad
7. Line guide
8. Spring
9. Housing
10. Cotter pin

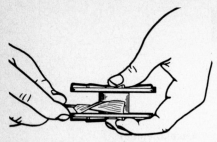

Fig. MC11—Tape end of new line to center of spool as shown.

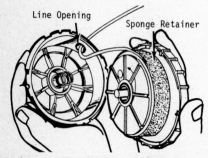

Fig. MC12—Install foam pad with line protruding from between pad and spool. Wind line in direction indicated on spool.

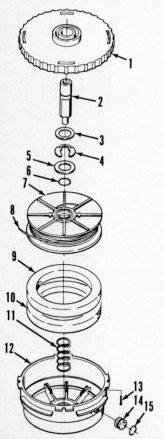

Fig. MC14—Exploded view of the single strand semi-automatic trimmer head used on some late models.

1. Cover
2. Drive shaft adapter
3. Washer
4. Retainer
5. Washer
6. Retainer
7. Spool
8. Line
9. Foam pad
10. Foam pad
11. Spring
12. Housing
13. Cotter pin
14. Line guide
15. Retainer

tion to lock in position then install cotter pin (13-Fig. MC10).

Late Style Single Strand Trimmer Head

Late style single strand semi-automatic trimmer head is shown in Fig. MC14. Line may be manually advanced with engine stopped by pushing in on housing (12) while pulling on line. Procedure may have to be repeated until desired line length is obtained. To advance line with engine running, operate trimmer engine at full rpm and tap housing (12) on the ground. Each time housing is tapped on the ground, a measured amount of trimmer line is advanced.

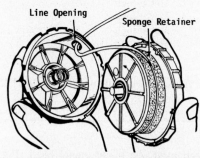

Fig. MC15—Install foam pads with line protruding from between pads. Wind line in direction indicated by arrow on spool.

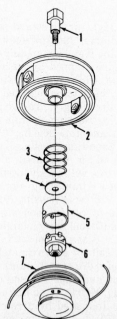

Fig. MC16—Exploded view of the dual strand semi-automatic trimmer head used on some models.

1. Drive shaft adapter
2. Housing
3. Spring
4. Washer
5. Outer cam
6. Inner cam
7. Spool & button

To renew trimmer line, remove cotter pin (13). Twist housing (12) counterclockwise and remove housing. Remove foam pads (9 and 10) and any remaining line from spool (7). Clean spool and inner area of housing. Cut off approximately 25 feet (7.6 mm) of 0.080 inch (2 mm) monofilament line and tape one end of line to spool (Fig. MC11). Wind line on spool in direction indicated by arrow on spool (Fig. MC15). Install foam pads so line is protruding from center of pads (Fig. MC15). Insert end of line through line guide and install spool, housing and spring. Push housing and twist in clockwise direction to lock in position then install cotter pin (13-Fig. MC14).

Dual Strand Trimmer Head

Heavy duty dual strand trimmer head is shown in Fig. MC16. To manually advance line with engine stopped, push in on button (7) and pull on each line. Procedure may have to be repeated to obtain desired line length. To extend line with engine running, operate trimmer at full operating rpm and tap button (7) on the ground. Line will automatically advance a measured amount.

To renew trimmer line, hold drum firmly and turn spool in direction shown in Fig. MC17 to remove slack.

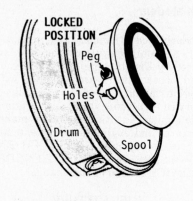

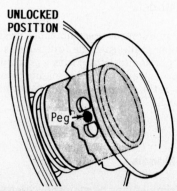

Fig. MC17—To remove spool, hold drum firmly and turn spool in direction shown to take up slack, then twist with a sudden snap until plastic peg is between holes as shown in lower view.

Twist with a hard snap until plastic peg is between holes. Pull spool out of drum. Remove old line from spool. Spool will hold approximately 20 feet (6 m) of monofilament line. Insert one end of new line through hole on spool (Fig. MC18) and pull line through until line is the same length on both sides of hole. Wind both ends of line at the same time in direction indicated by arrow on spool. Wind line tightly and evenly from side to side and do not twist line. Insert ends of line through line guide openings, align pegs on drum with slots in spool and push spool into drum. Hold drum firmly, twist spool suddenly in direction shown in Fig. MC19 until peg enters hole with a click and locks spool in position. Trim extending lines to desired length.

BLADE

All Models So Equipped

Some models may be equipped with a four cutting edge blade (Fig. MC20) or a saw blade (Fig. MC21). To remove blade, rotate cup washer (2-Fig. MC20) or (2-Fig. MC21) and align hole in cup washer with hole in gear head housing. Insert a suitable tool into hole to prevent drive shaft from turning. Remove cotter pin (6-Fig. MC20 or MC21). Nut (5-Fig. MC20 or MC21) has left-hand threads. Remove nut (5), adapter and blade. Tighten nut (5) to 260 in.-lbs. (30 N·m) and install a new cotter pin.

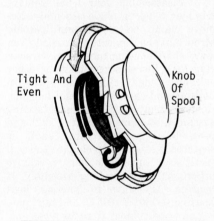

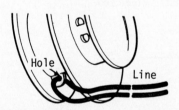

Fig. MC18—End of line must be inserted through hole on spool as shown in lower view. Wind line tightly in direction indicated by arrow on spool.

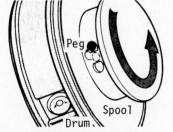

Fig. MC19—Hold drum firmly and twist suddenly to lock spool in position.

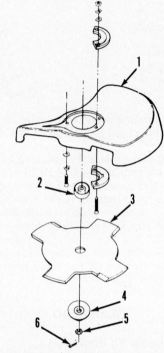

Fig. MC20—Exploded view of the four edge cutting blade used on some models.

1. Shield
2. Cup washer
3. Blade
4. Adapter washer
5. Nut
6. Cotter pin

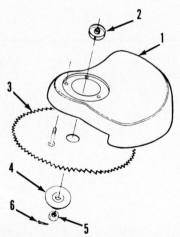

Fig. MC21—Exploded view of saw blade used on some models.

1. Shield
2. Cup washer
3. Saw blade
4. Adapter washer
5. Nut
6. Cotter pin

DRIVE SHAFT

Models With Curved Drive Shaft Housing

All models with a curved drive shaft housing are equipped with a flexible drive shaft enclosed in the drive shaft housing tube. Drive shaft has squared ends which engage adapters at each end. Drive shaft should be removed for maintenance at 20 hour intervals of use. To remove, separate drive shaft housing from engine. Mark locations of drive shaft ends and pull drive shaft out of housing. Clean drive shaft and lubricate with lithium base grease. Reinstall drive shaft in housing with the drive shaft end previously at engine now at trimmer head end. Reversing drive shaft in this manner will extend drive shaft life.

Models With Straight Drive Shaft Housing

Models with straight drive shaft housings are equipped with a solid steel drive shaft supported in drive shaft housing tube. Drive shaft requires no regular maintenance; however, if drive shaft has been removed, lubricate drive shaft with lithium base grease before reinstallation.

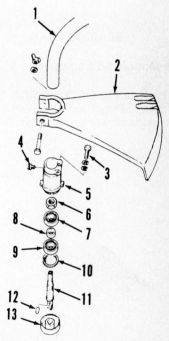

Fig. MC24—Exploded view of bearing head used on some models.

1. Drive shaft housing
2. Shield
3. Clamp bolt
4. Locating screw
5. Housing
6. Nut
7. Bearing
8. Spacer
9. Bearing
10. Snap ring
11. Arbor (output) shaft
12. Pin
13. Cup washer

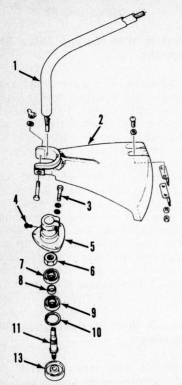

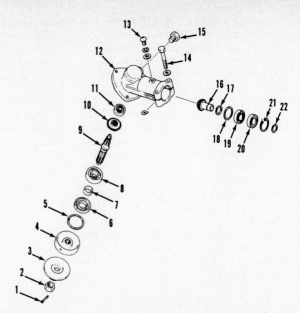

Fig. MC26—Exploded view of gear head used on heavy duty trimmers and brush cutters.

1. Cotter pin
2. Nut
3. Adapter plate
4. Cup washer
5. Snap ring
6. Seal
7. Spacer
8. Bearing
9. Arbor shaft
10. Gear
11. Bearing
12. Housing
13. Locating screw
14. Clamp bolt
15. Check plug
16. Input shaft
17. Spacer
18. Spacer
19. Bearing
20. Bearing
21. Snap ring
22. Snap ring

Fig. MC25—Exploded view of bearing head assembly used on some models.

1. Drive shaft housing	7. Bearing
2. Shield	8. Spacer
3. Clamp bolt	9. Bearing
4. Locating screw	10. Snap ring
5. Housing	11. Arbor (output) shaft
6. Nut	13. Cup washer

BEARING HEAD

All Models So Equipped

Refer to Fig. MC24 and MC25 for an exploded view of the two different bearing heads used on some models. Bearing heads are equipped with sealed bearings and require no regular maintenance.

To disassemble either bearing head, remove clamp bolt (3-Fig. MC24 or Fig. MC25) and locating screw (4). Separate bearing head from drive shaft housing. Remove trimmer head or blade assembly and cup washer (13). Remove snap ring (10) and use a suitable puller to remove arbor shaft and bearing assembly. Remove nut (6) and press bearings from arbor shaft as required.

GEAR HEAD

All Models So Equipped

Refer to Fig. MC26 for an exploded view of the gear head used on heavy duty string trimmers and brush cutters. Check plug (15) should be removed and gear head housing lubricant level checked at 30 hour intervals of use. Gear head should be 2/3 full of lithium base grease. Do not use a pressure grease gun to install grease as bearing seal and housing damage will occur.

To disassemble gear head, remove trimmer head or blade assembly. Remove clamp bolts (14) and locating screw (13) and separate gear head from drive shaft housing tube. Remove snap ring (21). Insert screwdriver or other suitable wedge into clamp splits in housing and carefully expand housing. Remove input shaft (16) and bearing assembly. Remove snap ring (22) and press bearings from input shaft as required. Remove snap ring (5) and seal (6). Use a suitable puller to remove arbor shaft and bearing assembly. If bearing (11) stays in housing, heat housing to 140° F (60° C) and tap housing on wooden block to remove bearing. Press bearings and gear from arbor shaft as required.

PIONEER/PARTNER

GASOLINE POWERED
STRING TRIMMERS

Model	Engine Manufacturer	Engine Model	Displacement
B180	Kawasaki	KE18	18.4 cc
B250	Kawasaki	KE24	24.1 cc
B370	Husqvarna	....	44.0 cc
B440	Husqvarna	....	44.0 cc

ENGINE INFORMATION

All Models

Pioneer/Partner line trimmers and brush cutters are equipped with a Kawasaki or Husqvarna two-stroke air-cooled gasoline engines. Engines may be identified by engine manufacturer, trimmer model number or engine displacement. Refer to KAWASAKI ENGINE SERVICE or HUSQVARNA ENGINE SERVICE sections of this manual.

FUEL MIXTURE

All Models

Manufacturer recommends mixing regular grade gasoline (unleaded is an acceptable substitute) with a good quality two-stroke air cooled engine oil at a 25:1 ratio. Do not use fuel containing alcohol.

STRING TRIMMER

Models B180 And B250

Refer to Fig. PR10 for an exploded view of the dual strand manual trimmer head used on Models B180 and B250. To extend line, stop trimmer engine and wait until all head rotation has stopped. Loosen lock knob (6) (left-hand thread) until line ends may be pulled from housing. Pull lines until desired length has been obtained. Correct line length is 3.4-4.7 inches (10-12 cm).

To renew line, remove lock knob (6) and housing (5). Remove any remaining line on spool (2) and clean spool and housing. Install new line on spool. Wind line in direction indicated by arrow on spool. Diameter when new line is wound on spool must not exceed spool flange diameter. Insert line ends through line guides (4) then reinstall housing and lock knob.

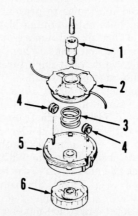

Fig. PR10—Exploded view of dual strand manual trimmer head used on Models B180 and B250.

1. Drive shaft adapter
2. Spool
3. Spring
4. Line guides
5. Lower housing
6. Lock knob

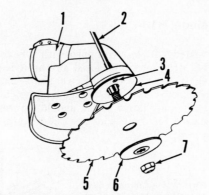

Fig. PR11—View showing parts assembly sequence to install blade on Models B370 and B440.

1. Gear head
2. Locking tool
3. Hole
4. Drive disc
5. Blade
6. Adapter washer
7. Nut (LH)

Models B370 And B440

Models B370 and B440 may be equipped with a trimmer head as an option. To install trimmer head, insert a locking rod (2-Fig. PR11) in hole in gear head and hole in drive disc (4). Some models have a slot at front of gear head housing instead of hole. Remove left-hand threaded nut (7), adapter washer (6) and blade (5). Some models may have a cover between nut (7) and adapter washer (6). Install trimmer head as shown in Fig. PR12. Tighten trimmer head to 20 N·m (15 ft.-lbs.).

To renew line in trimmer head, align hole in trimmer housing and line guide opening and feed new line onto spool while winding lower plate (Fig. PR13).

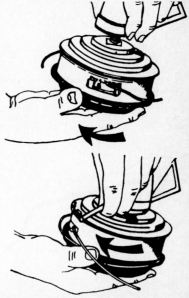

Fig. PR12—Trimmer head available for Models B370 and B440 has left-hand threads. Tighten trimmer head to 20 N·m (15 ft.-lbs.).

Fig. PR13—To renew line on Models B370 and B440 trimmer head, refer to text and follow sequence in illustration.

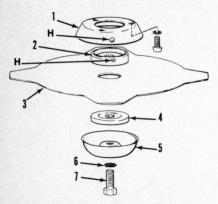

Fig. PR14—View showing parts assembly sequence to install blade on Model B250.

1. Anti-wrap guard
2. Cup washer
3. Blade
4. Adapter plate
5. Cover
6. Washer
7. Bolt (LH)

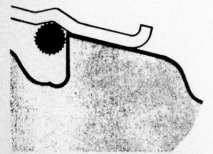

Fig. PR15—Sharpen front edge of tooth only. Make certain file holder is held firmly against the edge of tooth.

BLADE

Model B250

Model B250 may be equipped with a four cutting edge blade (Fig. PR14). To remove blade, rotate anti-wrap guard (1) until hole (H) in guard is aligned with hole (H) in cup washer (2). Insert a round tool into aligned holes to prevent blade rotation. Remove bolt (7) (left-hand thread), washer (6), cover (5) and adapter (4). Remove blade (3). When installing blade, tighten bolt (7) to 250 in.-lbs. (28 N·m).

Models B370 And B440

Models B370 and B440 may be equipped with a saw blade, a four cutting edge blade or a three cutting edge blade. To remove blade, carefully rotate blade until hole in upper driving disc is aligned with hole or slot in gear head housing. Insert a 4.5 mm (0.16 in.) round rod into holes to prevent blade rotation. Note nut retaining blade has left-hand threads and remove nut, cover, drive disc and blade. When installing blade, tighten left-hand thread nut to 35-50 N·m (26-30 ft.-lbs.).

To sharpen saw blade, use a 5.5 mm (7.32 in.) round file in file holder (part number 501 58 02-01). File front edge of tooth only with file holder firmly against the rear edge of tooth (Fig. PR15). Alternate filing one tooth to the right and the next tooth to the left at a 25° angle (Fig. PR16). Sharpen outer edge of tooth at a 5° angle (Fig. PR17). Use tooth set gage (part number 501 31 77-01) to adjust tooth set when teeth have been filed down 50 percent (Fig. PR18). Correct tooth set should provide 1 mm (0.04 in.) distance between tooth tips (Fig. PR19).

DRIVE SHAFT

Model B180

Model B180 is equipped with a flexible drive shaft enclosed in the drive shaft housing tube. Drive shaft has squared ends which engage adapters at each end. Drive shaft should be removed for maintenance at 20 hour intervals of use. To remove, separate drive shaft housing from engine. Clean drive shaft and lubricate with lithium base grease. Reinstall drive shaft in housing.

Models B250, B370 And B440

Models B250, B370 and B440 are equipped with a solid steel drive shaft supported in drive shaft housing tube. Drive shaft requires no regular maintenance; however, if drive shaft has been removed, lubricate drive shaft with lithium base grease before reinstallation.

BEARING HEAD

Model B180

Model B180 is equipped with sealed bearing housing (3-Fig. PR20). No regular maintenance is required and no service parts are available.

GEAR HEAD

Model B250

Model B250 is equipped with the gear head shown in Fig. PR21. Gear head lubricant level should be checked at 50 hour intervals of use by removing check plug (9). Gear head housing should be 2/3 full of lithium base grease. Do not use a pressure grease gun to install grease as bearing seal and housing damage will occur.

To disassemble gear head, remove trimmer head or blade assembly. Remove locating screw (7) and clamp bolt (8) then separate gear head from drive shaft housing. Remove spacer (16) and seal (15). Remove snap ring (14) and use a suitable puller to remove arbor shaft (12) and bearing assembly. If bearing (10) stays in housing, heat housing to 140° F (60° C) and tap housing on wooden block to remove bearing. Remove gear (11) from arbor shaft. Press bearing (13) from arbor shaft as required. Remove snap ring (1). Insert a screwdriver into clamp split in gear head housing and carefully expand housing. Remove input shaft (5) and bearing

Fig. PR16—Alternate filing one tooth to the right and the next tooth to the left. File at a 25° angle.

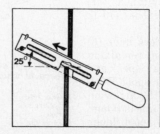
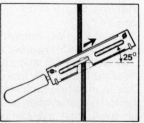

assembly. Remove snap ring (2) and press bearings (3 and 4) as required.

Models B370 And B440

Models B370 and B440 are equipped with gear head shown in Fig. PR22. Gear head lubricant level should be checked at 50 hour intervals of use. To check, remove check plug (11). Gear

head housing should be kept 3/4 full of lithium base grease.

To disassemble gear head, remove trimmer head or blade assembly. Remove the four screws (3) retaining cover (5) to housing and use puller (part number 502 50 09-01) to remove cover. Remove clamp bolts (14) and locating screw (15). Separate gear head assembly from drive shaft housing tube. Remove sleeve (19) using remover (part number 502 51 09-01). Heat housing (13) to 140° F (60° C) and remove input shaft (16) and bearing assembly and arbor shaft (9) and bearing assembly. If bearing (10) remains in housing, tap housing against a wooden block while housing is still hot to remove bearing. Remove snap ring (21) and press bearings (17 and 18) from input shaft as required. Remove bearing (7) and spacer (8) as required.

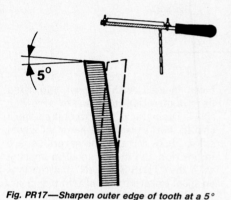

Fig. PR17—Sharpen outer edge of tooth at a 5° angle.

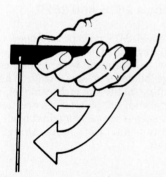

Fig. PR18—Use set gage (part number 501 31 77-01) to adjust tooth set when teeth have been filed down approximately 50 percent.

Fig. PR19—Tooth set should provide 1 mm (0.04 in.) distance between tooth tips.

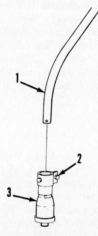

Fig. PR20—View of bearing head assembly used on Model B180.

1. Drive shaft housing
2. Clamp bolt
3. Bearing head

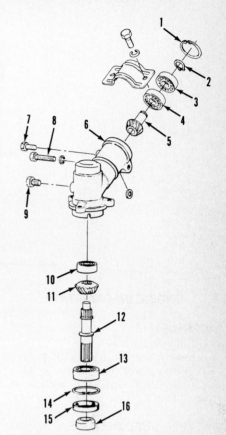

Fig. PR21—Exploded view of gear head used on Model B250.

1. Snap ring		9. Check plug
2. Snap ring		10. Bearing
3. Bearing		11. Gear
4. Bearing		12. Arbor shaft
5. Input gear		13. Bearing
6. Housing		14. Snap ring
7. Bolt		15. Seal
8. Clamp bolt		16. Spacer

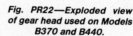

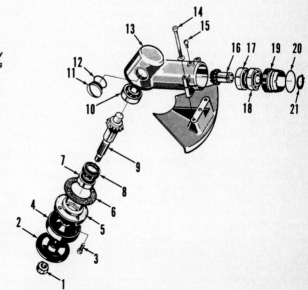

Fig. PR22—Exploded view of gear head used on Models B370 and B440.

1. Nut (LH)
2. Adapter plate
3. Screw
4. Drive disc
5. Cover
6. Gasket
7. Bearing
8. Spacer
9. Arbor shaft
10. Bearing
11. Check plug
12. Sealing ring
13. Housing
14. Clamp bolts
15. Locating screw
16. Input gear
17. Bearing
18. Bearing
19. Sleeve
20. "O" ring
21. Snap ring

POULAN

GASOLINE POWERED STRING TRIMMERS

Model	Engine Manufacturer	Engine Model	Displacement
2600	Poulan	....	26.2 cc
2610	Poulan	....	26.2 cc
2615	Poulan	....	26.2 cc
2620	Poulan	....	26.2 cc

ENGINE INFORMATION

All Models

All models are equipped with Poulan 2600 series power head. Refer to KIORITZ ENGINE SERVICE section of this manual.

FUEL MIXTURE

All Models

Manufacturer recommends mixing regular grade gasoline (unleaded is an acceptable substitute) with a good quality two-stroke air cooled engine oil at a 16:1 ratio. Do not use fuel containing alcohol.

STRING TRIMMER

Models 2600, 2610 And 2615

Models 2600, 2610 and 2615 are equipped with a single strand semi-automatic advance line trimmer head shown in Figs. PN10 and PN11. Fig. PN10 shows an exploded view of early style trimmer head which may be identified by the rough portion of upper housing (2). Fig. PN11 shows an exploded view of late style trimmer head which may be identified by the smooth portion of upper housing (2). Service procedure for both heads is similar.

To extend line with trimmer engine stopped, push in on button (7) while pulling on line end. Procedure may have to be repeated to obtain desired line length. To extend line with trimmer engine running, operate trimmer engine at full rpm and tap button (7) on the ground. Each time button (7) is tapped on the ground a measured amount of new line will be advanced.

To renew line, remove cover (8), button (7) and spool (6). Clean all parts thoroughly and remove any remaining old line from spool. Wind approximately 30 feet (9 m) of 0.080 inch (2 mm) monofilament line on spool in direction indicated by arrow on spool. Insert line end through line guide opening in housing (2) and install spool, button and cover.

Model 2620

Model 2620 is equipped with a dual strand manual trimmer head shown in Fig. PN12. To extend line, stop trimmer engine and wait until all trimmer head rotation has stopped. Push in on plate (8) while pulling each line out of housing (2).

To renew trimmer line, remove screw (9), plate (8), spring (6) and spool (7). Remove any remaining line from each side of spool. Clean spool, housing and plate. Insert ends of two new lines in holes located within spool and wind lines in direction indicated by arrow on spool. Diameter of line wound on spool should not exceed diameter of spool sides. Make certain line savers (3) are in position and install spool in housing with the "THIS SIDE IN" instructions on spool toward inside of trimmer head. Install spring (6), cover (8) and screw (9).

BLADE

Models 2615 And 2620

Model 2615 may be equipped with a four cutting edge blade and Model 2620 may be equipped with a four cutting edge blade or a saw blade. When installing blade on either model, make certain all adapter plates are centered and seated squarely against blade, then tighten nut (left-hand thread) securely.

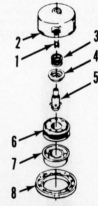

Fig. PN10—Exploded view of old style single strand semi-automatic trimmer head used on some models.

1. Drive shaft adapter
2. Housing
3. Spring
4. Spring adapter
5. Drive cam
6. Spool
7. Button
8. Cover

Fig. PN11—Exploded view of late style single strand semi-automatic trimmer head used on some models.

1. Line guide
2. Housing
3. Spring
4. Spring adapter
5. Drive cam
6. Spool
7. Button
8. Cover

DRIVE SHAFT

Models 2600, 2610 And 2615

Models 2600, 2610 and 2615 are equipped with a flexible drive shaft enclosed in the drive shaft housing tube. Drive shaft has squared ends which engage adapters at each end. Drive shaft should be removed for maintenance at 10 hour intervals of use. To remove, separate drive shaft housing from engine. Mark locations of drive shaft ends and pull drive shaft out of housing. Clean drive shaft and lubricate with lithium base grease. Reinstall drive shaft in housing. Make certain drive shaft ends are installed at original locations.

Model 2620

Model 2620 is equipped with a solid steel drive shaft supported in bearings located in drive shaft housing tube. Drive shaft requires no regular maintenance; however, if drive shaft has been removed, lubricate drive shaft with lithium base grease before reinstallation. When renewing bearings (1-Fig. PN13), mark position of old bearings in drive shaft housing tube before removing. Install new bearings at old bearing locations.

BEARING HEAD

Early Models 2600, 2610 And 2615

Early Models 2600, 2610 and 2615 are equipped with the bearing head shown in Fig. PN14. To disassemble bearing head, remove trimmer head assembly. Remove locating screw (2) and slip bearing head off of drive shaft housing tube. Remove dust cover (6), spacer (5) and arbor shaft (4). Lubricate arbor shaft with lithium base grease before installation.

Late Models 2600, 2610 And 2615

Late Models 2600, 2610 and 2615 are equipped with the bearing head shown in Fig. PN15. Bearing head is equipped with sealed bearings and requires no regular maintenance.

To disassemble bearing head, remove trimmer head or blade assembly. Remove clamp bolt (2) and locating screw (3). Separate bearing head assembly from drive shaft housing. Remove shield (6) and bracket (5) (as equipped). Remove cup washer (13) and washer (12). Carefully press drive shaft adapter (1) out of bearings. Remove snap rings (7 and 11). Press bearings (8 and 10) and spacer (9) from housing.

GEAR HEAD

Model 2620

Model 2620 is equipped with the gear head shown in Fig. PN16. Check plug

Fig. PN14—Exploded view of drive shaft and bearing head used on early Models 2600 and 2610.

1. Drive shaft housing	5. Spacer
2. Locating screw	6. Dust cover
3. Bearing housing	7. Nut
4. Arbor shaft	

Fig. PN12—Exploded view of dual strand manual trimmer head used on Model 2620.

1. Lock ring cap	
2. Housing	6. Spring
3. Line guide	7. Spool
4. Drive shaft adapter	8. Cover
5. Lock ring	9. Screw

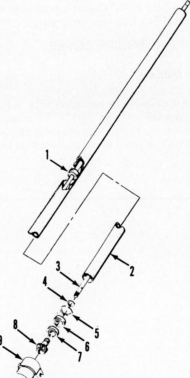

Fig. PN13—Exploded view of drive shaft and housing assembly used on Model 2620.

1. Bushing	
2. Drive shaft housing	6. Bearing
3. Drive shaft	7. Bearing
4. Snap ring	8. Input shaft
5. Snap ring	9. Bearing head housing

Fig. PN15—Exploded view of bearing head assembly used on late Model 2600 and 2610 and all 2615 models.

1. Arbor shaft	
2. Clamp bolt	8. Bearing
3. Locating screw	9. Spacer
4. Housing	10. Bearing
5. Bracket (as equipped)	11. Snap ring
6. Shield	12. Washer
7. Snap ring	13. Cup washer

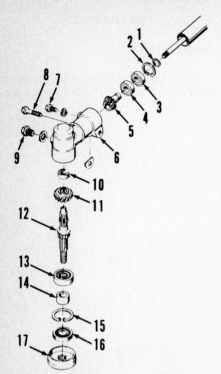

Fig. PN16—Exploded view of gear head assembly used on Model 2620.

1. Snap ring	10. Bearing
2. Snap ring	11. Gear
3. Bearing	12. Arbor shaft
4. Bearing	13. Bearing
5. Input shaft	14. Spacer
6. Housing	15. Snap ring
7. Bolt	16. Seal
8. Bolt	17. Cup washer
9. Check plug	

(9) should be removed and gear head lubricant checked at 10 hour intervals of use. Gear head housing should be 2/3 full of lithium base grease.

To disassemble gear head, remove trimmer head or blade assembly. Remove clamp bolt and head locating screw, then separate gear head from drive shaft housing. Remove cup washer (17) and spacer (14). Remove snap

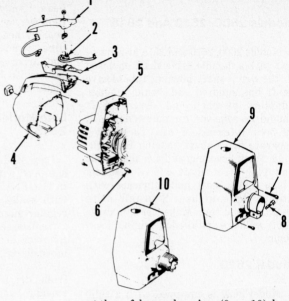

Fig. PN17—Exploded view of engine cover assembly used on all models.

1. Throttle trigger cover
2. Ignition switch
3. Throttle trigger
4. Handle
5. Fan housing
6. Spacer
7. Screw
8. Clamp bolt
9. Cover (clamp style)
10. Cover (threaded style)

ring (2) and use a suitable puller to remove input shaft (5) and bearing assembly. Remove snap ring (1) and press bearings (3 and 4) from input shaft as required. Remove seal (16) and snap ring (15). Use suitable puller to remove arbor shaft (12) and bearing assembly. Press bearing (13) and gear (11) from shaft as required. If bearing (10) remains in housing (6), heat housing to 140° F (60° C) and tap housing on wooden block to remove bearing.

ENGINE COVER

All Models

All models are equipped with a full engine cover (Fig. PN17). To remove engine cover, separate engine assembly from drive shaft housing. Note that two

styles of lower housing (9 or 10) have been used. Style (9) is secured to drive shaft housing by a clamp bolt (8). Style (10) has a threaded collar on drive shaft tube which connects to threads on housing. Remove the four 10-24 screws and separate housings (5) and (9 or 10) slightly. Disconnect ignition wire from module and separate fuel line so junction fitting stays with crankcase side of fuel line. Separate housing completely. Remove the three 8-24 screws from inner side of housing (5) and remove the air baffle. Remove the five 10-24 screws located under air baffle and separate housing (4) from housing (5). Remove fuel tank cap and remove fuel tank. Remove the four screws securing carburetor cover plate and remove carburetor cover. Disconnect spark plug, remove the four 10-24 screws at drive shaft housing side of cover (9 or 10), then remove cover (9 or 10).

ROBIN
GASOLINE POWERED
STRING TRIMMERS

Model	Engine Manufacturer	Engine Model	Displacement
NB02	Fuji	EC01	15.4 cc
NB04	Fuji	EC04	37.7 cc
NB16*	Fuji	EC01	15.4 cc
NB23*	Fuji	EC02	22.5 cc
NB30	Fuji	EC03	30.5 cc
HT01B	Fuji	EC01	15.4 cc
HT02B	Fuji	EC02	22.5 cc

* Designates Models NB16F, NB16S or NB23F, NB23S and NB23T.

ENGINE INFORMATION

All models are equipped with Fuji two-stroke air-cooled gasoline engines. Refer to the FUJI ENGINE SERVICE section of this manual. Engine may be identified by engine model number and engine displacement.

FUEL MIXTURE

All Models

Manufacturer recommends mixing regular grade gasoline (unleaded gaso-

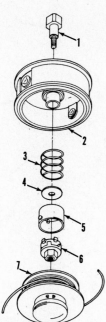

Fig. RB10—Exploded view of the dual strand semi-automatic trimmer head used on Models NB02, NB16 and NB23.

1. Drive shaft adapter
2. Housing
3. Spring
4. Washer
5. Outer cam
6. Inner cam
7. Spool

line is an acceptable substitute) and a good quality two-stroke air-cooled engine oil at a 24:1 ratio. Do not use gasoline containing alcohol.

STRING TRIMMER

Models NB02-NB16-NB23 With Semi-Automatic Head

Models NB02, NB16 and NB23 may be equipped with a dual strand semi-auto-

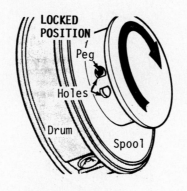

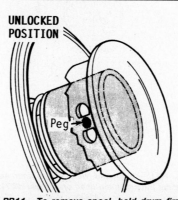

Fig. RB11—To remove spool, hold drum firmly and turn spool in direction shown to take up slack, then twist with a sudden snap until plastic peg is between holes as shown in lower view.

matic trimmer head shown in Fig. RB10. To extend line with trimmer engine stopped, push in on spool/button (7) while pulling on each line. Procedure may have to be repeated until desired line length is obtained. To extend line with trimmer engine running, operate trimmer at full rpm and tap spool/button (7) on the ground. Each time button is tapped on the ground, a measured amount of line will be advanced.

To renew trimmer line, hold drum firmly and turn spool in direction shown in Fig. RB11 to remove slack. Twist with a hard snap until plastic peg is between holes. Pull spool out of drum. Remove old line from spool. Spool will

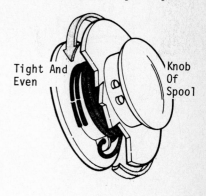

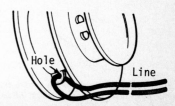

Fig. RB12—End of line must be inserted through hole on spool as shown in lower view. Wind line tightly in direction indicated by arrow on spool.

hold approximately 20 feet (6 m) of monofilament line. Insert one end of new line through hole on spool (Fig. RB12) and pull line through until line is the same length on both sides of hole. Wind both ends of line at the same time in direction indicated by arrow on spool. Wind tightly and evenly from side to side and do not twist line. Insert ends of line through line guide openings, align pegs on drum with slots in spool and push spool into drum. Hold drum firmly, twist spool suddenly in direction shown in Fig. RB13 until peg enters hole with a click and locks spool in position.

Models NBQ2-NB16-NB23 Low Profile Manual Head

Models NB02, NB16 and NB23 may be equipped with Low Profile manual trimmer head shown in Fig. RB14. To

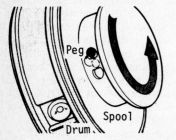

Fig. RB13—Hold drum firmly and twist suddenly to lock spool in position.

extend line, stop trimmer engine and wait until all head rotation has stopped. Loosen knob (6) until spool (4) may be turned to advance line. Tighten knob when desired line length has been obtained.

To renew line, remove lock knob (6), spring (5) and spool (4). Remove any remaining old line. Wind new line in direction indicated by arrow on spool. Do not exceed spool diameter with line. Insert line ends through line guides (3) of housing (2) and install spool, spring and lock knob.

Models NB04-NB30 With Four Strand Manual Head

Models NB04 and NB30 may be equipped with a four strand manual head shown in Fig. RB15. To extend line, loosen lock knob (8) and pull each of the four lines out until desired line length is obtained. Tighten lock knob (8).

To renew line, remove lock knob (8), cover (7), spools (5 and 3) and spring (4). Remove any remaining old line. Wind new line on spools in direction indicated by arrow on spool. Do not wrap line to greater diameter than diameter of spool. Insert line ends through line guides (6), then install spools, spring, cover (7) and lock knob (8).

Models NB04-NB30 With Dual Strand Manual Head

Models NB04 and NB30 use a manual trimmer head (Fig. RB16) similar to the manual Low Profile head (Fig. RB14) used on Models NB02, NB16 and NB23. Refer to preceding paragraph for service information.

BLADE

All Models

All models may be equipped with a four cutting edge blade, an eight cutting edge blade or a saw blade. Models NB16, NB23 will be equipped with 8 inch blades; Model NB02 will be equipped with 9 inch blades and Models NB04 and NB30 will be equipped with 10 inch blades. Refer to Fig. RB17 for correct parts installation sequence for blade installation.

To sharpen the four cutting edge blade, refer to Fig. RB18. Blade edge should have a length of 1.18-1.58 inch (30-40 mm). Do not grind the chamfered section of the blade root. Make certain the root of cutting blade remains chamfered to prevent breakage. Sharpen all teeth equally to maintain blade balance.

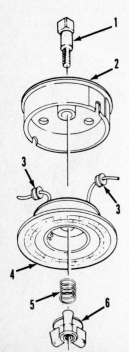

Fig. RB14—Exploded view of low profile manual trimmer head used on Models NB02, NB16 and NB23.

1. Drive shaft adapter
2. Housing
3. Line guides
4. Spool
5. Spring
6. Lock knob

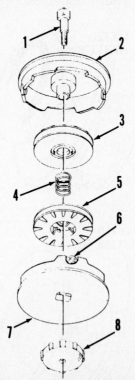

Fig. RB15—Exploded view of the four strand manual trimmer head used on Models NB04 and NB30.

1. Drive shaft adapter
2. Upper housing
3. Spool
4. Spring
5. Spool
6. Line guides
7. Lower housing
8. Lock knob

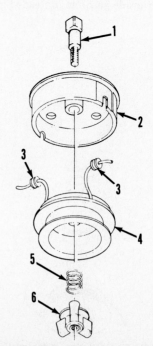

Fig. RB16—Exploded view of the dual strand manual trimmer head used on Models NB04 and NB30.

1. Drive shaft adapter
2. Housing
3. Line guides
4. Spool
5. Spring
6. Lock knob

To sharpen the eight cutting edge blade, refer to Fig. RB19. Sharpened section must NOT be closer than 0.08 inch (2 mm) to the root. Root chamfer should have a 0.08 inch (2 mm) radius. Sharpen all teeth equally to maintain blade balance.

To sharpen the saw blade, refer to Fig. RB20. Maintain a 0.04-0.08 inch (1-2 mm) radius at the tooth root. Maintain a 0.08-0.09 inch (2-2.5 mm) tooth set. Sharpen all teeth equally to maintain blade balance.

DRIVE SHAFT

Models NB16-NB23

Models NB16 and NB23 are equipped with a flexible drive shaft supported in a drive shaft housing tube (Fig. RB21). Flexible drive shaft (12) should be removed, cleaned and lubricated with lithium base grease at 30 hour intervals of use.

Model NB02

Model NB02 is equipped with a solid steel drive shaft supported in renewable bushings located in drive shaft housing tube (Fig. RB22). Drive shaft requires no regular maintenance; however, if removed, lubricate with lithium base grease before reinstallation. Drive shaft bushings (9) may be renewed. Mark locations of old bushings in drive shaft housing before removing so that

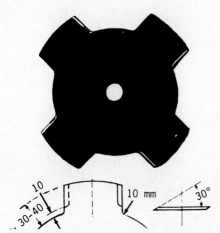

Fig. RB17—Exploded view of blade assembly used all models.

1. Gear head
2. Grass guard
3. Cup washer
4. Blade
5. Tool
6. Adapter plate
7. Washer
8. Nut

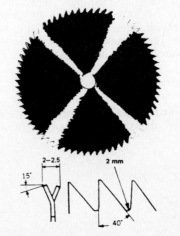

Fig. RB20—View of saw blade available for some models. Sharpen to dimensions shown and outlined in text.

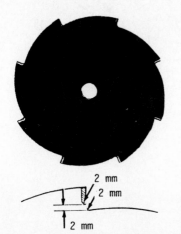

Fig. RB18—View of the four cutting edge blade available for some models. Sharpen to dimensions shown and outlined in text.

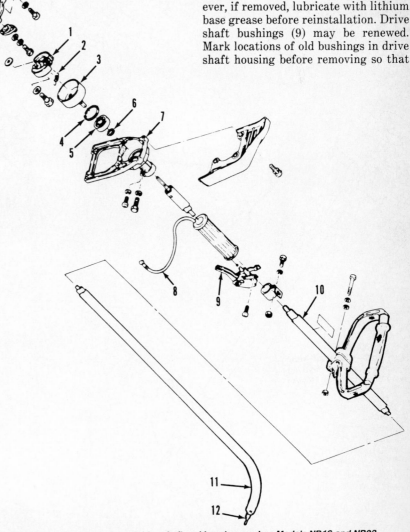

Fig. RB19—View of the eight cutting edge blade available for some models. Sharpen to dimensions shown and outlined in text.

Fig. RB21—Exploded view of drive shaft and housing used on Models NB16 and NB23.

1. Clutch assy.
2. Clutch spring
3. Clutch drum
4. Snap ring
5. Bearing
6. Snap ring
7. Housing
8. Throttle cable
9. Throttle trigger
10. Drive shaft housing
11. Drive shaft housing
12. Drive shaft

new bushings can be installed at the same locations.

Model NB04

Model NB04 is equipped with a solid steel drive shaft supported in renewable bushings located in drive shaft housing tube (Fig. RB23). Drive shaft requires no regular maintenance; however, if drive shaft is removed, lubricate

with lithium base grease before reinstallation. Drive shaft bushings (10) may be renewed. Mark locations of old bushings in drive shaft housing before removing old bushings. Note bushings may be held in position by pins (9) through drive shaft housing and bushing. Install new bushings at the same location as old bushings.

Model NB30

Model NB30 is equipped with a solid steel drive shaft supported in drive

shaft bushings and sealed ball bearings (Fig. RB24). Drive shaft requires no regular maintenance; however, if drive shaft is removed, lubricate with lithium base grease before reinstallation. Drive shaft bushings may be renewed. Mark locations of old bushings in drive shaft housing before removing so that new bushings can be installed at the same locations. Note some bushings may be held in position by pins through drive shaft housing and bushing.

BEARING HEAD

Models NB16 And NB23

Models NB16 and NB23 are equipped with sealed bearings in bearing head

Fig. RB22—Exploded view of drive shaft and housing used on Model NB02.
1. Clutch drum
2. Snap ring
3. Bearing
4. Housing
5. Housing
6. Snap ring
7. Bushing
8. Clamp
9. Bushing
10. Drive shaft housing
11. Collar
12. Throttle trigger
13. Throttle cable
14. Seal
15. Snap ring
16. Bearing
17. Bearing
18. Snap ring
19. Input shaft

Fig. RB23—Exploded view of drive shaft and housing assembly used on Model NB04.
1. Clutch drum
2. Snap ring
3. Bearing
4. Snap ring
5. Washer
6. Spacer
7. Snap ring
8. Drive shaft housing
9. Pin
10. Bushing
11. Drive shaft

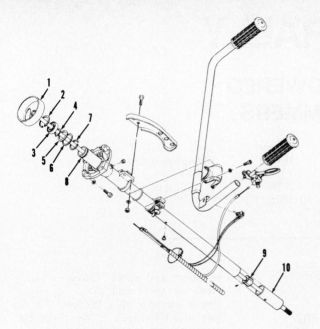

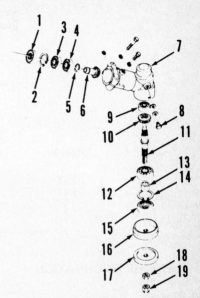

Fig. RB24—Exploded view of drive shaft and housing used on Model NB30.

1. Clutch drum
2. Snap ring
3. Bearing
4. Snap ring
5. Washer
6. Spacer
7. Snap ring
8. Housing
9. Bushing
10. Drive shaft housing

Fig. RB27—Exploded view of gear head used on Model NB02.

1. Seal	
2. Snap ring	11. Arbor shaft
3. Bearing	12. Bearing
4. Bearing	13. Spacer
5. Snap ring	14. Snap ring
6. Input shaft	15. Seal
7. Housing	16. Cup washer
8. Check plug	17. Adapter plate
9. Bearing	18. Nut
10. Gear	19. Jam nut

housing located at lower end of drive shaft housing tube (Fig. RB26). Bearing head requires no regular maintenance. To renew bearings (3 and 4), remove trimmer head or blade assembly and separate bearing head from drive shaft housing tube. Remove snap ring (5) and use a suitable puller to remove arbor shaft (2) and bearing assembly. Press bearings from arbor shaft as required.

GEAR HEAD

Model NB02

Model NB02 is equipped with gear head shown in Fig. RB27. Remove check plug (8) at 30 hour intervals of use and make certain gear head housing is 2/3 full of lithium base grease. Do not use a pressure type grease gun to pump grease into housing as bearing seal or housing damage may occur.

To disassemble gear head, separate gear head from drive shaft housing. Remove blade, adapters and spacer (13). Remove seal (1) and snap ring (2). Insert screwdriver or other suitable wedge into gear head housing clamp splits and carefully expand housing. Remove input shaft (6) and bearing assembly. Remove snap ring (5) and press bearings (3 and 4) off input shaft as required. Remove snap ring (14) and use a suitable puller to remove arbor (11) and bearing assembly. If bearing (9) stays in housing, heat housing to 140° F (60° C) and tap housing on wooden block to remove bearing.

Models NB04 And NB30

Models NB04 and NB30 are equipped with gear head shown in Fig. RB28. Re-

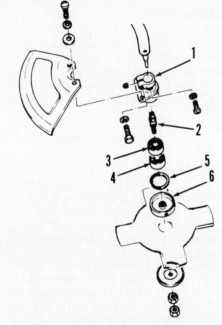

Fig. RB26—Exploded view of bearing head assembly used on Models NB16 and NB23.

1. Housing	4. Bearing
2. Arbor shaft	5. Snap ring
3. Bearing	6. Cup washer

move check plug (8) at 30 hour intervals of use and make certain gear head housing is 2/3 full of lithium base grease. Do not use pressure grease gun to pump grease into gear head housing as bearing seal or housing damage may occur.

To disassemble gear head, separate gear head from drive shaft housing. Remove trimmer head or blade assembly. Remove snap ring (2). Insert screwdriver or suitable wedge into gear head housing clamp split and carefully expand housing. Remove input shaft (4) and bearing assembly. Remove snap

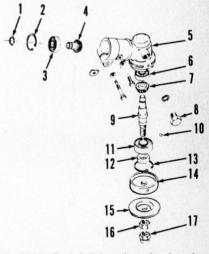

Fig. RB28—Exploded view of gear head used on Models NB04 and NB30.

1. Snap ring	
2. Snap ring	10. Pin
3. Bearing	11. Bearing
4. Input shaft	12. Spacer
5. Housing	13. Snap ring
6. Bearing	14. Cup washer
7. Gear	15. Adapter plate
8. Check plug	16. Nut
9. Arbor shaft	17. Jam nut

ring (1) and bearing (3) as required. Remove snap ring (13) and use a suitable puller to remove arbor shaft (9) and bearing assembly. If bearing (6) stays in housing, heat housing to 140° F (60° C) and tap housing on wooden block to remove bearing. Remove bearing (11) and gear (7) from arbor shaft as required.

ROPER/RALLY

GASOLINE POWERED STRING TRIMMERS

Model	Engine Manufacturer	Engine Model	Displacement
FE32	PPP	99E	31.0 cc
FE33	PPP	99E	31.0 cc

ENGINE INFORMATION

All Models

All models are equipped with a two-stroke air-cooled gasoline engine manufactured by Piston Powered Products (PPP). Refer to PISTON POWERED PRODUCTS ENGINE SERVICE section of this manual.

FUEL MIXTURE

All Models

Manufacturer recommends mixing 6 ounces (177 mL) of a good quality two-stroke air-cooled engine oil with 1 gallon (3.8 L) of regular grade (unleaded grade is an acceptable substitute) gasoline.

STRING TRIMMER

All Models

All models are equipped with a single line semi-automatic trimmer head (Fig. RY10). To extend line with engine stopped, push in on bump button (20) and pull on line until desired length is obtained. To extend line with engine running, operate trimmer engine at full rpm and tap bump button (20) on the ground. Line will automatically advance a measured amount.

To renew trimmer line, hold drum (15) and unscrew bump button (20). Remove spool (19). Clean inner surface of drum and spool. Check indexing teeth on spool and drum for wear. Insert one end of a 25 foot (7.6 m) length of 0.080 inch (2 mm) monofilament line into one of the holes in spool from the inside out, and back through the second hole to the inside. Wind line in direction indicated by arrow on spool and clip line in one of the line lock slots (LS) on spool. Insert line end through line guide in drum and install spool and bump button. Pull line to release from line lock slot on spool.

DRIVE SHAFT

All Models

All models are equipped with a flexible drive shaft enclosed in the tube housing. Drive shaft has squared ends which engage adapters at each end. Drive shaft should be removed for maintenance at 10 hour intervals of use. Remove and clean drive shaft. Inspect for damage. Coat with a good quality high temperature wheel bearing grease and install drive shaft. Make certain

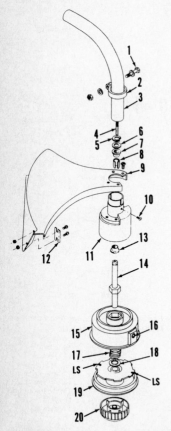

Fig. RY10—Exploded view of single strand semi-automatic trimmer head used on all models.

1. Bolt
2. Clamp
3. Drive shaft housing
4. Drive shaft
5. Retaining ring
6. Washer
7. Bushing
8. Bushing
9. Shield
10. Locating screw
11. Bushing housing
12. Line length trimmer
13. Bushing
14. Shaft
15. Drum
16. Line guide
17. Spring
18. Retainer
19. Spool
20. Bump button
LS. Line slot

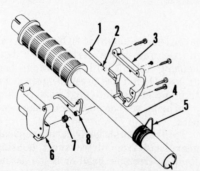

Fig. RY12—Exploded view of throttle trigger and cable assembly used on all models.

1. Throttle cable housing
2. Inner throttle cable
3. Throttle trigger housing
4. Drive shaft housing
5. Strap bracket
6. Throttle trigger housing
7. Spring
8. Throttle trigger

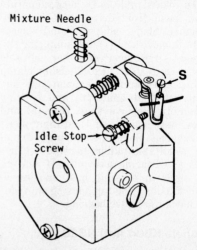

Fig. RY15—Loosen screw (S) and move throttle cable and housing to provide correct throttle trigger free play. Refer to text.

ends of drive shaft are properly located into upper and lower square drive adapters when installing.

LOWER DRIVE SHAFT BUSHINGS

All Models

All models are equipped with drive shaft support bushings (7 and 13-Fig.

RY10) located in bushing housing (11). Assemble in sequence shown.

THROTTLE TRIGGER AND CABLE

All Models

Throttle trigger assembly is located on drive shaft housing tube (Fig. RY12) on all models. Throttle cable inner wire

(2) should be lubricated at each end at 20 hour intervals of use with SAE 30 oil. Throttle cable should be adjusted to provide 0.02-0.04 inch (0.5-1.0 mm) throttle trigger movement before carburetor throttle lever begins to move. Adjust by loosening set screw (S-Fig. RY15) and moving cable housing and inner wire to provide specified free play. Tighten set screw (S) to maintain adjustment.

RYAN

GASOLINE POWERED
STRING TRIMMERS

Model	Engine Manufacturer	Engine Model	Displacement
261	PPP	99E	31.0 cc
265	PPP	99E	31.0 cc
275	PPP	99E	31.0 cc
285	PPP	99E	31.0 cc

ENGINE INFORMATION

All Models

All models are equipped with a two-stroke air-cooled gasoline engine manufactured by Piston Powered Products (PPP). Refer to PISTON POWERED PRODUCTS ENGINE SERVICE section of this manual.

FUEL MIXTURE

All Models

Manufacturer recommends mixing 6 ounces (177 mL) of a good quality two-stroke air-cooled engine oil with 1 gallon (3.8 L) of regular grade (unleaded grade is an acceptable substitute) gasoline.

STRING TRIMMER

Models 261, 265 And 275

Models 261, 265 and 275 are equipped with a single line semi-automatic trimmer head (Fig. RN10). To extend line with engine stopped, push in on bump button (20) and pull on line until desired length is obtained. To extend line with engine running, operate trimmer engine at full rpm and tap bump button (20) on the ground. Line will automatically advance a measured amount.

To renew trimmer line, hold drum (15) and unscrew bump button (20). Remove spool (19). Clean inner surface of drum and spool. Check indexing teeth on spool and drum for wear. Insert one end of a 25 foot (7.6 m) length of 0.080 inch (2 mm) monofilament line into one of the holes in spool from the inside out, and back through the second hole to the inside. Wind line

in direction indicated by arrow on spool until all but about 3 inches (76.2 mm) of line is wrapped, then clip line temporarily in one of the line lock slots (LS)

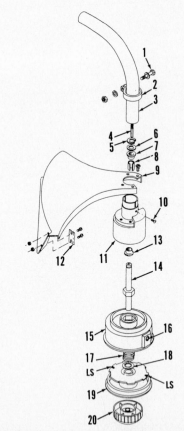

Fig. RN10—Exploded view of single strand semi-automatic trimmer head used on Models 261, 265 and 275.

1. Bolt
2. Clamp
3. Drive shaft housing
4. Drive shaft
5. Retaining ring
6. Washer
7. Bushing
8. Bushing
9. Shield
10. Locating screw
11. Bushing housing
12. Line length trimmer
13. Bushing
14. Shaft
15. Drum
16. Line guide
17. Spring
18. Retainer
19. Spool
20. Bump button
LS. Line slot

on spool. Insert line end through line guide in drum and install spool and bump button. Pull line to release from line lock slot on spool after assembly is complete.

Model 285

Model 285 is equipped with a semi-automatic dual strand trimmer head (Fig. RN14). To extend line with engine off, push bump button (8) in and pull lines out. Procedure may have to be repeated until desired line length has been obtained. To extend line with engine running, operate trimmer engine at full operating rpm and tap bump button on the ground. Each time bump button is tapped on the ground, approximately 1 inch (25 mm) of new line will be advanced.

To renew line, hold drum (2) and unscrew bump button (8). Remove spool (7) and remove any remaining old line. Clean spool and inner surface of drum. Check indexing teeth in drum and on spool. Loop a 25 foot (7.6 m) length of 0.080 inch (2 mm) monofilament line into two equal lengths. Insert the two line ends into the two holes in spool from the bottom and pull line out until loop is against spool. Wind both strands of line around spool in direction indicated by arrow on spool. Wind in tight even layers. Clip lines into line slots (6). Insert line ends through line guides (3) in drum and install spool and bump button. Pull line ends to free from line slots.

BLADE

Model 285

Model 285 may be equipped with a four cutting edge blade for weeds, grass and light brush (Fig. RN18). To install

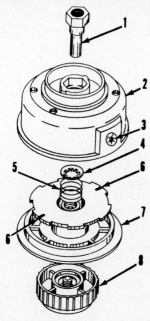

Fig. RN14—Exploded view of dual strand semi-automatic trimmer head used on Model 285.

1. Adapter
2. Drum
3. Line guide
4. Retainer
5. Spring
6. Line slot
7. Spool
8. Bump button

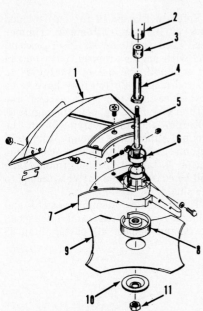

Fig. RN18—Exploded view of weed, grass and light brush blade assembly used on Model 285.

1. Shield
2. Drive shaft housing
3. Retainer & bushing
4. Drive shaft adapter
5. Head drive shaft
6. Clamp assy.
7. Bearing housing assy.
8. Blade adapter
9. Blade
10. Lower blade adapter
11. Nut

blade, refer to Fig. RN18 for assembly sequence. Tighten nut (11) to 225-250 in.-lbs. (26-28 N·m).

DRIVE SHAFT

All Models

All models are equipped with a flexible drive shaft enclosed in the tube housing. Drive shaft has squared ends which engage adapters at each end. Drive shaft should be removed for maintenance at 10 hour intervals of use. Remove and clean drive shaft, then inspect shaft for damage. Coat with a good quality high temperature wheel bearing grease and install drive shaft. Make certain ends of drive shaft are properly located into upper and lower square drive adapters when installing.

LOWER DRIVE SHAFT BUSHINGS

Models 261, 265 And 275

Models 261, 265 and 275 are equipped with drive shaft support bushings (7 and 13-Fig. RN10) located in bushing housing (11). Assemble in sequence shown.

BEARING HEAD

Model 285

Model 285 is equipped with a sealed bearing head assembly (7-Fig. RN18). Unit is sealed and no service parts are available.

THROTTLE TRIGGER AND CABLE

All Models

Throttle trigger assembly is located on drive shaft housing tube (Fig. RN22) on all models. Throttle cable inner wire (2) should be lubricated at each end at 20 hour intervals of use with SAE 30 oil. Throttle cable should be adjusted to provide 0.02-0.04 inch (0.5-1.0 mm) throttle trigger movement before carburetor throttle lever begins to move. Adjust by loosening set screw (S-Fig. RN23) and moving cable housing and inner wire to provide specified free play. Tighten set screw (S) to maintain adjustment.

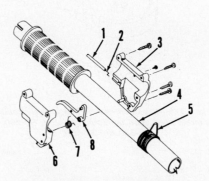

Fig. RN22—Exploded view of throttle trigger and cable assembly used on all models.

1. Throttle cable housing
2. Inner throttle cable
3. Throttle trigger housing
4. Drive shaft housing
5. Strap bracket
6. Throttle trigger housing
7. Spring
8. Throttle trigger

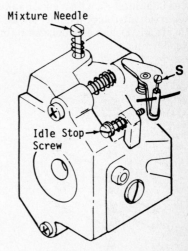

Fig. RN23—Loosen screw (S) and move throttle cable and housing to provide correct throttle trigger free play. Refer to text.

SACHS-DOLMAR

GASOLINE POWERED STRING TRIMMERS

Model	Engine Manufacturer	Engine Model	Displacement
LT-16	Fuji	EC01	15.4 cc
LT-250	Sachs	....	33.0 cc
BC-250	Sachs	....	33.0 cc
BC-330	Sachs	....	33.0 cc
BC-400	Sachs	....	40.0 cc

ENGINE INFORMATION

Model LT-16 is equipped with an engine manufactured by Fuji. All other models are equipped with Sachs-Dolmar engine. Refer to appropriate FUJI or SACHS-DOLMAR ENGINE SERVICE sections of this manual.

FUEL MIXTURE

Model LT-16

Manufacturer recommends mixing regular grade gasoline with an octane rating of at least 87, with a good quality two-stroke air-cooled engine oil at a ratio of 24:1. Do not use fuel containing alcohol.

All Other Models

Sachs-Dolmar recommends mixing SACHS-DOLMAR two-stroke engine oil with regular grade gasoline at a ratio of 40:1. When using regular two-stroke engine oil, mix at a ratio of 25:1. Do not use fuel containing alcohol.

STRING TRIMMER

Model LT-16

Refer to Fig. SD10 for an exploded view of the semi-automatic trimmer head used on Model LT-16. To extend line with engine stopped, push button (9) and pull line out of line guide to desired length. Button may have to be pushed several times. To extend line with engine running, operate engine at full rpm and tap button (9) on the ground. A measured amount of line will automatically be advanced each time button is tapped on the ground. Line will be cut off by the cutter attached to the shield.

To renew line, unsnap cover (10) and remove cover, button and line spool. Clean and inspect all parts. Wind 25

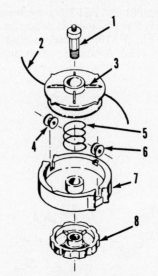

Fig. SD11—Exploded view of manual dual strand trimmer head used on Models LT-250, BC-250, BC-330 and BC-400.

1. Bolt   5. Spring
2. Line   6. Line guide
3. Spool   7. Hub
4. Line guide   8. Knob

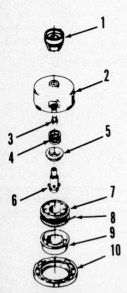

Fig. SD10—Exploded view of semi-automatic trimmer head used on Model LT-16.

1. Adapter   6. Drive post
2. Hub   7. Spool
3. Line guide   8. Line
4. Spring   9. Button
5. Spring adapter   10. Cover

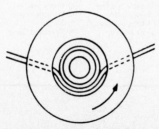

Fig. SD12—When installing new line, insert line end through the two holes in spool and pull line through until equal in length at each side. Wind lines in the direction indicated by arrow on spool.

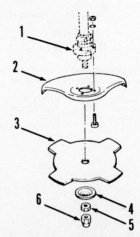

Fig. SD13—Exploded view of four cutting edge blade used on Model BC-250.

1. Bearing head   4. Adapter
2. Shield   5. Nut
3. Blade   6. Jam nut

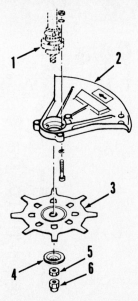

Fig. SD14—Exploded view of the eight cutting edge blade used on Model BC-250.

1. Bearing head
2. Shield
3. Blade
4. Adapter
5. Nut
6. Jam nut

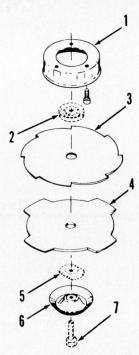

Fig. SD16—Exploded view of four and eight cutting edge blades available for Models LT-250, BC-250, BC-330 and BC-400.

1. Anti-Wind plate
2. Adapter
3. Eight edge blade
4. Four edge blade
5. Adapter
6. Cap
7. Bolt

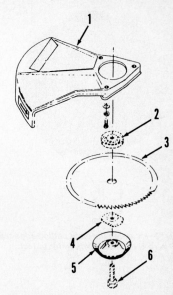

Fig. SD17—Exploded view of saw blade available for Models BC-330 and BC-400.

1. Shield
2. Adapter
3. Blade
4. Adapter
5. Cap
6. Bolt

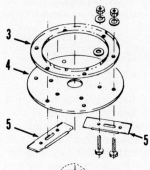

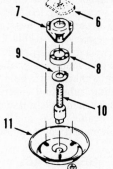

Fig. SD15—Exploded view of mulch cutting blade available for Models BC-330 and BC-400.

1. Anti-Wind plate
2. Adapter
3. Spacer
4. Blade plate
5. Blades
6. Adapter
7. Support bearing housing
8. Bearing
9. Washer
10. Arbor
11. Sliding cup

feet (7.6 m) of 0.080 inch (2 mm) monofilament line on spool in direction indicated by arrow on spool. Insert end of line through line guide (3) and install spool (7) in drum (2). Install button (9) and cover (10).

Models LT-250, BC-250, BC-330 And BC-400

Refer to Fig. SD11 for an exploded view of the manual dual strand trimmer head used. To advance trimmer line, shut off engine and wait until all head rotation has stopped. Loosen knob (8) (left-hand threads) until locating teeth between spool (3) and body (7) are disengaged. Carefully pull out each line to a length of 4 inches (101 mm). Make certain locating teeth are engaged and tighten knob (8).

To renew line, remove knob (8) (left-hand threads), body (7), spring (5), spool (3) and bolt (1). Remove any remaining line. Spool will hold approximately 25 feet (7.6 m) of monofilament line. Insert one end of line through the two holes in the spool (Fig. SD13). Pull line through holes until line is equal length at each side. Wind both ends of line in direction indicated by arrow on spool. Insert line ends through line guides in body and install bolt, spool, spring, body and knob.

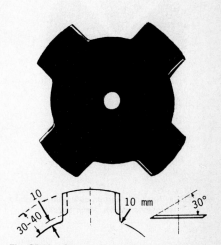

Fig. SD18—Sharpen four cutting edge blade to dimensions shown on all models except Model BC-250. Refer to text.

BLADE

Model BC-250 may be equipped with a four cutting edge blade (Fig. SD13) or an eight cutting edge blade (Fig. SD14). Model BC-330 and BC-400 may be equipped with a mulch cutting blade (Fig. SD15), a four cutting edge blade (4-Fig. SD16), an eight cutting edge blade (3-Fig. SD16) or a multi-tooth saw blade (Fig. SD17). Refer to appropriate illustration for installation sequence.

The mulch cutting blade should be sharpened using the same procedure as used for the four cutting edge blade.

To sharpen the four cutting edge blade, refer to Fig. SD18. Blade edge should have a length of 1.18-1.58 inch (30-40 mm) for all models except Model

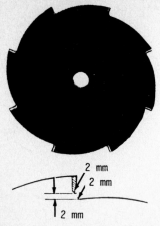

Fig. SD19—Sharpen the eight cutting edge blade to dimensions shown. Refer to text.

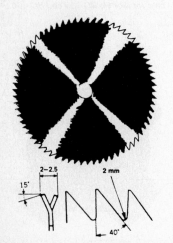

Fig. SD20—Set and sharpen saw blade teeth to dimensions shown. Refer to text.

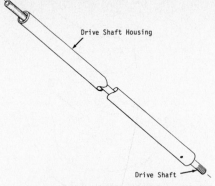

Fig. SD21—Models BC-250, BC-330 and BC-400 are equipped with a solid drive shaft.

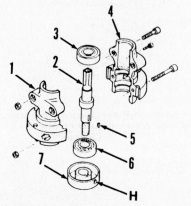

Fig. SD22—Exploded view of bearing head used on Model LT-250.

1. Housing	5. Key
2. Arbor	6. Bearing
3. Bearing	7. Cup washer
4. Housing	H. Hole

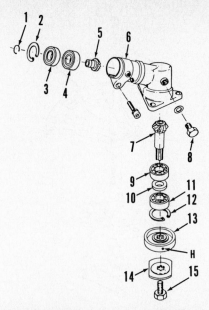

Fig. SD23—Exploded view of gear head used on some models. Refer also to Fig. SD24. Note hole (H) in cup washer can be aligned with hole in drive shaft housing to insert a 5/32 inch Allen wrench or similar tool to prevent drive shaft rotation when removing or installing cutting head or blade.

1. Snap ring	9. Bearing
2. Snap ring	10. Spacer
3. Bearing	11. Bearing
4. Bearing	12. Snap ring
5. Input shaft	13. Cup washer
6. Housing	14. Adapter
7. Arbor (output) shaft	15. Bolt
8. Check plug	H. Hole

BC-250. Model BC-250 should be sharpened to a length of 0.59-0.79 inch (15-20 mm). Do not grind the chamfered section of the blade root. Make certain the root of cutting blade remains chamfered to prevent breakage. Sharpen all teeth equally to maintain blade balance.

To sharpen the eight cutting edge blade, refer to Fig. SD19. Sharpened section must be kept 0.08 inch (2 mm) from the root. Root chamfer should have a 0.08 inch (2 mm) radius. Sharpen all teeth equally to maintain blade balance.

To sharpen the saw blade, refer to Fig. SD20. Maintain a 0.04-0.08 inch (1-2 mm) radius at the tooth root. Maintain a 0.08-0.09 inch (2-2.5 mm) tooth set. Sharpen all teeth equally to maintain blade balance.

DRIVE SHAFT

Models LT-16 And LT-250

Both models are equipped with a flexible drive shaft. Drive shaft should be removed, cleaned and lubricated at 20 hour intervals of use. Use a good quality lithium base grease. Drive shaft may be removed by separating drive shaft housing (tube) and engine.

Models BC-250, BC-330 And BC-400

Models BC-250, BC-330 and BC-400 are equipped with a solid steel drive shaft (Fig. SD21) supported in bushings in drive shaft housing. No regular maintenance is required.

BEARING HEAD

Model LT-16

Model LT-16 bearing head is an integral part of the drive shaft housing. If

bearing head becomes worn or damaged, entire housing assembly must be renewed.

Model LT-250

Refer to Fig. SD22 for an exploded view of bearing head used on LT-250 models. Bearings (3 and 6) are sealed and require no regular maintenance. To disassemble bearing head, remove bolts and separate gear head housing (1 and 4). Remove arbor and bearing assembly. Press cup washer (7) from arbor. Remove key (5) and press bearings from arbor as necessary. Note hole (H) in cup washer is an aid to tighten or remove cutting head or blade assemblies. Align hole in cup washer with hole in drive shaft housing tube and insert a 5/32 inch Allen wrench or similar tool into hole to prevent drive shaft turning while removing cutting head or blade.

GEAR HEAD

Models BC-250, BC-330 And BC-400

Models BC-250, BC-330 and BC-400 may be equipped with the gear head assembly shown in Fig. SD23 or

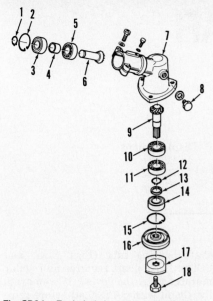

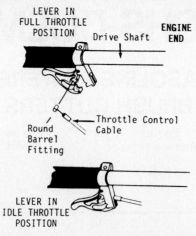

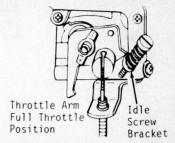

LEVER IN
FULL THROTTLE
POSITION

ENGINE
END

Drive Shaft

Throttle Control
Cable

Round
Barrel
Fitting

LEVER IN
IDLE THROTTLE
POSITION

Fig. SD25—Engine speed is controlled by throttle trigger located on drive shaft housing tube. Inner wire of cable should be lubricated with SAE 30 oil at 20 hour intervals of use.

Throttle Arm
Full Throttle
Position

Idle
Screw
Bracket

Fig. SD26—Threaded end of throttle cable should be adjusted as outlined in text.

Fig. SD24—Exploded view of gear head used on some models. Refer also to Fig. SD23.

1. Snap ring	10. Bearing
2. Snap ring	11. Bearing
3. Bearing	12. Snap ring
4. Spacer	13. Spacer
5. Bearing	14. Bearing
6. Input shaft	15. Snap ring
7. Housing	16. Cup washer
8. Check plug	17. Adapter
9. Arbor (output) shaft	18. Bolt

SD24. Gear head should be lubricated at 30 hour intervals of use. Remove check plug (8-Fig. SD23 or SD24) and fill gear head housing approximately 2/3 full with a good quality lithium base grease. Do not use a pressure grease gun to fill gear head as damage to bearing seals and housing will occur.

To disassemble gear head shown in Fig. SD23, separate gear head from drive shaft housing and drive shaft. Remove cutting head or blade. Pull cup washer (13) from arbor shaft. Remove snap ring (12). Heat gear head housing to approximately 212° F (100° C) and remove arbor shaft and bearing assembly. Press bearings (11) from arbor

shaft (7). Remove spacer (10). Press bearing (9) from arbor shaft. Remove snap ring (2). Insert screwdriver or suitable wedge in clamp split in housing and carefully expand housing. Remove input shaft and bearing assembly. Remove snap ring (1) and press bearings (3 and 4) from input shaft. After reassembly, fill gear head approximately 2/3 full with lithium base grease. Do not use a pressure grease gun to fill gear head.

To disassemble gear head shown in Fig. SD24, separate gear head from drive shaft housing and drive shaft. Remove cutting head or blade. Remove cup washer (16). Remove snap ring (15) and heat gear head housing to 212° F (100° C). Remove arbor shaft and bearing assembly. Remove snap ring (2) and insert a screwdriver or similar wedge into housing clamp splits and carefully expand housing. Remove input shaft and bearing assembly. Remove snap ring (1). Press bearing (3), spacer (4) and bearing (5) from input shaft. After reassembly, fill gear head approxi-

mately 2/3 full with a good quality lithium base grease. Do not use a pressure grease gun to fill gear head.

THROTTLE TRIGGER AND CABLE

Model LT-16

Throttle trigger located on drive shaft housing tube controls engine rpm. Throttle cable should be lubricated at each end by applying SAE 30 oil to inner throttle wire (Fig. SD25 and SD26). Lubricate throttle cable at 20 hour intervals of use. Cable should be threaded in or out of cable bracket at carburetor so that throttle arm contacts idle screw bracket at full throttle and return to idle screw when throttle trigger is released (Fig. SD26).

Models LT-250, BC-250, BC-330 And BC-400

Throttle trigger located on drive shaft housing tube controls engine rpm. Throttle cable should be lubricated at each end by applying SAE 30 oil to inner throttle wire. Throttle cable should be adjusted at knurled nut at throttle cable junction at engine. Loosen jam nut and adjust knurled nut to provide 0.08-0.10 inch (2-3 mm) cable movement before carburetor actuation begins. Tighten jam nut.

SACHS-DOLMAR

GASOLINE POWERED
BRUSH CUTTERS

Model	Engine Manufacturer	Engine Model	Displacement
BC-225-E	Fuji	....	22.5 cc
BC-377	Fuji	....	37.7 cc
BC-377-EES	Fuji	....	37.7 cc

ENGINE INFORMATION

Models BC-225-E, BC-377 and BC-377-EES brushcutters are equipped with Fuji two-stroke air-cooled gasoline engines. Identify engine by engine displacement or trimmer model number and refer to appropriate FUJI ENGINE SERVICE section of this manual.

FUEL MIXTURE

Manufacturer recommends mixing regular grade gasoline with an octane rating of at least 87, with a good quality two-stroke air-cooled engine oil at a ratio of 24:1. Do not use fuel containing alcohol.

BLADE

Model BC-225-E is equipped with a four cutting edge blade and Models BC-377 and BC-377-EES are equipped with a saw type blade (Fig. SD30). To remove blade from all models, align hole in cup washer with hole in gear head. Insert suitable tool (5-Fig. SD30) to prevent turning of arbor in gear head and remove jam nut (8) and nut (7). Remove adapter (6) and blade. When reassembling, tighten nut (7) to 130-215 in.-lbs. (15-24 N·m).

DRIVE SHAFT

All models are equipped with a solid steel drive shaft supported in sealed ball bearings and bushings in drive shaft housing tube (Figs. SD31 and SD32). Drive shaft requires no regular maintenance; however, if removed, lightly oil with SAE 30 oil before reinstalling drive shaft.

GEAR HEAD

Model BC-225-E

Refer to Fig. SD33 for an exploded view of the gear head used on Model BC-225-E. Remove check plug (8) and

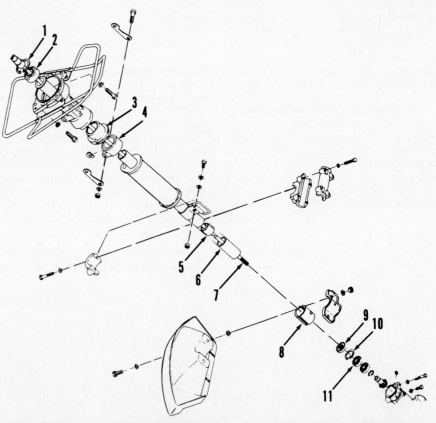

Fig. SD30—Exploded view of saw blade available for Models BC-377 and BC-377-EES.

1. Gear head
2. Anti-wrap plate
3. Cup washer
4. Saw blade
5. Tool
6. Adapter
7. Nut
8. Jam nut

Fig. SD31—Exploded view of drive shaft and housing used on Model BC-225-E. Solid drive shaft is supported at each end in ball bearings and along drive shaft housing by bushings (5).

1. Snap ring
2. Bearing
3. Rubber vibration dampner
4. Locating collar
5. Bushing
6. Drive shaft housing
7. Drive shaft
8. Split spacer
9. Seal
10. Snap ring
11. Bearing

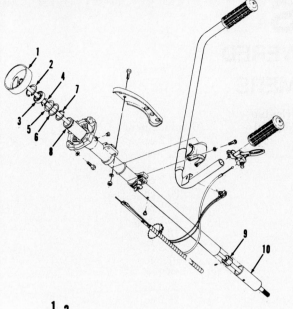

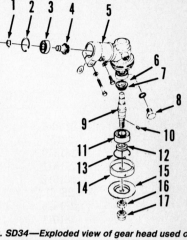

Fig. SD32—Exploded view of drive shaft and housing assembly used on Models BC-377 and BC-377-EES. Solid drive shaft is supported at each end by ball bearings and along drive shaft housing by bushings (9).

1. Drum & drive shaft assy.
2. Snap ring
3. Bearing
4. Snap ring
5. Spacer
6. Washer
7. Snap ring
8. Housing holder
9. Bushings
10. Housing

Fig. SD34—Exploded view of gear head used on Models BC-377 and BC-377-EES.

1. Snap ring
2. Snap ring
3. Bearing
4. Input shaft & gear
5. Housing
6. Bearing
7. Gear
8. Check plug
9. Arbor (output) shaft
10. Key
11. Bearing
12. Spacer
13. Snap ring
14. Cup washer
15. Adapter
16. Nut
17. Jam nut

Fig. SD33—Exploded view of gear head assembly used on Models BC-225-E.

1. Seal
2. Snap ring
3. Bearing
4. Bearing
5. Snap ring
6. Input shaft
7. Housing
8. Check plug
9. Bearing
10. Gear
11. Arbor (output) shaft
12. Bearing
13. Spacer
14. Snap ring
15. Bearing
16. Cup washer
17. Adapter
18. Nut
19. Jam nut

pump a good quality lithium base grease into gear head housing until grease appears at lower seal (15) at 30 hour intervals of use.

To disassemble gear head, separate gear head from drive shaft housing. Remove blade. Remove seal (15) and snap ring (14). Use a suitable puller to remove arbor shaft (11) and bearing assembly. If bearing (9) stays in housing, heat housing to 140° F (60° C) and tap housing on wooden block to remove bearing. Remove seal (1) and snap ring (2). Insert screwdriver or suitable wedge into housing clamp split and carefully expand housing to remove input shaft (6) and bearing assembly. Remove snap ring (5) and press bearings (3 and 4) from input shaft.

Models BC-377 And BC-377-EES

Models BC-377 and BC-377-EES are equipped with gear housing shown in Fig. SD34. Remove check plug (8) at 30 hour intervals of use and make certain gear head housing is 2/3 full of a good quality lithium base grease. Do not use a pressure type grease gun to pump grease into housing as bearing seal damage will occur.

To disassemble gear head, separate gear head from drive shaft housing. Remove blade, adapters and spacer. Remove snap ring (13) and use a suitable puller to remove arbor (9) and bearing assembly. If bearing (6) stays in housing, heat housing to 140° F (60° C) and tap housing on wooden block to remove bearing. Remove snap ring (2). Insert screwdriver or suitable wedge into gear head housing clamp split and carefully expand housing to remove input shaft (4) and bearing assembly. Remove necessary snap rings to remove bearings and gears from shafts.

THROTTLE TRIGGER AND CABLE

Throttle trigger located on drive shaft housing tube controls engine rpm by a cable and housing assembly running from trigger to carburetor. Inner wire of throttle cable should be lubricated at each end with SAE 30 oil at 20 hour intervals of use. Adjusting nuts are installed on throttle cable housing at carburetor end to provide throttle cable adjustment. Cable should be adjusted so that carburetor throttle plate will be fully opened at high speed position of throttle trigger; however, throttle trigger should have 0.08-0.10 inch (2-3 mm) movement before beginning to operate throttle lever on carburetor.

SEARS
GASOLINE POWERED
STRING TRIMMERS

Model	Engine Manufacturer	Engine Model	Displacement
28151	Kioritz	.....	21.2 cc
281510	Kioritz	.....	21.2 cc
281511	Kioritz	.....	21.2 cc
281512	Kioritz	.....	21.2 cc
28161	Kioritz	.....	30.1 cc
281610	Kioritz	.....	30.1 cc
281611	Kioritz	.....	30.1 cc
28171	Kioritz	.....	13.8 cc
281711	Kioritz	.....	13.8 cc
79545	Fuji	.....	37.7 cc
79555	Poulan	.....	26.2 cc
79556	Fuji	.....	28.0 cc
79558	Poulan	.....	26.2 cc
79559	Fuji	.....	28.0 cc
79623	Fuji	.....	37.7 cc
79812	Poulan	.....	26.2 cc
79813	Poulan	.....	26.2 cc
79814	Fuji	.....	28.0 cc
79821	Fuji	.....	28.0 cc
79822	Fuji	.....	28.0 cc

ENGINE INFORMATION

All Models

Sears and Sears "Brushwacker" line trimmers and brush cutters are equipped with Kioritz, Fuji or Poulan two-stroke air-cooled gasoline engines. Identify engine manufacturer by trimmer model number or engine displacement and refer to appropriate POULAN, KIORITZ or FUJI ENGINE SERVICE section in this manual.

FUEL MIXTURE

All Models

Manufacturer recommends mixing regular grade gasoline (unleaded is an acceptable substitute) with a good quality two-stroke air-cooled engine oil at a 25:1 ratio. Do not use fuel containing alcohol.

STRING TRIMMER

All Models

Single Strand Semi-Automatic Head. All models may be equipped with a single strand semi-automatic line trimmer head shown in Figs. SR10 and SR11. Fig. SR10 shows an exploded view of early style trimmer head which may be identified by the rough portion of upper housing (2). Fig. SR11 shows an exploded view of late style trimmer head which may be identified by the smooth portion of upper housing (2). Service procedure for both heads is similar.

To extend line with trimmer engine stopped, push in on button (7) while pulling on line end. Procedure may have to be repeated to obtain desired line length. To extend line with trimmer engine running, operate trimmer engine at full rpm and tap button (7) on the ground. Each time button (7) is tapped on the ground a measured amount of new line will be advanced.

To renew line, remove cover (8), button (7) and spool (6). Clean all parts thoroughly and remove any remaining old line from spool. Wind approximately 30 feet (9 m) of 0.080 inch (2 mm) monofilament line on spool in

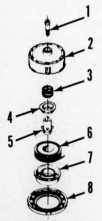

Fig. SR10—Exploded view of old style single strand semi-automatic trimmer head used on some early models.

1. Drive shaft adapter
2. Housing
3. Spring
4. Spring adapter
5. Drive cam
6. Spool
7. Button
8. Cover

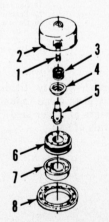

Fig. SR11—Exploded view of late style single strand semi-automatic trimmer head used on some models.

1. Line guide
2. Housing
3. Spring
4. Spring adapter
5. Drive cam
6. Spool
7. Button
8. Cover

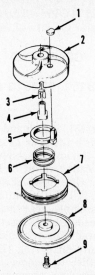

Fig. SR12—Exploded view of dual strand manual trimmer head used on some models.

1. Lock ring cap
2. Housing
3. Line guide
4. Drive shaft adapter
5. Lock ring
6. Spring
7. Spool
8. Cover
9. Screw

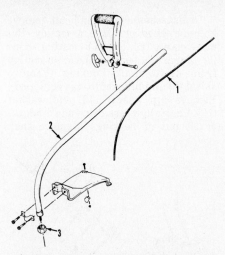

Fig. SR13—Exploded view of typical flexible drive shaft (1), drive shaft housing tube (2) and dust cover (3) used on some models. Note this style drive shaft and housing are also used with heavy duty bearing head models.

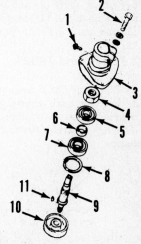

Fig. SR14—Exploded view of bearing head used on Models 28152, 28171 and 281711.

1. Locating screw
2. Clamp bolt
3. Bearing housing
4. Nut
5. Bearing
6. Spacer
7. Bearing
8. Snap ring
9. Arbor shaft
10. Cup washer
11. Pin

direction indicated by arrow on spool. Insert line end through line guide opening in housing (2) and install spool, button and cover.

Dual Strand Manual Head. Some models may be equipped with a dual strand manual trimmer head shown in Fig. SR12. To extend line, stop trimmer engine and wait until all trimmer head rotation has stopped. Push in on plate (8) while pulling each line out of housing (2).

To renew trimmer line, remove screw (9), plate (8), spring (6) and spool (7). Remove any remaining line from each side of spool. Clean spool, housing and plate. Insert ends of two new 0.095 inch (2.4 mm) lines in holes located within spool and wind lines in direction indicated by arrow on spool. Diameter of line wound on spool should not exceed diameter of spool sides. Make certain line savers (3) are in position and install spool in housing with the "THIS SIDE IN" instructions on spool toward inside of trimmer head. Install spring (6), cover (8) and screw (9).

BLADE

All Models So Equipped

Some models may be equipped with a four cutting edge grass and weed blade or a saw blade. When installing blade, make certain all adapter plates are centered and seated squarely against blade and tighten nut (left-hand thread) securely.

DRIVE SHAFT

Flexible Drive Shaft Models

Most models equipped with a flexible drive shaft (1-Fig. SR13) have a curved drive shaft housing tube (2). Drive shaft has squared ends which engage adapters at each end. Drive shaft should be removed for maintenance at 20 hour intervals of use. To remove, separate drive shaft housing from engine. Mark locations of drive shaft ends and pull drive shaft out of housing. Clean drive shaft and lubricate with lithium base grease. Reinstall drive shaft in housing making certain ends are not reversed.

Solid Drive Shaft

Models equipped with a solid steel drive shaft have a straight drive shaft housing tube. Drive shaft requires no regular maintenance; however, if drive shaft has been removed, lubricate drive shaft with lithium base grease before reinstallation.

BEARING HEAD

Models 79812 And 79813

Models 79812 and 79813 are equipped with a bearing head which is an integral part of drive shaft housing (Fig. SR13). Bearing head requires no regular maintenance and service parts are not available.

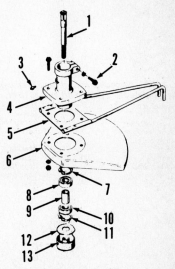

Fig. SR15—Exploded view of bearing head used on Models 79814 and 79821.

1. Drive shaft adapter
2. Clamp bolt
3. Locating screw
4. Housing
5. Bracket (as equipped)
6. Shield
7. Snap ring
8. Bearing
9. Spacer
10. Bearing
11. Snap ring
12. Washer
13. Drive disc

Models 281512, 28171 And 281711

Models 281512, 28171 and 281711 are equipped with the bearing head shown in Fig. SR14. Bearing head is equipped with sealed bearings and requires no regular maintenance.

To disassemble bearing head, remove trimmer head assembly and cup washer (10). Remove clamp bolt (2) and locating screw (1). Separate bearing head from drive shaft housing tube. Remove snap ring (8) and use a suitable puller to remove arbor shaft (9) and bearing assembly. Remove nut (4), bearing (5), spacer (6) and bearing (7) as required.

Models 79814 And 79821

Models 79814 and 79821 are equipped with the bearing head shown in Fig. SR15. Bearing head is equipped with sealed bearings and requires no regular maintenance.

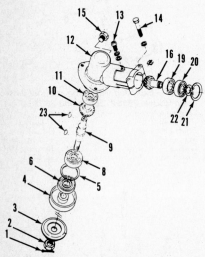

To disassemble bearing head, remove trimmer head or blade assembly. Remove clamp bolt (2) and locating screw (3). Separate bearing head assembly from drive shaft housing. Remove shield (6) and bracket (5) (as equipped). Remove cup washer (13) and washer (12). Carefully press drive shaft adapter (1) out of bearings. Remove snap

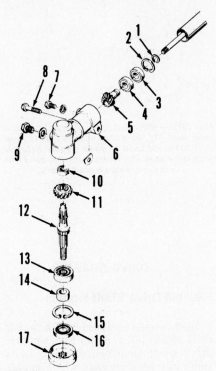

rings (7 and 11). Press bearings (8 and 10) and spacer (9) out of housing.

GEAR HEAD

Models 28151, 281510 And 281511

Models 28151, 281510 and 281511 are equipped with the gear head shown in Fig. SR16. Remove check plug (15) and check lubricant level at 50 hour intervals of use. Gear head housing should be kept 2/3 full of lithium base grease.

To disassemble gear head, remove trimmer head or blade assembly. Separate gear head from drive shaft housing tube. Remove snap ring (19) and use suitable puller to remove input shaft (14) and bearing assembly. Remove snap ring (18) and press bearings (16 and 17) from input shaft as required. Remove seal (5) and snap ring (6). Use suitable puller to remove arbor shaft (8) and bearing assembly. Press bearings from arbor shaft as required. Remove gear (9). If bearing (10) stays in housing (11), heat housing to 140° F (60° C) and tap housing on wooden block to remove bearing.

Models 28161, 281610 And 281611

Models 28161, 281610 and 281611 are equipped with the gear head shown in Fig. SR17. Remove check plug (15) and check lubricant level at 50 hour intervals of use. Gear head housing should be kept 2/3 full of lithium base grease.

To disassemble gear head, remove trimmer head or blade assembly. Separate gear head from drive shaft housing tube. Remove snap ring (25) and use suitable puller to remove input shaft and bearing assembly (20). Remove plug (16). Remove seal (7) and snap ring (8). Remove snap ring (14). Press arbor and bearing assembly from housing (19).

Model 79822

Model 79822 is equipped with the gear head shown in Fig. SR18. Check plug (9) should be removed and gear

Fig. SR16—Exploded view of gear head used on Models 28151, 281510 and 281511.

1. Cotter pin	12. Housing
2. Nut	13. Screw
3. Adapter plate	14. Clamp bolt
4. Adapter plate	15. Level check plug
5. Snap ring	16. Gear
6. Seal	19. Bearing
8. Bearing	20. Bearing
9. Arbor shaft	21. Snap ring
10. Gear	22. Snap ring
11. Bearing	23. Keys

Fig. SR18—Exploded view of gear head used on Model 79822.

1. Snap ring	
2. Snap ring	10. Bearing
3. Bearing	11. Gear
4. Bearing	12. Arbor shaft
5. Input shaft	13. Bearing
6. Housing	14. Spacer
7. Clamp bolt	15. Snap ring
8. Bolt	16. Seal
9. Check plug	17. Cup washer

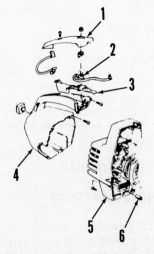

Fig. SR17—Exploded view of gear head used on Models 28161, 281610 and 281611.

1. Cotter pin	
2. Nut	14. Snap ring
3. Adapter plate	15. Level check plug
4. Adapter plate	16. Plug
5. Arbor shaft	17. Nut
6. Keys	18. Clamp bolt
7. Seal	19. Housing
8. Snap ring	20. Gear
9. Bearing	21. Spacer
10. Spacer	22. Bearing
11. Gear	23. Bearing
12. Snap ring	24. Snap ring
13. Bearing	25. Snap ring

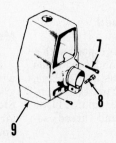

Fig. SR19—Exploded view of engine cover used on some models.

1. Throttle housing cover
2. Ignition switch
3. Throttle trigger
4. Handle
5. Fan housing
6. Spacer
7. Screw
8. Clamp bolt
9. Cover

head lubricant checked at 10 hour intervals of use. Gear head housing should be kept 2/3 full of lithium base grease.

To disassemble gear head, remove trimmer head or blade assembly. Remove clamp bolt and head locating screw and separate gear head from drive shaft housing. Remove cup washer (17) and spacer (14). Remove snap ring (2) and use a suitable puller to remove input shaft (5) and bearing assembly. Remove snap ring (1) and press bearings (3 and 4) from input shaft as required. Remove seal (16) and snap ring (15). Use suitable puller to remove arbor shaft (12) and bearing assembly. Press bearing (13) and gear (11) from shaft as required. If bearing

(10) remains in housing (6), heat housing to 140° F (60° C) and tap housing on wooden block to remove bearing.

ENGINE COVER

Models 79812, 79813, 79814, 79821 And 79822

Models 79812, 79813, 79814, 79821 and 79822 are equipped with a full engine cover (Fig. SR19). To remove engine cover, remove clamp bolt (8) and separate engine assembly from drive shaft

housing. Remove the four 10-24 screws and separate housings (5) and (9) slightly. Disconnect ignition wire from module and separate fuel line so junction fitting stays with crankcase side of fuel line. Separate housings completely. Remove the three 8-24 inch screws from inner side of housing (5) and remove the air baffle. Remove the five 10-24 screws located under air baffle and separate housing (4) from housing (5). Remove fuel tank cap and remove fuel tank. Remove the four screws securing carburetor cover plate and remove carburetor cover. Disconnect spark plug and remove the four 10-24 screws at drive shaft housing side of cover (9) and remove cover (9).

SHINDAIWA

GASOLINE POWERED STRING TRIMMERS

Model	Engine Manufacturer	Engine Model	Displacement
F20	Shindaiwa	....	19.8 cc
T20	Shindaiwa	....	21.1 cc
T25	Shindaiwa	....	24.1 cc
C25	Shindaiwa	....	24.1 cc
C35	Shindaiwa	....	33.6 cc
BP35	Shindaiwa	....	33.6 cc
B40	Shindaiwa	....	39.4 cc

ENGINE INFORMATION

All Models

All models are equipped with a two-stroke air-cooled gasoline engine manufactured for Shindaiwa. Engine may be identified by trimmer model or by engine displacement. Refer to appropriate SHINDAIWA ENGINE SERVICE section of this manual.

FUEL MIXTURE

All Models

Shindaiwa recommends mixing regular grade gasoline (unleaded regular gasoline is an acceptable substitute) with an octane rating of at least 87 with a good quality two-stroke, air-cooled engine oil at a ratio of 25:1.

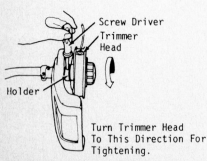

Fig. SH9—Use a 5/32 inch Allen wrench or similar tool inserted into hole in cup washer and drive shaft housing to prevent drive shaft from turning when removing trimmer head.

STRING TRIMMER

All Models

Refer to Figs. SH10 and SH11 for an exploded view of trimmer heads. To remove either head from drive shaft tube (housing), insert a tool into cup washer and bearing head (Fig. SH9) to lock head in position. Turn head counterclockwise to remove.

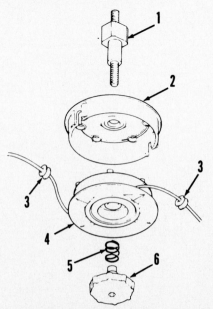

Fig. SH10—Exploded view of trimmer head used on some models. Use only 0.095 inch (2.4 mm) diameter trimmer line.

1. Adapter
2. Drum
3. Line guides
4. Spool
5. Spring
6. Knob

To renew line on head shown in Fig. SH10, unscrew knob (6) and release. Remove spool housing (2), spring (5) and spool (4). Wind new 0.095 inch (2.4 mm) monofilament line on spool evenly. Insert line ends through line guides and reinstall spool, spring and housing. To adjust line length, loosen knob (6) and turn trimmer head base counterclockwise. Pull both lines to 4 inch (102 mm) lengths. Tighten knob.

To renew line on trimmer head shown in Fig. SH11, unscrew knob (6) and remove. Remove spool housing (5) and spool (2). Wind new monofilament line onto spool evenly. Models F20 and T20 use 0.080 inch (2 mm) line, Models T25 and C25 use 0.095 inch (2.4 mm) line and Model C35 uses 0.105 inch (2.7 mm) line. Insert line ends through line guides (3) in housing. Reinstall spool, housing and knob.

BLADE

All models except Model F20 may be equipped with a steel brush blade. To install or remove blade, insert tool (5- Fig. SH12) into hole in upper adapter (1) and gear head to prevent drive shaft turning. Remove bolt (4), lower adapter (3) and blade.

DRIVE SHAFT

Model F20

Model F20 is equipped with a flexible steel drive shaft. Drive shaft should be removed and lubricated at 20 hour intervals of use. Use a good quality lithium base grease.

All Other Models

Models T20, T25, C25, C35 and B40 are equipped with a solid high carbon steel drive shaft splined at each end. Model BP35 is equipped with both a flexible drive shaft portion and a solid high carbon steel drive shaft. Solid drive shaft is supported in bushings located in drive shaft housing. Any discoloration or wear on steel drive shaft indicates bushing wear in housing. On Model T20, refer to Fig. SH13 and install bushings at equal distances with dimension (D) as 9.84 inches (250 mm). On Models T25 and C25, bushings are installed as shown in Fig. SH14. On Model BP35, refer to Fig. SH13 and install bushings at equal distances with dimension (D) as 11.02 inches (280 mm). On Model B40, refer to Fig. SH13 and install bushings at equal distances with

dimension (D) as 9.17 inches (233 mm). On all models, lubricate inside of housing and all bushings with oil for easier installation. Lubricate drive shaft with lithium base grease and install in housing and bushings.

BEARING HEAD

Model F20

Model F20 is equipped with a flange type bearing head equipped with sealed type bearings. Bearing head requires no regular maintenance except external cleaning.

To disassemble bearing head, refer to Fig. SH15. Remove trimmer head. Remove clamp bolt (2) and locating screw (1). Separate bearing head from drive shaft housing. Remove snap ring (8) and use suitable puller to remove arbor and bearing assembly. Remove bearings from arbor shaft as required.

GEAR HEAD

Models T20, T25, C25, C35, BP35 And B40

Refer to Fig. SH17 for cut-away view of gear head used on all models. Gear head should be lubricated at 50 hour intervals. Remove trimmer head or blade assembly. Remove grease plug from side of gear head housing. Pump a

good quality lithium base grease into housing through plug opening until grease appears at bearing seal (Fig. SH18). Failure to remove trimmer head

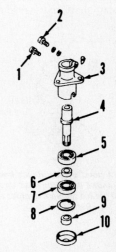

Fig. SH15—Exploded view of bearing head used on Model F20.

1. Locating screw	6. Spacer
2. Clamp bolt	7. Bearing
3. Housing	8. Snap ring
4. Arbor	9. Spacer
5. Bearing	10. Adapter plate

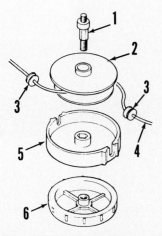

Fig. SH11—Exploded view of trimmer head used on some models. Use only 0.080 inch (2 mm) diameter trimmer line.

1. Adapter	4. Line
2. Spool	5. Drum
3. Line guides	6. Knob

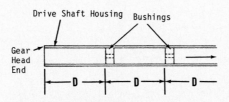

Fig. SH13—Bushings are installed in drive shaft housing as shown. Refer to text for correct dimension (D) according to model being serviced.

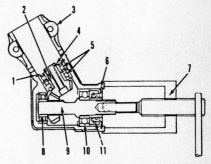

Fig. SH17—Cut-away view of gear head used on all models so equipped.

1. Snap ring	
2. Input shaft & gear	
3. Housing	7. Puller
4. Snap ring	8. Bearing
5. Bearings	9. Arbor shaft & gear
6. Snap ring	10. Bearing
	11. Seal

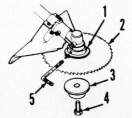

Fig. SH12—Use a 5/32 inch Allen wrench or similar tool to lock drive shaft when installing brush blade.

1. Upper adapter plate	
2. Blade	4. Screw
3. Lower adapter plate	5. Tool

Fig. SH14—Bushings for Models T25 and C25 are installed at locations shown.

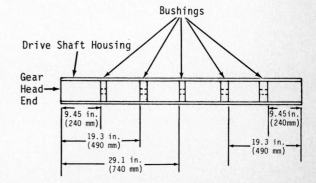

or blade before lubricating gear head may result in bearing, seal or housing damage.

To disassemble gear head, remove clamp bolts and head locating screws (Fig. SH19). Separate head from drive shaft and housing. Remove snap ring (1-Fig. SH17). Insert suitable puller bolt through input shaft and thread a nut on bolt against input gear (Fig. SH20). Remove input shaft and bearing assembly. Remove snap ring (4-Fig. SH17) and press bearings from input shaft. Remove snap ring (6). Install suitable puller as illustrated in Fig. SH17 and remove oil seal, bearing and arbor shaft assembly. To remove bearing (8), heat gear head housing to 212° F (100° C) and hit gear case sharply against a flat wooden surface. Remove seal (11) and press bearing (10) from arbor shaft.

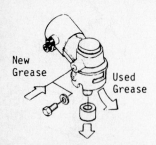

Fig. SH18—A good quality lithium base grease should be pumped into gear head through filler opening until grease appears at arbor shaft seal. Refer to text.

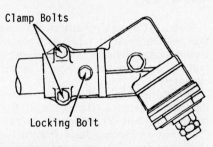

Fig. SH19—To separate gear head from drive shaft housing, remove clamp bolts and locking (head locating) bolt.

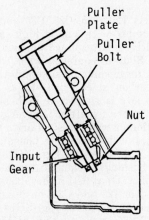

Fig. SH20—To remove input shaft, gear and bearing assembly, install puller as shown.

SMC

GASOLINE POWERED STRING TRIMMERS

Model	Engine Manufacturer	Engine Model	Displacement
GT-140	Kioritz	....	13.8 cc
GT-200	Kioritz	....	21.2 cc

ENGINE INFORMATION

All Models

All models are equipped with Kioritz two-stroke air-cooled engines. Identify engine model by trimmer model or engine displacement. Refer to KIORITZ ENGINE SERVICE section of this manual.

FUEL MIXTURE

All Models

Manufacturer recommends mixing regular grade gasoline (unleaded is an acceptable substitute) with a good quality two-stroke air-cooled engine oil at a 25:1 ratio. Do not use fuel containing alcohol.

STRING TRIMMER

Model GT-140

Model GT-140 is equipped with a single strand semi-automatic trimmer head shown in Fig. SC10. Line may be manually advanced with engine stopped by pushing in on housing (9) while pulling on line. Procedure may have to be repeated to obtain desired line length. To advance line with engine running, operate engine at full rpm and tap housing (9) on the ground. Each time housing is tapped on the ground, a measured amount of trimmer line will be advanced.

To renew trimmer line, remove cotter key (10) and twist housing (9) counterclockwise to remove housing. Remove foam pad (6) and any remaining line on spool (3). Clean spool and inside of housing. Cut off approximately 25 feet (7.6 m) of 0.080 inch (2 mm) monofilament line and tape one end of line to spool (Fig. SC12). Wind line on spool in direction indicated by arrow on spool (Fig. SC14). Install foam pad with line end protruding from between foam pad

and spool as shown in Fig. SC14. Insert line end through line guide and install housing and spring assembly on spool. Push in on housing and twist housing to lock into position. Install cotter key through hole in housing and cover.

Model GT-200

Model GT-200 is equipped with a single strand semi-automatic trimmer head shown in Fig. SC11. Line may be manually advanced with engine stopped by pushing in on housing (12) while pulling on line. Procedure may have to be repeated until desired line length is obtained. To advance line with engine running, operate trimmer engine at full rpm and tap housing (12) on the ground. Each time housing is tapped on the ground, a measured amount of trimmer line is advanced.

To renew trimmer line, remove cotter pin (13). Twist housing (12) counterclockwise and remove housing. Remove

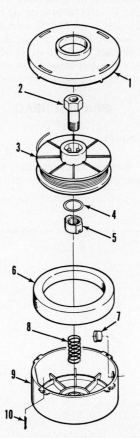

Fig. SC10—Exploded view of single strand semi-automatic trimmer head used on Model GT-140.

1. Cover
2. Drive adapter
3. Spool
4. "O" ring
5. Drive adapter nut
6. Foam pad
7. Line guide
8. Spring
9. Housing
10. Cotter pin

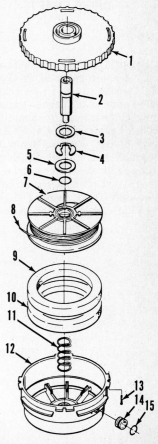

Fig. SC11—Exploded view of single strand semi-automatic trimmer head used on Model GT-200.

1. Cover
2. Drive adapter
3. Washer
4. Retainer
5. Washer
6. Retainer ring
7. Spool
8. Line
9. Foam pad
10. Foam pad
11. Spring
12. Housing
13. Cotter pin
14. Line guide
15. Retainer

Fig. SC12—Tape one end of new line to center of spool as shown.

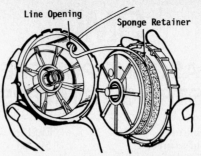

Fig. SC13—Install foam pads with line protruding from between pads. Wind line in direction indicated by arrow on spool.

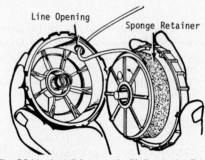

Fig. SC14—Install foam pad with line protruding between pad and spool as shown. Wind line in direction indicated by arrow on spool.

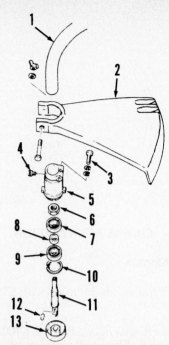

Fig. SC15—Exploded view of bearing head used on all models. Bearings (7 and 9) are sealed bearings and require no regular maintenance.

1. Drive shaft housing	
2. Shield	8. Spacer
3. Bolt	9. Bearing
4. Screw	10. Snap ring
5. Housing	11. Arbor (output) shaft
6. Nut	12. Pin
7. Bearing	13. Cup washer

foam pads (9 and 10) and any remaining line from spool (7). Clean spool and inner area of housing. Cut off approximately 25 feet (7.6 mm) of 0.080 inch (2 mm) monofilament line and tape one end of line to spool (Fig. SC12). Wind line on spool in direction indicated by arrow on spool (Fig. SC13). Install foam pads (9 and 10-Fig. SC11) so line is protruding from center of foam pads (Fig. SC13). Insert end of line through line guide and install spool, housing and spring. Push in on housing and twist housing to lock in position and install cotter pin (13-Fig. SC11).

DRIVE SHAFT

All Models

All models are equipped with a flexible drive shaft enclosed in the drive shaft housing tube. Drive shaft has squared ends which engage adapters at each end. Drive shaft should be removed for maintenance at 50 hour intervals of use. Remove screw (4-Fig. SC15) and bolt (3) at bearing head housing and separate bearing head from drive shaft housing. Pull flexible drive shaft from housing. Lubricate drive shaft with lithium base grease and reinstall in drive shaft housing with end which was previously at clutch end bearing head end. Reversing drive shaft ends extends drive shaft life. Make certain ends of drive shaft are properly located into upper and lower square drive adapters when installing.

BEARING HEAD

All Models

All models are equipped with the bearing head shown in Fig. SC15. Bearing head is equipped with sealed bearings and requires no regular maintenance. To disassemble bearing head, remove screw (4) and bolt (3) and separate bearing head from drive shaft housing tube. Remove trimmer head assembly and cup washer (13). Remove snap ring (10) and use a suitable puller to remove arbor shaft (11) and bearing assembly. Remove nut (6) and press bearings (7 and 9) and spacer (8) from arbor shaft as required.

SNAPPER

GASOLINE POWERED STRING TRIMMERS

Model	Engine Manufacturer	Engine Model	Displacement
210SS	Mitsubishi	T110	21.2 cc
240SS	Mitsubishi	T140	24.1 cc
311	PPP	99E	31.0 cc
410	Mitsubishi	T200-P-D	40.6 cc

ENGINE INFORMATION

Snapper trimmers and brush cutters are equipped with Mitsubishi or Piston Powered Products (PPP) engines. Identify engine by manufacturer, model number and engine displacement. Refer to appropriate MITSUBISHI ENGINE SERVICE section or PISTON POWERED PRODUCT ENGINE SERVICE sections of this manual.

FUEL MIXTURE

All Models

Manufacturer recommends mixing a good quality regular or unleaded gasoline with a good quality two-stroke air cooled engine oil at a 32:1 ratio.

STRING TRIMMER

Models 210SS And 311

Models 210SS and 311 are equipped with a dual strand semi-automatic trimmer head (Fig. SP10). To extend line with engine stopped, push up on bump button (6) and pull each line out. Procedure may have to be repeated until desired line length is obtained.

To extend line with engine running, operate trimmer at full rpm and tap bump button (6) on the ground. Each time bump button is tapped on the ground, a measured amount of line will be automatically advanced.

To renew trimmer line, hold hub (2) and push spool (5) upward against hub. Twist spool to the left until tabs lock the spool to the hub. Tabs can be viewed through the four holes in the hub. Remove bolt (7) and bump button (6). Twist spool to the right to unlock tabs and pull spool downward to remove. Loop 40 feet (12 m) of 0.095 inch (2.4 mm) monofilament line into two equal lengths. Insert line ends through the two holes in spool as shown in Fig. SP11. Wind both lines in direction indicated by arrow on spool. Snap lines into

lock tabs (LT-Fig. SP10) of spool and insert line ends through the line guide holes in hub. Install spool and bump button. Install bolt. Pull lines to free from lock tabs.

Models 240SS And 410

Models 240SS and 410 are equipped with heavy duty manual, dual strand trimmer heads (Fig. SP12). To extend line, stop trimmer engine and wait until all head rotation stops. Loosen knob (9). Pull each line end until desired line length has been obtained. Tighten knob when adjustment is complete.

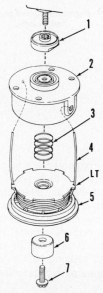

Fig. SP10—Exploded view of semi-automatic trimmer head used on Models 210SS and 311. This trimmer head was also available as an option for all other models.

1. Spacer
2. Hub
3. Spring
4. Line
5. Spool
6. Bump button
7. Bolt
LT. Lock tab (line)

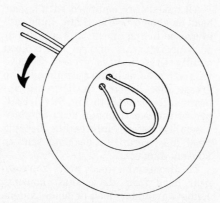

Fig. SP11—Insert line ends through holes in spool and pull line out in two equal lengths. Wind line in direction indicated by arrow on spool.

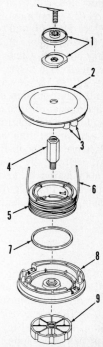

Fig. SP12 — Exploded view of manual dual strand trimmer head used on Models 240SS and 410. This head was available as an option on all other models.

1. Adapters
2. Upper housing
3. Line guides
4. Bolt
5. Spool
6. Line
7. "O" ring
8. Lower housing
9. Lock knob

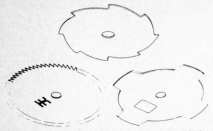

Fig. SP13—An optional four cutting edge blade, eight cutting edge blade or saw blade is available. Refer to text.

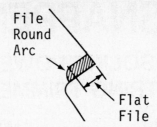

Fig. SP15—It is important to maintain an arc when filing blade teeth to prevent blade cracking. Refer to text.

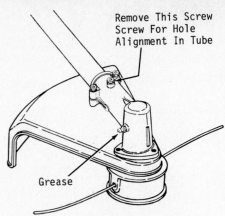

Fig. SP16—To lubricate head, pump grease into housing at grease fitting until grease appears at lower seal.

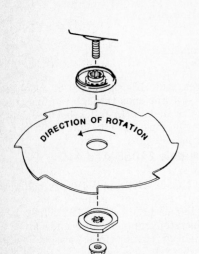

Fig. SP14—Blade should be installed as shown.

To renew line, cut 15 feet (4.6 m) of 0.095 inch (2.4 mm) monofilament line. Remove lock knob (9) and remove lower housing (8) and spool (5). Remove any remaining old line. Clean all parts of trimmer head. Use a wet soapy cloth. Pull line guides (3) down (do not remove) and clean outside surfaces. Apply a few drops of oil into cavities after cleaning. Loop new line into two equal lengths and insert line ends through holes at center of spool. Pull line ends out until stopped by spool. Wind in direction indicated by arrow on spool. Insert line ends in line guides and reinstall spool, lower housing and lock knob.

BLADE

Optional four cutting edge blade, eight cutting edge blade or eighty tooth saw blade are available for some models (Fig. SP13 or Fig. SP14). Blade is installed as shown in Fig. SP14.

To sharpen saw blade, refer to Fig. SP15. Check blade for nicks or cracks and discard blade if damage is found. Sharpen blade cutting edges as shown in Fig. SP15. Maintain radius at base of tooth to prevent blade cracking. Note also that idle speed of engine must be lowered when blade is installed.

DRIVE SHAFT

Model 311

Model 311 trimmer is equipped with a flexible drive shaft. Drive shaft should be removed, cleaned and lubricated with lithium base grease at 10 hour intervals of use. Mark ends of drive shaft before removing. Reinstall drive shaft with engine end at trimmer head end. Reversing drive shaft end for end extends drive shaft life. Note that if drive shaft extends more than 3/4 inch (19 mm) from the edge of drive shaft housing tube, the shaft is not fully engaged in drum.

Models 210SS, 240SS And 410

Models 210SS, 240SS and 410 are equipped with a solid steel drive shaft supported in five bushings installed in drive shaft housing tube. No regular maintenance is required; however, if drive shaft is removed, lubricate with a lithium base grease before installation. To renew bushings, mark location of old bushings in drive shaft housing before removing old bushings. Install new bushings at old bushing locations.

GEAR HEAD

All Models

All models are equipped with a gear head as shown in Fig. SP16. Lubricate at grease fitting shown in Fig. SP16 at 50 hour intervals of use. Use a good quality lithium base grease. Remove trimmer head or blade assembly. Pump grease into housing until grease appears at lower seal (15-Fig. SP17). Failure to remove trimmer head or blade assembly before lubricating bearing head may result in bearing, seal or housing damage.

To disassemble gear head, separate gear head from drive shaft housing. Remove trimmer head or blade, adapters and spacer. Remove snap ring (2). Insert screwdriver or suitable wedge into gear head housing clamp split and

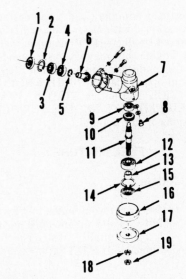

Fig. SP17—Exploded view of gear head used on all models.

1. Seal	
2. Snap ring	11. Arbor (output) shaft
3. Bearing	12. Bearing
4. Bearing	13. Spacer
5. Snap ring	14. Snap ring
6. Input shaft & gear	15. Seal
7. Housing	16. Cup washer
8. Grease fitting	17. Adapter
9. Bearing	18. Nut
10. Output gear	19. Jam nut

carefully expand housing to remove input shaft (6) and bearing assembly. Remove necessary snap rings to remove bearings and gears from shafts. Remove snap ring (14) and use a suitable puller to remove arbor (11) and bearing assembly. If bearing (9) stays in housing, heat housing to 140°F (60°C) and tap housing on wooden block to remove bearing.

THROTTLE TRIGGER AND CABLE

Throttle trigger located on handle attached to drive shaft housing tube controls engine rpm by a cable and housing assembly running from trigger to carburetor. Inner wire of throttle cable should be lubricated at each end with SAE 30 oil at 20 hour intervals of use.

Model 311 throttle cable is adjusted by loosening screw (S-Fig. SP18) at carburetor throttle lever and moving cable to provide 0.02-0.04 inch (0.5-1.0 mm) throttle trigger movement before carburetor throttle lever begins to move. Tighten screw (S) to maintain adjustment.

Models 210SS, 240SS and 410 are equipped with a throttle cable adjustment nut (3-Fig. SP19). Throttle cable should be adjusted at nut to provide 0.02-0.04 inch (0.5-1.0 mm) cable movement before carburetor throttle lever begins to move.

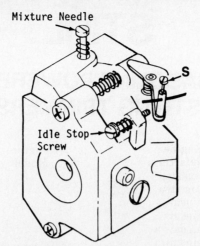

Fig. SP18—Screw (S) secures inner throttle cable in position on Model 311. Refer to text.

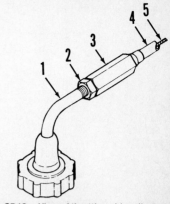

Fig. SP19—View of throttle cable adjustment nut on Models 210SS, 240SS and 400. Refer to text for adjustment procedure.

1. Housing
2. Jam nut
3. Adjustment nut
4. Housing
5. Inner cable

STIHL

GASOLINE POWERED STRING TRIMMERS

Model	Engine Manufacturer	Engine Model	Displacement
FS50	Komatsu	....	16.0 cc
FS51	Komatsu	....	16.0 cc
FS60	Shindaiwa	....	19.8 cc
FS62	Shindaiwa	....	19.8 cc
FS65	Shindaiwa	....	19.8 cc
FS66	Shindaiwa	....	19.8 cc
FS80	Komatsu	....	22.5 cc
FS81	Komatsu	....	22.5 cc
FS90	Stihl	O15	32.0 cc
FS96	Stihl	O15	32.0 cc
FS150	Stihl	O15	32.0 cc
FS151	Stihl	O15	32.0 cc
FS200	Stihl	O20	32.0 cc
FS202	Stihl	O20	35.0 cc
FS353	Stihl	O8S	56.0 cc
FS410	Stihl	O41	61.0 cc

ENGINE INFORMATION

All Models

All models are equipped with a two-stroke air-cooled gasoline engine manufactured by Stihl, Komatsu or Shindaiwa. Engine may be identified by trimmer model or engine displacement. Refer to appropriate STIHL, KOMATSU or SHINDAIWA ENGINE SERVICE section of this manual.

FUEL MIXTURE

All Models

Manufacturer recommends mixing regular grade gasoline (unleaded regular gasoline is an acceptable substitute) with an octane rating of at least 87 with a good quality two-stroke, air-cooled engine oil at a ratio of 25:1.

STRING TRIMMER

All Models

Stihl string trimmers may be equipped with the Stihl "AUTOCUT" dual strand semi-automatic trimmer head or the Stihl "POLYMATIC" dual strand manual trimmer head. Refer to appropriate paragraph for model being serviced.

Autocut Trimmer Head. To extend new trimmer line with engine running, operate trimmer engine at full rpm with trimmer head horizontal above the ground and tap head release button (5-Fig. SL10) on the ground. Each time button is tapped on the ground appropriately 5 cm (2 in.) of line is advanced.

To renew line, push cover latches (3) on housing (2) in and remove cover (4), button (5) and spool. Remove any remaining old line from spool. Clean spool and inside of housing. Wind new line onto spool in direction indicated by arrow on spool. Insert line ends through line guide (1) opening and reinstall spool, button and cover.

To install trimmer head assemble parts in sequence shown in Fig. SL12. Note trimmer head has left-hand threads and trimmer head is self-tightening as trimmer is used.

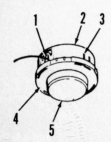

Fig. SL10—View of "AUTOCUT" semi-automatic trimmer head used on some models.

1. Line guide
2. Housing
3. Housing latch area
4. Cover
5. Button

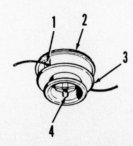

Fig. SL11—View of "POLYMATIC" manual trimmer head used on some models.

1. Line guide
2. Housing
3. Cover & spool
4. Lock knob

Fig. SL12—When installing trimmer head, parts should be assembled in sequence shown.

1. Thrust plate
2. Shaft (LH threads)
3. Washer
4. Washer
5. Trimmer head

Polymatic Trimmer Head. To extend trimmer line stop trimmer engine and wait until all trimmer head rotation has stopped. Loosen lock knob (4-Fig. SL11) until lines may be pulled from housing. Tighten lock knob.

To renew line, remove lock knob (4), cover (3) and spool. Remove any remaining old line. Clean spool and housing (2). Wind new line onto spool in direction indicated by arrow on spool. Insert line ends through line guide (1) openings and install spool, cover and lock knob.

To install trimmer head, assemble parts in sequence shown in Fig. SL12. Note trimmer head has left-hand threads and is self-tightening as trimmer is used.

BLADE

A "Polycut" blade is available for some models. To install, refer to Fig. SL13. Note that "Polycut" head has left-hand threads and is self-tightening as trimmer is used. Base of trimmer head is marked to indicate minimum blade length. If blade length is less than indicated, renew blades.

A "Rotocut 200" (Fig. SL14) is available for some models. To install, place blade (3) on thrust plate (1). Install

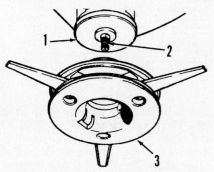

Fig. SL13—View of "Polycut" trimmer head available for some models.

1. Thrust plate
2. Shaft (LH threads)
3. "Polycut" trimmer head

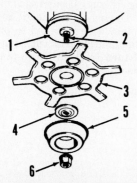

Fig. SL14—View of "Rotocut 200" blade available for some models.

1. Thrust plate
2. Shaft (LH threads)
3. Blade
4. Washer
5. Cover
6. Nut (LH)

thrust washer (4) over shaft (2) and install cover (5). Install nut (6) (left-hand threads). A round pin may be inserted through hole in side of gear head to prevent head rotation during tightening.

Models equipped with a gear head may be equipped with a variety of weed and grass blades (Fig. SL15). Heavy duty units may be equipped with a

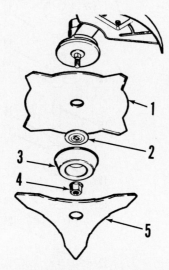

Fig. SL15—Exploded view of weed and grass blades available for some models.

1. Four cutting edge blade
2. Washer
3. Cover
4. Nut (LH)
5. Three cutting edge blade

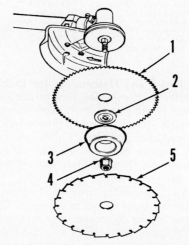

Fig. SL16—Exploded view of two different type saw blades available for some models.

1. Saw blade
2. Washer
3. Cover
4. Nut (LH)
5. Chisel tooth saw blade

brush or a saw blade (Fig. SL16). Blades are installed using procedure outlined for installation of "Rotocut 200" blade.

DRIVE SHAFT

Flexible Drive Shaft Models

Models equipped with a flexible drive shaft should have drive shaft removed, cleaned and lubricated with lithium base grease at 20 hour intervals of use.

Solid Drive Shaft Models

Some models are equipped with a solid drive shaft supported in bushings located in drive shaft housing tube. Drive shaft requires no regular maintenance; however, if drive shaft is removed, lubricate drive shaft with lithium base grease before reinstallation. Drive shaft may be supported in two, three or five bushings located in drive shaft housing tube. To renew bushings, mark location of old bushings in drive shaft housing tube and remove old bushings. Install new bushings at old bushing locations. Note early FS410 models are equipped with two bushings and late FS410 models are equipped with three bushings. Three bushings may be installed in early models by referring to Fig. SL17 for new bushing location. A 4.1 mm (0.016 in.) hole must be drilled in housing at location shown for spring clip which retains bushing.

BEARING HEAD

All Models So Equipped

Bearing head is shown in Fig. SL18. Bearing head is equipped with sealed bearings and requires no regular maintenance.

To disassemble bearing head, remove trimmer head assembly. Remove clamp bolt (2) and locating screw (1). Separate bearing head from drive shaft housing. Remove snap ring (8) and use suitable puller to remove arbor and bearing assembly. Remove bearings from arbor shaft as required.

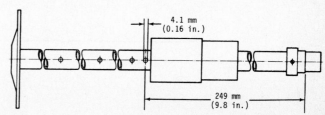

Fig. SL17—Exploded view of FS410 model drive shaft tube showing dimensions used to install a third drive shaft bushing in drive shaft housing. Refer to text.

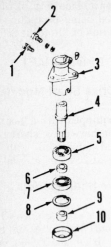

Fig. SL18—Exploded view of bearing head used on some models.

1. Locating screw	6. Spacer
2. Clamp bolt	7. Bearing
3. Housing	8. Snap ring
4. Arbor	9. Spacer
5. Bearing	10. Adapter plate

GEAR HEAD

All Models So Equipped

Trimmer may be equipped with a gear head with a one-piece gear head housing or a two-piece gear head housing. Refer to appropriate paragraph for model being serviced.

One-Piece Housing. Refer to Fig. SL19 for an exploded view of the one-piece housing gear head used on some models. Check plug (9) should be removed and housing filled 2/3 full of lithium base grease at 20 hour intervals of use.

To disassemble gear head, remove trimmer head or blade assembly. Remove clamp bolt and locating screw (8). Separate trimmer head from drive shaft housing tube. Remove snap ring (1) and use a suitable puller to remove input shaft (6) and bearing assembly. Remove snap ring (2). Remove shim (3), bearings (4 and 5) as required. Remove snap ring (17) and use a suitable puller to remove arbor shaft (15) and bearing assembly. Press bearings and gear from shaft as required. If bearing (12) remains in housing (10), heat housing to 140° C (280° F) and tap housing on wooden block to remove bearing.

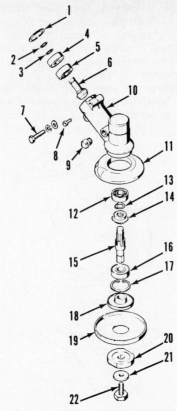

Fig. SL19—Exploded view of the one-piece housing gear head used on some models.

1. Snap ring	12. Bearing
2. Snap ring	13. Shim
3. Shim	14. Output gear
4. Bearing	15. Arbor (output) shaft
5. Bearing	16. Bearing
6. Input shaft	17. Snap ring
7. Clamp bolt	18. Adapter
8. Locating screw	19. Thrust plate
9. Check plug	20. Washer
10. Housing	21. Washer
11. Anti-wrap guard	22. Bolt

Two-Piece Housing. Refer to Fig. SL20 for an exploded view of the two-piece housing gear head used on some models. Check plug (1) should be removed and gear head lubricant level checked at 20 hour intervals of use. Gear head should contain 40 cc of SAE 90 gear lubricant.

To disassemble gear head, remove trimmer head or blade assembly. Remove clamp bolt and separate gear head from drive shaft housing tube. Remove screws and separate lower gear head housing (21) from upper gear head housing (2). Press arbor shaft (14) and gear assembly out of the thrust plate

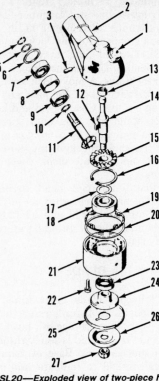

Fig. SL20—Exploded view of two-piece housing gear head used on some models.

1. Check plug	15. Output gear
2. Housing	16. Snap ring
3. Locating screws	17. Shim
4. Snap ring	18. Bearing
5. Shim	19. Gasket
6. Shim	20. Shim
7. Bearing	21. Housing
8. Spacer	22. Bolt
9. Bearing	23. Seal
10. Shim	24. Adapter
11. Input shaft	25. Thrust plate
12. Key	26. Washer
13. Needle bearing	27. Nut (LH)
14. Arbor shaft	

and ball bearing. Remove snap ring (16). Heat housing to 140° C (280° F) and press bearing (18) out of housing. Remove seal (23). Press gear (15) off of arbor shaft. Remove the two locating screws (3). Heat housing to 140° C (280° F) and press input shaft (11) and bearing assembly out of housing. Remove snap rings and press bearings from input shaft as required. Remove needle bearing (13) only if bearing is to be renewed. During gear head assembly, shims should be installed to provide a slight amount of gear backlash. Shafts should turn freely with no binding or tight spots.

TANAKA
GASOLINE POWERED
STRING TRIMMERS

Model	Engine Manufacturer	Engine Model	Displacement
TBC-160,			
TBC-162,			
TBC-205	Tanaka	....	26 cc
TBC-202,			
TBC-215	Tanaka	....	20 cc
TBC-232,			
TBC-233	Tanaka	....	22.6 cc
TBC-301,			
TBC-303,			
TBC-321,			
TBC-322	Tanaka	....	30.5 cc
TBC-373	Tanaka	....	37.4 cc
TBC-501	Tanaka	....	50.2 cc

ENGINE INFORMATION

All Models

Tanaka (TAS) two-stroke air-cooled gasoline engines are used on all Tanaka line trimmers and brush cutters. Identify engine by engine displacement and refer to the TANAKA (TAS) ENGINE SERVICE section of this manual.

FUEL MIXTURE

All Models

Manufacturer recommends mixing regular grade gasoline (unleaded is an acceptable substitute) with a good quality two-stroke air cooled engine oil at a 25:1 ratio. Do not use fuel containing alcohol.

STRING TRIMMER

All Models

A dual strand manual feed trimmer head is available for most models (Fig. TA10). To extend line, loosen lock knob (6) until line may be pulled from housing. Pull line to desired length and tighten lock knob (6).

To renew line, remove lock knob (6), spring (5) and spool (4). Remove any remaining old line and install new line on spool. Wind line in direction indicated by arrow on spool and insert line ends through line guides (3). Install spool, spring and lock knob.

BLADE

All Models

All models may be equipped with a four cutting edge grass, weed and brush blade and all models except Models TBC-160 and TBC-162 may be equipped with a saw blade. Always make certain cup washer above blade and adapter plate below blade are centered and fit flat against surface of blade when installing blade.

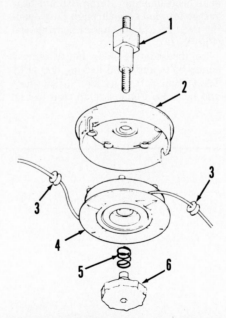

Fig. TA10—Exploded view of dual strand manual feed trimmer head available for most models.
1. Drive shaft adapter
2. Housing
3. Line guides
4. Spool
5. Spring
6. Lock knob

DRIVE SHAFT

Models TBC-160 And TBC-162

Models TBC-160 and TBC-162 are equipped with a flexible drive shaft supported in a flexible liner located in the curved drive shaft housing tube. Drive shaft should be removed, cleaned and lubricated with lithium base grease at 30 hour intervals of use. Flexible drive shaft housing liner may be pulled from housing as required and renewed.

All Other Models

All other models are equipped with a solid drive shaft supported in a straight drive shaft housing tube. Drive shaft is supported in bushings located in drive shaft housing tube. Drive shaft requires no regular maintenance; however, if drive shaft is removed, lubricate shaft with lithium base grease before reinstallation.

BEARING HEAD

Models TBC-160 And TBC-162

Models TBC-160 and TBC-162 are equipped with bearing head similar to the bearing head shown in Fig. TA11. Bearing head is equipped with sealed bearings and requires no regular maintenance.

To disassemble bearing head, remove trimmer head. Remove clamp bolt (1) and locating screw (2). Separate bearing head from drive shaft housing tube.

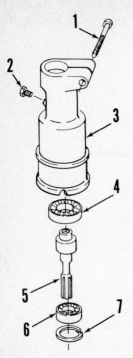

Fig. TA11—Exploded view of bearing head used on Models TBC-160 and TBC-162.

1. Clamp bolt
2. Locating screw
3. Housing
4. Bearing
5. Arbor shaft
6. Bearing
7. Snap ring

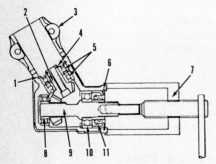

Fig. TA12—Cross-section view of gear head used on most models.

1. Snap ring
2. Input shaft & gear
3. Housing
4. Snap ring
5. Bearings
6. Snap ring
7. Puller
8. Bearing
9. Arbor shaft & gear
10. Bearing
11. Seal

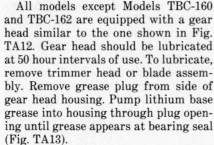

Fig. TA13—A good quality lithium base grease should be pumped into gear head housing through filler opening until grease appears at arbor shaft seal. Refer to text.

Remove snap ring (7). Use a suitable puller (part numbers 015-29338-000 and 015-29339-000) to remove arbor shaft (5) and bearing (6). If bearing (4) remains in housing (3), use puller (part numbers 016-29338-000 and 016-29339-000) to remove bearing. Press bearing (6) from arbor shaft as required. To reassemble, install bearing (4) in housing, then install arbor shaft (5) in bearing (4) and housing. Press bearing (6) onto arbor shaft and into housing until snap ring (7) can be installed.

GEAR HEAD

All Models Except Models TBC-160 And TBC-162

All models except Models TBC-160 and TBC-162 are equipped with a gear head similar to the one shown in Fig. TA12. Gear head should be lubricated at 50 hour intervals of use. To lubricate, remove trimmer head or blade assembly. Remove grease plug from side of gear head housing. Pump lithium base grease into housing through plug opening until grease appears at bearing seal (Fig. TA13).

To disassemble gear head, remove clamp bolts and head locking bolt (Fig. TA14). Separate head from drive shaft and housing. Remove snap ring (6-Fig.

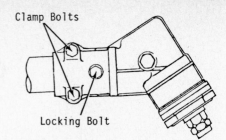

Fig. TA14—To separate gear head from drive shaft housing, remove clamp bolts and locking (head locating) bolt.

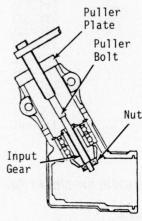

Fig. TA15—To remove input shaft, gear and bearing assembly, install puller as shown.

TA12). Install suitable puller (part number 015-29339-000) as illustrated in Fig. TA12 and remove oil seal, bearing and arbor shaft assembly. Remove gear (9) from housing. Remove snap ring (1). Insert suitable puller bolt (part numbers 016-29338-000 and 016-29339-000) through input shaft and thread a nut on bolt against input gear (Fig. TA15). Remove input shaft and bearing assembly. Remove snap ring (4-Fig. TA12) and press bearings from input shaft. To remove bearing (8), heat gear head housing to 212° F (100° C) and tap housing against wooden block.

TORO

GASOLINE POWERED STRING TRIMMERS

Model	Engine Manufacturer	Engine Model	Displacement
30900	Kioritz	....	21.2 cc
30910	Kioritz	....	21.2 cc
30920	Kioritz	....	30.1 cc
51600	Kioritz	....	13.8 cc
51625	Kioritz	....	13.8 cc
51700	Kioritz	....	21.2 cc
TC-3000	Mitsubishi	T140	24.1 cc
TC-4000	Mitsubishi	T140	24.1 cc
TC-5000	Mitsubishi	T180	32.5 cc

ENGINE INFORMATION

Early model Toro trimmers are equipped with Kioritz engines and later models are equipped with Mitsubishi engines. Identify engine by manufacturer and engine displacement and refer to appropriate KIORITZ ENGINE SERVICE or MITSUBISHI ENGINE SERVICE sections of this manual.

FUEL MIXTURE

All Models

Manufacturer recommends mixing regular grade gasoline with an octane rating of at least 87, with a good quality two-stroke engine oil at a ratio of 32:1. Do not use fuel containing alcohol.

STRING TRIMMER

Models 30900, 30910 And 30920

Models 30900, 30910 and 30920 are equipped with a dual strand semi-automatic trimmer head shown in Fig. TO10. To manually advance line with engine stopped, push in on button (7) and pull on each line. Procedure may have to be repeated to obtain desired line length. To extend line with engine running, operate trimmer at full operating rpm and tap button (7) on the ground. Line will automatically advance a measured amount.

To renew trimmer line, hold drum firmly and turn spool in direction shown in Fig. TO11 to remove slack. Twist with a hard snap until plastic peg is between holes. Pull spool out of drum. Remove old line from spool. Spool will

hold approximately 20 feet (6 mm) of monofilament line. Insert one end of new line through hole on spool (Fig. TO12) and pull line through until line is the same length of both sides of hole. Wind both ends of line at the same time in direction indicated by arrow on spool. Wind tightly and evenly from side to side and do not twist line. Insert ends of line through line guide openings, align pegs on drum with slots in spool and push spool into drum. Hold drum firmly, twist spool suddenly in direction shown in Fig. TO13 until peg

enters hole with a click and locks spool in position. Trim extended lines to desired lengths.

Models 51600 And 51625

Models 51600 and 51625 are equipped with the dual strand semi-automatic trimmer head shown in Fig. TO14. To extend line with trimmer engine stopped, push in on spool button (8) while pulling on line ends. Procedure may have to be repeated until desired

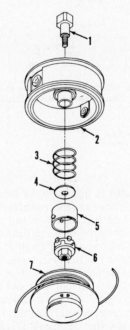

Fig. TO10—Exploded view of the dual strand semi-automatic line trimmer head used on Models 30900, 30910 and 30920.

1. Drive shaft adapter
2. Housing
3. Spring
4. Washer
5. Outer drive cam
6. Inner drive cam
7. Spool

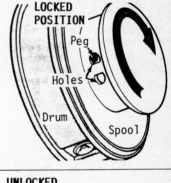

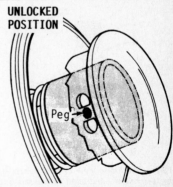

Fig. TO11—To remove spool, hold drum firmly and turn spool in direction shown to take up slack, then twist with a sudden snap until plastic peg is between holes as shown in lower view.

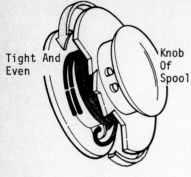

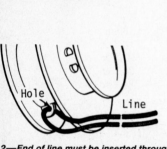

Fig. TO12—End of line must be inserted through hole on spool as shown in lower view. Wind line tightly in direction indicated by arrow on spool.

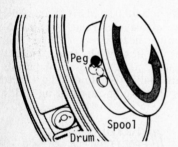

Fig. TO13—Hold drum firmly and twist suddenly in direction indicated to lock spool in position.

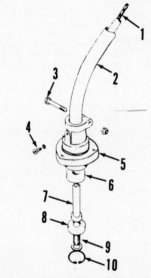

Fig. TO15—Exploded view of four strand fixed line trimmer head used on Model 51700 with 0.130 inch (3.3 mm) line. Dual strand fixed line trimmer head with 0.105 inch (2.7 mm) line used on Model TC-3000 is similar.

1. Cup washer
2. Plate
3. Plate
4. Nut (LH)
5. Cotter pin

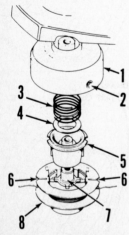

Fig. TO14—Exploded view of dual strand semi-automatic trimmer head used on Models 51600 and 51625.

1. Housing
2. Line guide
3. Spring
4. Washer
5. Outer drive cam
6. Line slots
7. Inner drive cam
8. Spool

Fig. TO16—Exploded view of drive shaft housing and gear head assembly used on Model 51625.

1. Drive shaft
2. Drive shaft housing
3. Clamp bolt
4. Locating screw
5. Bearing housing
6. Bearing
7. Arbor shaft
8. Bearing
9. Spacer
10. Snap ring

line length is obtained. To extend line with trimmer engine running, operate trimmer at full rpm and tap trimmer head on the ground. Each time trimmer head is tapped on the ground, a measured amount of line will be advanced.

To renew line, insert widest possible screwdriver into slot in spool cap and twist to "pop" off spool assembly (8). Remove any remaining old line and install new line on spool. Wind line in direction indicated by arrow on spool and clip the two ends in line slots (6). Insert line ends in line guides (2) and install spool in housing (1). Pull on line ends to release from line slots (6).

Model 51700

Model 51700 is equipped with a four strand fixed line trimmer head shown in Fig. TO15. Trimmer head is equipped with two 14 inch (35.6 cm) lengths of 0.130 inch (3.3 mm) monofilament line (6) secured to trimmer head plate (2) by plate (3), left-hand thread nut (4) and cotter pin (5). Lines clip in locking slots in trimmer head plate (2) also.

Model TC-3000

Model TC-3000 is equipped with a dual strand fixed line trimmer head similar to trimmer head used on Model 51700. Trimmer head is equipped with a single 16 inch (40.6 cm) length of 0.105 inch (2.7 mm) line.

Models TC-4000 And TC-5000

Models TC-4000 and TC-5000 are equipped with a dual strand manual trimmer head similar to the dual strand semi-automatic trimmer head used on Models 51600 and 51625. To extend line, pull out on cutting head and rotate it counterclockwise to advance line. Model TC-4000 trimmer head is equipped with 0.080 inch (2 mm) line and Model TC-5000 trimmer head is equipped with 0.105 inch (2.7 mm) line.

BLADE

Models 30920, 51700, TC-3000, TC-4000 And TC-5000

Models 30920, 51700, TC-3000, TC-4000 and TC-5000 may be equipped with an eight cutting edge grass, weed and brush blade or a saw blade. Units equipped with a blade should be equipped with shoulder harness.

DRIVE SHAFT

Models 30900, 30910, 51600 And 51625

Models 30900, 30910, 51600 and 51625 are equipped with a flexible drive shaft mounted in the drive shaft housing tube. Drive shaft should be removed, cleaned and lubricated with lithium base grease at 50 hour intervals of use. To remove drive shaft, remove clamp bolt (3–Fig. TO16) and locating screw (4). Separate bearing head assembly (5) from drive shaft housing (2). Pull drive shaft (1) out of lower end of drive shaft housing. When reinstalling drive shaft, make certain drive shaft ends fully engage adapters at engine and bearing head ends.

Models 30920, 51700, TC-3000, TC-4000 And TC-5000

Models 30920, 51700, TC-3000, TC-4000 and TC-5000 are equipped with a solid drive shaft supported in drive shaft housing in five renewable bushings. Toro recommends removing, cleaning and lubricating drive shaft at 50 hour intervals of use. To renew any or all of the five drive shaft bushings, mark bushing locations in drive shaft housing. Use a wooden dowel to remove old bushings and to install new bushings at the same locations from which old bushings were removed.

BEARING HEAD

Models 30900, 30910 And 51600

Models 30900, 30910 and 51600 are equipped with the bearing head shown in Fig. TO17. Bearing head is equipped with sealed bearings (5 and 7) and requires no regular maintenance.

To disassemble bearing head, remove trimmer head assembly and cup washer (10). Remove clamp bolt (2) and locating screw (1). Separate bearing head from drive shaft housing tube. Remove snap ring (8) and use a suitable puller (part number 897603-05330) to remove arbor shaft (9) and bearing assembly. Remove nut (4), bearing (5), spacer (6) and bearing (7) as required.

Model 51625

Model 51625 is equipped with the bearing head shown in Fig. TO16. Bearing head is equipped with sealed bearings (6 and 8) and requires no regular maintenance. To disassemble bearing head, remove trimmer head assembly and cup washer. Remove snap ring (10) and use a suitable puller (part number 897603-05330) to remove arbor shaft (7) and bearing assembly. Press bearings from shaft as required. If bearing (6) remains in housing (5), it may be necessary to slightly heat bearing housing and tap housing on wooden block to remove bearing.

GEAR HEAD

Model 30920

Model 30920 is equipped with the gear head shown in Fig. TO18. Gear head lubricant should be checked at 50 hour intervals of use. To check lubricant, remove check plug (15). Gear head should be kept 2/3 full of lithium base grease.

To disassemble gear head, remove trimmer head or blade assembly. Separate gear head from drive shaft housing tube. Remove snap ring (25) and use a suitable puller to remove input shaft and bearing assembly (20). Remove

plug (16), seal (7), snap ring (8), and snap ring (14). Press arbor and bearing assembly from housing (19). Remove required snap rings to remove gears and bearings.

Models 51700, TC-3000, TC-4000 And TC-5000

Refer to Fig. TO19 for an exploded view of gear head used on Model 51700. Models TC-3000, TC-4000 and TC-5000 use a similar gear head. On all models, gear head lubricant should be checked at 50 hour intervals of use. To check, remove check plug (12). Gear head housing should be kept 2/3 full of lithium base grease.

To disassemble gear head, remove trimmer head or blade assembly. Remove cup washer (21) and key (17). Remove snap ring (2). Use suitable puller (part number 897603-05330) to remove input shaft (8) and bearing assembly. Remove seal (20) and snap ring (19). Use suitable puller (part number 897703-04130) to remove arbor shaft (16) and bearing assembly. If bearing

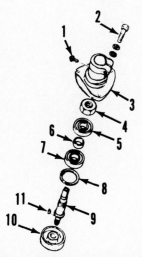

Fig. TO17—Exploded view of bearing head used on Models 30900, 30910 and 51600.

1. Locating screw
2. Clamp bolt
3. Bearing housing
4. Nut
5. Bearing
6. Spacer
7. Bearing
8. Snap ring
9. Arbor shaft
10. Cup washer
11. Pin

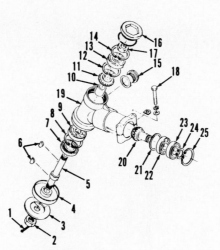

Fig. TO18—Exploded view of gear head used on Model 30920.

1. Cotter pin
2. Nut
3. Adapter plate
4. Cup washer
5. Arbor shaft
6. Keys
7. Seal
8. Snap ring
9. Bearing
10. Spacer
11. Gear
12. Snap ring
13. Bearing
14. Snap ring
15. Level check plug
16. Plug
17. Nut
18. Clamp bolt
19. Housing
20. Gear
21. Spacer
22. Bearing
23. Bearing
24. Snap ring
25. Snap ring

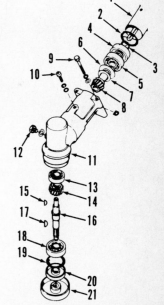

Fig. TO19—Exploded view of gear head used on Models 51700, TC-3000, TC-4000 and TC-5000.

1. Drive shaft housing
2. Snap ring
3. Snap ring
4. Bearing
5. Bearing
6. Spacer washer
7. Spacer washer
8. Input gear
9. Clamp bolt
10. Locating screw
11. Housing
12. Check plug
13. Bearing
14. Gear
15. Key
16. Arbor shaft
17. Key
18. Bearing
19. Snap ring
20. Seal
21. Cup washer

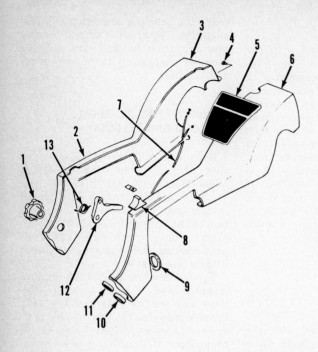

Fig. TO20—Exploded view of engine cover assembly used on Model 51625.

1. Lock knob
2. Screw
3. Cover half
4. Screw
5. Decal
6. Cover half
7. Ignition switch leads
8. Ignition switch
9. Grommet
10. Grommet
11. Grommet
12. Throttle trigger
13. Throttle trigger spring

(13) stays in gear head housing (11), heat housing slightly and tap housing on wooden block to remove bearing. Press bearings from shafts as required.

ENGINE COVER

Model 51625

Model 51625 is equipped with a partial engine cover (Fig. TO20). To remove engine cover, carefully remove decal (5) or cut down housing seam. Remove the eight screws and lock knob (1) securing engine cover halves together and carefully separate the cover. Note positions of internal parts. Lift out the stop switch (8). Disconnect throttle cable at throttle trigger (12). Remove throttle trigger and spring (13).

TML (TRAIL)

GASOLINE POWERED STRING TRIMMERS

Model	Engine Manufacturer	Engine Model	Displacement
BC-35	TML	150528	35.0 cc
LT-35	TML	150528	35.0 cc

ENGINE INFORMATION

All Models

All models are equipped with a two-stroke air-cooled gasoline engine manufactured by TML (Trail). Refer to TML (TRAIL) ENGINE SERVICE section of this manual.

FUEL MIXTURE

All Models

Manufacturer recommends mixing regular grade (unleaded is an acceptable substitute) gasoline with a good quality two-stroke air-cooled engine oil at a ratio of 20:1. Do not use fuel containing alcohol.

STRING TRIMMER

All Models

Trimmer may be equipped with a single strand (Fig. TL10) or a dual strand (Fig. TL16) manual trimmer head. Refer to appropriate paragraph for model being serviced.

Single Strand Trimmer Head. Refer to Fig. TL10 for an exploded view of the single strand trimmer head used on some models. To extend line, stop trimmer engine and wait until all head rotation has stopped. Pull down on spool cover (Fig. TL11) and rotate top in direction of arrow (Fig. TL12) while pulling line out of head. Procedure may have to be repeated until line end reaches mark on trimmer head (Fig. TL13) provided to gage correct line length.

To renew line, push in on spool cover (5-Fig. TL10) and unscrew knob (8). Refer to Fig. TL14. Remove knob (8-Fig. TL10), spring (7), spool cover (5) and spool (3). Remove any remaining line and clean spool and inside of spool cover. Insert the end of the new line into "V" shaped slot in spool (Fig. TL15). Wind line in direction indicated by arrow on spool. Insert line through line guide in spool cover and reinstall spool, spool cover, spring and knob.

Dual Strand Trimmer Head. Refer to Fig. TL16 for exploded view of the dual strand manual trimmer head used on some models. To extend line, stop trimmer engine and wait until all head rotation has stopped. Loosen knob (6). Pull each line end at the same time until each line is extended 6 inches (15 cm). Tighten knob (6).

To renew line, cut 15 feet (4.6 m) of 0.095 inch (2.4 mm) monofilament line. Remove lock knob (6) and remove lower housing (5) and spool (4). Remove any remaining old line. Clean all parts of trimmer head. Pull line guides (2) down (do not remove) and clean outside surfaces with a wet soapy cloth. Apply a few drops of oil into cavities after cleaning. Loop new line into two equal lengths and insert line ends through holes at center of spool. Pull line ends out until stopped by spool. Wind both ends onto spool in direction indicated

Fig. TL13—Spool is marked to indicate correct line length.

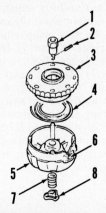

Fig. TL10—Exploded view of single strand manual trimmer head used on some models.

1. Adapter	5. Spool cover
2. Pin	6. Line guide
3. Spool	7. Spring
4. Line	8. Lock knob

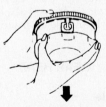

Fig. TL11—To extend line, pull down on spool cover and rotate. Refer to Fig. TL12.

Fig. TL12—Pull out line as cover is rotated. Refer to text.

Fig. TL14—To remove spool, push up on cover and remove lock knob. Refer to text.

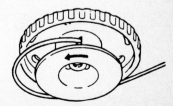

Fig. TL15—Wind new line on spool in direction indicated by arrow on spool.

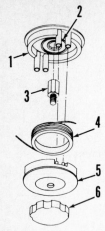

Fig. TL16—Exploded view of dual strand manual trimmer head used on some models.

1. Upper cover
2. Line guides
3. Adapter
4. Spool
5. Lower cover
6. Lock knob

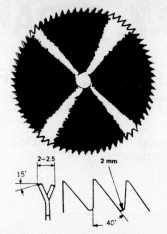

Fig. TL18—Some models may be equipped with an eighty tooth saw blade. Refer to illustration and text for sharpening procedure.

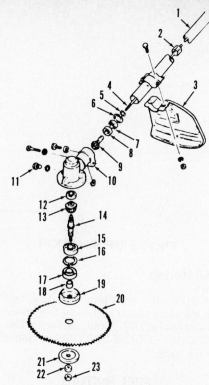

Fig. TL19—Exploded view of drive shaft housing and gear head assembly.

1. Drive shaft housing
2. Bushings
3. Shield
4. Drive shaft
5. Snap ring
6. Snap ring
7. Bearing
8. Bearing
9. Input shaft
10. Housing
11. Check plug
12. Bearing
13. Output gear
14. Arbor (output) shaft
15. Bearing
16. Snap ring
17. Seal
18. Spacer
19. Adapter
20. Blade
21. Adapter
22. Nut
23. Jam nut

Fig. TL17—Some models may be equipped with a four cutting edge blade. Refer to illustration and text for sharpening procedure.

by arrow on spool. Insert line ends through line guides in upper cover and install spool, lower cover and lock knob.

BLADE

All Models

Trimmer may be equipped with a four cutting edge blade (Fig. TL17) or an eighty tooth saw blade (Fig. TL18). Blade should be installed with parts assembled in sequence shown in Fig. TL19.

To sharpen the four cutting edge blade, refer to Fig. TL17. Blade edge

should have a length of 1.18-1.58 inch (30-40 mm). Do not grind the chamfered section of the blade root. Make certain the root of cutting blade remains chamfered to prevent cracking or breakage. Sharpen all teeth equally to maintain blade balance.

To sharpen the eighty tooth saw blade, refer to Fig. TL18. Maintain a 0.04-0.08 inch (1-2 mm) radius at the tooth root. Maintain a 0.08-0.09 inch (2-2.5 mm) tooth set. Sharpen all teeth equally to maintain blade balance.

DRIVE SHAFT

All Models

All models are equipped with a solid steel drive shaft (4-Fig. TL19) which is supported in drive shaft housing (1) in four renewable bushings (2). Drive shaft and bushings require no regular maintenance; however, before removing bushings (2), mark bushing locations in drive shaft housing. Install new bushings at old bushing locations. When installing drive shaft, lightly lubricate with SAE 30 oil prior to installation.

GEAR HEAD

All Models

All models are equipped with gear head shown in Fig. TL19. At 30 hour intervals of use, lubricate gear head by removing trimmer head or blade as-

sembly and check plug (11). Pump lithium base grease into gear head housing until grease appears at lower seal (17).

To disassemble gear head, separate gear head from drive shaft housing. Remove trimmer head or blade. Remove snap ring (6). Insert screwdriver or suitable wedge in gear head housing clamp split. Carefully expand housing and remove input shaft (9) and bearing assembly. Remove snap ring (5) and press bearings (8 and 7) from input shaft as necessary. Remove spacer (18) and seal (17). Remove snap ring (16). Use suitable puller to remove arbor shaft (14) and bearing assembly. Remove bearing (15) and gear (13) from arbor shaft as necessary. If bearing (12) stays in housing, heat housing to 140° F (60° C) and tap housing on wooden block to remove bearing.

WARDS

GASOLINE POWERED STRING TRIMMERS

Model	Engine Manufacturer	Engine Model	Displacement
2049	Tecumseh	AV520	85.0 cc
24206	Kioritz	....	16.0 cc
24207	Kioritz	....	21.2 cc
24369	Tecumseh	AV520	85.0 cc
XEC-24300	Kioritz	....	13.8 cc
XEC-24340	Kioritz	....	13.8 cc
XEC-24341	Kioritz	....	16.0 cc
XEC-24342	Kioritz	....	21.2 cc
XEC-24358	Kioritz	....	13.8 cc
XEC-24359	Kioritz	....	21.2 cc
XEC-24361	Kioritz	....	30.8 cc

ENGINE INFORMATION

All Models

Wards line trimmers and brush cutters may be equipped with Kioritz or Tecumseh two-stroke air-cooled gasoline engines. Identify engine model by engine manufacturer, trimmer model number or engine displacement. Refer to KIORITZ ENGINE SERVICE or TECUMSEH ENGINE SERVICE section of this manual.

FUEL MIXTURE

All Models

Manufacturer recommends mixing regular grade gasoline (unleaded is an acceptable substitute) with a good quality two-stroke air-cooled engine oil at a 25:1 ratio. Do not use fuel containing alcohol.

STRING TRIMMER

Models XEC-24359 And XEC-24361

Semi-Automatic Dual Strand Trimmer Head. Models XEC-24359 and XEC-24361 may be equipped with dual strand trimmer head as shown in Fig. WD10. To manually advance line with engine stopped, push in on button (7) and pull on each line. Procedure may have to be repeated to obtain desired line length. To extend line with engine running, operate trimmer at full operating rpm and tap button (7) on the ground. Line will automatically extend a measured amount.

To renew trimmer line, hold drum firmly and turn spool in direction shown in Fig. WD11 to remove slack. Twist with a hard snap until plastic peg is between holes. Pull spool out of drum. Remove old line from spool. Spool will hold aproximately 20 feet (6 m) of monofilament line. Insert one end of new line through hole on spool (Fig. WD12) and pull line through until line is the same length on both sides of hole. Wind both ends of line at the same time in direction indicated by arrow on spool. Wind tightly and evenly from side to side and do not twist line. Insert ends of line through line guide openings, align pegs on drum with slots in spool and push spool into drum. Hold drum firmly, twist spool suddenly in direction shown in Fig. WD13 until peg enters hole with a click and locks spool in posi-

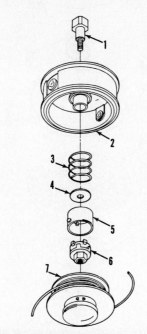

Fig. WD10—Exploded view of dual strand semi-automatic trimmer head used on some models.
1. Bolt
2. Drum
3. Spring
4. Washer
5. Outer drive
6. Inner cam
7. Spool

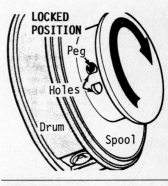

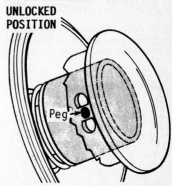

Fig. WD11—To remove spool, hold housing firmly and turn spool in direction shown to take up slack, then twist with a sudden snap until plastic peg is between holes as shown in lower view.

tion. Trim extending lines to correct lengths.

Manual Advance Dual Strand Trimmer Head. Models XEC-24359 and XEC-24361 may be equipped with manual advance dual strand trimmer head shown in Fig. WD14. To extend line, loosen lock knob (6) approximately one turn. Pull out the line on each side until line lengths are 6 inches (152 mm).

To renew line, remove slotted screw (8) and washer (7). Unscrew ball lock (6). Remove cover (5) and spring (3). Remove spool (4). Cut two 12 foot (4 m) lengths of 0.095 inch (2.4 mm) monofilament line. Insert one end of each line through the slot and into the locating hole on bottom side of spool. Line ends should extend approximately 1/4 inch (6.4 mm) through locating holes. Hold lines tight and wind in a counterclockwise direction using care not to cross the lines. Insert the end of each line into each slot leaving approximately 6 inches (152 mm) of line extending from

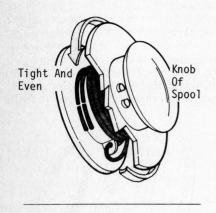

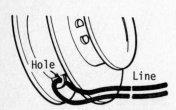

Fig. WD12—End of line must be inserted through hole on spool as shown in lower view. Wind line tightly in direction indicated by arrow on spool.

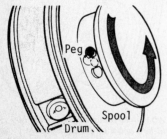

Fig. WD13—Hold drum firmly and twist suddenly to lock spool in position.

spool. Place spool into drum and feed one line through each of the line guides. Install spring, cover, ball lock, washer and screw.

Models XEC-24300, XEC-24340, XEC-24341, XEC-24342, XEC-24358, 24206 And 24207

Models XEC-24300, XEC-24340, XEC-24341, XEC-24342, XEC-24358, 24206 and 24207 may be equipped with a semi-automatic single strand trimmer head shown in Fig. WD15. Line may be manually advanced with engine stopped by pushing in on housing (12) and pulling line out as required.

To renew line, remove cotter pin (13-Fig. WD15). Rotate housing (12) counterclockwise and remove housing and line spool (7). Remove foam pads (9 and 10) and any remaining old line. Clean spool and inner surface of outer housing (12). Check indexing teeth on spool and in housing. Cut off approximately 25 feet (7.6 mm) of 0.080 inch (2 mm) monofilament line and tape one end of line to spool (Fig. WD16). Wind line on spool in direction indicated by arrow on spool (Fig. WD17). Install foam pads (9 and 10) with line between them as shown in Fig. WD17. Insert line end through line guide (14-Fig.

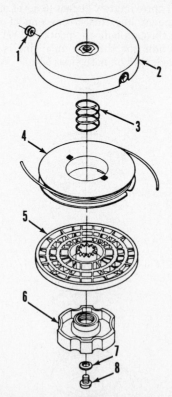

Fig. WD14—Exploded view of manual trimmer head used on some models. This head is no longer available.

1. Line guide	5. Cover
2. Hub	6. Ball lock
3. Spring	7. Washer
4. Spool	8. Screw

WD15) opening and install spool and housing. Push in on housing and rotate housing clockwise to lock in position, then install cotter pin (13).

Models 2049 And 24369

Models 2049 and 24369 may be equipped with a four strand trimmer head shown in Fig. WD18.

To renew trimmer line, remove bolt (8) and cover (7). Remove spools (6) and remove any remaining old line. Clean inside of upper body. Wind new monofilament line on the four spools (6). Place spools (6) back in upper body (1), install springs (5) and install cover (7). Install bolt (8) and tighten securely.

BLADE

Models XEC-24359, XEC-24361, 2049 And 24369

Models XEC-24359, XEC-24361, 2049 and 24369 may be equipped with a 10

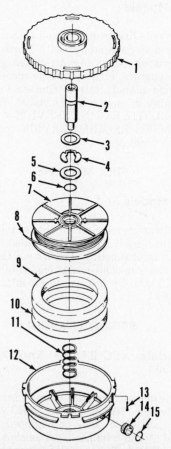

Fig. WD15—Exploded view of semi-automatic trimmer head used on some models.

1. Plate	
2. Adapter	9. Foam pad
3. Washer	10. Foam pad
4. Retainer ring	11. Spring
5. Washer	12. Hub
6. Retainer ring	13. Cotter pin
7. Spool	14. Line guide
8. Line	15. Retainer

inch saw blade. When installing blade, make certain all adapter plates are centered and seated squarely against blade and tighten nut (left-hand thread) securely.

DRIVE SHAFT

Models 24206, 24207, XEC-24300, XEC-24340, XEC-24341, XEC-24342 And XEC-24358

Models 24206, 24207, XEC-24300, XEC-24340, XEC-24341, XEC-24342 and XEC-24358 are equipped with flexible drive shafts supported in a curved drive shaft housing. Drive shaft should be removed at 18 hour intervals of use, cleaned and lubricated with lithium base grease. Reverse positions of drive shaft ends (engine end now at trimmer head end) and install drive shaft in housing. Reversing drive shaft ends each time it is lubricated will extend drive shaft life.

Models 2049, 24369, XEC-24358 And XEC-24361

Models 2049, 24369, XEC-24358 and XEC-24361 are equipped with a solid drive shaft supported in a straight drive shaft housing tube. No regular maintenance is required; however, if drive shaft is removed, lubricate drive shaft with lithium base grease before reinstallation.

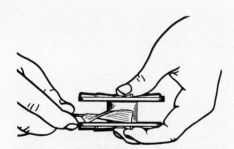

Fig. WD16—Tape one end of line to center of spool as shown.

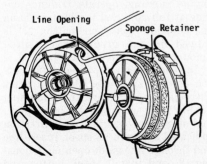

Fig. WD17—Foam pads are installed on spool with trimmer line between them.

BEARING HEAD

All Models So Equipped

Bearing heads used on all models except Models 2049 and 24369 are shown in Fig. WD19 or WD20. Bearing heads are equipped with sealed bearings and require no regular maintenance. To disassemble either bearing head, remove screw (1) and clamp screw (2). Remove adapter plate (10) and snap ring (8). Use suitable puller to remove bearing and arbor assemblies. Remove nut (4) and remove bearings and spacer as required.

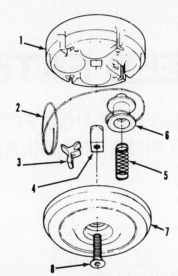

Fig. WD18—Exploded view of four strand trimmer head used on Models 2049 and 24369.

1. Upper housing
2. Line
3. Line retainer
4. Arbor post
5. Spring
6. Spools
7. Cover
8. Screw

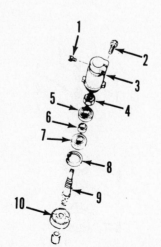

Fig. WD19—Exploded view of bearing head used on some models.

1. Screw
2. Clamp screw
3. Housing
4. Nut
5. Bearing
6. Spacer
7. Bearing
8. Snap ring
9. Shaft
10. Adapter plate & key

Bearing head used on Models 2049 and 24369 is shown in Fig. WD21. Bearing head is equipped with sealed bearings and requires no regular maintenance.

To disassemble bearing head, remove trimmer head or blade assembly. Re-

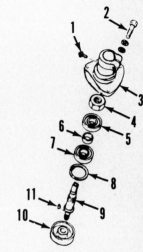

Fig. WD20—Exploded view of bearing head used on some models.

1. Screw
2. Clamp screw
3. Housing
4. Nut
5. Bearing
6. Spacer
7. Bearing
8. Snap ring
9. Shaft
10. Adapter
11. Key

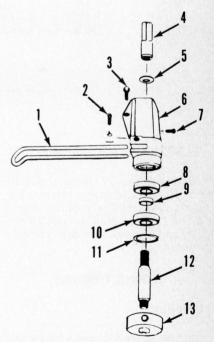

Fig. WD21—Exploded view of bearing head used on Models 2049 and 24369.

1. Wire bracket
2. Bolt
3. Bolt
4. Drive shaft adapter
5. Washer
6. Housing
7. Locating screw
8. Bearing
9. Spacer
10. Bearing
11. Snap ring
12. Arbor shaft
13. Cup washer

move clamp bolt (3) and locating screw (7). Separate gear head from drive shaft housing tube. Remove snap ring (11). Secure head assembly in a vise. Place a 1-3/8 inch wooden dowel with a 3/4 inch hole drilled through center over arbor shaft, against the square coupling end. Tap wooden dowel with a mallet to remove arbor shaft and bearing assembly. Disassemble bearings, coupling and arbor assembly as required.

To reassemble, place coupling (4) and washer (5) on arbor (12). Press one bearing onto arbor. Install assembly into housing. Install spacer (9) and press remaining bearing onto arbor and into housing. Install snap ring.

WEED EATER

ELECTRIC POWERED STRING TRIMMERS

Model	Volts	Amps	Cutting Swath	Line Diameter	Rpm
1208	120	2.0	8 in.	0.065 in.	N/A
1210	120	2.8	10 in.	0.065 in.	N/A
1214	120	3.5	14 in.	0.065 in.	N/A
1216	120	4.5	16 in.	0.080 in.	N/A

N/A—Rpm specifications not available.

ELECTRICAL REQUIREMENTS

All models require electrical circuits with 120-volt alternating current. Extension cord length should not exceed 100 feet (30.5 m). Make certain all circuits and connections are properly grounded at all times.

STRING TRIMMER

All Models

All models are equipped with a single strand semi-automatic trimmer head shown in Fig. WE1. Models 1208 and 1210 are equipped with 35 feet (10.7 m) of 0.065 inch (1.6 mm) line, Model 1214 is equipped with 50 feet (15.2 m) of 0.065 inch (1.6 m) line and Model 1216 is

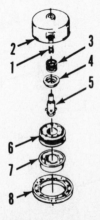

Fig. WE1—Exploded view of single strand semi-automatic trimmer head used on all models.

1. Line guide
2. Housing
3. Spring
4. Spring adapter
5. Drive cam
6. Spool
7. Button
8. Cover

equipped with 40 feet (12.2 m) of 0.080 inch (2.0 mm) line.

To extend line with trimmer engine stopped, push in on button (7) while pulling on line end. Procedure may have to be repeated to obtain desired line length. To extend line with trimmer engine running, operate trimmer engine at full rpm and tap button (7) on the ground. Each time button (7) is tapped on the ground a measured amount of new line will be advanced.

To renew line, remove cover (8), button (7) and spool (6). Clean all parts thoroughly and remove any remaining old line from spool. Wind correct length and diameter line on spool in direction indicated by arrow on spool. Insert line end through line guide opening in housing (2) and install spool, button and cover.

WEED EATER

GASOLINE POWERED STRING TRIMMERS

Model	Engine Manufacturer	Engine Model	Displacement
XR-50	Poulan	....	26.2 cc
XR-70	Poulan	....	26.2 cc
XR-80	Fuji	....	28.0 cc
XR-90	Poulan	....	26.2 cc
XR-100	Poulan	....	26.2 cc
1600	Poulan	....	26.2 cc
1700	Fuji	....	28.0 cc
1000	Fuji	....	37.7 cc
657	Tecumseh	AV520	85.0 cc

ENGINE INFORMATION

All Models

Weed Eater line trimmers and brush cutters may be equipped with Poulan, Fuji or Tecumseh two-stroke air-cooled gasoline engines. Identify engine manufacturer, engine model number or engine displacement and refer to appropriate POULAN ENGINE SERVICE, FUJI ENGINE SERVICE or TECUMSEH ENGINE SERVICE section in this manual.

FUEL MIXTURE

All Models

Manufacturer recommends mixing regular grade gasoline (unleaded is an acceptable substitute) with a good quality two-stroke air-cooled engine oil at a 25:1 ratio. Do not use fuel containing alcohol.

STRING TRIMMER

Models XR-50, XR-70 And XR-80

Models XR-50, XR-70 and XR-80 are equipped with a single strand semi-automatic trimmer head shown in Figs. WE10 and WE11. Fig. WE10 shows an exploded view of early style trimmer head which may be identified by the rough portion of upper housing (2). Fig. WE11 shows an exploded view of late style trimmer head which may be identified by the smooth portion of upper housing (2). Service procedure for both heads is similar.

To extend line with trimmer engine stopped, push in on button (7) while pulling on line end. Procedure may have to be repeated to obtain desired line length. To extend line with trimmer engine running, operate trimmer engine at full rpm and tap button (7) on the ground. Each time button (7) is tapped on the ground a measured amount of new line will be advanced.

To renew line, remove cover (8), button (7) and spool (6). Clean all parts thoroughly and remove any remaining old line from spool. Wind approximately 30 feet (9 m) of 0.080 inch (2 mm) monofilament line on spool in direction indicated by arrow on spool. Insert line end through line guide opening in housing (2) and install spool, button and cover.

Models XR-90, XR-100 And 1000

Models XR-90, XR-100 and 1000 are equipped with a dual strand manual trimmer head shown in Fig. WE12. To extend line, stop trimmer engine and wait until all trimmer head rotation has stopped. Push in on plate (8) while pulling each line out of housing (2).

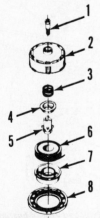

Fig. WE10—Exploded view of old style single strand semi-automatic trimmer head used on early Models XR-50, XR-70 and XR-80.

1. Drive shaft adapter
2. Housing
3. Spring
4. Spring adapter
5. Drive cam
6. Spool
7. Button
8. Cover

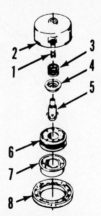

Fig. WE11—Exploded view of late style single strand semi-automatic trimmer head used on late Models XR-50, XR-70 and XR-80.

1. Line guide
2. Housing
3. Spring
4. Spring adapter
5. Drive cam
6. Spool
7. Button
8. Cover

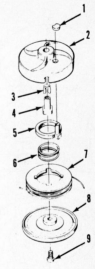

Fig. WE12—Exploded view of dual strand manual trimmer head used on Models XR-90, XR-100 and 1000.

1. Lock ring cap
2. Housing
3. Line guide
4. Drive shaft adapter
5. Lock ring
6. Spring
7. Spool
8. Cover
9. Screw

To renew trimmer line, remove screw (9), plate (8), spring (6) and spool (7). Remove any remaining line from each side of spool. Clean spool, housing and plate. Insert ends of two new 0.095 inch (2.4 mm) lines in holes located within spool and wind lines in direction indicated by arrow on spool. Total diameter of line wound on spool should not exceed diameter of spool sides. Make certain line savers (3) are in position and install spool in housing with the "THIS SIDE IN" instructions on spool toward inside of trimmer head. Install spring (6), cover (8) and screw (9).

Model 657

Model 657 is equipped with a four strand trimmer head shown in Fig. WE13. To renew trimmer line, remove bolt (8) and cover (7). Remove spools (6) and remove any remaining old line. Clean inside of rotary head. Wind new monofilament line on the four spools (6). Place spools (6) back in upper body (1), install springs (5) and install cover (7). Install bolt (8) and tighten securely.

BLADE

Model XR-80 And 1700

Models XR-80 and 1700 may be equipped with a four cutting edge grass and weed blade. Make certain weed blade conversion kit (part number 701566) is installed with blade. When installing blade, make certain all adapter plates are centered and seated squarely

against blade and tighten nut (left-hand thread) securely.

Models XR-90, XR-100, 1000 And 657

Models XR-90, XR-100, 1000 and 657 may be equipped with a 10 inch saw blade. When installing blade, make certain all adapter plates are centered and seated squarely against blade and tighten nut (left-hand thread) securely.

DRIVE SHAFT

Models XR-50, XR-70, XR-80, 1600, 1700 And 657

Models XR-50, XR-70, XR-80, 1600, 1700 and 657 are equipped with a flexible drive shaft (1-Fig. WE14) enclosed in the drive shaft housing tube (2). Drive shaft has squared ends which engage adapters at each end. Drive shaft should be removed for maintenance at 20 hour intervals of use. To remove, separate drive shaft housing from engine. Mark locations of drive shaft ends and pull drive shaft out of housing. Clean drive shaft and lubricate with lithium base grease. Reinstall drive shaft in housing.

Models XR-90, XR-100 And 1000

Models XR-90, XR-100 and 1000 are equipped with a solid steel drive shaft supported in drive shaft housing tube. Drive shaft requires no regular maintenance; however, if drive shaft has been

removed, lubricate drive shaft with lithium base grease before reinstallation.

BEARING HEAD

Models XR-50, XR-70 And 1600

Models XR-50, XR-70 and 1600 are equipped with a bearing head which is an integral part of drive shaft housing (Fig. WE14). No regular maintenance is required and no service parts are available.

Models XR-80 And 1700

Models XR-80 and 1700 are equipped with the bearing head shown in Fig. WE15. Bearing head is equipped with sealed bearings and requires no regular maintenance.

To disassemble bearing head, remove trimmer head or blade assembly. Remove clamp bolt (2) and locating screw (3). Separate bearing head assembly from drive shaft housing. Remove shield (6) and bracket (5) (as equipped). Remove cup washer (13) and washer (12). Carefully press drive shaft adapter (1) out of bearings. Remove snap rings (7 and 11). Press bearings (8 and 10) and spacer (9) out of housing.

Model 657

Model 657 is equipped with the bearing head assembly shown in Fig. WE16. Bearing head is equipped with

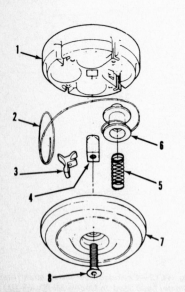

Fig. WE13—Exploded view of the four strand trimmer head used on Model 657.

1. Upper housing	5. Spring
2. Line	6. Spool
3. Line retainer	7. Cover
4. Arbor post	8. Screw

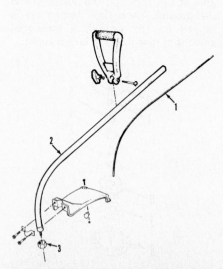

Fig. WE14—Exploded view of flexible drive shaft (1), drive shaft housing tube (2) and dust cover (3) used on Models XR-50, XR-70 and 1600. Models XR-80 and 1600 are equipped with a similar drive shaft; however, these models are equipped with a heavy duty bearing head.

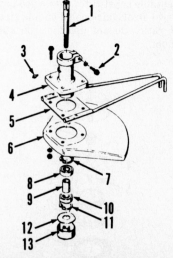

Fig. WE15—Exploded view of bearing head used on Models XR-80 and 1600.

1. Drive shaft adapter	
2. Clamp bolt	
3. Locating screw	8. Bearing
4. Housing	9. Spacer
5. Bracket (as equipped)	10. Bearing
6. Shield	11. Snap ring
7. Snap ring	12. Washer
	13. Drive disc

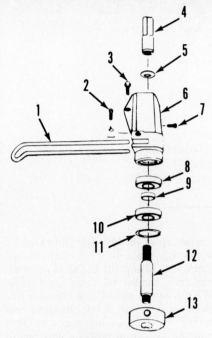

Fig. WE16—Exploded view of bearing head used on Model 657.

1. Wire bracket
2. Screw
3. Bolt
4. Drive shaft adapter
5. Washer
6. Housing
7. Locating screw
8. Bearing
9. Spacer
10. Bearing
11. Snap ring
12. Arbor shaft
13. Cup washer

sealed bearings and requires no regular maintenance.

To disassemble bearing head, remove trimmer head or blade assembly. Remove clamp bolt (3) and locating screw (7). Separate gear head from drive shaft housing tube. Remove snap ring (11). Secure head assembly in a vise. Place a 1-3/8 inch wooden dowel with a 3/4 inch hole drilled through center over arbor shaft, against the square coupling end. Tap wooden dowel with a mallet to remove arbor shaft and bearing assembly. Disassemble bearings, coupling and arbor assembly as required.

To reassemble, place coupling (4) and washer (5) on arbor (12). Press one bearing onto arbor. Install assembly into housing. Install spacer (9) and press remaining bearing onto arbor and into housing. Install snap ring.

GEAR HEAD

Models XR-90, XR-100 And 1000

Models XR-90, XR-100 and 1000 are equipped with the gear head shown in Fig. WE17. Check plug (9) should be removed and gear head lubricant checked at 10 hour intervals of use. Gear head housing should be kept 2/3 full of lithium base grease.

To disassemble gear head, remove trimmer head or blade assembly. Remove clamp bolt and head locating screw and separate gear head from drive shaft housing. Remove cup washer (17) and spacer (14). Remove snap ring (2) and use a suitable puller to

remove input shaft (5) and bearing assembly. Remove snap ring (1) and press bearings (3 and 4) from input shaft as required. Remove seal (16) and snap ring (15). Use suitable puller to remove arbor shaft (12) and bearing assembly. Press bearing (13) and gear (11) from shaft as required. If bearing (10) remains in housing (6), heat housing to 140° F (60° C) and tap housing on wooden block to remove bearing.

ENGINE COVER

Models XR-50, XR-70, XR-80, XR-90, XR-100, 1600 And 1700

Models XR-50, XR-70, XR-80, XR-90, XR-100, 1600 and 1700 are equipped with a full engine cover (Fig. WE18). To remove engine cover, remove clamp bolt (8) and separate engine assembly from drive shaft housing. Remove the four 10-24 screws and separate housings (5) and (9) slightly. Disconnect ignition wire from module and separate fuel line so junction fitting stays with crankcase side of fuel line. Separate housings completely. Remove the three 8-24 inch screws from inner side of housing (5) and remove the air baffle. Remove the five 10-24 screws located under air baffle and separate housing (4) from housing (5). Remove fuel tank cap and remove fuel tank. Remove the four screws securing carburetor cover plate and remove carburetor cover. Disconnect spark plug, remove the four 10-24 screws at drive shaft housing side of cover (9), then remove cover.

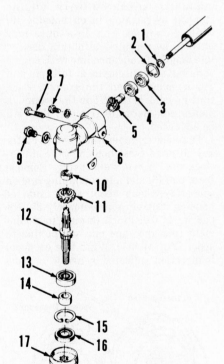

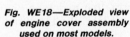

Fig. WE17—Exploded view of gear head used on Models XR-90, XR-100 and 1000.

1. Snap ring
2. Snap ring
3. Bearing
4. Bearing
5. Input shaft
6. Housing
7. Clamp bolt
8. Bolt
9. Check plug
10. Bearing
11. Gear
12. Arbor shaft
13. Bearing
14. Spacer
15. Snap ring
16. Seal
17. Cup washer

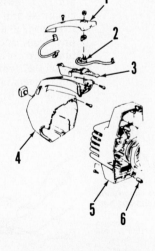

Fig. WE18—Exploded view of engine cover assembly used on most models.

1. Throttle housing cover
2. Ignition switch
3. Throttle trigger
4. Handle
5. Fan housing
6. Spacer
7. Screw
8. Clamp bolt
9. Cover

WESTERN AUTO

GASOLINE POWERED STRING TRIMMERS

Model	Engine Manufacturer	Engine Model	Displacement
95-2027-1	Kioritz	G2	16.0 cc
95-2028-9	Kioritz	H-1A	21.2 cc

ENGINE INFORMATION

All Models

All models are equipped with Kioritz two-stroke air-cooled engines. Identify engine model by trimmer model or engine displacement. Refer to KIORITZ ENGINE SERVICE section of this manual.

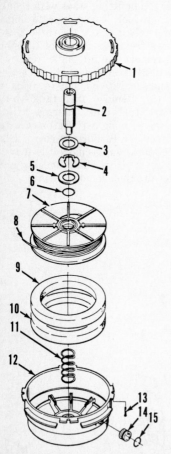

Fig. WA10—Exploded view of single strand semi-automatic trimmer head for Model 95-2027-1.

1. Cover
2. Drive shaft adapter
3. Washer
4. Retainer ring
5. Washer
6. Retainer ring
7. Spool
8. Line
9. Foam pad
10. Foam pad
11. Spring
12. Housing
13. Cotter pin
14. Line guide
15. Retainer

FUEL MIXTURE

All Models

Manufacturer recommends mixing regular grade gasoline (unleaded is an acceptable substitute) with a good quality two-stroke air-cooled engine oil at a 25:1 ratio. Do not use fuel containing alcohol.

STRING TRIMMER

Model 95-2027-1

Model 95-2027-1 is equipped with a single strand semi-automatic trimmer head shown in Fig. WA10. Line may be manually advanced with engine stopped by pushing in on housing (12) while pulling on line. Procedure may have to be repeated until desired line length is obtained. To advance line with engine running, operate trimmer engine at full rpm and tap housing (12) on the ground. Each time housing is tapped on the ground, a measured amount of trimmer line is advanced.

To renew trimmer line, remove cotter pin (13). Twist housing (12) counterclockwise and remove housing. Remove foam pads (9 and 10) and any remaining line from spool (7). Clean spool and inner area of housing. Cut off approximately 25 feet (7.6 m) of 0.080 inch (2 mm) monofilament line and tape one end of line to spool (Fig. WA11). Wind

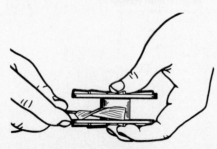

Fig. WA11—Tape new trimmer line end to center of spool as shown.

line on spool in direction indicated by arrow on spool (Fig. WA12). Install foam pads (9 and 10) so line is protruding from center of foam pads (Fig. WA12). Insert end of line through line guide and install spool, housing and spring. Push in on housing and twist housing to lock in position and install cotter pin (13-Fig. WA10).

Model 95-2028-9

Model 95-2028-9 is equipped with a single strand semi-automatic trimmer head shown in Fig. WA13. Line may be manually advanced with engine stopped by pushing in on housing (9) while pulling on line. Procedure may have to be repeated to obtain desired line length. To advance line with engine running, operate engine at full rpm and tap housing (9) on the ground. Each time housing is tapped on the ground, a measured amount of trimmer line will be advanced.

To renew trimmer line, remove cotter key (10) and twist housing (9) counterclockwise to remove housing. Remove foam pad (6) and any remaining line on spool (3). Clean spool and inside of housing. Cut off approximately 25 feet (7.6 m) of 0.080 inch (2 mm) monofilament line and tape one end of line to spool (Fig. WA11). Wind line on spool in direction indicated by arrow on spool

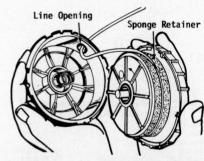

Fig. WA12—Install foam pads with line protruding from center of pads as shown. Wind line in direction indicated by arrow on spool.

(Fig. WA14). Install foam pad with line end protruding from between foam pad and spool as shown in Fig. WA14. Insert line end through line guide and install housing and spring assembly on spool. Push in on housing and twist housing to lock into position. Install cotter key through hole in housing and cover.

BLADE

Model 95-2028-9

Model 95-2028-9 may be equipped with a 60 tooth saw blade or an eight tooth weed and grass blade. To install blade with trimmer head removed, rotate cup washer (13–Fig. WA16) until hole in cup washer aligns with hole in gear head housing. Install a round tool into hole to prevent drive shaft turning. Install blade and lower adapter plate. Install and tighten nut. Install a new split pin in arbor to prevent nut loosening.

DRIVE SHAFT

All Models

All models are equipped with a flexible drive shaft enclosed in the drive shaft housing tube. Drive shaft has squared ends which engage adapters at each end. Drive shaft should be removed for maintenance at 50 hour intervals of use. Remove screw (4-Fig. WA15 or Fig. WA16) and bolt (3) at bearing head housing, then separate bearing head from drive shaft housing. Pull flexible drive shaft from housing. Lubricate drive shaft with lithium base grease and reinstall in drive shaft housing with end which was previously at clutch end at bearing head end. Reversing drive shaft ends extends drive shaft life. Make certain ends of drive shaft engage upper and lower square drive adapters when installing.

BEARING HEAD

Model 95-2027-1

Model 95-2027-1 is equipped with the bearing head shown in Fig. WA15. Bearing head is equipped with sealed bearings (7 and 9) and requires no regular maintenance. To disassemble bearing head, remove bolt (3) and screw (4) and separate bearing head from drive shaft housing tube. Remove trimmer head or blade assembly. Remove cup washer (13) and snap ring (10). Use a suitable puller to remove arbor shaft (11) and bearing assembly. Remove nut (6) and press bearings from arbor shaft as required.

Model 95-2028-9

Model 95-2028-9 is equipped with the bearing head shown in Fig. WA16. Bearing head is equipped with sealed bearings (7 and 9) and requires no regular maintenance. To disassemble bearing head, remove bolt (3) and screw (4) and separate bearing head from drive shaft housing tube. Remove trimmer head or blade assembly. Remove cup washer (13) and snap ring (10). Use suitable puller to remove arbor shaft (11) and bearing assembly. Remove nut (6) and press bearings from arbor shaft as required.

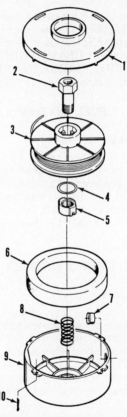

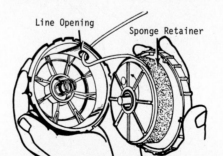

Fig. WA13—Exploded view of single strand semi-automatic trimmer head for Model 95-2028-9.

1. Cover	6. Foam pad
2. Drive shaft adapter	7. Line guide
3. Spool	8. Spring
4. "O" ring	9. Housing
5. Drive adapter nut	10. Cotter pin

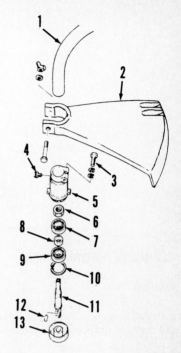

Fig. WA15—Exploded view of bearing head assembly used on Model 95-2027-1.

1. Drive shaft housing	7. Bearing
tube	8. Spacer
2. Shield	9. Bearing
3. Bolt	10. Snap ring
4. Screw	11. Arbor (output) shaft
5. Housing	12. Pin
6. Nut	13. Cup washer

Line Opening   Sponge Retainer

Fig. WA14—Install foam pad with line protruding from between pad and spool as shown. Wind line in direction indicated by arrow on spool.

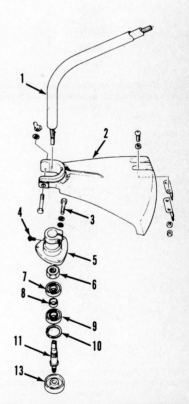

Fig. WA16—Exploded view of gear head assembly used on Model 95-2028-9. Refer to Fig. WA15 for legend.

YARD PRO
GASOLINE POWERED STRING TRIMMERS

Model	Engine Manufacturer	Engine Model	Displacement
110	Poulan	....	26.2 cc
120	Poulan	....	26.2 cc
130	Fuji	....	28.0 cc
140	Poulan	....	26.2 cc

ENGINE INFORMATION

All Models

Yard Pro line trimmers and brush cutters may be equipped with Poulan or Fuji two-stroke air-cooled gasoline engines. Identify engine manufacturer and engine displacement, then refer to appropriate POULAN ENGINE SERVICE or FUJI ENGINE SERVICE section in this manual.

FUEL MIXTURE

All Models

Manufacturer recommends mixing regular grade gasoline (unleaded is an acceptable substitute) with a good quality two-stroke air-cooled engine oil at a 25:1 ratio. Do not use fuel containing alcohol.

STRING TRIMMER

All Models

All models may be equipped with a single strand semi-automatic advance line trimmer head shown in Figs. YP10 and YP11. Fig. YP10 shows an exploded view of early style trimmer head which may be identified by the rough portion of upper housing (2). Fig. YP11 shows an exploded view of late style trimmer head which may be identified by the smooth portion of upper housing (2). Service procedure for both early and late trimmer heads is similar.

To extend line with trimmer engine stopped, push in on button (7) while pulling on line end. Procedure may have to be repeated to obtain desired line length. To extend line with trimmer engine running, operate trimmer engine at full rpm and tap button (7) on the ground. Each time button (7) is tapped on the ground a measured amount of new line will be advanced.

To renew line, remove cover (8), button (7) and spool (6). Clean all parts thoroughly and remove any remaining old line from spool. Wind approximately 30 feet (9 m) of 0.080 inch (2 mm) monofilament line on spool in direction indicated by arrow on spool. Insert line end through line guide opening in housing (2) and install spool, button and cover.

BLADE

Model 130

Model 130 may be equipped with a four cutting edge grass and weed blade. Make certain weed blade conversion kit (part number 701566) is installed with blade. When installing blade, make certain all adapter plates are centered and seated squarely against blade, then tighten nut (left-hand thread) securely.

Model 140

Model 140 may be equipped with a 10 inch saw blade or an 8 inch, four cutting edge weed blade. When installing blade, make certain all adapter plates are centered and seated squarely against blade, then tighten nut (left-hand thread) securely.

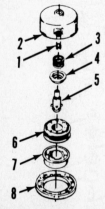

Fig. YP10—Exploded view of old style single strand semi-automatic trimmer head used on early models.

1. Drive shaft adapter
2. Housing
3. Spring
4. Spring adapter
5. Drive cam
6. Spool
7. Button
8. Cover

Fig. YP11—Exploded view of late style single strand semi-automatic trimmer head used on late models.

1. Line guide
2. Housing
3. Spring
4. Spring adapter
5. Drive cam
6. Spool
7. Button
8. Cover

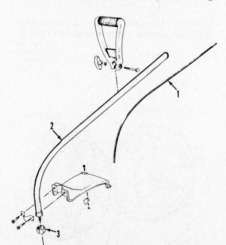

Fig. YP13—Exploded view of flexible drive shaft (1), drive shaft housing tube (2) and dust cover (3).

DRIVE SHAFT

All Models

All models are equipped with a flexible drive shaft (1-Fig. YP13) enclosed in the drive shaft housing tube (2). Drive shaft has squared ends which engage adapters at each end. Drive shaft should be removed for maintenance at 20 hour intervals of use. To remove, separate drive shaft housing from engine, then pull drive shaft out of housing. Clean drive shaft and lubricate with lithium base grease. Reinstall drive shaft in housing.

BEARING HEAD

Models 110 And 120

Models 110 and 120 are equipped with sealed bearing head which is an integral part of drive shaft housing (Fig. YP13). No regular maintenance is required and no service parts are available.

Model 130

Model 130 is equipped with the bearing head shown in Fig. YP14. Bearing head is equipped with sealed bearings and requires no regular maintenance.

To disassemble bearing head, remove trimmer head or blade assembly. Remove clamp bolt (2) and locating screw (3). Separate bearing head assembly from drive shaft housing. Remove shield (6) and bracket (5) (as equipped).

Remove cup washer (13) and washer (12). Carefully press drive shaft adapter (1) out of bearings. Remove snap rings (7 and 11). Press bearings (8 and 10) and spacer (9) out of housing.

GEAR HEAD

Model 140

Model 140 is equipped with the gear head shown in Fig. YP15. Check plug (9) should be removed and gear head lubricant checked at 10 hour intervals of use. Gear head housing should be kept 2/3 full of lithium base grease.

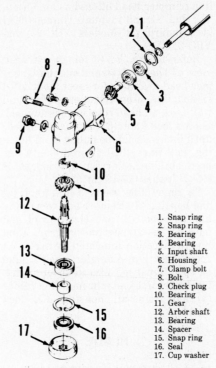

Fig. YP15—Exploded view of gear head assembly used on Model 140.

1. Snap ring
2. Snap ring
3. Bearing
4. Bearing
5. Input shaft
6. Housing
7. Clamp bolt
8. Bolt
9. Check plug
10. Bearing
11. Gear
12. Arbor shaft
13. Bearing
14. Spacer
15. Snap ring
16. Seal
17. Cup washer

To disassemble gear head, remove trimmer head or blade assembly. Remove clamp bolt and head locating screw and separate gear head from drive shaft housing. Remove cup washer (17) and spacer (14). Remove snap ring (2) and use a suitable puller to remove input shaft (5) and bearing assembly. Remove snap ring (1) and press bearings (3 and 4) from input shaft as required. Remove seal (16) and snap ring (15). Use suitable puller to remove arbor shaft (12) and bearing assembly. Press bearing (13) and gear (11) from shaft as required. If bearing (10) remains in housing (6), heat housing to 140° F (60° C) and tap housing on wooden block to remove bearing.

ENGINE COVER

All Models

All models are equipped with a full engine cover (Fig. YP16). To remove engine cover, remove clamp bolt (8) and separate engine assembly from drive shaft housing. Remove the four 10-24 screws and separate housings (5) and (9) slightly. Disconnect ignition wire from module and separate fuel line so junction fitting stays with crankcase side of fuel line. Separate housings completely. Remove the three 8-24 inch screws from inner side of housing (5) and remove the air baffle. Remove the five 10-24 screws located under air baffle and separate housing (4) from housing (5). Remove fuel tank cap and remove fuel tank. Remove the four screws securing carburetor cover plate and remove carburetor cover. Disconnect spark plug, remove the four 10-24 screws at drive shaft housing side of cover (9), then remove cover.

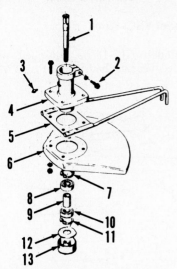

Fig. YP14—Exploded view of bearing head assembly used on Model 130.

1. Drive shaft adapter
2. Clamp bolt
3. Locating screw
4. Housing
5. Bracket (as equipped)
6. Shield
7. Snap ring
8. Bearing
9. Spacer
10. Bearing
11. Snap ring
12. Washer
13. Drive disc

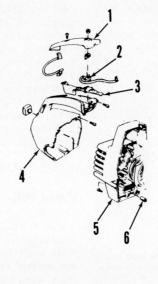

Fig. YP16—Exploded view of engine cover assembly used on all models.
1. Throttle housing cover
2. Ignition switch
3. Throttle trigger
4. Handle
5. Fan housing
6. Spacer
7. Screw
8. Clamp bolt
9. Housing

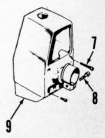

YAZOO

GASOLINE POWERED STRING TRIMMERS

Model	Engine Manufacturer	Engine Model	Displacement
YBC-16	Tanaka	....	16.0 cc
YBC-23	Tanaka	....	22.6 cc
YBC-31	Tanaka	....	30.5 cc

ENGINE INFORMATION

All Models

Yazoo line trimmers and brush cutters are equipped with Tanaka (TAS) two-stroke air-cooled engines. Engines may be identified by engine displacement. Refer to TANAKA (TAS) ENGINE SERVICE sections of this manual.

FUEL MIXTURE

All Models

Manufacturer recommends mixing regular grade gasoline (unleaded is an acceptable substitute) with a good quality two-stroke air-cooled engine oil at a 25:1 ratio. Do not use fuel containing alcohol.

STRING TRIMMER

All Models

Model YBC-16 is equipped with an eight blade plastic flexible blade with line trimmer head offered as an option. The dual strand manual trimmer head is standard on Models YBC-23 and YBC-31.

Refer to Fig. YA10 for an exploded view of the dual strand manual trimmer head available for most models. To extend line, stop trimmer engine and wait until all head rotation has stopped. Loosen lock knob (6) (left-hand thread) until line ends can be pulled from housing. Pull lines until desired length has been obtained. Correct line length is 3.4-4.7 inches (10-12 cm).

To renew line, remove lock knob (6) and housing (5). Remove any remaining line on spool (2) and clean spool and housing. Install new line on spool. Wind line in direction indicated by arrow on spool. New line diameter when wound on spool must not exceed spool diameter. Insert line ends through line guides (4) and reinstall housing and lock knob.

BLADE

Models YBC-23 And YBC-31

Models YBC-23 and YBC-31 may be equipped with a four cutting edge blade or a saw blade. To remove blade, rotate blade until hole (H-Fig. YA11) in guard is aligned with hole (H) in cup washer (2). Insert a round tool into aligned holes to prevent blade rotation. Remove bolt (7) (left-hand thread), washer (6), cover (5) and adapter (4). Remove blade (3). When installing blade, tighten bolt (7) to 250 in.-lbs. (28 N·m).

DRIVE SHAFT

Model YBC-16

Model YBC-16 is equipped with a flexible drive shaft enclosed in the drive shaft housing tube. Drive shaft has squared ends which engage adapters at each end. Drive shaft should be removed for maintenance at 20 hour intervals of use. To remove, separate drive shaft housing from engine, then pull drive shaft from housing. Clean drive shaft and lubricate with lithium base grease. Reinstall drive shaft in housing.

Models YBC-23 And YBC-31

Models YBC-23 and YBC-31 are equipped with a solid steel drive shaft supported in five renewable bushing assemblies located in drive shaft housing tube (Fig. YA12). Drive shaft requires no regular maintenance; however, if drive shaft has been removed, lubricate drive shaft with lithium base gease before reinstallation. To renew bushing assemblies, mark locations of old bushings on drive shaft housing, then remove all old bushings. Install new bushings with suitable driver at old bushing locations.

BEARING HEAD

Model YBC-16

Model YBC-16 is equipped with sealed bearing housing (3-Fig. YA13).

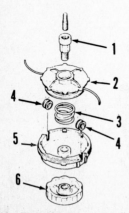

Fig. YA10—Exploded view of the dual strand manual trimmer head standard on most models.

1. Drive shaft adapter
2. Spool
3. Spring
4. Line guides
5. Housing
6. Lock knob

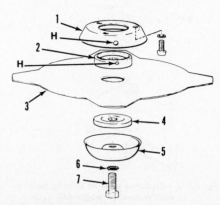

Fig. YA11—Exploded view of blade assembly available for Models YBC-23 and YBC-31.

1. Anti-wrap guard
2. Cup washer
3. Blade
4. Adapter plate
5. Cover
6. Washer
7. Bolt (LH)
H. Hole

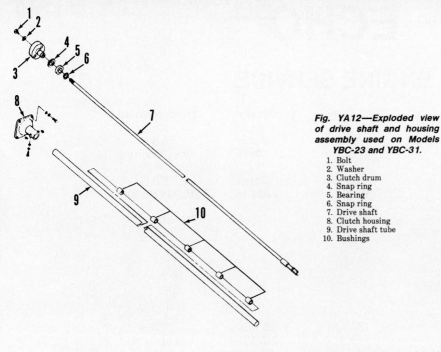

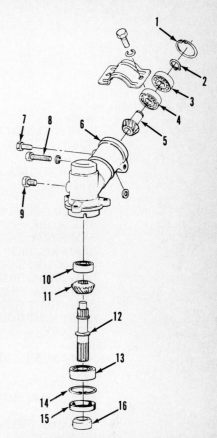

Fig. YA12—Exploded view of drive shaft and housing assembly used on Models YBC-23 and YBC-31.

1. Bolt
2. Washer
3. Clutch drum
4. Snap ring
5. Bearing
6. Snap ring
7. Drive shaft
8. Clutch housing
9. Drive shaft tube
10. Bushings

No regular maintenance is required and no service parts are available.

GEAR HEAD

Models YBC-23 And YBC-31

Models YBC-23 and YBC-31 are equipped with the gear head shown in Fig. YA 14. Gear head lubricant level should be checked at 50 hour intervals of use by removing check plug (9). Gear head housing should be 2/3 full of lithium base grease. Do not use a pressure grease gun to install grease as bearing seal and housing damage will occur.

To disassemble gear head, remove trimmer head or blade assembly. Remove locating screw (7) and clamp bolt (8) and separate gear head from drive shaft housing. Remove spacer (16) and seal (15). Remove snap ring (14) and use a suitable puller to remove arbor shaft (12) and bearing assembly. If bearing (10) stays in housing, heat housing to 140° F (60° C) and tap housing on wood-

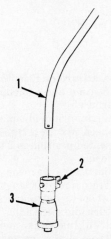

Fig. YA13—Bearing head assembly (3) is attached to drive shaft housing tube (1) by clamp (2). No service parts are available for bearing head.

Fig. YA14—Exploded view of gear head used on Models YBC-23 and YBC-31.

1. Snap ring	9. Check plug
2. Snap ring	10. Bearing
3. Bearing	11. Gear
4. Bearing	12. Arbor (output) shaft
5. Input shaft	13. Bearing
6. Housing	14. Snap ring
7. Locating screw	15. Seal
8. Clamp bolt	16. Spacer

en block to remove bearing. Remove gear (11) from arbor shaft. Press bearing (13) from arbor shaft as required. Remove snap ring (1). Insert a screwdriver into clamp split in gear head housing and carefully expand housing. Remove input shaft (5) and bearing assembly. Remove snap ring (2) and press bearings (3 and 4) from input shaft as required.

ECHO

ENGINE SERVICE

Model	Bore	Stroke	Displacement
SRM-140D, SRM-140DA, GT-140, GT-140A, GT-140B	26 mm (1.024 in.)	26 mm (1.024 in.)	13.8 cc (0.842 cu. in.)
GT-160, GT-160A, GT-160AE	28 mm (1.102 in.)	26 mm (1.024 in.)	16.0 cc (0.976 cu. in.)
SRM-200, SRM-200AE, SRM-200BE, SRM200D, SRM-200DA, SRM-200DB, SRM-200E, SRM-201F, SRM-201FA, SRM-202D, SRM-202DA, SRM-202F, SRM-202FA, SRM-210E, SRM-210AE, GT-200, GT-200A, GT-200B, GT-200BE	32.2 mm (1.268 in.)	26 mm (1.024 in.)	21.2 cc (1.294 cu. in.)
SRM-300, SRM-302ADX	28 mm (1.102 in.)	37 mm (1.457 in.)	30.1 cc (1.837 cu. in.)
SRM-300E, SRM-300E/1, SRM-300AE, SRM-300AE/1	35 mm (1.378 in.)	32 mm (1.260 in.)	30.8 cc (1.880 cu. in.)
SRM-400E, SRM-400AE, SRM-402DE	40 mm (1.575 in.)	32 mm (1.260 in.)	40.2 cc (2.452 cu. in.)

ENGINE INFORMATION

These two-cycle engines are used on Echo grass trimmers, weed trimmers and brush cutters. Engine has a detachable cylinder and two-piece crankcase. Crankshaft and connecting rod are considered an assembly and are not serviced separately. On all models, crankshaft/connecting rod assembly is supported by two ball bearing mains. All models except Model SRM-202FA use a diaphragm type carburetor which allows engine to be operated in any position. Model SRM-202FA uses a float type carburetor.

MAINTENANCE

SPARK PLUG. Recommended spark plug for all models is a Champion CJ8, or equivalent. Electrode gap is 0.6-0.7 mm (0.024-0.028 in.). Tighten spark plug to specified torque.

CARBURETOR. All engines are equipped with Walbro diaphragm type carburetors except Model SRM-202FA which is equipped with a Keihin float type carburetor. Refer to Fig. EC1 or EC2 for exploded view of carburetors. Refer to appropriate paragraphs for model being serviced.

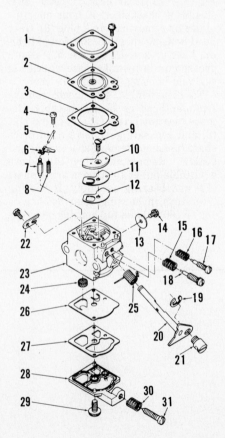

Walbro Carburetor. Refer to Fig. EC-1 for identification and exploded view of Walbro carburetor.

Initial adjustment of idle mixture (18) and high speed mixture (17) needles from a lightly seated position is 1 turn open for each needle.

Final adjustments are made with trimmer line at recommended length. Engine should be at operating temperature and running. Turn idle speed adjusting screw (31) until engine runs smoothly at 2500-3000 rpm. Adjust low speed needle (18) to obtain consistent idling and smooth acceleration. Readjust idle speed adjusting screw (31) as necessary. Open throttle fully and adjust high speed needle (17) about 1/8 turn counterclockwise from maximum high speed position.

Fig. EC1—Exploded view of Walbro carburetor.

1. Cover
2. Metering diaphragm
3. Gasket
4. Metering lever screw
5. Meter lever pin
6. Metering lever
7. Fuel inlet valve
8. Meter lever spring
9. Circuit plate screw
10. Circuit plate
11. Check valve
12. Gasket
13. Throttle valve
14. Shutter screw
15. Spring
16. Spring
17. High speed mixture needle
18. Idle mixture needle
19. "E" clip
20. Throttle shaft
21. Swivel
22. Throttle shaft clip
23. Body
24. Inlet screen
25. Return spring
26. Fuel pump diaphragm
27. Gasket
28. Cover
29. Cover screw
30. Spring
31. Idle speed screw

CAUTION: Do not go any leaner with high speed needle adjustment as it could result in improper lubrication and engine seizure could result.

Fuel inlet lever (6) should be flush with carburetor body (Fig. EC4). Carefully bend fuel inlet lever to obtain correct setting.

Keihin Carburetor. Refer to Fig. EC2 for identification and exploded view of Keihin float type carburetor.

To adjust idle speed, engine must be at operating temperature and running. Turn idle speed screw (1) to obtain 2500-3000 rpm idle. Counterclockwise rotation lowers idle speed and clockwise rotation increases idle speed. Screw rotation raises or lowers throttle valve (29).

Standard height of metering lever is 3.05 mm (0.120 in.) measured from top of rim of float chamber as shown in Fig. EC3.

Full load adjustment is obtained by changing position of "E" ring (27—Fig. EC2) on jet needle (28). To increase fuel volume, install clip at lower groove on jet needle. To reduce fuel volume, install "E" ring at higher groove on jet needle. Refer to Fig. EC5.

IGNITION SYSTEM. Engines may be equipped with a magneto type ignition with breaker points and condenser or a CDI (capacitor-discharge) ignition system which requires no regular maintenance and has no breaker points or condensers. Ignition module (CDI) is located outside of flywheel. Refer to appropriate paragraph for model being serviced.

Breaker Point Ignition System. Breaker points may be located behind recoil starter or behind flywheel. Note location of breaker points and refer to following paragraphs for service.

To inspect or service magneto ignition with breaker points and condenser located behind recoil starter and cover, first remove fan cover. Refer to Fig. EC6 and check pole gap between flywheel and ignition coil laminations. Gap should be 0.35-0.40 mm (0.014-0.016 in.). To adjust pole gap, loosen two retaining screws in coil (threads or retaining screws must be treated with Loctite or equivalent), place correct gage between flywheel and coil laminations. Pull coil to flywheel by hand as shown, then tighten screws and remove feeler gage.

Breaker points are accessible after removal of starter case, nut and pawl carrier.

NOTE: Nut and pawl carrier are both left-hand thread.

To adjust point gap and ignition timing, disconnect stop switch wire from stop switch. Connect one lead from a timing tester (Echo 990510-00031) or equivalent to stop switch wire. Ground remaining timing tester lead to engine body. Position flywheel timing mark as shown in Fig. EC7 and set breaker point gap to 0.3-0.4 mm (0.012-0.014 in.). Rotate flywheel and check timing with timing tester. Readjust as necessary.

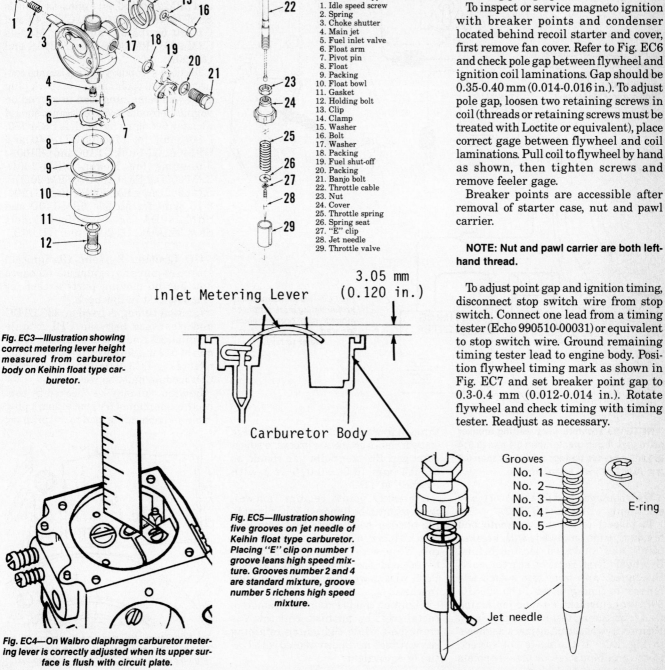

Fig. EC2—Exploded view of Keihin float type carburetor.

1. Idle speed screw
2. Spring
3. Choke shutter
4. Main jet
5. Fuel inlet valve
6. Float arm
7. Pivot pin
8. Float
9. Packing
10. Float bowl
11. Gasket
12. Holding bolt
13. Clip
14. Clamp
15. Washer
16. Bolt
17. Washer
18. Packing
19. Fuel shut-off
20. Packing
21. Banjo bolt
22. Throttle cable
23. Nut
24. Cover
25. Throttle spring
26. Spring seat
27. "E" clip
28. Jet needle
29. Throttle valve

Fig. EC3—Illustration showing correct metering lever height measured from carburetor body on Keihin float type carburetor.

Fig. EC4—On Walbro diaphragm carburetor metering lever is correctly adjusted when its upper surface is flush with circuit plate.

Fig. EC5—Illustration showing five grooves on jet needle of Keihin float type carburetor. Placing "E" clip on number 1 groove leans high speed mixture. Grooves number 2 and 4 are standard mixture, groove number 5 richens high speed mixture.

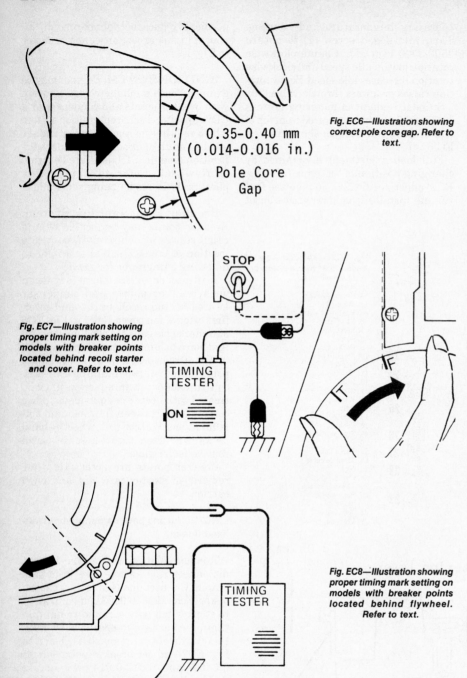

Fig. EC6—Illustration showing correct pole core gap. Refer to text.

Fig. EC7—Illustration showing proper timing mark setting on models with breaker points located behind recoil starter and cover. Refer to text.

Fig. EC8—Illustration showing proper timing mark setting on models with breaker points located behind flywheel. Refer to text.

0.35-0.40 mm (0.014-0.016 in.)

Pole Core Gap

NOTE: Be accurate when setting breaker point gap. A gap greater than 0.4 mm (0.014 in.) will advance timing; a gap less than 0.3 mm (0.012 in.) will retard timing.

With point gap and flywheel correctly set, timing will be 23° BTDC.

To inspect or service magneto and breaker points on models with breaker points and condenser located behind flywheel, first remove starter case. Disconnect wire from stop switch and connect to timing tester (Echo 990510-0031) or equivalent. Ground remaining lead from timing tester to engine body. Position flywheel timing mark as shown in Fig. EC8. If timing is not correct, loosen retaining screw on breaker points

through flywheel slot openings. Squeeze screwdriver in crankcase groove to adjust point gap. Breaker point gap should be 0.3-0.4 mm (0.012-0.016 in.) with flywheel at TDC.

If breaker points require renewal, flywheel must be removed. When installing breaker points note that stop lead (black) from condenser must pass under coil. White wire from coil must pass between condenser bracket and oiler felt. Push wire down to avoid contact with flywheel.

If ignition coil is loosened or removed, install coil by pushing coil towards crankshaft while tightening retaining screws which have been treated with Loctite or equivalent.

NOTE: Be accurate when setting breaker point gap. A gap greater than 0.4 mm (0.016 in.) will advance timing; a gap less than 0.3 mm (0.012 in.) will retard timing.

With point gap and flywheel correctly set, timing will be 30° BTDC. Tighten flywheel nut to specified torque.

Primary and secondary ignition coil resistance may be checked with an ohmmeter without removing coil.

To check primary coil resistance, connect ohmmeter to disconnected ignition coil primary lead and ground remaining lead to engine. Primary coil resistance should register 0.5-0.8 ohms for Models GT-140A, GT-140B, GT-160 and GT-160A; 0.5-0.6 ohms for Models SRM-200D, SRM-200DA, SRM-200DB, SRM-202DA and SRM-202FA; 0.6-0.8 ohms for Models SRM-140D, SRM-140DA, GTL-140 and GT-200 or 0.5-0.7 ohms for Models SRM-200, SRM-302ADX, GT-200A and GT-200B.

To check secondary coil resistance connect one lead of ohmmeter to spark plug cable and remaining lead to ground on engine. Secondary coil resistance should register 6-9 ohms for Models SRM-200, 7-10 ohms for Models GTL-140 and GT-140A, GT-140B, GT-160 and GT160A; 5-6 ohms for Models SRM-200D, SRM-200DA, SRM-200DB, SRM-202DB, SRM-202DA, SRM-202FA and GT200; 8-10 ohms for Models SRM-140D and SRM-140DA or 8-9.5 for Models SRM-302ADX, GT-200A and GT200B.

CD Ignition System. CD ignition system requires no regular maintenance and has no moving parts except for magnets cast in flywheel.

Ignition timing is fixed at 30° BTDC and clearance between CDI module laminations and flywheel should be 0.3 mm (0.012 in.). To check ignition timing refer to Fig. EC9. If timing is not correct, CDI module must be renewed.

Ignition coil may be checked by connecting one ohmmeter lead to spark plug cable and remaining lead to coil primary

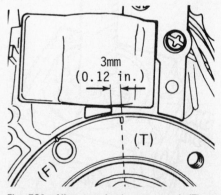

Fig. EC9—Align top dead center mark (T) on flywheel with laminations as shown to check timing on models with CD ignition. Refer to text.

3mm (0.12 in.)

(T)

(F)

lead; ohmmeter should register 0.0-0.2 ohms for all models. Connect ohmmeter lead to coil primary lead (red) wire and remaining ohmmeter lead to either the coil exciter lead (grounded wire), if so equipped, or to coil laminations. Ohmmeter should register 0.5-1.5k ohms for models with exciter lead or 1.5-3.0k ohms for remaining models. On models so equipped, connect one ohmmeter lead to exciter lead and remaining lead to coil laminations; ohmmeter should register 120-200 ohms.

CARBON. Muffler and cylinder exhaust ports should be cleaned periodically to prevent loss of power due to carbon build-up. Remove muffler cover and baffle plate and scrape muffler free of carbon. With muffler cover removed, position engine so piston is at top dead center and carefully remove carbon from exhaust ports with wooden scraper. Be careful not to damage the edges of exhaust ports or to scratch piston. Do not attempt to run engine without muffler baffle plate or cover.

LUBRICATION. Engine is lubricated by mixing oil with the fuel. Thoroughly mix two-cycle air-cooled engine oil at 20:1 ratio for Models SRM-200D, SRM-200DA, SRM-200DB, SRM-202DA, SRM-202FA, SRM-140D, SRM-140DA, SRM-302ADX and GTL-140. Thoroughly mix Echo special two-cycle engine oil at a 32:1 ratio for all other models. Do not use premium gasoline.

TIGHTENING TORQUES. Recommended tightening torque specifications are as follows:
Spark plug . . . . 17 N·m
(150 in.-lbs.)
Cylinder cover
(as equipped) . . . . 1.5-1.9 N·m
(13-17 in.-lbs.)
Cylinder:
SRM-200D, SRM-200DA,
SRM-200DB, SRM-202D,
SRM-202DA, SRM-202FA . . 3-4 N·m
(30-35 in.-lbs.)
SRM-140D, SRM-140DA,
SRM-200, SRM-200E,
SRM-200AE, SRM-200BE,
SRM-200F, SRM-200FA,
SRM-210E, SRM-210AE,
GT160, GT-160A, GT-160AE,
GT-200, GT-200BE,
GTL-140 . . . . 5.7-6 N·m
(50-55 in.-lbs.)
SRM-400, SRM-300,
SRM-300E, SRM-300E/1,
SRM-300AE, SRM-300AE/1,
SRM-400E, SRM-400AE,
SRM-402DE . . . . 7-8 N·m
(65-75 in.-lbs.)
SRM-302ADX . . . . 8-9 N·m
(13-17 in.-lbs.)
Crankcase:
SRM-140D, SRM-140DA,
SRM-302ADX, GTL-140 4.5-5.7 N·m
(40-50 in.-lbs.)
All others . . . . 4-5 N·m
(35-45 in.-lbs.)
Flywheel nut:
SRM-302ADX, GT-140, GT-160,

GT-200 . . . . 8-10 N·m
(70-90 in.-lbs.)
SRM-200, SRM-200AE,
SRM-200BE, SRM-210E,
SRM-210AE, GT-160AE,
GT-200BE . . . . 14-16 N·m
(120 to 140 in.-lbs.)
SRM-140D, SRM-140DA,
SRM-200D, SRM-200DA,
SRM-200DB, SRM-202DA,
SRM-202FA, SRM-300,
SRM-300E, SRM-300E/1,
SRM-300AE, SRM-300AE/1,
GTL-140 . . . . 20-24 N·m
(175-210 in.-lbs.)

PISTON, PIN AND RINGS. Rings are pinned to prevent ring rotation on all models. Piston may be equipped with one or two compression rings according to model and application.

Cylinder is removed and pulled off piston. On models with needle bearings in connecting rod small end, make certain needle bearings are not lost when separating piston from connecting rod.

Standard ring end gap for all models is 0.3 mm (0.012 in.). If ring end gap is 0.5 mm (0.020 in.) or more, renew rings and/or cylinder bore.

Standard ring side clearance in piston groove for all models is 0.06 mm (0.0024 in.). If ring side clearance is 0.10 mm (0.004 in.) or more, renew ring and/or piston.

Standard piston pin bore diameter in piston is 6.0 mm (0.2362 in.) for

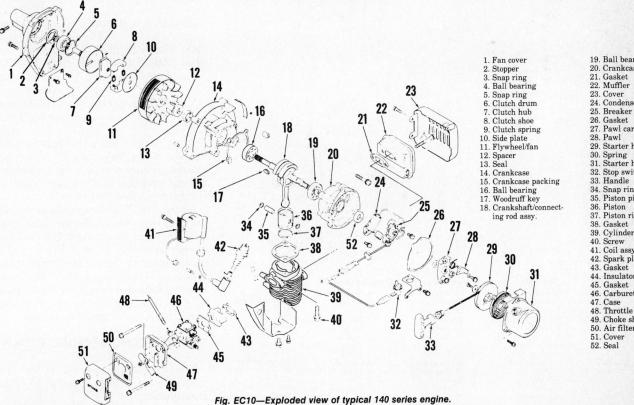

1. Fan cover	19. Ball bearing
2. Stopper	20. Crankcase half
3. Snap ring	21. Gasket
4. Ball bearing	22. Muffler
5. Snap ring	23. Cover
6. Clutch drum	24. Condenser
7. Clutch hub	25. Breaker points
8. Clutch shoe	26. Gasket
9. Clutch spring	27. Pawl carrier
10. Side plate	28. Pawl
11. Flywheel/fan	29. Starter hub
12. Spacer	30. Spring
13. Seal	31. Starter housing
14. Crankcase	32. Stop switch
15. Crankcase packing	33. Handle
16. Ball bearing	34. Snap ring
17. Woodruff key	35. Piston pin
18. Crankshaft/connect-	36. Piston
ing rod assy.	37. Piston ring
	38. Gasket
	39. Cylinder
	40. Screw
	41. Coil assy.
	42. Spark plug
	43. Gasket
	44. Insulator
	45. Gasket
	46. Carburetor
	47. Case
	48. Throttle cable
	49. Choke shutter
	50. Air filter
	51. Cover
	52. Seal

Fig. EC10—Exploded view of typical 140 series engine.

SRM-140D model, 8.997 mm (0.3542 in.) for SRM-302ADX model, 10.0 mm (0.3937 in.) for SRM-300E and SRM-300AE models and 8.0 mm (0.3049 in.) for all other models. If piston pin bore diameter is 6.3 mm (0.2374 in.) or more for SRM-140D model, 9.027 mm (0.3554 in.) or more for SRM-302ADX model, 10.03 mm (0.3949 in.) or more for SRM-300E and SRM-300AE models for 8.03 mm (0.3161 in.) or more for all other models, renew piston.

Standard piston pin diameter is 6.0 mm (0.2362 in.) for SRM-140D model, 9.0 mm (0.3543 in.) for SRM-302ADX model, 10.0 mm (0.3957 in.) for SRM-300E and SRM-300AE models and 8.0 mm (0.3150 in.) for all other models. If piston pin diameter is 5.98 mm (0.2354 in.) or less for SRM-140D model, 8.98 mm (0.3535 in.) or less for SRM-302ADX model, 8.0 mm (0.3150 in.) or less for SRM-300E and SRM-300AE models or 7.98 mm (0.3142 in.) or less for all other models, renew pin.

Standard piston skirt diameter is 25.90 mm (1.020 in.) for models with 26 mm bore, 27.90 mm (1.101 in.) for models with 28 mm (1.102 in.) bore, 32.1 mm (1.264 in.) for models with 32.2 mm (1.268 in.) bore, 34.90 mm (1.374 in.) for models with 35 mm (1.378 in.) bore and 39.90 mm (1.571 in.) for models with 40 mm (1.575 in.) bore. If piston diameter is 0.10 mm (0.004 in.) or less than standard, renew piston.

When installing piston, rings must be correctly positioned over pins in ring grooves. Install piston on connecting rod with arrow on top of piston towards exhaust side of engine. Make certain piston pin retaining rings are correctly seated in piston pin bore of piston. Use care when slipping piston into cylinder that cylinder does not rotate.

CYLINDER. Cylinder bores of all models are chrome plated and should be renewed at the first sign of aluminum showing through plated surface or if surface is scored or flaking.

CRANKSHAFT AND CONNECTING ROD ASSEMBLY. The crankshaft and connecting rod are serviced as an assembly only and crankshaft and connecting rod are not available separately.

To remove crankshaft and connecting rod assembly on all models, remove fan housing and clutch assembly. Remove carburetor, muffler and fuel tank. Remove starter assembly, flywheel, magneto, points and condenser or ignition module (as equipped). Carefully remove cylinder, separate piston from connecting rod and remove piston. Separate crankcase halves and remove crankshaft and connecting rod assembly.

Ball bearing type main bearings are used on all models. Bearings may be removed and installed using a suitable puller.

Standard connecting rod side clearance on crankpin journal is 0.55-060 mm (0.022-0.026 in.) for Models SRM-140D, SRM-140DA, GT-140, GT-140A, GT-140B, GTL-140, GT-160, GT-160A, GT-160AE, GT-200, GT-200A, GT-200B and GT-200BE. If side clearance is 0.7 mm (0.028 in.) or more for any of these models, crankshaft and connecting rod assembly must be renewed. Standard connecting rod side clearance for all other models is 0.25-0.30 mm (0.010-0.012 in.), and if side clearance is 0.40 mm (0.016 in.) or more, connecting rod and crankshaft assembly must be renewed.

Connecting rod piston pin bearing bore standard and maximum diameters are as follows:

Models
SRM-140D
Standard diameter	6.0 mm (0.2362 in.)
Maximum diameter	6.06 mm (0.2386 in.)

SRM-140D, GT-140, GT-160, GTL-140
Standard diameter	8.0 mm (0.3150 in.)
Maximum diameter	8.06 mm (0.3173 in.)

SRM-200D, SRM-200DA, SRM-200DB, SRM-202DA, SRM-202FA
Standard diameter	11.0 mm (0.4336 in.)
Maximum diameter	11.03 mm (0.4341 in.)

SRM200, SRM-200AE, SRM-200BE, SRM-210E, SRM-210AE, SRM-302ADX, GT-200, GT-200BE
Standard diameter	12.0 mm (0.4729 in.)
Maximum diameter	12.03 mm (0.4734 in.)

SRM-300, SRM-300E, SRM-300AE, SRM-400E, SRM-400AE, SRM-402DE
Standard diameter	14.0 mm (0.5517 in.)
Maximum diameter	14.03 mm (0.5522 in.)

When reassembling crankcase on all models, use a light coat of sealer on crankcase halves as sealing crankcase against pressure and vacuum leaks is critical to engine operation.

Always install new crankcase seals and packing when reassembling crankcase. Seal lips must face inward. Use caution during assembly so seal lips are not damaged during crankcase installation over ends of crankshaft. Packing excess must be trimmed from cylinder surface to avoid crankcase leaks. Tighten crankcase bolts to specified torque.

KIORITZ-ECHO SPECIAL TOOLS

The following special tools are available from Echo Central Service Distributors.

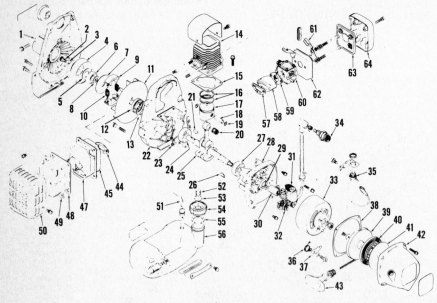

Fig. EC11—Exploded view of typical 200 series engine.

1. Fan cover	14. Cylinder	26. Woodruff key	39. Starter drum	53. Check valve
2. Bolt	15. Gasket	27. Ball bearing	40. Spring	54. Cap
3. Washer	16. Piston rings	28. Crankcase half	41. Plate	55. Gasket
4. Clutch drum	17. Piston	29. Seal	42. Starter housing	56. Fuel tank
5. Spacer	18. Piston pin	30. Sleeve	43. Handle	57. Gasket
6. Ball bearing	19. Snap ring	31. Coil assy.	44. Gasket	58. Insulator
7. Plate	20. Needle bearing	32. Breaker points	45. Case	59. Gasket
8. Spacer	21. Woodruff key	33. Flywheel	47. Baffle	60. Carburetor
9. Clutch shoe	22. Crankcase half	34. Spark plug	48. Gasket	61. Choke shutter
10. Clutch spring	23. Packing	35. Stop switch	49. Case	62. Case
11. Fan	24. Ball bearing	36. Spring	50. Cover	63. Air filter
12. Seal	25. Crankshaft/connect-	37. Pawl	51. Fuel line	64. Cover
13. Snap ring	ing rod assy.	38. Gasket	52. Vent	

FLYWHEEL HOLDER
897712-06030 . . .   SRM-140,
        SRM-140DA
897712-07930 . . .   GTL-140
897501-03932 . . .   SRM-200D,
SRM-200DA, SRM200DB,
SRM-202DA, SRM-202FA,
        SRM-302ADX
895115-00330 . . .   GT-160AE,
GT-200BE, SRM-200,
SRM-200E, SRM-200AE,
SRM-200BE, SRM-201F,
SRM-201FA, SRM-210E,
SRM-210AE, SRM-300E,
SRM-300AE, SRM-400E,
SRM-400AE, SRM-402DD

MAGNETO SPANNER AND GAGE
895115-00330 . . .   All models

BEARING WEDGE SET
897701-06030 . . .   SRM140D,
SRM-140DA, GT-140A,
GTL-140, GT-160,
GT-160AE, GT-200,
GT-200A, GT-200B,
GT-200BE, SRM-200,
SRM-200AE, SRM-200BE,
SRM-200E, SRM-201F,
SRM-201FA, SRM-202DA,
SRM202-FA, SRM-210E,
SRM-210AE, SRM-300E,
SRM-300AE, SRM-400E,
        SRM-400AE
897701-02830 . . .   SRM-200D,
SRM-200DA, SRM-200DB,
SRM-202DA, SRM-202FA,
        SRM-300

DRIVERS
897718-06030 . . .   SRM-140D,
SRM-140DA, SRM-200,
SRM-200AE, SRM-200BE,
SRM-200E, GT-140A,
GT140-B, GT-160,
GT-160A, GTL-140,
GT-200, SRM-302ADX
897718-02830 . . .   SRM-300E,
SRM-300AE, SRM-400E,
SRM-400AE, SRM-402DD

PISTON PIN TOOL
097702-06030 . . .   All models

PRESSURE TESTER
990510-0020 . . .   All models

TIMING TESTER
990510-00031 . . .   All models

FUJI
ENGINE SERVICE

Model	Bore	Stroke	Displacement
EC01A	28.0 mm	25.0 mm	15.4 cc
	(1.10 in.)	(0.98 in.)	(0.94 cu. in.)
EC02E	31.5 mm	26.0 mm	20.3 cc
	(1.24 in.)	(1.02 in.)	(1.24 cu. in.)
EC02R	31.5 mm	28.0 mm	22.5 cc
	(1.24 in.)	(1.10 in.)	(1.37 cu. in.)
EC03-1R	36.0 mm	28.0 mm	28.0 cc
	(1.42 in.)	(1.10 in.)	(1.71 cu. in.)
EC03-2R	36.0 mm	30.0 mm	30.5 cc
	(1.42 in.)	(1.18 in.)	(1.86 cu. in.)
EC04-3R	40.0 mm	30.0 mm	37.7 cc
	(1.58 in.)	(1.18 in.)	(2.30 cu. in.)

ENGINE INFORMATION

Fuji two-stroke air-cooled gasoline engines are used by several manufacturers of string trimmers and brush cutters.

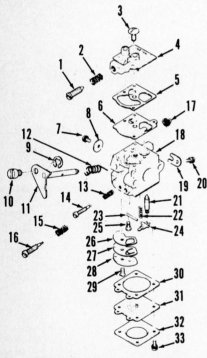

Fig. FI50—Exploded view of Walbro diaphragm type carburetor used on some models.

1. Idle speed screw
2. Spring
3. Screw
4. Pump cover
5. Gasket
6. Pump diaphragm
7. Screw
8. Throttle plate
9. "E" clip
10. Cable clamp
11. Throttle shaft
12. Spring
13. Spring
14. Low speed needle
15. Spring
16. High speed needle
17. Screen
18. Body
19. Clip
20. Screw
21. Fuel inlet needle
22. Spring
23. Pin
24. Fuel lever
25. Screw
26. Gasket
27. Gasket
28. Circuit plate
29. Screw
30. Gasket
31. Main diaphragm
32. Cover
33. Screw

MAINTENANCE

SPARK PLUG. Recommended spark plug for all models is a Champion CJ6, or equivalent. Specified electrode gap is 0.6-0.7 mm (0.024-0.028 in.).

CARBURETOR. Fuji engines may be equipped with a Walbro diaphragm type carburetor, a Walbro WZ variable venturi diaphragm type carburetor, a TK piston valve type diaphragm carburetor, a Teikei diaphragm type carburetor, a float type carburetor or a DPK carburetor. Refer to appropriate paragraph for model being serviced.

Walbro Diaphragm Carburetor. Initial setting of the Walbro diaphragm type carburetor is one turn out from a lightly seated position for both mixture needles.

Make final adjustments with engine at operating temperature and running. Trimmer line should be at recommended length. Operate trimmer engine at full throttle and turn high speed mixture needle (16-Fig. FI50) until engine begins to run smoothly as needle is turned in, then turn needle out 1/8 turn. Allow engine to idle and adjust idle mixture needle (14) until engine idles smoothly and will accelerate without hesitation. Adjust idle speed screw (1) so engine idles just below clutch engagement speed.

During servicing inspect fuel pump and metering diaphragms for pin holes, tears or other damage. Diaphragms should be flexible. Metal button must be tight on metering diaphragm. When assembling the carburetor, the metering diaphragm lever should be flush with floor of cavity as shown in Fig. FI51. If necessary, adjust by carefully bending diaphragm lever.

Walbro WZ Series Carburetor. Refer to Fig. FI52 for an exploded view of the Walbro WZ series carburetor. Initial setting for low speed adjustment screw (25) is at the middle of the five notches. Initial setting for the high speed mixture needle (42) is 1-1/2 turns open from a lightly seated position.

Final adjustment is made with string trimmer line at recommended length or blade assembly installed. Engine must be at operating temperature and running. Operate engine at full rpm and adjust high speed mixture needle to obtain approximately 11000 rpm. Release throttle and allow engine to idle. Adjust idle speed screw (30) to obtain 3000-3300 rpm. If idle rpm cannot be obtained at idle speed screw, turn low speed mixture screw one notch at a time to obtain 3000-3300 rpm. Turning low speed mixture screw counterclockwise richens fuel mixture and turning low speed mixture screw clockwise leans fuel mixture.

To disassemble Walbro WZ series carburetor, remove air filter cover (36), filter element (35), spring (34) and plate (33). Remove the four screws (1), metal

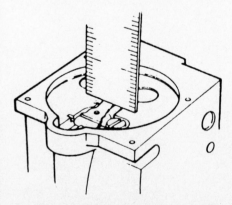

Fig. FI51—Metering valve lever should be flush with carburetor body.

Fig. FI52—Exploded view of Walbro WZ variable venturi carburetor used on some models.

1. Screw
2. Plate
3. Primer bulb
4. Screw
5. Cover
6. Gasket
7. Plate
8. Diaphragm
9. Gasket
10. Fuel inlet needle
11. Spring
12. Fuel inlet lever
13. Pin
14. Gasket
15. Diaphragm
16. Cover
17. Screw
18. Bracket
19. Screw
20. Bolt
21. Nut
22. Gasket
23. Body
24. Throttle valve assy.
25. Low speed mixture needle
26. Throttle cable swivel
27. Screw
28. Bracket
29. Spring
30. Idle speed screw
31. "E" ring
32. Metal sleeve support
33. Plate
34. Spring
35. Air filter
36. Cover
37. Wick
38. Gasket
39. Plate
40. Cap
41. Sleeve
42. High speed mixture needle
43. Spring

plate (2) and primer bulb (3). Remove screw (4), then separate pump cover (5), gasket (6), plate (7), pump diaphragm (8) and gasket (9) from carburetor body (23). Remove fuel strainer screen from port (44) in carburetor body. Remove the four screws (17), cover (16), diaphragm (15) and gasket (14). Use a small screwdriver to "pop" pin (13) from plastic retainers, then remove pin, fuel inlet lever (12), fuel needle (10) and spring (11). Remove high speed mixture needle (42) and spring (43). Remove metal sleeve (41) and pull throttle barrel assembly (24) from body as required. Do not disassemble throttle barrel. Clear plastic end cap (40) is bonded to the plastic carburetor body at the factory and should not be removed.

Clean carburetor in a cleaning solution approved for the all plastic body of the carburetor. Inspect all parts for wear or damage. Tip of fuel inlet needle

should be smooth and free of grooves. Fuel inlet lever spring (11) free length should be 8.7 mm (0.34 in.). When reassembling carburetor, fuel inlet lever (12) should be adjusted to obtain 1.65 mm (0.059 in.) between carburetor body surface and top of lever as shown (D-Fig. FI53).

TK Series Carburetor. Refer to Fig. FI54 for an exploded view of the TK

diaphragm type carburetor. Initial setting for the low speed mixture needle (18) is 3/4 turn open from a lightly seated position. Initial setting for the high speed mixture needle (21) is 2 turns open from a lightly seated position.

Final adjustments are made with trimmer head line at recommended length or blade assembly installed. Engine should be at operating temperature and running. Idle speed screw (17) should be adjusted to obtain 2500-3000 engine rpm. Trimmer head or blade should not rotate at this speed. Adjust low speed mixture needle to obtain maximum rpm at idle, then turn needle to richen mixture slightly. Readjust idle speed screw (17) to obtain 2500-3000 engine rpm at idle. Operate engine at full throttle and adjust high speed mixture needle to obtain maximum engine rpm, then turn needle counterclockwise 1/6 turn to richen fuel mixture slightly.

To disassemble carburetor, unscrew cap (13) and remove throttle valve assembly. Remove carburetor from engine. Remove fuel pump retaining screws (39) and separate pump cover (38), diaphragm (37) and gasket (36) from pump plate (35). Remove sealing rings (34). Remove the four metering cover screws (33). Remove metering cover (32), diaphragm (31) and gasket (30). Remove screw (29), pin (28), fuel inlet lever (27), fuel inlet needle (26) and spring (25). Remove low speed mixture needle (18) and high speed mixture needle (21).

Fig. FI54—Exploded view of TK diaphragm type carburetor used on some models.

1. Air filter cover
2. Gasket
3. Screen
4. Bracket
5. Filter
6. Screen
7. Housing
8. Throttle valve
9. Fuel needle
10. Clip
11. Spring seat
12. Spring
13. Cap
14. Nut
15. Throttle cable adjuster
16. Spring
17. Idle speed screw
18. Low speed mixture needle
19. Spring
20. Spring
21. High speed mixture needle
22. "O" ring
23. Tube
24. Body
25. Spring
26. Fuel inlet needle
27. Fuel inlet lever
28. Pin
29. Screw
30. Gasket
31. Diaphragm
32. Cover
33. Screw
34. Sealing rings
35. Fuel pump plate
36. Gasket
37. Diaphragm
38. Fuel pump cover
39. Screws
40. Stud
41. Choke lever
42. Choke plate
43. Washer
44. Nut

Fig. FI53—View showing correct method for measuring dimension (D). Refer to text.

1. Fuel inlet lever
2. Fuel inlet needle
3. Spring
4. Carburetor body

131

Clean and inspect all parts for wear or damage. Inspect fuel inlet needle and renew if needle tip is worn, grooved or damaged. Fuel inlet lever spring (25) should have a free length of 9.5 mm (0.35 in.). Diaphragms should be soft and flexible. Install fuel inlet lever (27) and carefully bend lever to obtain 2.1 mm (0.08 in.) distance (D-Fig. FI53) between carburetor body surface and fuel inlet lever. Clip (10-Fig. FI54)

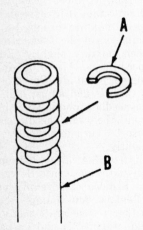

Fig. FI55—Fuel needle clip should usually be installed in the center groove.

should be installed in middle groove of fuel needle (Fig. FI55). Installing the clip in a lower groove richens the fuel mixture during transition from idle to high speed.

Teikei Diaphragm Type Carburetor. Refer to Fig. FI56 for an exploded view of the Teikei diaphragm type carburetor. Initial adjustment of fuel mixture needles from a lightly seated position is 1-1/4 turns open for low speed mixture needle (29) and 3/4 turn open for high speed mixture needle (28).

Final adjustments are made with trimmer line at recommended length or blade assembly installed. Engine must be at operating temperature and running. Operate trimmer engine at full throttle and adjust high speed mixture needle to obtain 9000 rpm. If an accurate tachometer is not available, do not adjust high speed mixture needle beyond initial setting. Operate trimmer engine at idle speed and adjust low speed mixture needle until a smooth idle is obtained and engine does not hesitate during acceleration. Adjust idle speed screw (1) until engine idles at just below clutch engagement speed.

To disassemble carburetor, remove the two screws (3) and separate cover (4) from carburetor body. Remove gasket (5) and pump diaphragm (6). Remove the four screws and separate metering diaphragm cover (21) from car-

buretor body. Remove diaphragm (19) and gasket (13). Remove screw (17), pin (18), fuel inlet lever (16), fuel inlet needle (14) and spring (15). Remove fuel mixture screws and springs.

Clean and inspect all parts. Diaphragms must not be torn or wrinkled. Inspect tip of fuel inlet needle. Renew needle if tip is grooved or damaged. Fuel lever (16) must be 2.0 mm (0.08 in.) from carburetor body as shown (D–Fig. FI53).

Float Type Carburetor. Refer to Fig. FI58 for an exploded view of the float type carburetor used on some models. Standard adjustment of pilot air screw (8) is one turn open from a lightly seated position.

Fuel needle clip (5) should be installed in the second groove (B-Fig. FI59) for EC02 models or in the third groove (C) for EC03 and EC04 models.

Float level should be 3.5 mm (0.138 in.) (D-Fig. FI60) from gasket surface at fuel inlet needle side and 3 mm (0.118 in.) from gasket surface at opposite side of float.

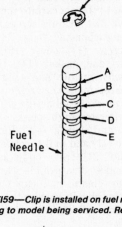

Fig. FI59—Clip is installed on fuel needle according to model being serviced. Refer to text.

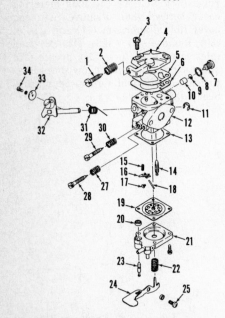

Fig. FI56—Exploded view of Teikei diaphragm type carburetor used on some models.

1. Idle speed screw
2. Spring
3. Screw
4. Pump cover
5. Gasket
6. Diaphragm
7. Plug
8. "O" ring
9. Screen
10. Felt
11. "E" ring
12. Body
13. Gasket
14. Fuel inlet needle
15. Spring
16. Fuel inlet lever
17. Screw
18. Pin
19. Diaphragm
20. Seat
21. Cover
22. Spring
23. Plunger
24. Primer lever
25. Screw
27. Spring
28. High speed mixture needle
29. Low speed mixture needle
30. Spring
31. Spring
32. Throttle shaft
33. Throttle plate
34. Screw

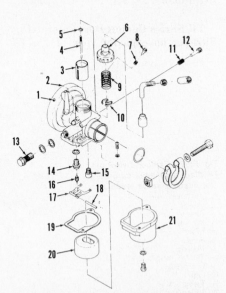

Fig. FI58—Exploded view of float type carburetor used on some models. Fitting (13) on some models may be equipped with a fuel shut-off valve.

1. Choke lever
2. Body
3. Throttle valve
4. Fuel needle
5. Clip
6. Cap
7. Spring
8. Air screw
9. Spring
10. Spring seat
11. Spring
12. Idle speed screw
13. Fitting
14. Fuel inlet needle seat
15. Main jet
16. Fuel inlet needle
17. Float lever
18. Pin
19. Gasket
20. Float
21. Float bowl

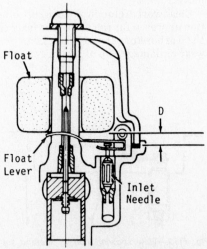

Fig. FI60—Float level should be measured as shown. Refer to text for specification for (D).

DPK Series Carburetor. Initial setting of the main fuel mixture needle (15-Fig. FI61) is 1-1/2 turns out from a lightly seated position. Make final adjustments with trimmer line at proper length or blade assembly installed and engine at operating temperature and running. Operate engine at wide open throttle and turn main fuel mixture needle until engine begins to run smoothly as needle is turned IN, then back out needle 1/8 turn. Normal range of adjustment is 1-2 turns out from a lightly seated position. Adjust idle speed screw so engine idles just below clutch engagement speed. Midrange mixture is determined by the position of clip (7) on jet needle (8). There are three grooves located at the upper end of the jet needle (Fig. FI55) and normal position of clip (7-Fig. FI61) is in the middle groove. The mixture will be leaner if clip is installed in the top groove or richer if clip is installed in the bottom groove.

DPK carburetor is equipped with an integral fuel pump (16, 17 and 18). During servicing inspect fuel pump and metering diaphragms for pin holes, tears or other damage. Diaphragms should be flexible. Metal button must be tight on metering diaphragm. When assembling the carburetor the metering diaphragm lever should be 2.1-2.4 mm (0.08-0.09 in.) below the carburetor body (Fig. FI53).

IGNITION SYSTEM. Fuji engines may be equipped with breaker point type ignition or electronic ignition system. Refer to appropriate paragraphs for models being serviced.

Breaker Point Type Ignition. Ignition condenser and contact set are located behind the flywheel. To adjust, remove flywheel and rotate crankshaft so that contact set is at widest open position. Adjust gap to 0.35 mm (0.014 in.).

Timing should be set at 26° BTDC on EC01 engine or 25° BTDC on EC02 engine. To check timing, rotate flywheel until the "F" mark cast on flywheel surface aligns with setting mark on crankcase (Fig. FI63). Carefully remove flywheel and make certain contact set is just beginning to open. Air gap between flywheel and ignition coil should be 0.5 mm (0.020 in.) for EC01 and EC02 engines or 0.2 mm (0.008 in.) for EC03 and EC04 engines.

Transistorized Ignition System. Transistorized ignition system is operating satisfactorily if spark will jump across the 3 mm (1/8 in.) gap of a test spark plug. If no spark is produced, check on/off switch and wiring. If switch and wiring are determined to be satisfactory, renew ignition module. Air gap between ignition module and flywheel should be 0.02 mm (0.008 in.).

LUBRICATION. All models are lubricated by mixing a good quality two-stroke air-cooled engine oil with gasoline. Refer to TRIMMER SERVICE section for correct fuel/oil mixture ratio recommended by trimmer manufacturer.

REPAIRS

TIGHTENING TORQUES. Recommended tightening torque specifications are as follows:

Clutch:
EC01 & EC02 . . . . .5-6 N·m
(47.6-56.3 in.-lbs.)
EC03 & EC04 . . . . 18-22 N·m
(156.0-197.0 in.-lbs.)

Crankcase:
EC01 & EC02 . . . . .3-4 N·m
(36.4-41.6 in.-lbs.)
EC03 & EC04 . . . . .4-7 N·m
(43.3-60.7 in.-lbs.)

Cylinder:
EC01 & EC02 . . . . .3-4 N·m
(36.4-41.6 in.-lbs.)
EC03 & EC04 . . . . 9-11 N·m
(78.0-95.3 in.-lbs.)

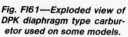
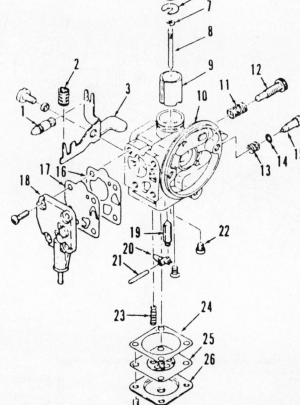

Fig. FI61—Exploded view of DPK diaphragm type carburetor used on some models.

1. Primer valve
2. Spring
3. Lever
4. Cap
5. Spring
6. Retainer
7. Clip
8. Jet needle
9. Throttle slide
10. Body
11. Spring
12. Idle speed screw
13. Spring
14. "O" ring
15. Main fuel mixture needle
16. Pump gasket
17. Pump diaphragm
18. Pump cover
19. Inlet needle valve
20. Metering lever
21. Pin
22. Jet
23. Spring
24. Gasket
25. Diaphragm
26. Cover

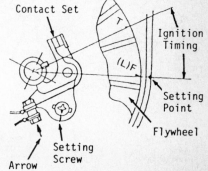

Fig. FI63—View showing location of timing mark on flywheel and crankcase. Refer to text.

Fig. FI64—Exploded view of ECO1 engine. ECO2 engine is similar.

1. Housing
2. Rewind spring
3. Pulley
4. Spring
5. Ratchet
6. Brake spring
7. Plate
8. Bolt
9. Nut
10. Flywheel
11. Ignition module
12. Seal
13. Crankcase half
14. Gasket
15. Bearing
16. Key
17. Crankshaft/connecting rod assy.
18. Bearing
19. Crankcase half
20. Seal
21. Bearing
22. Retainer
23. Piston pin
24. Piston
25. Rings
26. Cylinder
27. Gasket

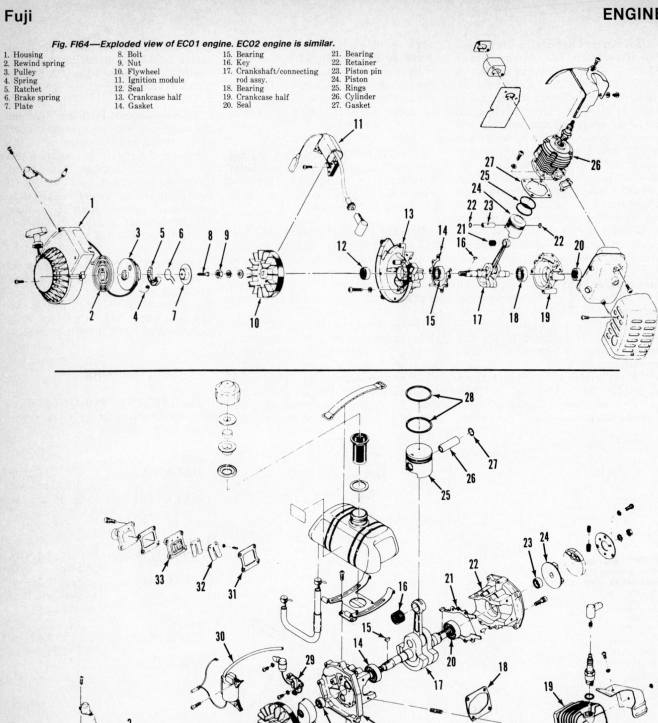

Fig. FI65—Exploded view of ECO4 engine. ECO3 engine is similar.

1. Housing
2. Rewind spring
3. Pulley
4. Spring
5. Ratchet
6. Brake spring
7. Plate
8. Bolt
9. Nut
10. Flywheel
11. Cover
12. Seal
13. Crankcase half
14. Bearing
15. Key
16. Bearing
17. Crankshaft/connecting rod assy.
18. Gasket
19. Cylinder
20. Bearing
21. Gasket
22. Crankcase half
23. Seal
24. Retainer
25. Piston
26. Piston pin
27. Retainer
28. Rings
29. Points & condenser
30. Ignition coil
31. Gasket
32. Reed
33. Reed plate

Flywheel:
EC01 . . . . 12-13 N·m
(104.0-121.3 in.-lbs.)
EC02 . . . . 13-15 N·m
(121.3-138.7 in.-lbs.)
EC03 & EC04 . . . . . . 14-18 N·m
(130.0-156.0 in.-lbs.)

Spark plug:
EC01 . . . . 14-19 N·m
(130.0-173.4 in.-lbs.)
EC02 . . . . 22-29 N·m
(190.7-260.1 in.-lbs.)
EC03 & EC04 . . . . . . 14-24 N·m
(130.0-216.7 in.-lbs.)

CRANKSHAFT AND CONNECTING ROD. Refer to FI64 for an exploded view of the EC01 engine which is typical of EC01 and EC02 engines or to Fig. FI65 for an exploded view of the EC04 engine which is typical of the EC03 and EC04 engines.

To disassemble engine, remove fuel tank, muffler cover and muffler. Remove rewind starter and cooling shroud. Remove carburetor, flywheel assembly and clutch. Carefully separate cylinder from crankcase and piston. Remove bolts retaining crankcase halves and separate crankcase. Remove piston pin retaining rings and remove piston. Press main bearings off crankshaft as required. If main bearings remain in crankcase halves, heat crankcase slightly to remove bearings.

Inspect all parts for wear or damage. Crankshaft and connecting rod are serviced as an assembly only. Do not remove connecting rod from crankshaft.

PISTON, PIN AND RINGS. To remove piston from all models, remove cooling shroud and recoil starter assembly. Remove carburetor and muffler. Remove all bolts retaining cylinder to crankcase and carefully work cylinder away from crankcase and piston. Remove piston pin retaining rings and press pin out of piston pin bore. Piston may now be removed. Remove bearing from connecting rod piston pin bearing bore.

When installing piston on connecting rod, "M" stamped on top of piston must be toward the larger crankcase side and piston pin must move smoothly in piston pin bearing installed in connecting rod.

Standard piston diameter is 28.0 mm (1.102 in.) for EC01 engine, 31.99 mm (1.221 in.) for EC02 engine, 35.96 mm (1.378 in.) for EC03 engine and 39.94 mm (1.536 in.) for EC04 engine. If piston measures 0.05 mm (0.002 in.) less than standard, renew piston.

If piston ring end gap exceeds 0.4 mm (0.016 in.) for EC01 engine, 0.6 mm (0.024 in.) for EC02 engine, 0.8 mm (0.031 in.) for EC03 engine or 1.0 mm (0.039 in.) for EC04 engine, renew rings and/or cylinder.

If piston ring side clearance exceeds 0.15 mm (0.006 in.), renew rings and/or piston.

Standard piston pin bore diameter in piston is 8.0 mm (0.315 in.) for EC01 and EC02 engine, 10.0 mm (0.394 in.) for EC03 engine or 12.0 mm (0.472 in.) for EC04 engine. If piston pin bore exceeds standard diameter by 0.02 mm (0.0008 in.) for EC01 and EC02 engine or 0.03 mm (0.0012 in.) for all other models, renew piston.

Standard piston pin diameter is 8.0 mm (0.315 in.) for EC01 and EC02 engines, 10.0 mm (0.394 in.) for EC03 engine or 12.0 mm (0.472 in.) for EC04 engine. Renew pin if diameter is 0.01 mm (0.0004 in.) less than standard for EC01 and EC02 engines, 0.014 mm (0.0006 in.) for EC03 engine or 0.017 mm (0.0007 in.) for EC04 engine.

CYLINDER. Cylinder may be unbolted and removed from crankcase after shroud, muffler, carburetor and starter housing are removed.

Renew cylinder if cylinder is scored, cracked or if piston to cylinder clearance with new piston installed exceeds 0.08 mm (0.003 in.) for EC01 engine, 0.12 mm (0.005 in.) for EC02 engine or 0.18 mm (0.007 in.) for EC03 and EC04 engines.

HOMELITE

ENGINE SERVICE

Model	Bore	Stroke	Displacement
ST-80, ST-100, ST-120, ST-160, ST-160A, ST-165, ST-180, ST-260	1-5/16 in. (33.34 mm)	1-3/16 in. (30.16 mm)	1.6 cu. in. (26.2 cc)
ST-200, ST-210, ST-310	1-7/16 in. (36.51 mm)	1-3/16 in. (30.16 mm)	1.9 cu. in. (31.2 cc)

ENGINE INFORMATION

These engines are used on Models ST-80, ST-100, ST-120, ST-160, ST-160A, ST-165, ST-180, ST-200, ST-210, ST-260 and ST-310 String Trimmers and Brushcutters.

MAINTENANCE

SPARK PLUG. Recommended spark plug is a Champion DJ7Y for Models ST-160, ST-180, ST-260 and ST-310. Champion DJ7J is recommended for all other models. Spark plug electrode gap should be 0.025 inch (0.6 mm).

CARBURETOR. Refer to the following table for carburetor applications:

Model	Carburetor
ST-80	Walbro WA-83
ST-100	Zama C1S-46
	Walbro WA-130
ST-120	Walbro WA-43A
	Zama C1S-H2A
ST-160	Walbro HDC-70
ST-160A, ST-165	Walbro HDC-75
	Zama C2S-H9
ST-180	Walbro HDC-70
ST-200	Walbro HDC-59
	Walbro HDC-69
ST-210	Walbro HDC-69
ST-260, ST-310	Walbro HDC-80

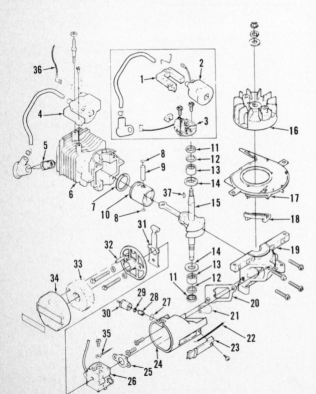

Fig. HL40-2—Exploded view of engine used on Models ST-80, ST-100 and ST-120. Early Model ST-100 trimmers are equipped with breaker point ignition shown in inset.

1. Coil core
2. Ignition coil
3. Breaker point assy.
4. Ignition module
5. Spark plug
6. Cylinder
7. Piston ring
8. Circlip
9. Piston pin
10. Piston
11. Seal
12. Seal spacer
13. Needle bearing
14. Thrust washer
15. Crankshaft
16. Flywheel
17. Air cover
18. Seal
19. Crankcase
20. Gasket
21. Reed valve petal
22. Throttle cable
23. Cable clamp
24. Carburetor housing
25. Gasket
26. Carburetor
27. "O" ring
28. Filter
29. Gasket
30. Fuel inlet
31. Choke
32. Filter support
33. Air filter
34. Cover
35. Ground wire (early ST-100)
36. Ground wire (solid state ign.)
37. Key

Walbro HDC-70 carburetor is equipped with an accelerator pump which uses a bladder to eject additional fuel through the main fuel orifice when needed.

Adjustment. UNIT MUST BE SHUT OFF when making adjustments and throttle cable must move freely. String on trimmer models must be extended to maximum recommended length. Initial setting of idle mixture needle is 1½ turns open. Initial setting of high speed mixture on models so equipped is ¾ turns open.

Adjust idle mixture needle so engine idles at highest speed and accelerates cleanly. Turn idle mixture needle 1/8 turn each time after checking unit operation then stopping trimmer engine. Adjust idle speed screw so engine idles at 2800-3200 rpm on Models ST-80, ST-100, ST-120, ST-160, ST-160A, ST-165, ST-180 and ST-260, or below clutch engagement speed on Models ST-200, ST-210 and ST-310. Check high speed mixture if adjustable.

Some models are equipped with a high speed mixture needle. On all other models the high speed mixture is calibrated at the factory and is not adjustable. With engine warm, adjust high speed mixture needle so engine fluctuates between two-stroke and four-stroke operation. Recheck idle adjustment.

MAGNETO AND TIMING. Early Model ST-100 is equipped with a conventional breaker-point, flywheel magneto. Breaker point gap should be 0.015 inch (0.038 mm). Ignition timing is not adjustable, however, an incorrect breaker point gap setting will affect ignition timing.

A solid-state ignition is used on all models except early ST-100 models. The ignition module is attached to the side of the engine cylinder. Ignition service is accomplished by replacing ignition com-

Illustrations Courtesy Homelite Div. of Textron, ©1987

ponents until faulty part is located. Air gap between ignition module and flywheel is adjustable and should be 0.015 inch (0.38 mm). Loosen ignition module mounting screws and adjust module position to set air gap.

LUBRICATION. The engine is lubricated by mixing oil with regular gasoline. Recommended oil is Homelite two-stroke oil mixed at ratio as designated on oil container. If Homelite oil is not available, a good quality oil designed for two-stroke engines may be used when mixed at a 16:1 ratio, however, an antioxidant fuel stabilizer (such as Sta-Bil) should be added to fuel mix. Antioxidant fuel stabilizer is not required with Homelite® oils as they contain fuel stabilizer so the fuel mix will stay fresh up to one year.

MUFFLER. Outer screen of muffler should be cleaned of debris every week or as required. Carbon should be removed from muffler and engine ports to prevent excessive carbon buildup and power loss. Do not allow loose carbon to enter cylinder and be careful not to damage exhaust port or piston.

REPAIRS

TIGHTENING TORQUE VALUES. Tightening torque values are listed in following table. Note: Values given are average figures in inch-pounds (in.-lbs. x 0.113 = N·m). To obtain minimum or maximum values, reduce or increase given values by 10 percent.

Flywheel	100
Clutch hub	100
Spark plug	150
Crankcase screws—socket head	35
Starter pulley screw	40-50

COMPRESSION PRESSURE. For optimum performance of all models, cylinder compression pressure should be 115-145 psi (792-1000 kPa) with engine at normal operating temperature. Engine should be inspected and repaired when compression pressure is 90 psi (621 kPa) or below.

CYLINDER, PISTON, PIN AND RINGS. Cylinder may be removed after unscrewing four screws in bottom of crankcase (19—Fig. HL40-2 or HL40-3). Be careful when removing cylinder as crankshaft assembly will be loose in crankcase. Care should be taken not to damage mating surfaces of cylinder and crankcase.

Inspect crankshaft bearings and renew if scored or worn. Thrust washers (14) should be installed with shoulder to outside. Crankshaft seals are installed with seal lip to inside. Cylinder and crankcase

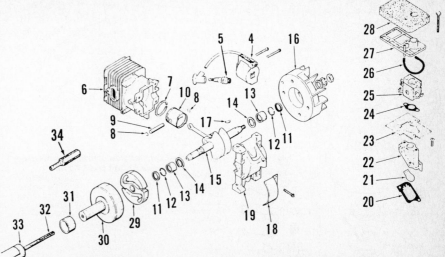

Fig. HL40-3—Exploded view of engine used on Models ST-160, ST-180, ST-200 and ST-210; adapter (34) is used in place of clutch components (29, 30 and 31) on Models ST-160 and ST-180.

4. Ignition module	11. Seal	18. Shroud	25. Carburetor
5. Spark plug	12. Seal spacer	19. Crankcase	26. Tubing
6. Cylinder	13. Needle bearing	20. Gasket	27. Filter support
7. Piston ring	14. Thrust washer	21. Reed valve petal	28. Air filter
8. Circlip	15. Crankshaft	22. Carburetor spacer	29. Clutch hub
9. Piston pin	16. Flywheel	23. Air baffle	30. Clutch drum
10. Piston	17. Key	24. Gasket	31. Bushing
			32. Drive shaft
			33. Drive tube
			34. Adapter

mating surfaces should be flat and free of nicks and scratches. Mating surfaces should be cleaned then coated with room temperature vulcanizing (RTV) silicone sealer before assembly.

Early model cylinders are equipped with an open exhaust port while a bridged exhaust port is used on late model cylinders. Early model piston is equipped with a piston ring locating pin in the piston ring groove. Piston ring installed on early model piston must be positioned so end gap indexes with locating pin in ring groove. Late model piston does not have piston ring locating pin and piston ring should be installed so end gap is opposite exhaust port.

Bearings, seals and thrust washers must be positioned correctly on crankshaft before final assembly. Use the following procedure for crankshaft installation: With piston assembly installed on rod, insert piston in cylinder being sure piston ring is aligned on locating pin on early models, or ring gap is opposite exhaust port on late models. Install thrust washers (14), bearings (13), seal spacers (12) and seals (11) on crankshaft. Place 0.0125 inch thick shims shown in Fig. HL40-5 between thrust washers and bearings as shown in Fig. HL40-6. Gently push seals toward crankshaft counterweights until assemblies are snug. Remove shims and complete assembly being careful not to disturb position of thrust washers, bearings and seals.

REED VALVE. All models are equipped with a reed valve induction system. Renew reed petal (21—Fig. HL40-2 or HL40-3) if cracked, bent or otherwise damaged. Do not attempt to straighten

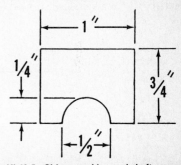

Fig. HL40-5—Shims used in crankshaft assembly may be made by cutting 0.0125 inch thick plastic, metal or other suitable material in the outline shown above. Refer to Fig. HL40-6 and text.

Fig. HL40-6—View showing placement of shims (Fig. HL40-5) between thrust washers (14—Fig. HL40-2, HL40-3 or HL40-4) and bearings (13) for correct crankshaft assembly. Refer to text.

a bent reed petal. Seating surface for reed petal should be flat, clean and smooth.

CLUTCH. Models ST-200 and ST-210 are equipped with a centrifugal clutch (29—Fig. HL40-3) which is accessible

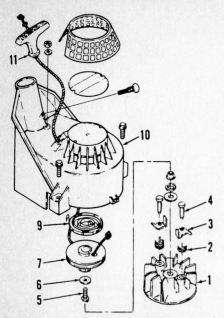

Fig. HL40-8—Exploded view of rewind starter used on Models ST-80, ST-100 and ST-120.

1. Flywheel	5. Screw
2. Spring	6. Washer
3. Pawl	7. Rope pulley
4. Pawl pin	9. Rewind spring
	10. Housing
	11. Rope handle

Fig. HL40-9—Exploded view of rewind starter used on Models ST-200 and ST-210.

1. Flywheel	7. Rope pulley
2. Spring	8. Nylon washer
3. Pawl	9. Rewind spring
4. Pawl pin	10. Housing
5. Screw	11. Rope handle
6. Washer	

after removing engine housing. Clutch hub (29) has left-hand threads. Inspect bushing (31) and renew if excessively worn. Install clutch hub (29) while noting "OUTSIDE" marked on side of hub.

REWIND STARTER. To service the rewind starter, proceed as follows:

Remove starter housing (10—Fig. HL40-8 or HL40-9). Pull starter rope and hold rope pulley with notch in pulley adjacent to rope outlet. Pull rope back through outlet so that it engages notch in pulley and allow pulley to completely unwind. Unscrew pulley retaining screw (5) and remove rope pulley being careful not to dislodge rewind spring in housing. Care must be taken if rewind spring is removed to prevent injury if spring is allowed to uncoil uncontrolled.

Rewind spring is wound in clockwise direction in starter housing. Rope is wound on rope pulley in clockwise direction as viewed with pulley in housing. To place tension on rewind spring, pass rope through rope outlet in housing and install rope handle. Pull rope out and hold rope pulley so notch on pulley is adjacent to rope outlet. Pull rope back through outlet between notch in pulley and housing. Turn rope pulley clockwise to place tension on spring. Release pulley and check starter action. Do not place more tension on rewind spring than is necessary to draw rope handle up against housing.

HOMELITE
ENGINE SERVICE

Model	Bore	Stroke	Displacement
ST-400	1¾ in. (44 mm)	1-1/8 in. (35 mm)	3.3 cu. in. (54 cc)

ENGINE INFORMATION

The 3.3 cu. in. (54 cc) displacement engine is used to power the ST-400 brushcutter.

MAINTENANCE

SPARK PLUG. Recommended spark plug is a Champion CJ6. Spark plug electrode gap should be 0.025 inch (0.6 mm).

CARBURETOR. Model ST-400 brushcutter is equipped with a Tillotson HS-207A carburetor.

To adjust carburetor, turn idle speed stop screw in until it just contacts throttle lever tab, then turn screw in ½-turn further. Turn idle and main fuel adjustment needles in gently until they just contact seats, then back each needle out one turn. With engine warm and running, adjust idle fuel needle so that engine runs smoothly, then adjust idle stop screw so that engine runs at 2600 rpm, or just below clutch engagement speed. Check engine acceleration and open idle fuel needle slightly if engine will not accelerate properly. Adjust main fuel needle under load so engine will neither slow down or smoke excessively.

GOVERNOR. The engine is equipped with an air-vane type governor; refer to Fig. HL43-1.

To adjust governor using vibrating reed or electronic tachometer, proceed as follows: With engine warm and running and throttle trigger released, adjust position of cable nuts (see Fig. HL43-1A) on remote control cable so that engine slow idle speed is 2500 rpm, or just below clutch engagement speed. Then when throttle trigger is fully depressed, engine no-load speed should be 6300 rpm. To adjust maximum governed no-load speed, loosen screw (14—Fig. HL43-1) and move speed adjusting plate (13) as required to obtain no-load speed of 6300 rpm. When adjusting maximum non-load speed, be sure that governor link (26) is reconnected at hole "A" in carburetor throttle shaft lever. Governor spring (12) is connected to third hole away from hole "A" (two open holes between link and spring). Be sure that governor linkage moves smoothly throughout range of travel.

MAGNETO AND TIMING. All engines are equipped with a solid-state ignition (Fig. HL43-4). Ignition service is accomplished by replacing ignition components until faulty part is located. Air gap between ignition module (3) and flywheel is adjustable and should be 0.015 inch (0.4 mm). Loosen ignition module mounting screws and adjust module position to set air gap.

LUBRICATION. The engine is lubricated by mixing oil with regular gasoline. Recommended oil is Homelite

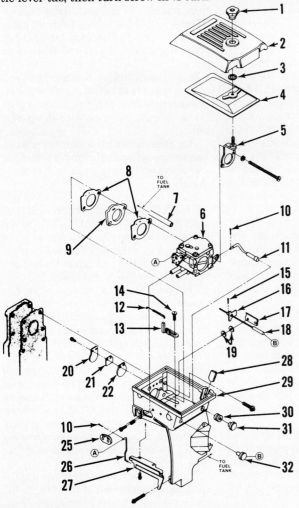

Fig. HL43-1—Exploded view of air box assembly on Model XL-12 engine.

1. Nut
2. Air filter cover
3. Retaining ring
4. Air filter element
5. Mounting bracket
6. Carburetor
7. Fuel line
8. Gasket
9. Spacer
10. Cotter pin
11. Choke rod
12. Governor spring
13. Adjusting plate
14. Screw
15. Cotter pin
16. Collar
17. Clamp
18. Throttle cable
19. Washers
20. Reed stop
21. Reed backup
22. Reed valve
25. Grommet
26. Governor link
27. Governor air vane
28. Felt plug
29. Air box
30. Grommet
31. Choke button
32. Throttle button

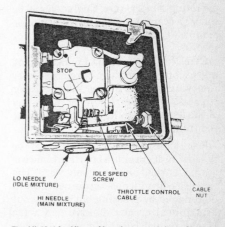

Fig. HL43-1A—View of brushcutter air box. Outside throttle cable nut is not shown.

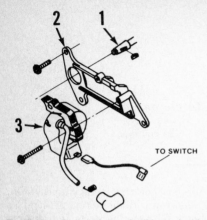

Fig. HL43-4—Exploded view of solid-state ignition.
1. Crankshaft
2. Stator plate
3. Ignition module

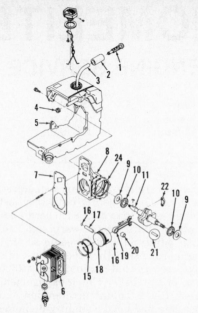

Fig. HL43-5—Exploded view of engine. Refer to Fig. HL43-5A for brushcutter drivecase.

1. Fuel pickup	11. Crankshaft
2. Fuel filter	15. Piston rings
3. Fuel line	16. Retaining ring
4. Grommet	17. Piston pin
5. Fuel tank	18. Piston
6. Cylinder	19. Connecting rod
7. Gasket	20. Needle bearing
8. Crankcase	21. Crankpin rollers (31)
9. Thrust washer	22. Rod cap
10. Thrust bearing	24. Gasket

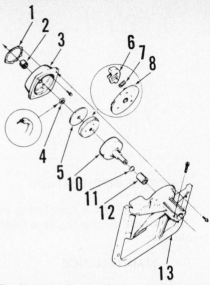

Fig. HL43-5A—Exploded view of ST-400 clutch assembly.

1. Gasket	5. Cover	10. Clutch drum
2. Bearing	6. Clutch shoe	11. Snap ring
3. Drivecase	7. Spring	12. Bearing
4. Seal	8. Clutch hub	13. Frame

two-stroke oil mixed at ratio as designated on oil container. If Homelite oil is not available, a good quality oil designed for two-stroke engines may be used when mixed at a 16:1 ratio, however, an anti-oxidant fuel stabilizer (such as Sta-Bil) should be added to fuel mix. Anti-oxidant fuel stabilizer is not required with Homelite® oils as they contain fuel stabilizer so the fuel mix will stay fresh up to one year.

CARBON. Muffler, manifold and cylinder exhaust ports should be cleaned periodically to prevent loss of power through carbon build up. Remove muffler and scrape free of carbon. With muffler or manifold removed, turn engine so that piston is at top dead center and carefully remove carbon from exhaust ports with a wooden scraper. Be careful not to damage chamfered edges of exhaust ports or to scratch piston. Do not run engine with muffler removed.

REPAIRS

COMPRESSION PRESSURE. For optimum performance, cylinder compression pressure should be 130-155 psi (896-1069 kPa) with engine at normal operating temperature. Engine should be inspected and repaired when compression is 90 psi (621 kPa) or below.

CONNECTING ROD. Connecting rod and piston assembly can be removed after removing cylinder from crankcase. Refer to Fig. HL43-5. Be careful not to lose any of the 31 needle rollers when detaching rod from crankpin.

Renew connecting rod if bent or twisted, or if crankpin bearing surface is scored, burned or excessively worn. The caged needle roller piston pin bearing can be renewed by pressing old bearing out and pressing new bearing in with Homelite tool No. 23756. Press on lettered end of bearing cage only.

It is recommended that the crankpin needle rollers be renewed as a set whenever engine is disassembled for service. When assembling connecting rod on crankshaft, stick 16 rollers in rod and 15 rollers in rod cap. Assemble rod to cap with match marks aligned, and with open end of piston pin towards flywheel side of engine. Wiggle the rod as cap retaining screws are being tightened to align the fractured mating surfaces of rod and cap.

PISTON, PIN AND RINGS. The piston is fitted with two pinned compression rings. Renew piston if scored, cracked or excessively worn, or if ring side clearance in top ring groove exceeds 0.0035 inch (0.09 mm).

Recommended piston ring end gap is 0.070-0.080 inch (1.8-2.0 mm); maximum allowable ring end gap is 0.085 inch (2.2 mm). Desired ring side clearance of groove is 0.002-0.003 inch (0.05-0.08 mm).

Piston, pin and rings are available in standard size only. Piston and pin are available in a matched set, and are not available separately.

Piston pin has one open and one closed end and may be retained in piston with snap rings or a Spirol pin. A wire retaining ring is used on exhaust side of piston on some models and should not be removed.

To remove piston pin remove the snap ring at intake side of piston. On piston with Spirol pin at exhaust side, drive pin from piston and rod with slotted driver (Homelite tool No. A-23949). On all other models, insert a 3/16-inch pin through snap ring at exhaust side and drive piston pin out.

When reassembling, be sure closed end of piston pin is to exhaust side of piston (away from piston pin ring locating pin). Install Truarc snap ring with sharp edge out.

The cylinder bore is chrome plated. Renew the cylinder if chrome plating is worn away exposing the softer base metal.

CRANKCASE, BEARING HOUSING AND SEALS. CAUTION: Do not lose crankcase screws. New screws of the same length must be installed in place of old screws. Refer to parts book if correct screw length is unknown.

The crankshaft is supported in two caged needle roller bearings and crankshaft end play is controlled by a roller bearing and hardened steel thrust washer at each end of the shaft. Refer to Fig. HL43-5.

The needle roller main bearings and crankshaft seals in crankcase and drivecase can be renewed using Homelite tools Nos. 23757 and 23758. Press bearings and seals from crankcase or bearing housing with large stepped end of tool No. 23757, pressing towards outside of either case.

To install new needle bearings, use the shouldered short end of tool No. 23757 and press bearings into bores from inner

Illustrations Courtesy Homelite Div. of Textron, ©1987

Fig. HL43-6—When installing flat reed valve, reed backup and reed stop, be sure reed is centered between two points indicated by black arrows.

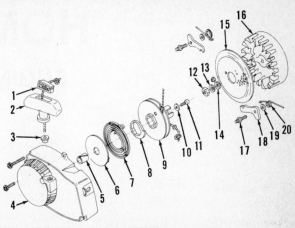

Fig. HL43-8—Exploded view of rewind starter.
1. Rope retainer
2. Handle
3. Bushing
4. Starter housing
5. Bushing
6. Washer
7. Rewind spring
8. Spring lock
9. Rope pulley
10. Washer
11. Screw
12. Nut
13. Lockwasher
14. Washer
15. Screen
16. Flywheel
17. Stud
18. Pawl
19. Washer
20. Spring

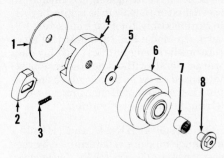

Fig. HL43-7—Exploded view of clutch used on saw engines.

1. Cover
2. Clutch shoe
3. Spring
4. Plate
5. Thrust washer
6. Clutch drum
7. Needle bearing
8. Nut

side of either case. Press on lettered end of bearing cage only.

To install new seals, first lubricate the seal and place seal on long end of tool No. 23758 so that lip of seal will be towards needle bearing as it is pressed into place.

To install crankshaft, lubricate thrust bearings (10) and place on shaft as shown. Place a hardened steel thrust washer to the outside of each thrust bearing. Insert crankshaft into crankcase being careful not to damage seal in crankcase. Place a seal protector sleeve (Homelite tool No. 23759) on crankshaft and gasket on shoulder of drivecase or pump housing. Lubricate seal protector sleeve, seal and needle bearing and mate drivecase or pump housing to crankshaft and crankcase. Use **NEW** retaining screws. Clean the screw threads and apply Loctite to threads before installing screws. Be sure the screws are correct length; screw length is critical. Tighten the screws alternately and remove seal protector sleeve from crankshaft.

CLUTCH. To service clutch on ST-400 models, unscrew cap screws securing frame (13—Fig. HL43-5A) to drivecase (3) and separate brushcutting unit from engine. Remove snap ring (11) and clutch drum (10). Rotate clutch hub in counterclockwise direction to remove clutch assembly. Inspect clutch components and renew any which are damaged or excessively worn.

REWIND STARTER. To disassemble starter, refer to exploded view in Fig. HL43-8 and proceed as follows: Pull starter rope out fully, hold pulley (9) and place rope in notch of pulley. Let pulley rewind slowly. Hold pulley while removing screw (11) and washer (10). Turn pulley counterclockwise until disengaged from spring, then carefully lift pulley off starter post. Turn open side of housing down and rap housing sharply against top of work bench to remove spring. CAUTION: Be careful not to dislodge spring when removing pulley as spring could cause injury if it should recoil rapidly.

Install new spring with loop in outer end over pin in blower housing and be sure spring is coiled in direction shown in Fig. HL43-8. Install pulley (9), turning pulley clockwise until it engages spring and secure with washer and screw. Insert new rope through handle and hole in blower housing. Knot both ends of the rope and harden the knots with cement. Turn pulley clockwise eight turns and slide knot in rope into slot and keyhole in pulley. Let starter pulley rewind slowly.

Starter pawl spring outer ends are hooked behind air vanes on flywheel in line with starter pawls when pawls are resting against flywheel nut. Pull starter rope slowly when installing blower housing so that starter cup will engage pawls.

HOMELITE

ENGINE SERVICE

Model	Bore	Stroke	Displacement
HK-18	1.14 in.	1.10 in.	1.12 cu. in
	(28.9 mm)	(27.9 mm)	(18.4 cc)
HK-24	1.26 in.	1.18 in.	1.47 cu. in.
	(32.0 mm)	(30.0 mm)	(24.1 cc)
HK-33	1.45 in.	1.22 in.	2.03 cu. in.
	(36.8 mm)	(30.9 mm)	(33.3 cc)

ENGINE INFORMATION

These engines are used as the power units for the Model HK-18, HK-24 and HK-33 Trimmer/Brushcutter.

MAINTENANCE

SPARK PLUG. Recommended spark plug is a Champion CJ8. Specified electrode gap is 0.025 inch (0.6 mm).

CARBURETOR. Initial setting for both mixture needles on Model HK-18 is one turn out from a lightly seated position. Initial setting of the high speed mixture needle on Models HK-24 and HK-33 is 1½ turns out from a lightly seated position. On all later models, the setting of the high speed mixture needle may be out as much as 2½ turns to obtain best performance.

After running engine so normal operating temperature is reached, run engine at wide open throttle (string must be at normal cutting length). Turn high speed mixture needle in so engine begins to run smoothly, then back out screw 1/8 turn. On Model HK-18, adjust idle mixture needle so engine idles smoothly and will accelerate without hesitation. Adjust idle speed screw on all models so engine idles just below clutch engagement speed (string head does not rotate).

On Models HK-24 and HK-33, midrange mixture is determined by the position of clip (7—Fig. HL45-1) on jet needle (8). There are three grooves located at the upper end of the jet needle (see Fig. HL45-2) and the normal position of clip (7) is in the middle groove. The mixture will be leaner if clip is installed in the top groove or richer if clip is installed in the bottom groove.

Model HK-18 is equipped with a Walbro WA series carburetor.

Models HK-24 and HK-33 are equipped with the slide-valve, diaphragm type carburetor shown in Fig. HL45-1. Carburetor is equipped with an integral fuel pump (16, 17 and 18). During servicing inspect fuel pump and metering diaphragms for pin holes, tears and other damage. Diaphragms should be flexible. Metal button must be tight on metering diaphragm. When assembling the carburetor note that the metering diaphragm lever should be flush with the

Fig. HL45-1—Exploded view of carburetor used on Models HK-24 and HK-33.

1. Tickler valve
2. Spring
3. Lever
4. Cap
5. Spring
6. Retainer
7. Clip
8. Jet needle
9. Throttle slide
10. Body
11. Spring
12. Idle speed screw
13. Spring
14. "O" ring
15. Main fuel mixture screw
16. Pump gasket
17. Pump diaphragm
18. Pump cover
19. Inlet needle valve
20. Metering lever
21. Pin
22. Jet
23. Spring
24. Gasket
25. Diaphragm
26. Cover

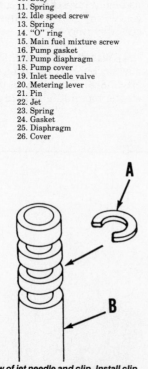

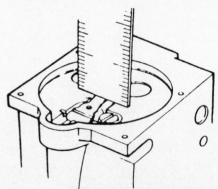

Fig. HL45-2—View of jet needle and clip. Install clip in middle groove for normal operation.

Fig. HL45-3—Adjust metering lever so lever just touches straightedge.

floor of cavity as shown in Fig. HL45-3. If necessary, adjust lever. Be sure retainer (6—Fig. HL45-1) is properly installed and secures jet needle and clip in throttle slide (9). Groove in side of throttle slide must engage pin in carburetor body when installing slide assembly.

IGNITION SYSTEM. All models use a transistorized ignition system consisting of a coil and an igniter. The flywheel-to-coil air gap is not adjustable.

The ignition system is operating satisfactorily if spark will jump across the 1/8 inch (3 mm) gap of a test spark plug (Homelite part JA-31316-4). If no spark is produced, check on/off switch and wiring.

The igniter may be tested with an ohmmeter as follows: Set ohmmeter to the R X 10K scale and connect the black ohmmeter lead to the igniter case and connect the red ohmmeter lead to the igniter lead tab. Ohmmeter needle should deflect from infinity to slightly more than zero ohms. Reverse the ohmmeter leads and the ohmmeter needle should again deflect from infinity to slightly more than zero ohms. The ohmmeter needle should not return all the way back to zero ohms after deflecting to infinity. Replace igniter if any faults are noted.

The coil may be tested wth an ohmmeter as follows: Set ohmmeter to the R X 1 scale and connect the red ohmmeter lead to the primary lead wire. Connect the black ohmmeter lead wire to the coil core. Specified resistance of the primary winding is 0.5 ohms for Model HK-18 and 0.6-0.7 ohms for Models HK-24 and HK-33. Connect the red ohmmeter lead to the spark plug wire and connect the black ohmmeter lead to the coil core. Specified resistance of the secondary coil winding is 0.97 ohms for Model HK-18 and 0.7-0.8 ohms for Models HK-24 and HK-33. Replace coil assembly if other test results are obtained.

REPAIRS

HOMELITE SPECIAL TOOLS. Special tools which will aid in servicing are as follows:

Tool No. and Description.
22828—Snap ring pliers.
JA-31316-4—Test spark plug.
94194—Compression gage.
94197—Carburetor tester.
17789—Carburetor repair tool kit.
94455—Alignment tool (for clutch drum removal).
A-98059—Flywheel puller.
98061-42—Tool kit (early models).
PR-24A—External snap ring pliers (Snap-On).
TM-30—Clutch head driver (Snap-On).

COMPRESSION PRESSURE. For optimum performance, compression pressure should be as follows with a hot engine and throttle and choke open. Crank engine until maximum pressure observed.

HK-18:
  Low . . . . .115 psi
      (793 kPa)
  High . . . . .145 psi
      (1000 kPa)
HK-24:
  Low . . . . .140 psi
      (965 kPa)
  High . . . . .170 psi
      (1172 kPa)
HK-33:
  Low . . . . .160 psi
      (1103 kPa)
  High . . . . .190 psi
      (1310 kPa)

A compression reading of 90 psi (620 kPa) or lower indicates a need for repairs.

TIGHTENING TORQUES. Engine tightening torques are listed below. All values are in inch-pounds (in.-lbs. x 0.113=N·m).
Air cleaner:
  HK-24 & HK-33 . . . . .14.5-17 in.-lbs.
Clutch pin to flywheel:
  HK-18 & HK-24 . . . . . .69-85 in.-lbs.
  HK-33 . . . . .120-137 in.-lbs.
Crankcase . . . . .30-34 in.-lbs.
Cylinder to crankcase:
  HK-24 & HK-33 . . . . . .30-34 in.-lbs.
Flywheel:
  HK-18 & HK-24 . . . . . .69-85 in.-lbs.
  HK-33 . . . . .120-137 in.-lbs.
Muffler . . . . .34-39 in.-lbs.
Rope pulley . . . . .120-137 in.-lbs.
Spark plug . . . . .103-146 in.-lbs.

CRANKSHAFT AND CONNECTING ROD. Refer to Figs. HL45-5 and HL45-6 for exploded views. Crankshaft is pressed together at connecting rod journal, therefore crankshaft and

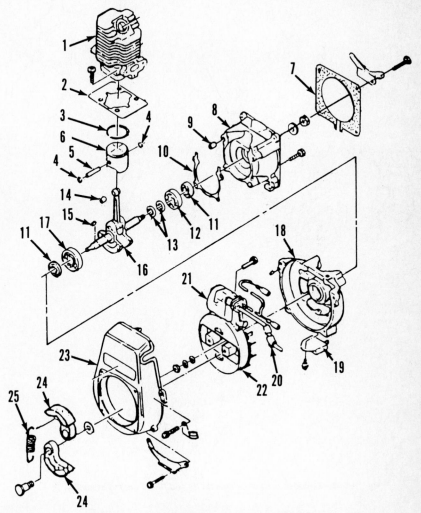

Fig. HL45-5—Exploded view of HK-18 engine assembly.

1. Cylinder	6. Piston	11. Seal	16. Crankshaft & rod assy	21. Coil
2. Gasket	7. Gasket	12. Bearing	17. Bearing	22. Flywheel
3. Ring	8. Crankcase	13. Shims	18. Crankcase	23. Shroud
4. Clip	9. Dowel pin	14. Bushing	19. Igniter	24. Clutch shoe
5. Piston pin	10. Gasket	15. Woodruff key	20. Tube	25. Clutch spring

connecting rod must be replaced as an assembly. Crankshaft is supported by ball bearings at both ends.

To remove crankshaft assembly, remove shroud and starter. On Model HK-18, unscrew starter pulley retaining nut and pry starter pulley off of crankshaft. On Models HK-24 and HK-33, the starter pulley is threaded onto crankshaft and is removed by unscrewing. On all models, remove flywheel, carburetor, muffler and cylinder. Split crankcase and remove crankshaft. Remove piston. Renew crankshaft assembly.

Inspect crankshaft assembly for damage and excessive wear. Be sure to inspect main bearings and roller bearing in small end of connecting rod.

Check crankshaft end play during reassembly. Crankshaft end play should be 0.002-0.010 inch (0.05-0.27 mm). Shims (13—Fig. HL45-5 or 21—Fig. HL45-6) are available in thicknesses of 0.004 inch (0.1 mm), 0.008 inch (0.2 mm), 0.016 inch (0.4 mm) and 0.024 inch (0.06 mm). To determine the correct shim pack thickness the following measurements must be taken: Magneto side of crankshaft half (dimension "A"); starter side of crankshaft half (dimension "B"); distance between outside edges of crankshaft counterweights (dimension "C"). Place a straightedge across gasket surface of magneto side of crankcase half. Measure the distance from the face of the outside bearing race to the bottom of the straightedge. This measurement is dimension "A". Place a straightedge across gasket surface of starter side of crankcase half. Measure the distance from the face of the outside bearing race to the bottom of the straightedge. This measurement is dimension "B". Using a vernier caliper, measure the distance between the machined surfaces of the crankshaft counterweights as shown in Fig. HL45-7. This measurement is dimension "C". Add dimensions "A" and "B", then deduct dimension "C". This will give the total thickness of the shim pack that will be needed. Refer to Table 1 for correct shim pack thickness. Shims must be installed on the starter side of crankshaft.

PISTON AND RINGS. Model HK-18 is equipped with one piston ring and Models HK-24 and HK-33 are equipped with two piston rings. Piston pin is retained in bore with two retaining rings.

Renew piston if scored, cracked, excessively worn or if side clearance in ring groove exceeds 0.027 inch (0.7 mm).

CYLINDER. Cylinder may be unbolted and removed from crankcase after shroud, muffler, carburetor and starter housing are removed.

Replace cylinder if scored, cracked or otherwise damaged. Use a crossing "X" pattern when retorquing cylinder retaining screws.

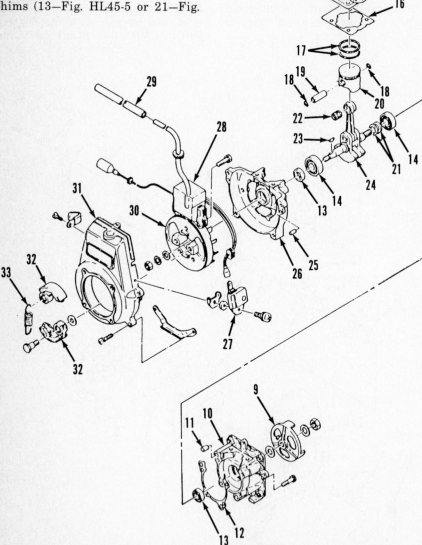

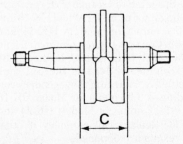

Fig. HL45-7—Measure distance (C) between machined surfaces of crankshaft counterweights to determine crankshaft end play.

Fig. HL45-6—Exploded view of Models HK-24 and HK-33 engine assembly.

9. Pulley	16. Gasket	23. Woodruff key
10. Crankcase	17. Rings	24. Crankshaft & rod
11. Dowel pin	18. Clips	assy.
12. Gasket	19. Piston pin	25. Dowel pin
13. Seal	20. Piston	26. Crankcase
14. Bearing	21. Shims	27. Igniter
15. Cylinder	22. Bushing	28. Coil
		29. Tube
		30. Flywheel
		31. Shroud
		32. Clutch shoe
		33. Clutch spring

Fig. HL45-8—Lobes on clutch shoes should be in position shown when assembling clutch.

CLUTCH. Install clutch shoes onto flywheel with the lobes positioned as shown in Fig. HL45-8. Clutch will not engage if shoes are installed backwards. Shoes and clutch drum should be inspected for excessive wear or damage and replaced if necessary.

RECOIL STARTER. Model HK-18. Refer to Fig. HL45-9 for an exploded view of starter assembly. To disassemble starter, remove starter assembly from engine. Pull rope 6 inches (15.2 cm) out of housing (8). Align notch in pulley (5) with rope hole in housing. While holding pulley and rope hole in alignment, pull slack rope back through rope hole in side housing. Hold rope in notch while slowly allowing pulley to unwind relieving spring (6) tension.

Remove the center screw and washer, then slowly lift pulley off center post of housing. Do not dislodge rewind spring. Use care if spring must be removed. Do not allow spring to uncoil uncontrolled.

Inspect rope and spring. Lubricate center post of housing with light grease prior to reassembly. Reassembly is reverse of disassembly procedure. Wind all but 6 inches (15.2 cm) of rope onto pulley before installing pulley in starter housing. Wrap rope around pulley in a counterclockwise direction as viewed from pawl side of pulley. Press down on pulley while turning to engage pulley with spring hook. Install retaining screw and washer. Three prewinds counterclockwise are required on the rewind spring. After assembly, check for rewind spring bottoming out. With rope pulled all the way out of starter, pulley should still rotate, counterclockwise. If pulley will not rotate any further with rope pulled out, then release one prewind from spring and recheck.

Models HK-24 and HK-33. Refer to Fig. HL45-10 for an exploded view of starter assembly. To disassemble starter, first remove starter assembly from engine. Slide rope guide (8) out of starter housing (10) and slip rope (6) into slot on pulley. Hold rope in notch while slowly allowing pulley to unwind, relieving spring (7) tension.

Remove the center screw, retainer (1), pawl (2) and springs (3 and 4). Slowly lift pulley off starter housing post while using a small screwdriver to release pulley from spring hook. Use care if spring must be removed. Do not allow spring to uncoil uncontrolled.

Inspect rope, pawl and springs for breakage and excessive wear and replace as needed. Lubricate center post of housing with light grease prior to reassembly. Reassembly is reverse of disassembly procedure. Install spring in a counterclockwise direction from outer end. Wind all but 6 inches (15.2 cm) of rope onto pulley before installing pulley in starter housing. Wrap rope around pulley in a counterclockwise direction as viewed from pawl side of pulley. Press down on pulley while turning to engage pulley with spring hook. Reinstall retaining screw, retainer, pawl, pawl spring and loop spring. Make sure loop spring is installed properly as shown in Fig. HL45-11. Three prewinds counterclockwise are required on the rewind spring. Recheck to be sure pulley rewinds completely when released.

CLEARANCE "0" (Inch)	CLEARANCE "0" (mm)	SHIM NO.
− .004" to − .001"	− 0.11 to + 0.03	NONE
+ .001" to + .005"	+ 0.03 to + 0.13"	.004"
+ .005" to + .009"	+ 0.13 to + 0.23	.008"
+ .009" to + .013"	+ 0.23 to + 0.33	.012"
+ .013" to + .017"	+ 0.33 to + 0.43	.016"
+ .017" to + .021"	+ 0.43 to + 0.53	.020"
+ .021" to + .025"	+ 0.53 to + 0.63	.024"

TABLE 1—Select shim to obtain specified end play.

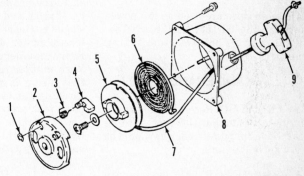

Fig. HL45-9—Exploded view of recoil starter used on Model HK-18.

1. "E" ring
2. Pulley
3. Spring
4. Pawl
5. Reel
6. Spring
7. Rope
8. Housing
9. Handle

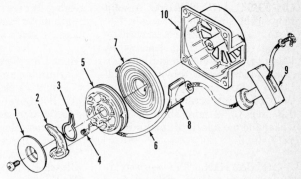

Fig. HL45-10—Exploded view of recoil starter used on Models HK-24 and HK-33.

1. Retainer
2. Pawl
3. Loop spring
4. Pawl spring
5. Pulley
6. Rope
7. Spring
8. Guide
9. Handle
10. Housing

Fig. HL45-11—Loop spring must be installed as shown.

Spring End

HOMELITE

ENGINE SERVICE

Model	Bore	Stroke	Displacement
ST-155	1-5/16 in.	1-1/8 in.	1.53 cu. in.
	(33.34 mm)	(28.84 mm)	(25 cc)
ST-175	1-5/16 in.	1-1/8 in.	1.53 cu. in.
	(33.34 mm)	(28.84 mm)	(25 cc)
ST-185	1-5/16 in.	1-1/8 in.	1.53 cu. in.
	(33.34 mm)	(28.84 mm)	(25 cc)
ST-285	1-5/16 in.	1-1/8 in.	1.53 cu. in.
	(33.34 mm)	(28.84 mm)	(25 cc)
ST-385	1-5/16 in.	1-1/8 in.	1.53 cu. in.
	(33.34 mm)	(28.84 mm)	(25 cc)

ENGINE INFORMATION

These engines are used as the power units for the ST-155, ST-175, ST-185, ST-285, and ST-385 Gasoline String Trimmers.

MAINTENANCE

SPARK PLUG. Recommended spark plug is a Champion DJ7Y or Autolite 2554. Spark plug electrode gap should be 0.025 inch (0.6 mm).

CARBURETOR. All models are equipped with either a Walbro or Zama fully adjustable diaphragm type carburetor with primer bulb.

MAGNETO AND TIMING. A solid state ignition is used on all models. The solid-state ignition system is serviced by renewing the spark plug, lead wires, and/or ignition module. Air gap between ignition module and flywheel is adjustable. Adjust air gap by loosening module retaining screws and place a 0.0125 inch (0.32 mm) shim between flywheel and module. Ignition timing is nonadjustable.

LUBRICATION. The engine is lubricated by mixing oil with unleaded gasoline. Recommended oil is Homelite two-stroke oil mixed at ratio as designated on oil container. If Homelite oil not available, a good quality oil designed for two-stroke engines may be used when mixed at a 16:1 ratio; however, an antioxidant fuel stabilizer (such as Sta-Bil) should be added to the fuel mix. Antioxidant fuel stabilizer is not required with Homelite® oils as they contain fuel stabilizer so the fuel mix will stay fresh up to one year.

MUFFLER. Spark screen in muffler should be cleaned or replaced periodically. Muffler and cylinder exhaust ports should be cleaned periodically to prevent loss of power due to carbon buildup. Remove muffler and scrape free of carbon. With muffler removed, turn engine so that piston is at top dead center and carefully remove carbon from exhaust ports with a wooden scraper. Be careful not to damage chamfered edges of exhaust ports or to scratch piston. DO NOT run engine with muffler removed.

REPAIRS

TIGHTENING TORQUE VALUES. Tightening torque values are listed in following table. Note: Values given are average figures in inch-pounds. To obtain minimum or maximum values, reduce or increase given values by 10 percent.

```
*Heat Dam Screws............40-50
*Carburetor and Air Box
    Mounting Screws...........30-40
Air Box Cover Screws........20-30
Muffler Screws..............40-50
*Crankcase Cover Screws.....40-50
*Cylinder Screws.............55-65
*Engine Housing Screws......40-50
Clutch Housing Screws.......40-50
*Module Mounting Screws.....30-40
Drive Connector...........100-150
Clutch Adapter Shaft......100-150
Starter Pulley Bracket Screw..30-40
Clutch....................80-100
Spark Plug...............120-180
```

*Requires Torx Driver Bit P/N 24982-02

COMPRESSION PRESSURE. For optimum performance of all models, cylinder compression pressure should be 95-105 GPSI with engine at normal operating temperature. Cold compression should be 100-110 GPSI.

RECOIL STARTER. To service the recoil starter, remove the engine housing from the powerhead. On Models ST-185 and ST-385 it will be necessary to first remove the tube adapter and clutch. See CLUTCH section for instructions regarding clutch disassembly.

Pull starter rope and hold rope pulley with notch in pulley adjacent to rope outlet. Pull rope back through outlet so that it engages notch in pulley and allow pulley to completely unwind. Unscrew pulley retaining screw and clamp. Remove rope pulley being careful not to dislodge rewind spring in housing. Care must be taken if rewind spring is removed to prevent injury if spring is allowed to uncoil uncontrolled.

Rewind spring is wound in clockwise direction in starter housing. Rope is wound on rope pulley in clockwise direction as viewed with pulley in housing. To place tension on rewind spring, pass rope through rope outlet in housing and install rope handle. Pull rope out and hold rope pulley so notch on pulley is adjacent to rope outlet. Pull rope back through outlet between notch in pulley and housing. Turn rope pulley clockwise to place tension on spring. Release pulley and check starter action. Do not place more tension on rewind spring than is necessary to draw rope handle up against housing. (2 to 3 prewinds)

CLUTCH. Models ST-185 and ST-385 are equipped with a double S-clutch. Remove tube adapter from engine housing to gain access to clutch. Remove one S-clutch at a time by turning counterclockwise. (R.H. thread) using spanner wrench A-93791. DO NOT attempt to remove both S-clutches together or damage to the clutch adapter shaft will occur.

CYLINDER, PISTON, PIN, RINGS.

The cylinder can be removed using the following procedure. Remove powerhead from engine housing. On Models ST-185 and ST-385 the tube adapter and clutch must first be removed. Refer to CLUTCH section for disassembly instructions.

Unless necessary, the muffler and carburetor need not be removed from the cylinder. Remove the shield and crankcase cover from the back of the crankcase. This will allow removal of the fuel tank giving access to the cylinder mounting screws. Remove the cylinder mounting screws and lift the cylinder from the crankcase. The cylinder has a chrome bore which should be inspected for excessive wear or damage.

Remove the piston and connecting rod assembly from the crankshaft crank pin. The piston, pin, connecting rod and caged needle bearings are serviced as a complete assembly only. Piston is equipped with a single piston ring. There is no piston ring locating pin in the land of the piston. When installing cylinder onto piston assembly, locate piston ring end gap towards the center of the exhaust port (away from the intake port).

CRANKSHAFT, CRANKCASE, AND SEALS.

To disassemble crankcase, remove the cylinder assembly as outlined in CYLINDER section. Remove the drive connector (ST-155, ST-175, ST-285) or clutch adapter (ST-185, ST-385) and flywheel.

All models use a half-crankshaft supported by two ball bearings. Remove the flywheel key and press the one-piece crankshaft through the two bearings into the crankcase. Inspect the crankshaft for damage or wear and replace as required.

Remove the outer (small) sealed ball bearing using a 9/16-inch (14 mm) rod. Insert the rod through the inner (large) ball bearing and main seal pressing on the inner race of the outer bearing. Remove the internal snap ring from the bearing bore. Press the main seal and inner bearing out of the crankcase. Inspect bearings and replace as required. Always install a new main seal when replacing main bearings. Service replacement crankcases are supplied with both main bearings, seal and retaining ring installed.

1. Tube adapter*
2. Connector & drum*
3. Clutch*
4. Flat washer*
5. Flat washer (1/8 in.)*
6. Engine housing
7. Spring & container
8. Starter pulley
9. Retaining bracket
10. Drive connector (ST-155, ST-175 & ST-385)
11. Flat washer (ST-155, ST-175 & ST-285)
12. Clutch adapter*
13. Rotor
14. Ignition module
15. Wire to stop switch
16. Ball bearing
17. Snap ring
18. Crankcase
19. Seal assy.
20. Ball bearing
21. Crankshaft
22. Piston & connecting rod
23. Piston ring
24. Gasket
25. Cylinder
26. Gasket
27. Cover
28. Shield
29. Heat dam & gasket
30. Carburetor
31. Air filter & housing
32. Stop switch (ST-155, ST-175 & ST-285)
33. Fuel tank & cap
34. Fuel filter
35. Muffler & gasket

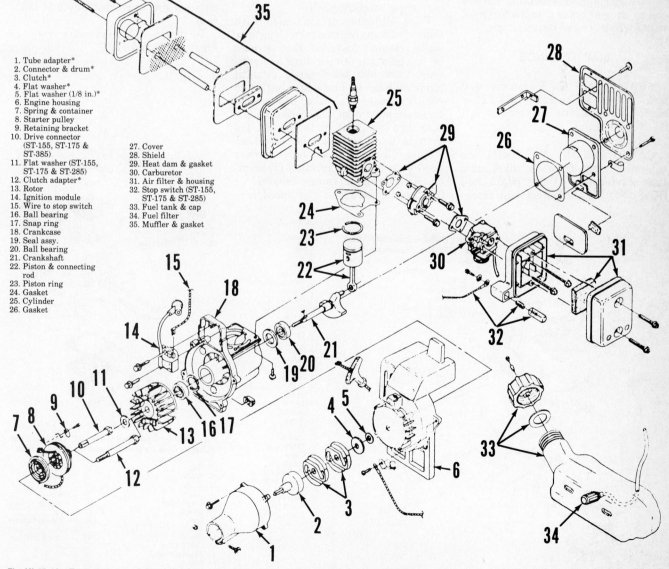

Fig. HL46-10—Exploded view of the engine assembly typical of the units used on Homelite ST-155, ST-175, ST-185, ST-285 and ST-385 string trimmers. Clutch parts marked with "*" are used on ST-185 models only.

HUSQVARNA
ENGINE SERVICE

Model	Bore	Stroke	Displacement
Husqvarna	36.0 mm (1.42 in.)	32.0 mm (1.26 in.)	36 cc (2.20 cu. in.)
Husqvarna	40.0 mm (1.57 in.)	32.0 mm (1.26 in.)	40 cc (2.44 cu. in.)
Husqvarna	42.0 mm (1.65 in.)	32.0 mm (1.26 in.)	44 cc (2.68 cu. in.)
Husqvarna	48.0 mm (1.89 in.)	36.0 mm (1.42 in.)	65 cc (3.96 cu. in.)

ENGINE INFORMATION

Husqvarna two-stroke air-cooled gasoline engines are used on Husqvarna string trimmers and brush cutters and by several other manufacturers of string trimmers and brush cutters.

MAINTENANCE

SPARK PLUG. Recommended spark plug is a Champion RCJ 7Y, or equivalent. Specified electrode gap is 0.5 mm (0.020 in.).

CARBURETOR. All models are equipped with Tillotson diaphragm type carburetor (Figs. HQ50 and HQ51). Service and adjustment procedure is similar for both carburetors.

Initial adjustment of fuel mixture needles from a lightly seated position is one turn open for the low speed mixture needle (24) and 3/4 turn open for the high speed mixture needle.

Final adjustments are made with trimmer line at recommended length or blade assembly installed. Engine must be at operating temperature and running. Turn idle speed screw in until trimmer head or blade just begins to rotate. Adjust low speed mixture needle to obtain maximum idle speed possible, then turn low speed mixture needle 1/6 turn in a counterclockwise direction. Adjust idle speed screw until trimmer head or blade stops rotating (approximately 2500 rpm). Operate trimmer at full throttle and adjust high speed mix-

ture needle to obtain maximum engine rpm, then turn high speed mixture needle 1/6 turn in a clockwise direction. Maximum engine rpm with trimmer blade or trimmer head installed and trimmer line at correct length is 12500 rpm.

To disassemble carburetor, refer to Figs. HQ50 and HQ51. If welch plugs

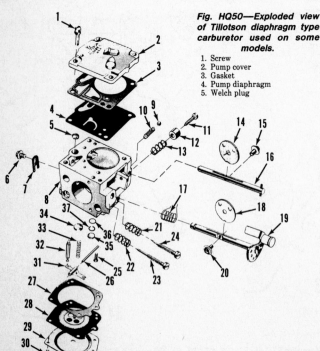

Fig. HQ50—Exploded view of Tillotson diaphragm type carburetor used on some models.

1. Screw
2. Pump cover
3. Gasket
4. Pump diaphragm
5. Welch plug
6. Screw
7. Clip
8. Body
9. Ball
10. Spring
11. Idle speed screw
12. Collar
13. Spring
14. Choke plate
15. Screw
16. Choke shaft
17. Spring
18. Throttle plate
19. Throttle shaft
20. Screw
21. Spring
22. Spring
23. High speed mixture needle
24. Low speed mixture needle
25. Screw
26. Pin
27. Gasket
28. Diaphragm
29. Cover
30. Screw
31. Fuel inlet lever
32. Fuel inlet needle
33. Spring
34. Welch plug
35. Welch plug
36. Retainer
37. Screen

Fig. HQ51—Exploded view of Tillotson diaphragm type carburetor used on some models.

1. Idle speed screw
2. Ball
3. Screw
4. Cover
5. Gasket
6. Diaphragm
7. Screen
8. Body
9. Clip
10. Screw
11. Check valve
12. Fuel inlet needle
13. Spring
14. Fuel inlet lever
15. Pin
16. Screw
17. Gasket
18. Diaphragm
19. Cover
20. Screw
21. Welch plug
22. Spring
23. High speed mixture needle
24. Low speed mixture needle
25. Spring
26. Spring
27. Throttle shaft
28. Screw
29. Throttle plate

are removed they must be replaced with new plugs and new plugs must be expanded with a punch and sealed with a sealant compound which will not be affected by gasoline. Fuel inlet lever must be flush with carburetor body after installation (Fig. HQ52).

IGNITION SYSTEM. All models are equipped with an electronic ignition system. Ignition system is considered satisfactory if spark will jump across the 3 mm (1/8 in.) gap of a test spark plug. If no spark is produced, check on/off switch and wiring. If switch and

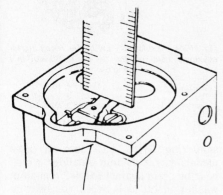

Fig. HQ52—Fuel inlet lever must be flush with carburetor body after installation.

wiring are satisfactory, install a new ignition module.

Correct air gap for ignition module is 0.35-0.40 mm (0.014-0.016 in.) for all models.

LUBRICATION. Engine is lubricated by mixing gasoline with a good quality two-stroke air-cooled engine oil. Refer to TRIMMER SERVICE section for correct fuel/oil mixture ratio recommended by trimmer manufacturer.

REPAIRS

CRANKSHAFT AND BEARINGS. Crankshaft is supported in crankcase at both ends in ball bearings. Crankshaft and connecting rod are considered an assembly and are not serviced separately.

To remove crankshaft and connecting rod assembly, refer to Figs. HQ53 and HQ54. Remove cooling shroud, recoil starter assembly, muffler, carburetor and flywheel. Remove centrifugal clutch assembly. Note that 65 cc (3.96 cu. in.) engine clutch hub assembly has left-hand threads and the nut retaining clutch hub to crankshaft on all other models has left-hand thread. Clutch assemblies for some models have been

changed and clutch must be replaced by a clutch of the same type. Refer to CLUTCH paragraphs. Remove cylinder retaining bolts and carefully work cylinder away from crankcase and piston. Remove crankcase retaining bolts and carefully separate crankcase halves. Remove crankshaft and connecting rod assembly.

It may be necessary to slightly heat crankcase halves to remove or install the ball bearing main bearings.

To reassemble engine, install ball bearings on crankshaft making certain

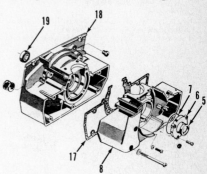

Fig. HQ54—Exploded view of crankcase assembly used on all engines except the 65 cc (3.96 cu. in.) engine.

5. Seal
6. Seal plate
7. "O" ring
8. Crankcase half
17. Gasket
18. Crankcase half
19. Bearing

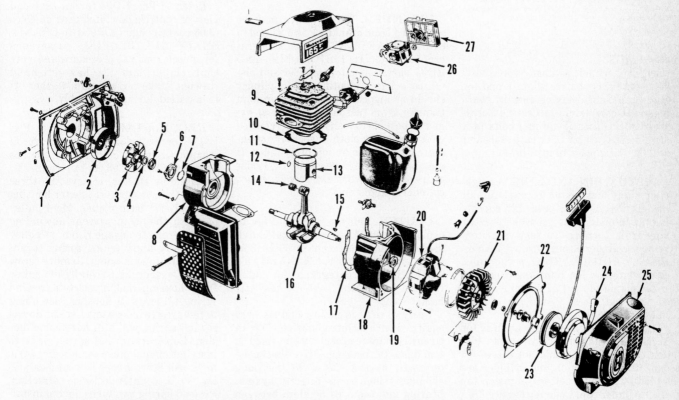

Fig. HQ53—Exploded view of the 65 cc (3.96 cu. in.) engine. All other engines are similar except for crankcase which is shown in Fig. HQ54.

1. Cover
2. Clutch drum
3. Clutch shoe assy.
4. Shim washer
5. Seal
6. Seal plate
7. "O" ring
8. Crankcase half
9. Cylinder
10. Gasket
11. Ring
12. Retainer
13. Piston
14. Bearing
15. Key
16. Crankshaft & connecting rod assy.
17. Gasket
18. Crankcase half
19. Seal
20. Ignition system
21. Flywheel
22. Shroud
23. Pulley
24. Rewind spring
25. Cover
26. Carburetor
27. Air cleaner

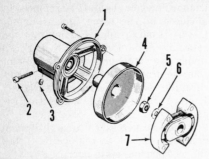

Fig. HQ55—Exploded view of clutch assembly used on all engines except the 65 cc (3.96 cu. in.) engine.

1. Clutch housing
2. Clamp bolt
3. Locating screw
4. Clutch drum
5. Nut (LH)
6. Washer
7. Clutch hub & shoe assy.

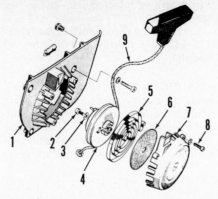

Fig. HQ57—Exploded view of the recoil starter assembly used on all engines except the 65 cc (3.96 cu. in.) engine.

1. Cover
2. Screw
3. Washer
4. Pulley
5. Rewind spring
6. Disc
7. Housing
8. Screw
9. Rope

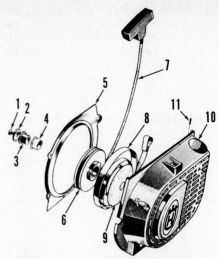

Fig. HQ58—Exploded view of the recoil starter assembly used on the 65 cc (3.96 cu. in.) engine.

1. Screw
2. Washer
3. Bearing
4. Bearing sleeve
5. Cover
6. Pulley
7. Rope
8. Rewind spring
9. Disc
10. Cover
11. Pin

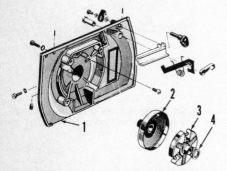

Fig. HQ56—Exploded view of clutch assembly used on the 65 cc (3.96 cu. in.) engine.

1. Cover
2. Clutch drum
3. Clutch hub & shoe assy.
4. Shim washer

they are seated against crankshaft. Heat crankcase halves slightly and install crankshaft making certain bearings seat completely in bearing bores. Tighten crankcase retaining bolts in a criss-cross pattern. Lubricate seals and seal "O" ring prior to installation.

PISTON, PIN AND RING. A single ring aluminum piston is used for all models. Piston is equipped with a locating pin in piston ring groove to prevent ring from turning. To remove piston, remove cylinder as outlined in CRANKSHAFT AND BEARING paragraphs. Remove piston pin retaining rings and press piston pin out of piston and connecting rod. Press piston pin bearing out of connecting rod as required.

Inspect piston and rings carefully for scoring, burning or excessive wear. Piston ring end gap should not exceed 0.6 mm (0.02 in.). Piston and cylinder are coded by stamped letters on piston top and cylinder top. Code letters are "A", "B" and "C". Install piston in cylinders with corresponding code letters only. Note that arrow on top of piston should be toward exhaust side of cylinder when piston is reinstalled.

Inspect piston for scratches, scoring or excessive wear. Renew piston as required.

CONNECTING ROD. Crankshaft and connecting rod are considered an assembly and are not serviced separately. To remove crankshaft and connecting rod assembly, refer to CRANKSHAFT AND BEARING paragraphs.

CYLINDER. The cylinder may be separated from crankcase as outlined in CRANKSHAFT AND BEARING paragraphs. Refer to PISTON, PIN AND RING paragraphs for cylinder and piston code letter identification. Cylinder should be inspected and any aluminum transfer from piston (especially at exhaust port area) should be removed with fine emery cloth. Inspect for cylinder coating wear at top of cylinder. If aluminum transfer has scored cylinder or if coating is worn excessively, renew cylinder and piston.

CLUTCH. Refer to Fig. HQ55 for an exploded view of the centrifugal clutch used on all engines except the 65 cc (3.96 cu. in.) engine. Refer to CRANKSHAFT AND BEARING paragraphs for clutch removal noting that nut (5) has left-hand threads.

Early 40 cc (2.44 cu. in.) engines were equipped with a clutch housing (1) with a bearing bore to accept a 9 mm thick 32 mm diameter bearing. Drive shaft used on these models has a 46 mm long shoulder which seats directly against bearing and requires no shim between bearing and drive shaft shoulder.

Late production engines are equipped with a 14 mm thick 35 mm diameter bearing. Bearing on these models are retained in clutch housing (1) with a snap ring. Drive shaft used on these models has a 44 mm shoulder which bearing seats against and a 2 mm shim washer installed between the bearing and drive shaft shoulder. Do not attempt to interchange parts between early and late models.

Refer to Fig. HQ56 for an exploded view of centrifugal clutch used on 65 cc (3.96 cu. in.) engines. Refer to CRANKSHAFT AND BEARING paragraphs for clutch removal procedure and note that clutch hub (3) has left-hand threads. Make certain shim washer (4) is installed during reassembly.

RECOIL STARTER. Refer to Fig. HQ57 for exploded view of the recoil starter assembly used on all engines except the 65 cc (3.96 cu. in.) engine. To disassemble starter, remove the three screws (8) and separate starter housing assembly (7) from engine. Hold pulley (4) with thumb to prevent unwinding and lift rope to engage notch on pulley (4). Slowly allow pulley spring to unwind with rope in notch. Remove screw (2) and washer (3). Carefully lift pulley from housing making certain rewind spring (5) stays in housing. Use pliers to remove rewind spring. Use caution as rewind spring will still have some tension. Lubricate rewind spring prior to installation and make certain disc (6) is installed. Starter rope is wound on pulley in a counterclockwise direction. Preload spring two turns during installation by turning pulley with rope engaging notch in pulley. Make certain that pulley can be turned at least 1/2 turn further after starter rope is pulled fully out. Spring preload should pull handle against housing when released. It may be necessary to pull starter rope slightly as starter housing assembly is installed to engage flywheel starter pawls with pulley.

Recoil starter for 65 cc (3.96 cu. in.) engines is shown in Fig. HQ58. To disassemble starter, remove starter housing assembly (10). Pull starter cord out of housing approximately 25 mm (1 ft.) and hold pulley (6) with thumb to prevent pulley movement. Pull rope slack into housing and slip rope into notch on edge of pulley. Carefully allow pulley to rewind until spring tension is removed. Remove screw (1), washer (2), bearing (3) and bearing sleeve (4). Carefully lift pulley (6) out of housing making certain rewind spring (8) remains in housing. Use pliers to remove rewind spring. Use caution as rewind spring will still have some tension. Lubricate rewind spring prior to installation and make certain disc (9) is installed. Preload spring two turns during installation and make sure handle rewinds against housing when released. It should be possible to turn pulley 1/2 turn more after starter rope has been pulled fully out. It may be necessary to pull starter rope slightly as starter housing assembly is installed to engage flywheel starter pawls with pulley.

KAWASAKI

ENGINE SERVICE

Model	Bore	Stroke	Displacement
KE18	28.9 mm	27.9 mm	18.4 cc
	(1.14 in.)	(1.10 in.)	(1.12 cu. in.)
KE24	32.0 mm	30.0 mm	24.1 cc
	(1.26 in.)	(1.18 in.)	(1.47 cu. in.)
TD18	28.9 mm	27.9 mm	18.4 cc
	(1.14 in.)	(1.10 in.)	(1.12 cu. in.)
TD24	32.0 mm	30.0 mm	24.1 cc
	(1.26 in.)	(1.18 in.)	(1.47 cu. in.)
TD33	36.8 mm	30.9 mm	33.3 cc
	(1.45 in.)	(1.22 in.)	(2.03 cu. in.)
TD40	40.0 mm	32.0 mm	40.2 cc
	(1.57 in.)	(1.26 in.)	(2.45 cu. in.)

ENGINE INFORMATION

Kawasaki two-stroke air-cooled gasoline engines are used by several manufacturers of string trimmers and brush cutters.

MAINTENANCE

SPARK PLUG. Recommended spark plug for all models except Model TD40 is a NGK BM6A. Recommended spark plug for Model TD40 is a NGK B7S. Specified electrode gap is 0.6 mm (0.025 in.) for all models.

CARBURETOR. Engines may be equipped with a DPK series diaphragm type carburetor (Fig. KA10), a Walbro WA diaphragm type carburetor (Fig. KA13) or a float type carburetor (Fig. KA15). Refer to the appropriate paragraphs for model being serviced.

DPK Series Carburetor. Initial setting of the main fuel mixture needle is 1½ turns out from a lightly seated position.

Make final adjustments with trimmer line at proper length or blade assembly installed. Engine should be at operating temperature and running. Operate engine at wide open throttle and turn main fuel mixture needle until engine begins to run smoothly as needle is turned IN, then back needle out 1/8 turn. Normal range of adjustment is 1-2 turns out from a lightly seated position.

Adjust idle speed screw so engine idles just below clutch engagement speed.

Midrange mixture is determined by the position of clip (7—Fig. KA10) on jet needle (8). There are three grooves located at the upper end of the jet needle (Fig. KA11) and normal position of clip (7—Fig. KA10) is in the middle groove. The mixture will be leaner if clip is installed in the top groove or richer if clip is installed in the bottom groove.

DPK carburetor is equipped with an integral fuel pump (16, 17 and 18). During servicing inspect fuel pump and metering diaphragms for pin holes, tears or other damage. Diaphragms should be flexible. Metal button must be tight on metering diaphragm. When assembling the carburetor note that the

Fig. KA10—Exploded view of DPK diaphragm type carburetor used on some models.

1. Tickler valve
2. Spring
3. Lever
4. Cap
5. Spring
6. Retainer
7. Clip
8. Jet needle
9. Throttle slide
10. Body
11. Spring
12. Idle speed screw
13. Spring
14. "O" ring
15. Main fuel mixture needle
16. Pump gasket
17. Pump diaphragm
18. Pump cover
19. Inlet needle valve
20. Metering lever
21. Pin
22. Jet
23. Spring
24. Gasket
25. Diaphragm
26. Cover

metering diaphragm lever should be 2.1-2.4 mm (0.08-0.09 in.) below the carburetor body (Fig. KA12).

Walbro WA Series Carburetor. Initial setting of the Walbro WA series carburetor is one turn out from a lightly seated position for both mixture needles.

Make final adjustments with engine at operating temperature and running. Operate trimmer engine at full throttle and turn high speed mixture needle (16—Fig. KA13) until engine begins to run smoothly as needle is turned IN, then back needle out 1/8 turn. Allow engine to idle and adjust idle mixture needle (14) until engine idles smoothly and will accelerate without hesitation. Adjust idle speed screw (1) so engine idles just below clutch engagement speed.

During servicing inspect fuel pump and metering diaphragms for pin holes, tears or other damage. Diaphragms should be flexible. Metal button must be tight on metering diaphragm. When assembling the carburetor, the metering diaphragm lever should be flush with floor of cavity as shown in Fig. KA14. If necessary, adjust by carefully bending diaphragm lever.

Float Type Carburetor. Adjustment of the float type carburetor is limited to float level adjustment and adjustment of the "E" clip to vary fuel needle adjustment.

To adjust float level, remove float bowl assembly (25—Fig. KA15). Invert carburetor throttle body and measure float level as shown in Fig. KA16. Dimension "D" should be 2.5 mm (0.09 in.). Carefully bend float lever to obtain correct float level.

Install "E" clip on fuel needle at the position marked (C) in Fig. KA17. Installation of "E" clip at positions (A or B) on fuel needle results in a leaner

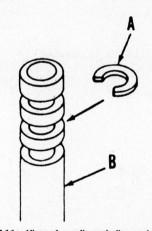

Fig. KA11—View of needle and clip used on DPK series diaphragm carburetor. Install clip (A) in middle groove for normal operation.

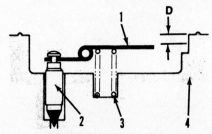

Fig. KA12—Dimension "D" should be 2.1-2.4 mm (0.08-0.09 in.).
1. Fuel lever
2. Fuel needle
3. Spring
4. Carburetor body

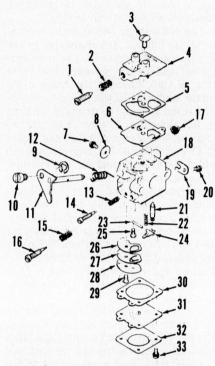

Fig. KA13—Exploded view of Walbro diaphragm type carburetor used on some models.

1. Idle speed screw	18. Body
2. Spring	19. Clip
3. Screw	20. Screw
4. Pump cover	21. Fuel inlet needle
5. Gasket	22. Spring
6. Pump diaphragm	23. Pin
7. Screw	24. Fuel lever
8. Throttle plate	25. Screw
9. "E" clip	26. Gasket
10. Cable clamp	27. Gasket
11. Throttle shaft	28. Circuit plate
12. Spring	29. Screw
13. Spring	30. Gasket
14. Low speed needle	31. Main diaphragm
15. Spring	32. Cover
16. High speed needle	33. Screw
17. Screen	

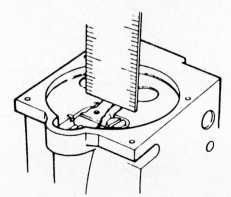

Fig. KA14—Metering valve lever should be flush with carburetor body.

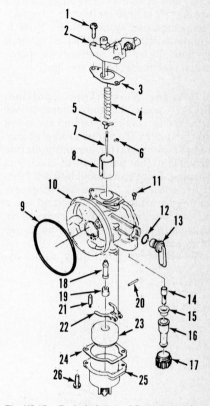

Fig. KA15—Exploded view of float type carburetor used on some models.

1. Screw	14. Strainer
2. Cover	15. Gasket
3. Gasket	16. Fitting
4. Spring	17. Nut
5. Spring seat	18. Jet
6. Clip	19. Jet
7. Fuel needle	20. Pin
8. Slide	21. Fuel inlet needle
9. Gasket	22. Float hinge
10. Body	23. Float
11. Screw	24. Gasket
12. "O" ring	25. Fuel bowl
13. Shut-off	26. Screw

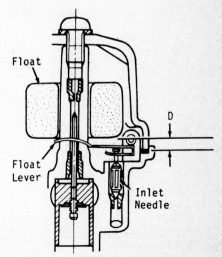

Fig. KA16—Dimension "D" should be 2.5 mm (0.09 in.) for correct float level setting.

fuel:air mixture and installation of "E" clip at the positions marked (D or E) results in a richer fuel:air mixture.

IGNITION SYSTEM. Models TD18, TD24 and TD33 may be equipped with a breaker point type ignition or a transistorized ignition system. Model TD40 is equipped with a transistorized ignition system. Refer to appropriate paragraphs for model being serviced.

Breaker Point Type Ignition. Breaker point set and condenser are attached to crankcase behind the recoil starter pulley. To adjust the point gap, remove recoil starter assembly. Rotate flywheel so that points are at maximum opening. Point gap should be 0.3-0.4 mm (0.012-0.016 in.). Loosen set screw retaining breaker point plate and use a screwdriver in supporting groove to rotate plate slightly to adjust point gap (Fig. KA18).

To adjust ignition timing, rotate fly-

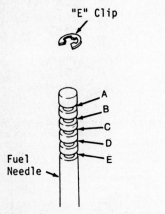

Fig. KA17—Refer to text for correct placement of fuel clip for model being serviced.

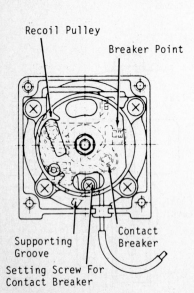

Fig. KA18—View showing location of ignition components. Refer to text.

wheel until "F" mark (line stamped on blades) is aligned with the crank case mark (Fig. KA19). Ignition points should just be beginning to open with flywheel at this position. Shift fixed point plate as required.

Transistorized Ignition System. Transistorized ignition system is operating satisfactorily if spark will jump across the 3 mm (1/8 in.) gap of a test spark plug. If no spark is produced, check on/off switch and wiring.

The coil may be tested with an ohmmeter as follows: Set ohmmeter to the R x 1 scale and connect the red ohmmeter lead to the primary lead wire (Fig. KA20). Connect the black ohmmeter lead wire to the coil core. Specified resistance of the primary winding is 0.5 ohms for 18.4 cc (1.12 cu. in.) engines, 0.6-0.7 ohms for 24.1 and 33.3 cc (1.47 and 2.03 cu. in.) engines and 0.9 ohms for 40.2 cc (2.45 cu. in.) engines. Connect the red ohmmeter lead to the spark plug wire and connect the black ohmmeter lead to the coil core (Fig. KA21). Specified resistance of the secondary coil windings is 9.7 ohms for 18.4 cc (1.12 cu. in.) engines, 7-8 ohms for 24.1 and 33.3 cc (1.47 and 2.03 cu. in.) engines and 11.5 ohms for 40.2 cc (2.45 cu. in.) engines. Renew coil if any faults are noted.

The igniter may be tested with an ohmmeter as follows: Set ohmmeter to the R x 10K scale and connect the black ohmmeter lead to the igniter case and connect the red ohmmeter lead to the igniter lead tab (Fig. KA22). Ohmmeter needle should deflect from infinity to slightly more than zero ohms. Reverse the ohmmeter leads and the ohmmeter

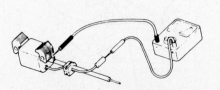

Fig. KA19—Align "F" timing mark on flywheel with timing mark on crankcase. Refer to text.

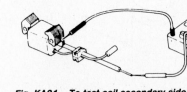

Fig. KA20—To test coil primary side, refer to text for proper test sequence.

needle should again deflect from infinity to slightly more than zero ohms. The ohmmeter needle should not return all the way back to zero ohms after deflecting to infinity. Renew igniter if any faults are noted.

LUBRICATION. All models are lubricated by mixing a good quality two-stroke air-cooled engine oil with gasoline. Refer to TRIMMER SERVICE section for correct fuel/oil mixture ratio recommended by trimmer manufacturer.

CARBON. Manufacturer recommends disassembling engine at 100 hour intervals of use and cleaning carbon from exhaust port, cylinder and from top of piston.

REPAIRS

COMPRESSION PRESSURE. For optimum performance, compression pressure should be as follows with engine at operating temperature and throttle and choke wide open. Crank engine until maximum pressure is observed.

18.4 cc (1.12 cu. in.) engine:
Low . . . . 793 kPa (115 psi)
High . . . . 1000 kPa (145 psi)

24.1 cc (1.47 cu. in.) engine:
Low . . . . 965 kPa (140 psi)
High . . . . 1172 kPa (170 psi)

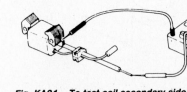

Fig. KA21—To test coil secondary side, refer to text for proper test sequence.

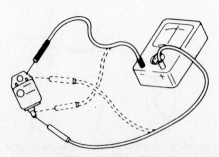

Fig. KA22—Refer to text for correct connection sequence for igniter tests using an ohmmeter.

33.3 cc (2.03 cu. in.) engine:
Low . . . . 1103 kPa
(160 psi)
High . . . . 1310 kPa
(190 psi)

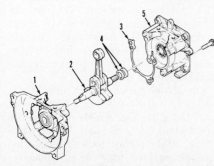

Fig. KA23—Exploded view of crankshaft and connecting rod assembly used on Models KE18, TD18, KE24, TD24 and TD33.

1. Crankcase half
2. Crankshaft & connecting rod assy.
3. Gasket
4. Shims
5. Crankcase half

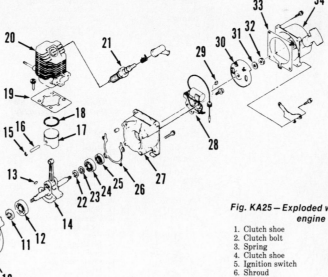

Fig. KA24—Exploded view of crankshaft and connecting rod assembly used on Model TD40.

1. Crankcase half
2. Crankshaft & connecting rod assy.
3. Gaskets
4. Shim
5. Crankcase half

40.2 cc (2.47 cu. in.) engine:
Low . . . . Not Available

High . . . . Not Available

A compression reading of 620 kPa (90 psi) or lower for any model indicates a need for repairs.

TIGHTENING TORQUES. Recommended tightening torque specifications are as follows:

Clutch pin to flywheel:
KE18, TD18,
KE24 & TD24 . . . . . . 8-10 N·m
(69-85 in.-lbs.)
TD33, TD40 . . . . . . 13-14 N·m
(120-137 in.-lbs.)

Crankcase:
KE18, TD18, KE24,
TD24 & TD33 . . . . . . .3-4 N·m
(30-34 in.-lbs.)
TD40 . . . . .5-7 N·m
(52-61 in.-lbs.)

Cylinder to crankcase:
KE18, TD18, KE24,
TD24 & TD33 . . . . . . .3-4 N·m
(30-34 in.-lbs.)
TD40 . . . . .7-9 N·m
(61-78 in.-lbs.)

Flywheel:
KE18, TD18,
KE24 & TD24 . . . . . . .8-10 N·m
(69-85 in.-lbs.)

TD33 & TD40 . . . . . 30-34 N·m
(260-304 in.-lbs.)

Spark plug:
All models . . . . 12-16 N·m
(103-146 in.-lbs.)

CRANKSHAFT AND CONNECTING ROD. Refer to Fig. KA23 for an exploded view of crankshaft and connecting rod assembly used on 18.4, 24.1 and 33.3 cc (1.12, 1.47 and 2.03 cu. in.) engines or to Fig. KA24 for 40.2 cc (2.45 cu. in.) engine. On all models, crankshaft is pressed together at connecting rod journal, therefore crankshaft and connecting rod must be renewed as an assembly. Crankshaft is supported by ball bearings at both ends. For exploded views of engine assemblies refer to Fig. KA25 for Models KE18 and TD18, to Fig. KA26 for Models KE24, TD24 and TD33 and to Fig. KA27 for Model TD40.

To remove crankshaft assembly refer to appropriate exploded view and remove engine cooling shroud and recoil starter assembly. On Models KE18, TD18 and TC40, unscrew starter pulley retaining nut and pry starter pulley off of crankshaft. On Models KE24, TD24 and TD33, the starter pulley is threaded onto crankshaft and is removed by unscrewing. On all models, remove flywheel, carburetor, muffler and cylinder. Split crankcase and remove crankshaft. Remove piston.

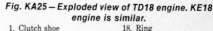

Fig. KA25 — Exploded view of TD18 engine. KE18 engine is similar.

1. Clutch shoe
2. Clutch bolt
3. Spring
4. Clutch shoe
5. Ignition switch
6. Shroud
7. Nut
8. Ignition coil
9. Flywheel
10. Crankcase half
11. Seal
12. Bearing
13. Key
14. Crankshaft & connecting rod assy.
15. Retainer
16. Piston pin
17. Piston
18. Ring
19. Gasket
20. Cylinder
21. Spark plug
22. Shim
23. Shim
24. Bearing
25. Seal
26. Gasket
27. Crankcase half
28. Point & condenser (as equipped)
29. Felt
30. Pulley
31. Washer
32. Nut
33. Gasket
34. Starter housing

Inspect crankshaft assembly for damage or excessive wear. Inspect main bearings and roller bearing (as equipped) in small end of connecting rod. Renew parts as required.

To reassemble, crankshaft end play must be correctly set. Shims are available for Models KE18, TD18, KE24, TD24 and TD33 in the sizes listed in chart in Fig. KA28. Shims are available for Model TD40 in the sizes listed in chart in Fig. KA29. Note that all shim sizes are measured in millimeters only. All measurements and dimensions must be in millimeters to correctly set crankshaft end play.

On Models KE18, TD18, KE24, TD24 and TD33, correct crankshaft end play is 0.05-0.268 mm (0.002-0.011 in.). Refer to Fig. KA30 and measure dimensions "A", "B" and "C" as illustrated. Make certain gasket is installed on one surface only when measurements are taken. Add dimension "A" to dimension "B". Subtract dimension "C" from the total of "A" plus "B". This will result in dimension "D". Refer to the chart in Fig. KA28 for the correct shim or combination of shims to correctly set crankshaft end play.

On Model TD40 correct crankshaft end play is 0.045-0.305 mm (0.002-0.012 in.). Refer to Fig. KA31 and measure dimensions "A", "B" and "C" as illustrated. Make certain gasket is installed on one surface only when measurements are made. Add dimension "A" to dimension "B". Subtract dimension "C" from the total of "A" plus "B". This will result in dimension "D". Refer to the chart in Fig. KA29 for the correct shim or combination of shims to correctly set crankshaft end play.

Crankcase bolts should be tightened to specified torque in a criss-cross pattern for Models KE18, TD18, KE24, TD24 and TD33. Refer to Fig. KA32 for Model TD40 bolt tightening sequence. Ends of gasket may have to be trimmed after installation.

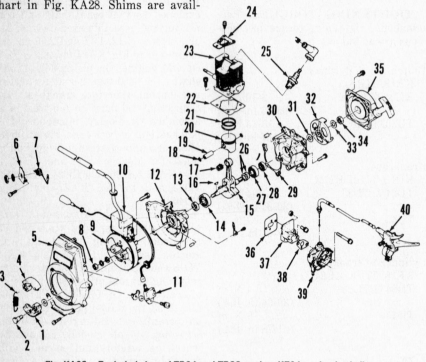

Fig. KA26—Exploded view of TD24 and TD33 engine. KE24 engine is similar.

1. Clutch shoe
2. Clutch bolt
3. Spring
4. Clutch shoe
5. Shroud
6. Bracket
7. Ignition switch
8. Nut
9. Flywheel
10. Ignition coil
11. Igniter
12. Crankcase half
13. Seal
14. Bearing
15. Crankshaft & connecting rod assy.
16. Key
17. Bearing
18. Retainer
19. Piston pin
20. Piston
21. Rings
22. Gasket
23. Cylinder
24. Retainer
25. Spark plug
26. Shims
27. Bearing
28. Seal
29. Gasket
30. Crankcase half
31. Washer
32. Pulley
33. Washer
34. Nut
35. Starter housing
36. Gasket
37. Insulator
38. Gasket
39. Carburetor
40. Throttle trigger assy.

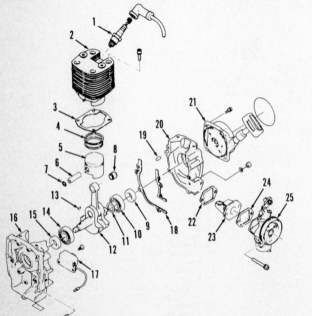

Fig. KA27—Exploded view of TD40 engine assembly.

1. Spark plug
2. Cylinder head
3. Gasket
4. Rings
5. Piston
6. Piston pin
7. Retainer ring
8. Bearing
9. Seal
10. Bearing
11. Shim
12. Crankshaft & connecting rod assy.
13. Key
14. Bearing
15. Seal
16. Crankcase half
17. Igniter
18. Gaskets
19. Dowel pin
20. Crankcase half
21. Starter housing
22. Gasket
23. Insulator
24. Gasket
25. Carburetor

Shim No.	Shim Thickness (mm)
①	0.1
②	0.2
③	0.4
④	0.6

Clearance (D)	Shim No.
-0.11 ~ under +0.03	None
+0.03 ~ under +0.13	①
+0.13 ~ under +0.23	②
+0.23 ~ under +0.33	② + ①
+0.33 ~ under +0.43	③
+0.43 ~ under +0.53	③ + ①
+0.53 ~ under +0.63	④

Fig. KA28—Refer to text for procedure to determine correct shim thickness and number. Note all dimensions are in millimeters.

Shim No.	Shim Thickness (mm)
①	0.1
②	0.2
③	0.4
④	0.6

TA 40	TA 51
Clearance (D)	Thickness Of Shim
-0.10 ~ -0.09	None
-0.08 ~ 0.01	①
0.02 ~ 0.13	②
0.14 ~ 0.22	① + ②
0.23 ~ 0.34	③
0.35 ~ 0.43	① + ②
0.44 ~ 0.54	④
0.55 ~ 0.64	① + ④
0.65 ~ 0.76	② + ④
0.77 ~ 0.84	① + ② + ⑥

Fig. KA29—Refer to text for procedure to determine correct shim thickness and number. Note all dimensions are in millimeters.

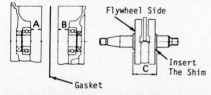

Fig. KA30—Illustration showing measurement locations to determine correct thickness and number of shims required on Models KE18, TD18, KE24, TD24 and TD33. Refer to text.

PISTON, PIN AND RINGS. Piston for Models KE18 and TD18 is equipped with one piston ring. Piston for Models KE24, TD24, TD33 and TD40 are equipped with two piston rings. On all models, piston is equipped with a locating pin (Fig. KA33) in piston ring groove (grooves) to prevent ring rotation. A needle bearing is installed in connecting rod pin bearing bore of all models except Models KE18 and TD18. On Models KE18 and TD18, piston pin rides directly in connecting rod bore.

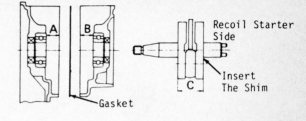

Fig. KA31—Illustration showing measurement locations to determine correct thickness and number of shims required on Model TD40. Refer to text.

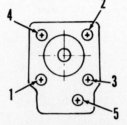

Fig. KA32—Tighten crankcase bolts in sequence shown to specified torque.

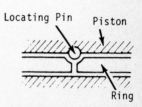

Fig. KA33—Piston ring or rings on all models are held in position by locating pin.

To remove piston from all models, remove cooling shroud and recoil starter assembly. Remove carburetor and muffler. Remove all bolts retaining cylinder to crankcase and carefully work cylinder off of crankcase and piston. Remove retaining rings (3 and 6—Fig. KA34) and press pin (5) out of piston pin bore. Piston (4) may now be removed. Remove bearing (7) (as equipped) from connecting rod piston pin bearing bore.

When installing piston on connecting rod, arrow on piston top must point toward flywheel side of engine and piston pin must move smoothly in piston pin bearing installed in connecting rod.

Correct piston ring end gap is 0.7 mm (0.03 in.). Correct ring groove clearance for top ring is 0.17 mm (0.007 in.). Correct ring groove clearance for second ring of models so equipped is 0.15 mm (0.006 in.).

Correct piston to cylinder clearance is 0.15 mm (0.006 in.) for all models.

CYLINDER. Cylinder may be unbolted and removed from crankcase after shroud, muffler, carburetor and starter housing are removed.

Renew cylinder if bore is scored, cracked or if piston to cylinder clearance with new piston installed exceeds 0.15 mm (0.006 in.).

CLUTCH. Refer to Fig. KA35 for an exploded view of clutch shoe installation. Tighten clutch pin bolts (1) to specified torque. If clutch engages low idle speeds, clutch spring (2) may be stretched or damaged. Clutch shoes, spring and drum should be inspected for excessive wear or damage any time clutch drum is removed. Renew parts as required.

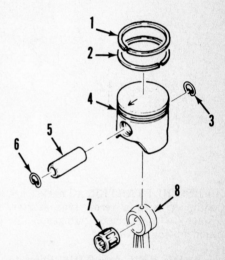

Fig. KA34—Exploded view of typical piston assembly. Note Models KE18 and TD18 are equipped with one ring only and connecting rod is not equipped with needle bearing (7).

1. Top ring   5. Piston pin
2. Second ring   6. Retainer
3. Retainer   7. Needle bearing
4. Piston   8. Connecting rod

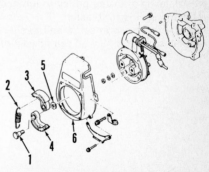

Fig. KA35—Exploded view of clutch shoe arrangement typical of most models.

1. Clutch pin (bolt)   4. Clutch shoe
2. Clutch spring   5. Washer
3. Clutch shoe   6. Shroud

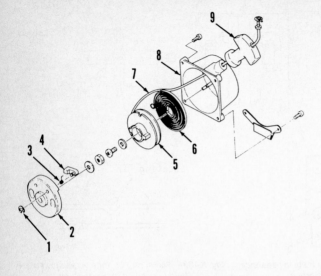

Fig. KA36—Exploded view of recoil starter used on Models KE18 and TD18.
1. "E" ring
2. Pulley
3. Spring
4. Pawl
5. Reel
6. Spring
7. Rope
8. Housing
9. Handle

Fig. KA38—Loop spring must be installed as shown.

way out of starter. Pulley should still be able to rotate counterclockwise. If pulley will not rotate any further with rope pulled out, release one turn of preload.

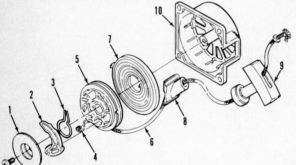

Fig. KA37—Exploded view of recoil starter used on Models KE24, TD24, TD33 and TD40.
1. Retainer
2. Pawl
3. Loop spring
4. Pawl spring
5. Pulley
6. Rope
7. Spring
8. Guide
9. Handle
10. Housing

Models KE24, TD24, TD33 And TD40. Refer to Fig. KA37 for an exploded view of starter assembly. To disassemble starter, first remove starter assembly from engine. Slide rope guide (8) out of starter housing (10) and slip rope (6) into slot on pulley. Hold rope in notch while slowly allowing pulley to unwind relieving spring (7) tension.

Remove the center screw, retainer (1), pawl (2) and springs (3 and 4). Slowly lift pulley off starter housing post while using a small screwdriver to release pulley from spring hook. Use care if spring must be removed. Do not allow spring to uncoil uncontrolled.

Inspect rope, pawl and springs for breakage or excessive wear and renew as needed. Lubricate center post of housing with light grease prior to reassembly. Reassembly is reverse of disassembly procedure. Install spring in a counterclockwise direction from outer end. Wind all but 6 inches (15.2 cm) of rope onto pulley before installing pulley in starter housing. Wrap rope around pulley in a counterclockwise direction as viewed from pawl side of pulley. Press down on pulley while turning to engage pulley with spring hook. Reinstall retaining screw, retainer, pawl, pawl spring and loop spring. Make sure loop spring is installed properly as shown in Fig. KA38. Preload the rewind spring three turns. Recheck to be sure pulley rewinds completely when released.

RECOIL STARTER. All models are equipped with a recoil type starter. Refer to appropriate paragraph for model being serviced.

Models KE18 And TD18. Refer to Fig. KA36 for an exploded view of starter assembly. To disassemble starter, remove starter assembly from engine. Pull rope 6 inches (15.2 cm) out of housing (8). Align notch in pulley (5) with rope hole in housing. While holding pulley and rope hole in alignment, pull slack rope back through rope hole in side housing. Hold rope in notch while slowly allowing pulley to unwind relieving spring (6) tension.

Remove the center screw and washer, then slowly lift pulley off center post of housing. Do not dislodge rewind spring. Use care if spring must be removed. Do not allow spring to uncoil uncontrolled.

Inspect rope and spring. Lubricate center post of housing with light grease prior to reassembly. Reassembly is reverse of disassembly procedure. Wind all but 6 inches (15.2 cm) of rope onto pulley before installing pulley in starter housing. Wrap rope around pulley in a counterclockwise direction as viewed from pawl side of pulley. Press down on pulley while turning to engage pulley with spring hook. Install retaining screw and washer. Recommended preload is three turns counterclockwise. Check rewind spring for bottoming after assembly, by pulling rope all the

KIORITZ
ENGINE SERVICE

Model	Bore	Stroke	Displacement
Kioritz	26.0 mm	26.0 mm	13.8 cc
	(1.02 in.)	(1.02 in.)	(0.84 cu. in.)
Kioritz	28.0 mm	26.0 mm	16.0 cc
	(1.10 in.)	(1.02 in.)	(0.98 cu. in.)
Kioritz	32.2 mm	26.0 mm	21.2 cc
	(1.27 in.)	(1.02 in.)	(1.29 cu. in.)
Kioritz	28.0 mm	37.0 mm	30.1 cc
	(1.10 in.)	(1.46 in.)	(1.84 cu. in.)
Kioritz	40.0 mm	32.0 mm	40.2 cc
	(1.56 in.)	(1.26 in.)	(2.45 cu. in.)

ENGINE INFORMATION

Kioritz two-stroke air-cooled gasoline engines are used by several manufacturers of string trimmers and brush cutters.

MAINTENANCE

SPARK PLUG. Recommended spark plug is a Champion CJ8, or equivalent. Specified electrode gap for all models is 0.6-0.7 mm (0.024-0.28 in.).

CARBURETOR. Kioritz engines may be equipped with a Walbro diaphragm type carburetor with a built in fuel pump (Fig. KZ50) or a Zama diaphragm type carburetor (Fig. KZ52). Refer to appropriate paragraph for model being serviced.

Walbro Diaphragm Type Carburetor. Initial adjustment of fuel mixture needle from a lightly seated position is 1-1/8 turn open for low speed mixture needle (18—Fig. KZ50) and 1-1/4 turn open for high speed mixture needle.

Final adjustments are made with trimmer line at recommended length. Engine should be at operating temperature and running. Turn idle speed screw (31) to obtain 2500-3000 rpm, or just below clutch engagement speed. Adjust low speed mixture needle (18) to obtain consistent idling and smooth acceleration. Readjust idle speed screw (31) as required. Open throttle fully and adjust high speed mixture needle (17) to obtain highest engine rpm, then turn high speed mixture needle counterclockwise 1/8 turn.

To disassemble carburetor, remove the four screws retaining cover (1) to carburetor body. Remove cover (1), diaphragm (2) and gasket (3). Remove screw (4), pin (5), fuel inlet lever (6), spring (8) and fuel inlet needle (7). Remove screw (9) and remove circuit

plate (10), check valve (11) and gasket (12). Remove screw (29), cover (28), gasket (27) and diaphragm (26). Remove inlet screen (24). Remove high and low speed mixture needles and springs. Re-

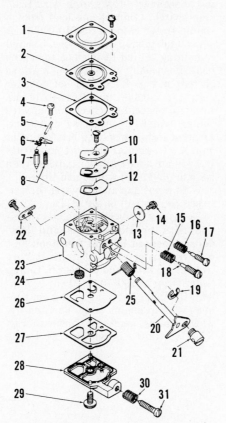

Fig. KZ50—Exploded view of Walbro carburetor used on some models.

1. Cover
2. Metering diaphragm
3. Gasket
4. Metering lever screw
5. Metering lever pin
6. Metering lever
7. Fuel inlet valve
8. Metering lever spring
9. Circuit plate screw
10. Circuit plate
11. Check valve
12. Gasket
13. Throttle valve
14. Shutter screw
15. Spring
16. Spring
17. High speed mixture needle
18. Idle mixture needle
19. "E" clip
20. Throttle shaft
21. Swivel
22. Throttle shaft clip
23. Body
24. Inlet screen
25. Return spring
26. Fuel pump diaphragm
27. Gasket
28. Cover
29. Cover screw
30. Spring
31. Idle speed screw

move throttle plate (13) and shaft (20) as required.

Carefully inspect all parts. Diaphragms should be flexible and free of cracks or tears. When reassembling, fuel inlet lever (6) should be flush with carburetor body (Fig. KZ51). Carefully bend fuel inlet lever to obtain correct setting.

Zama Diaphragm Type Carburetor. Initial adjustment of low speed (16—Fig. KZ52) and high speed (17) mixture needles is one turn open from a lightly seated position.

Final adjustments are made with trimmer line at recommended length. Engine should be at operating temperature and running. Turn idle speed screw (27) to obtain 2500-3000 rpm, or just below clutch engagement speed. Adjust low speed mixture needle (16) to obtain consistent idling and smooth acceleration. Readjust idle speed screw (27) as required. Open throttle fully and adjust high speed mixture needle (17) to obtain highest engine rpm, then turn high speed mixture needle counterclockwise 1/8 turn.

To disassemble carburetor, remove screw (26), pump cover (25), gasket (24) and diaphragm (23). Remove fuel inlet screen (22). Remove the two screws (1)

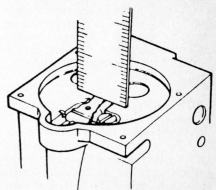

Fig. KZ51—Fuel inlet lever should be flush with carburetor body.

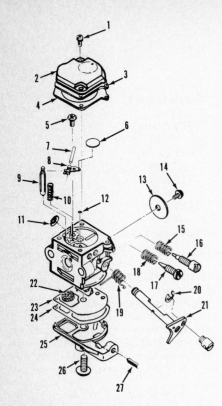

Fig. KZ52—Exploded view of Zama diaphragm carburetor used on some models.

1. Screw	15. Spring
2. Cover	16. Low speed mixture
3. Diaphragm	needle
4. Gasket	17. High speed mixture
5. Screw	needle
6. Fuel metering lever	18. Spring
disc	19. Spring
7. Pin	20. "E" ring
8. Fuel inlet lever	21. Throttle shaft
9. Fuel inlet needle	22. Screen
10. Spring	23. Diaphragm
11. "E" ring	24. Gasket
12. Disc	25. Cover
13. Throttle plate	26. Screw
14. Screw	27. Idle speed screw

and remove cover (2), diaphragm (3) and gasket (4). Remove screw (5), pin (7), metering disc (6), fuel inlet lever (8), fuel inlet needle (9) and spring (10). Remove fuel mixture needles and springs. Remove "E" clip (11), throttle plate (13) and throttle shaft (21) as required.

Inspect all parts for wear or damage. Diaphragms should be flexible with no cracks or wrinkles. Fuel inlet lever (8) with metering disc (6) removed, should be flush with carburetor fuel chamber floor (Fig. KZ51).

IGNITION SYSTEM. Engines may be equipped with a magneto type ignition with breaker points and condenser or a CDI (capacitor-discharge) ignition system which requires no regular maintenance and has no breaker points. Ignition module (CDI) is located outside of flywheel. Refer to appropriate paragraph for model being serviced.

Breaker Point Ignition System. Breaker points may be located behind recoil starter or behind flywheel. Note location of breaker points and refer to following paragraphs for service.

To inspect or service magneto ignition with **breaker points and condenser located behind recoil starter and cover,** first remove fan cover. Refer to Fig. KZ53 and check pole gap between flywheel and ignition coil laminations. Gap should be 0.35-0.40 mm (0.014-0.016 in.). To adjust pole gap, loosen two retaining screws in coil (threads of retaining screws should be treated with Loctite or equivalent), place correct gage between flywheel and coil laminations. Pull coil to flywheel by hand as shown, then tighten screws and remove feeler gage.

Breaker points are accessible after removal of starter case, nut and pawl carrier. Nut and pawl carrier both have left-hand threads.

To adjust point gap and ignition timing, disconnect stop switch wire from stop switch. Connect one lead from a timing tester (Kioritz 990510-00031) or equivalent to stop switch wire. Ground remaining timing tester lead to engine body. Position flywheel timing mark as shown in Fig. KZ54 and set breaker point gap to 0.3-0.4 mm (0.012-0.014 in.). Rotate flywheel and check timing with timing tester. Readjust as necessary. Be accurate when setting breaker point gap. A gap greater than 0.4 mm (0.014 in.) will advance timing; a gap less than 0.3 mm (0.012 in.) will retard timing.

With point gap and flywheel correctly set, timing will be 23° BTDC.

To inspect or service magneto ignition with **breaker points and condenser located behind flywheel,** first remove starter case. Disconnect wire from stop switch and connect to timing tester (Kioritz 990510-00031) or equivalent. Ground remaining lead from timing tester to engine body. Position flywheel timing mark as shown in Fig. KZ55. If timing is not correct, loosen

retaining screw on breaker points through flywheel slot openings. Squeeze screwdriver in crankcase groove to adjust point gap. Breaker point gap should be 0.3-0.4 mm (0.012-0.016 in.) with flywheel at TDC.

If breaker points require renewal, flywheel must be removed. When installing breaker points note that stop lead (black) from condenser must pass under coil. White wire from coil must pass between condenser bracket and oiler felt. Push wire down to avoid contact with flywheel.

Ignition coil air gap between coil and flywheel should be 0.4 mm (0.016 in.). Retaining screws should be treated with Loctite or equivalent.

Be accurate when setting breaker point gap. A gap greater than 0.4 mm (0.016 in.) will advance timing; a gap less than 0.3 mm (0.012 in.) will retard timing.

With point gap and flywheel correctly set, timing will be 30° BTDC. Tighten flywheel nut.

Primary and secondary ignition coil resistance may be checked with an ohmmeter without removing coil.

To check primary coil resistance, connect ohmmeter to disconnected ignition coil primary lead and ground remaining lead to engine. Primary coil resistance should register 0.5-0.8 ohms.

To check secondary coil resistance connect one lead of ohmmeter to spark plug cable and remaining lead to ground on engine. Secondary coil resistance should register 5-10 ohms.

CD Ignition System. CD ignition system requires no regular maintenance and has no moving parts except for magnets cast in flywheel.

Ignition timing is fixed at 30° BTDC and clearance between CDI module laminations and flywheel should be 0.3 mm (0.012 in.). To check ignition timing, refer to Fig. KZ56. If timing is not correct, CDI module must be renewed.

Fig. KZ53—Illustration showing correct pole core gap. Refer to text.

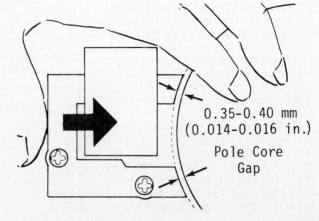

0.35-0.40 mm
(0.014-0.016 in.)

Pole Core Gap

Ignition coil may be checked by connecting one ohmmeter lead to spark plug cable and remaining lead to coil primary lead; ohmmeter should register 0.0-0.2 ohms for all models. Connect ohmmeter lead to coil primary lead (red) wire and remaining ohmmeter lead to either the coil exciter lead (grounded wire), if so equipped, or to coil laminations. Ohmmeter should register 0.5-1.5k ohms for models with exciter lead or 1.5-3.0k ohms for remaining models. Connect one ohmmeter lead to exciter lead, of models so equipped, and remaining ohmmeter lead to coil laminations; ohmmeter should register 120-200 ohms.

CARBON. Muffler and cylinder exhaust ports should be cleaned periodically to prevent loss of power due to carbon build-up. Remove muffler cover and baffle plate and scrape muffler free of carbon. With muffler cover removed, position engine so piston is at top dead center and carefully remove carbon from exhaust ports with wooden scraper. Be careful not to damage the edges of exhaust ports or to scratch piston. Do not attempt to run engine without muffler baffle plate or cover.

LUBRICATION. Engine lubrication is obtained by mixing a good quality two-stroke air-cooled engine oil with gasoline. Refer to TRIMMER SERVICE section for fuel/oil mixture ratio recommended by trimmer manufacturer.

REPAIRS

COMPRESSION PRESSURE. For optimum performance, minimum compression pressure should be 621 kPa (90 psi). Compression test should be performed with engine cold and throttle and choke plates at wide open positions.

TIGHTENING TORQUES. Recommended tightening torque specifications are as follows:

Spark plug:
  All models . . . . 14-15 N·m
                   (168-180 in.-lbs.)
Cylinder cover:
  All models so equipped 1.5-1.9 N·m
                   (13-17 in.-lbs.)
Cylinder:
  13.8, 16.0
   & 21.2 cc engine . . . . .5.7-6.0 N·m
                   (50-55 in.-lbs.)
  All other engines . . . .7.0-8.0 N·m
                   (65-75 in.-lbs.)
Crankcase:
  All models . . . . .4.5-5.7 N·m
                   (40-50 in.-lbs.)

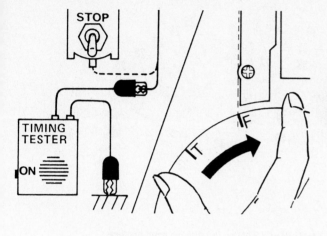

Fig. KZ54—Illustration showing proper timing mark setting for engines with breaker points located behind recoil starter and cover. Refer to text.

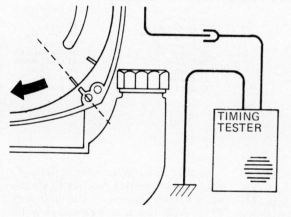

Fig. KZ55—Illustration showing proper timing mark setting for engines with breaker points located behind flywheel. Refer to text.

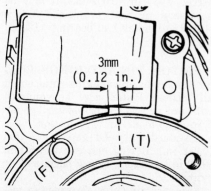

Fig. KZ56—Align top dead center mark (T) on flywheel with laminations as shown to check timing on models with CD ignition. Refer to text.

Fig. KZ57—Exploded view of engine similar to the 13.8, 16.0 and 21.2 cc (0.84, 0.98 and 1.29 cu. in.) displacement engines.

1. Clutch drum
2. Hub
3. Ignition module
4. Clutch springs
5. Clutch shoes
6. Plate
7. Flywheel
8. Seal
9. Key
10. Crankcase
11. Gasket
12. Bearing
13. Crankshaft & connecting rod assy.
14. Bearing
15. Crankcase cover
16. Seal
17. Ratchet assy.
18. Nut
19. Thrust washer
20. Bearing
21. Thrust washer
22. Retainer
23. Piston pin
24. Piston
25. Ring
26. Gasket
27. Cylinder

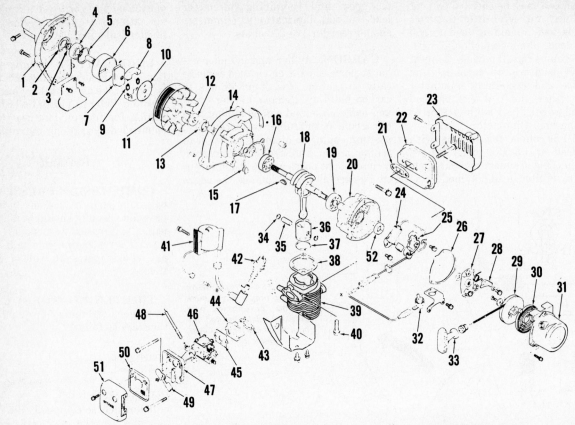

Fig. KZ58 — Exploded view of engine similar to 30.1 and 40.2 cc (1.84 and 2.45 cu. in.) displacement engines.

1. Fan cover	12. Spacer	22. Muffler	33. Handle	43. Gasket

1. Fan cover
2. Stopper
3. Snap ring
4. Ball bearing
5. Snap ring
6. Clutch drum
7. Clutch hub
8. Clutch shoe
9. Clutch spring
10. Side plate
11. Flywheel/fan

12. Spacer
13. Seal
14. Crankcase
15. Crankcase packing
16. Ball bearing
17. Woodruff key
18. Crankshaft/connect-
    ing rod assy.
19. Ball bearing
20. Crankcase half
21. Gasket

22. Muffler
23. Cover
24. Condenser
25. Breaker points
26. Gasket
27. Pawl carrier
28. Pawl
29. Starter hub
30. Spring
31. Starter housing
32. Stop switch

33. Handle
34. Snap ring
35. Piston pin
36. Piston
37. Piston ring
38. Gasket
39. Cylinder
40. Screw
41. Coil assy.
42. Spark plug

43. Gasket
44. Insulator
45. Gasket
46. Carburetor
47. Case
48. Throttle cable
49. Choke shutter
50. Air filter
51. Cover
52. Seal

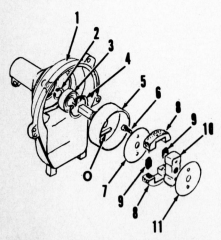

Fig. KZ59—Exploded view of clutch assembly.

O. Opening
1. Clutch housing
2. Snap ring
3. Bearing
4. Snap ring
5. Clutch drum

6. Screw
7. Plate
8. Clutch shoes
9. Clutch springs
10. Hub
11. Plate

**CRANKSHAFT AND CONNECT-
ING ROD.** The crankshaft and connecting rod are serviced as an assembly
only and crankshaft and connecting rod
are not available separately.

To remove crankshaft and connecting
rod assembly remove fan housing and
clutch assembly. Remove carburetor,
muffler and fuel tank. Remove starter
assembly, flywheel and ignition module. Carefully remove cylinder (27—Fig.
KZ57). Remove retaining rings (22) and
use a suitable piston pin puller to
remove pin (23). Note thrust washers
(19 and 21) are installed on some engines and will fall when piston pin and
piston are removed. Separate crankcase
halves and remove crankshaft and connecting rod assembly. Carefully press
ball bearings (12 and 14) off crankshaft
as required. If bearings remain in
crankcase, it may be necessary to heat
crankcase halves slightly to remove
bearings.

Inspect all parts for wear or damage.
Standard connecting rod side clearance
on crankpin journal is 0.55-0.60 mm
(0.022-0.026 in.). If side clearance is 0.7
mm (0.028 in.) or more, crankshaft and
connecting rod assembly must be renewed. Crankcase runout should not
exceed 0.05 mm (0.002 in.). It may be
necessary to heat crankcase halves
slightly to install ball bearings (12 and
14).

PISTON, PIN AND RINGS. Rings
are pinned to prevent ring rotation on
all models. Piston may be equipped
with one or two compression rings according to model and application.

Standard ring end gap is 0.3 mm
(0.012 in.). If ring end gap is 0.5 mm
(0.02 in.) or more, renew rings and/or
cylinder.

Standard ring side clearance in piston groove is 0.06 mm (0.0024 in.). If
ring side clearance is 0.10 mm (0.004 in.)

or more, renew ring and/or piston.

When installing piston, rings must be correctly positioned over pins in ring grooves. Install piston on connecting rod with arrow on top of piston towards exhaust side of engine. Make certain piston pin retaining rings are correctly seated in piston pin bore of piston. Use care when installing piston into cylinder that cylinder does not rotate.

CYLINDER. The cylinder bore has a chrome plated surface and must be re-newed if plating is worn through or scored excessively. Worn spots will appear dull and may be easily scratched while chrome plating will be bright and much harder.

CLUTCH. Refer to Fig. KZ59 for an exploded view of centrifugal clutch assembly used on 13.8, 16.0 and 21.2 cc (0.84, 0.98 and 1.29 cu. in.) engines. Snap ring (4) is removed from snap ring bore through opening (O) in clutch drum. Drive clutch drum (5) out and remove snap ring (2). Remove ball bearing (3). Check shoes for wear or oil, check clutch springs for fatigue and renew parts as necessary. If removal of clutch hub is necessary, it is screwed on crankshaft with left-hand threads.

To remove clutch from all other engines, remove fan cover. Remove screw retaining clutch drum to crankshaft. Remove ball bearing from clutch drum. Check shoes for wear or oil, check clutch springs for fatigue and renew parts as necessary.

KOMATSU

ENGINE SERVICE

Model	Bore	Stroke	Displacement
Komatsu	28.0 mm	26.0 mm	16.0 cc
	(1.10 in.)	(1.06 in.)	(0.96 cu. in.)

ENGINE INFORMATION

Komatsu 16 cc (0.96 cu. in.) two-stroke air-cooled gasoline engine is used by several manufacturers of string trimmers and brush cutters. Engine is equipped with a cantilevered type crankshaft supported in two ball bearings at flywheel side only. Refer to following sections for other Komatsu engine models.

MAINTENANCE

SPARK PLUG. Recommended spark plug is a NGK BMR-6, or equivalent. Specified electrode gap for all models is 0.6-0.7 mm (0.024-0.28 in.).

CARBURETOR. A Teikei diaphragm type carburetor is used. Refer to Fig. KU2 for an exploded view of the Teikei diaphragm type carburetor. Initial adjustment of fuel mixture needles from a lightly seated position is 1¼ turns open for low speed mixture needle (29) and 3/4 turn open for high speed mixture needle (28).

Final adjustments are made with trimmer line at recommended length or blade assembly installed. Engine must be at operating temperature and running. Operate trimmer engine at full throttle and adjust high speed mixture needle to obtain 9000 rpm. If an accurate tachometer is not available, do not adjust high speed mixture needle beyond initial setting. Operate trimmer engine at idle speed and adjust low speed mixture needle until a smooth idle is obtained and engine does not hesitate during acceleration. Adjust idle speed screw (1) until engine idles at just below clutch engagement speed.

To disassemble carburetor, remove the two screws (3) and separate cover (4) from carburetor body. Remove gasket (5) and pump diaphragm (6). Remove the four screws and separate metering diaphragm cover (21) from carburetor body. Remove diaphragm (19) and gasket (13). Remove screw (17), pin (18), fuel inlet lever (16), fuel inlet needle (14) and spring (15). Remove fuel mixture needles and springs.

Clean and inspect all parts. Diaphragms must not be torn or wrinkled. Inspect tip of fuel inlet needle. Renew needle if tip is grooved or damaged. Fuel lever (16) must be 2.0 mm (0.08 in.) from carburetor body after installation (D-Fig. KU3).

IGNITION SYSTEM. An electronic ignition system is used and ignition system is considered satisfactory if spark will jump across the 3 mm (1/8 in.) gap of a test spark plug. If no spark is produced, check on/off switch wiring and module air gap. If switch and wiring are satisfactory ignition module may be checked using an ohmmeter. Primary module winding should register 0.6-1.0 ohms and secondary module winding should register 6.3k ohms. Air gap between module and flywheel should be 0.2-0.3 mm (0.008-0.012 in.).

LUBRICATION. Engine is lubricated by mixing a good quality two-stroke air-cooled engine oil with gasoline. Refer to TRIMMER SERVICE sections for correct fuel/oil mixture ratio recommended by trimmer manufacturer.

REPAIRS

COMPRESSION PRESSURE. For optimum performance, compression pressure should be 586 kPa (85 psi) and not less than 393 kPa (57 psi). Compression should be checked with engine at operating temperature and with throttle valve and choke wide open.

CRANKSHAFT AND CONNECTING ROD. Crankshaft is supported at flywheel side only in two ball bearing installed in crankcase half (Fig. KU4). To remove crankshaft, remove recoil starter and fan housing assembly and cooling shrouds. Remove air filter assembly, muffler and carburetor. Remove flywheel and ignition module. Remove the two cylinder retaining bolts and carefully pull cylinder away from crankcase. Pull cylinder straight off piston, do not twist. Remove piston pin retaining rings (11 and 9), then use a

Fig. KU2—Exploded view of Teikei diaphragm type carburetor used on some models.

1. Idle speed screw
2. Spring
3. Screw
4. Pump cover
5. Gasket
6. Diaphragm
7. Plug
8. "O" ring
9. Screen
10. Felt
11. "E" ring
12. Body
13. Gasket
14. Fuel inlet needle
15. Spring
16. Fuel inlet lever
17. Screw
18. Pin
19. Diaphragm
20. Seat
21. Cover
22. Spring
23. Plunger
24. Primer lever
25. Screw
27. Spring
28. High speed mixture needle
29. Low speed mixture needle
30. Spring
31. Spring
32. Throttle shaft
33. Throttle plate
34. Screw

Fig. KU3—Throttle lever must be flush with carburetor body surface.

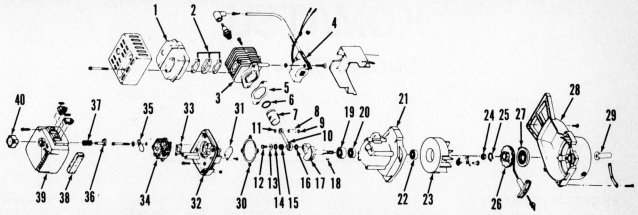

Fig. KU4—Exploded view of the 16 cc (0.96 cu. in.) Komatsu engine. Refer to Fig. KU5 also.

1. Muffler	8. Piston pin	15. Bearing
2. Gaskets	9. Retainer	16. Shim washer
3. Cylinder	10. Connecting rod	17. Crankshaft
4. Ignition module	11. Retainer	18. Key
5. Gasket	12. Bolt	19. Bearing
6. Ring	13. Washer	20. Seal
7. Piston	14. Shim washer	21. Crankcase

22. Bearing	29. Drive shaft adapter
23. Flywheel	30. Gasket
24. Nut	31. Reed plate
25. Snap ring	32. Crankcase plate
26. Pulley	33. Gasket
27. Recoil spring	34. Carburetor
28. Fan housing	

35. Choke plate
36. Choke shaft
37. Spring
38. Air filter element
39. Air filter housing
40. Choke knob

suitable piston pin puller to remove piston pin. Remove piston. Remove crankcase cover bolts, then carefully separate crankcase cover (32) from crankcase (21). Remove connecting rod retaining bolt (12). Remove washer (13) and shim (14). Slip connecting rod (10) from crankshaft journal. Remove bearing (15), shim (16) and key (18). Refer to Fig. KU5, then remove snap ring (10) and shim (9). Press crankshaft out of crankcase and bearing assembly. Note shim (2) located between bearing (3) and crankshaft counterweight. Press main bearings (3 and 8) out of crankcase housing. Remove snap rings (4 and 7), then press seal (6) out of crankcase housing.

Inspect all parts for wear or damage and renew parts as required. When installing crankshaft in crankcase and main bearings, vary thickness of shims (2 and 9—Fig. KU5) to obtain 0.1-0.3 mm (0.004-0.010 in.) end play. Refer to Fig. KU6 and install shim (16) on crankshaft connecting rod journal. Lubricate bearing (15), then install bearing on crankshaft journal. Slip connecting rod over bearing and install shim (14). Install washer (13) on connecting rod retaining bolt (12). Treat threads on connecting rod retaining bolt with a mild thread locking compound prior to installation. Tighten bolt to 2 N·m (1.5 ft.-lbs.). Refer to PISTON, PIN AND RINGS paragraphs for piston installation. Rotate crankshaft after joining crankcase halves and installing piston to make certain connecting rod and piston skirt clear crankshaft counterweight.

PISTON, PIN AND RINGS. The single ring aluminum piston is equipped with a locating pin in ring groove to

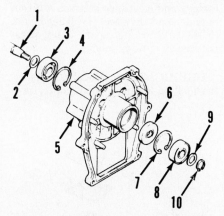

Fig. KU5—Exploded view of main bearing assembly sequence.

1. Crankshaft	6. Seal
2. Shim	7. Snap ring
3. Main bearing	8. Bearing
4. Snap ring	9. Shim
5. Crankcase	10. Snap ring

Fig. KU6—Exploded view of connecting rod bearing assembly sequence on crankpin. Refer to text.

10. Connecting rod	
12. Bolt	15. Bearing
13. Washer	16. Shim washer
14. Shim washer	17. Crankshaft

prevent ring rotation. Make certain ring end gap is correctly positioned at locating pin before installing piston in cylinder. Arrow on top of piston should point toward exhaust side of cylinder after piston installation.

CYLINDER. The cylinder bore has a chrome plated surface and must be renewed if plating is worn through or scored excessively. Worn spots will appear dull and may be easily scratched while chrome plating will be bright and much harder.

CLUTCH. Engine may be equipped with a direct drive adapter as shown at (29—Fig. KU4) or a centrifugal clutch as shown in Fig. KU7. To remove clutch, remove housing (2). Clutch shoes (7) may be removed after removing springs (6 and 8) and plate (5).

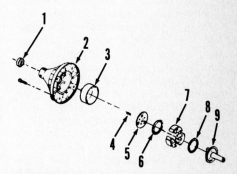

Fig. KU7—Exploded view of centrifugal clutch assembly.

1. Collar	6. Spring
2. Clutch housing	7. Clutch shoe assy.
3. Clutch drum	8. Spring
4. Screw	9. Adapter
5. Plate	

KOMATSU

ENGINE SERVICE

Model	Bore	Stroke	Displacement
G2E	34.0 mm	28.0 mm	25.4 cc
	(1.36 in.)	(1.10 in.)	(1.55 cu. in.)

ENGINE INFORMATION

Komatsu G2E two-stroke air-cooled gasoline engine is used by several manufacturers of string trimmers and brush cutters. Engine is equipped with a cantilevered type crankshaft supported in two ball bearings at flywheel side only. Refer to preceding and following sections for other Komatsu engine models.

MAINTENANCE

SPARK PLUG. Recommended spark plug is a NGK BMR-6, or equivalent. Specified electrode gap for all models is 0.6-0.7 mm (0.024-0.28 in.).

CARBURETOR. Model G2E engine is equipped with a diaphragm type carburetor with a built in fuel pump (Fig. KU10).

Initial adjustment of fuel mixture needles from a lightly seated position is one turn open for the low speed mixture needle (24) and 3/4 turn open for the high speed mixture needle (23).

Final adjustments are made with trimmer line at recommended length or blade assembly installed. Engine must be at operating temperature and running. Turn idle speed screw in until trimmer head or blade just begins to rotate. Adjust low speed mixture needle to obtain maximum idle speed possible, then turn low speed mixture needle 1/6 turn in a counterclockwise direction. Adjust idle speed screw until trimmer head or blade stops rotating (approximately 2500 rpm). Operate trimmer at full throttle and adjust high speed mixture needle to obtain maximum engine rpm, then turn high speed mixture needle 1/6 turn in a clockwise direction.

To disassemble carburetor, refer to Fig. KU10. Welch plugs are removed they must be replaced with new plugs and new plugs must be expanded with punch and sealed with a sealant compound which will not be affected by gasoline. Fuel inlet lever must be flush with carburetor body after installation (Fig. KU11).

IGNITION SYSTEM. Model G2E engine is equipped with an electronic ignition system. Ignition system is considered satisfactory if spark will jump across the 3 mm (1/8 in.) gap of a test spark plug. If no spark is produced, check on/off switch, wiring and clearance between ignition module and flywheel. If switch and wiring are satisfactory and clearance between ignition module and flywheel is 0.2-0.3 mm (0.008-0.012 in.) but spark is not present, renew ignition module.

LUBRICATION. Model G2E is lubricated by mixing a good quality two-

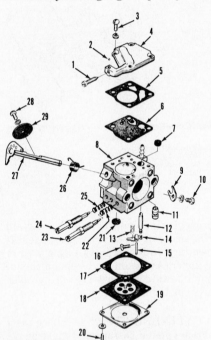

Fig. KU10—Exploded view of the diaphragm carburetor used on Model G2E engine.

1. Idle speed screw
2. Ball
3. Screw
4. Pump cover
5. Gasket
6. Diaphragm
7. Screen
8. Body
9. Retainer
10. Screw
11. Check valve
12. Fuel inlet needle
13. Spring
14. Fuel inlet lever
15. Pin
16. Screw
17. Gasket
18. Diaphragm
19. Cover
20. Screw
21. Welch plug
22. Spring
23. High speed mixture needle
24. Low speed mixture needle
25. Spring
26. Spring
27. Throttle shaft
28. Screw
29. Throttle plate

stroke air-cooled engine oil with gasoline. Refer to TRIMMER SERVICE section for correct fuel/oil mixture ratio recommended by trimmer manufacturer.

REPAIRS

COMPRESSION PRESSURE. For optimum performance, compression pressure should be 586 kPa (85 psi) and not less than 393 kPa (57 psi). Compression should be checked with engine at operating temperature and with throttle valve and choke wide open.

CRANKSHAFT AND CONNECTING ROD. Crankshaft is supported at flywheel side only in two ball bearings installed in crankcase half (Fig. KU12). To remove crankshaft, remove recoil starter and fan housing assembly and cooling shrouds. Remove air filter assembly, muffler, carburetor, flywheel and ignition module. Remove the two cylinder retaining bolts and carefully pull cylinder away from crankcase. Pull cylinder straight off piston, do not twist. Remove piston pin retaining rings (9 and 11), then use a suitable piston pin puller to remove piston pin. Remove piston. Remove crankcase cover bolts, then carefully separate crankcase cover (32) from crankcase (21). Remove connecting rod retaining bolt (12). Remove washer (13) and shim (14). Slip connecting rod (10) from crank-

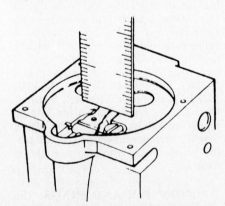

Fig. KU11—Throttle lever must be flush with carburetor body surface.

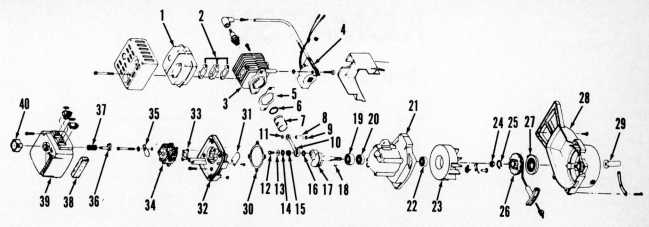

Fig. KU12—Exploded view of Model G2E engine. Refer to Fig. KU13 also.

1. Muffler	8. Piston pin	15. Bearing
2. Gaskets	9. Retainer	16. Shim washer
3. Cylinder	10. Connecting rod	17. Crankshaft
4. Ignition module	11. Retainer	18. Key
5. Gasket	12. Bolt	19. Bearing
6. Ring	13. Washer	20. Seal
7. Piston	14. Shim washer	21. Crankcase

22. Bearing	29. Drive shaft adapter	35. Choke plate
23. Flywheel	30. Gasket	36. Choke shaft
24. Nut	31. Reed plate	37. Spring
25. Snap ring	32. Crankcase plate	38. Air filter element
26. Pulley	33. Gasket	39. Air filter housing
27. Recoil spring	34. Carburetor	40. Choke knob
28. Fan housing		

shaft journal. Remove bearing (15), shim (16) and key (18). Refer to Fig. KU13, then remove snap ring (10) and shim (9). Press crankshaft out of crankcase and bearing assembly. Note shim (2) is located between bearing (3) and crankshaft counterweight. Press main bearings (3 and 8) out of crankcase housing. Remove snap rings (4 and 7), then press seal (6) out of crankcase housing.

Inspect all parts for wear or damage and renew parts as required. When installing crankshaft in crankcase and main bearings, vary thickness of shims (2 and 9—Fig. KU13) to obtain 0.1-0.3 mm (0.004-0.010 in.) end play. Refer to Fig. KU14 and install shim (16) on crankshaft connecting rod journal. Lubricate bearing (15) and install bearing on crankshaft journal. Slip connecting

rod over bearing and install shim (14). Install washer (13) on connecting rod retaining bolt (12). Treat threads on connecting rod retaining bolt with a mild thread locking compound prior to installation. Tighten bolt to 2 N·m (1.5 ft.-lbs.). Refer to PISTON, PIN AND RINGS paragraphs for piston installation. Rotate crankshaft after joining crankcase halves and installing piston to make certain connecting rod and piston skirt clear crankshaft counterweight.

PISTON, PIN AND RINGS. The single ring aluminum piston is equipped with a locating pin in ring groove to prevent ring rotation. Make certain ring end gap is correctly positioned at locating pin before installing piston in

cylinder. Cupped side of piston skirt must be toward crankshaft counterweight after installation.

CYLINDER. The cylinder bore has a chrome plated surface and must be renewed if plating is worn through or scored excessively. Worn spots will appear dull and may be easily scratched while chrome plating will be bright and much harder.

CLUTCH. Komatsu G2E engine may be equipped with a direct drive adapter as shown at (29—Fig. KU12) or a centrifugal clutch as shown in Fig. KU15. To remove clutch, remove housing (2). Clutch shoes (7) may be removed after removing springs (6 and 8) and plate (5).

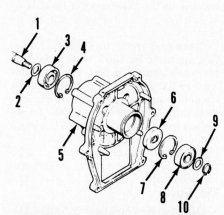

Fig. KU13—Exploded view of main bearing assembly sequence.

1. Crankshaft	6. Seal
2. Shim	7. Snap ring
3. Main bearing	8. Bearing
4. Snap ring	9. Shim
5. Crankcase	10. Snap ring

Fig. KU14—Exploded view of connecting rod bearing assembly sequence on crankpin. Refer to text.

10. Connecting rod	
12. Bolt	15. Bearing
13. Washer	16. Shim washer
14. Shim washer	17. Crankshaft

Fig. KU15—Exploded view of centrifugal clutch assembly.

1. Collar	
2. Clutch housing	6. Spring
3. Clutch drum	7. Clutch shoe assy.
4. Screw	8. Spring
5. Plate	9. Adapter

KOMATSU

ENGINE SERVICE

Model	Bore	Stroke	Displacement
G2D	32.0 mm	28.0 mm	22.5 cc
	(1.28 in.)	(1.10 in.)	(1.37 cu. in.)
G2K	34.0 mm	28.0 mm	25.4 cc
	(1.36 in.)	(1.10 in.)	(1.55 cu. in.)
G4K	40.0 mm	33.0 mm	41.5 cc
	(1.60 in.)	(1.32 in.)	(2.53 cu. in.)

ENGINE INFORMATION

Komatsu two-stroke air-cooled gasoline engines are used by several manufacturers of string trimmers and brush cutters. Refer to preceding section for other Komatsu engine models.

MAINTENANCE

SPARK PLUG. Recommended spark plug for G2D and G2K models is a NGK BM-7A, or equivalent. Recommended spark plug for G4K model is a NGK BPM-6A. Specified electrode gap for all models is 0.6-0.7 mm (0.024-0.28 in.).

CARBURETOR. Models G2D and G2K are equipped with Walbro WZ variable venturi diaphragm type car-

buretor and Model G4K is equipped with a DPK diaphragm type carburetor. Refer to the appropriate paragraph for model being serviced.

Walbro WZ Series Carburetor. Refer to Fig. KU47 for an exploded view of the Walbro WZ series carburetor. Initial setting for low speed adjustment screw (25) is at the middle of the five notches. Initial setting for the high speed mixture needle (42) is 1-1/2 turns open from a lightly seated position.

Final adjustment is made with string trimmer line at recommended length of blade assembly installed. Engine must be at operating temperature and running. Operate engine at full rpm and adjust high speed mixture needle to obtain approximately 11000 rpm. Release throttle and allow engine to idle. Adjust idle speed screw (30) to obtain

3000-3300 rpm. If idle rpm cannot be obtained at idle speed screw, turn low speed mixture needle one notch at a time to obtain 3000-3300 rpm. Turning low speed mixture needle counterclockwise richens fuel mixture and turning low speed mixture needle clockwise leans fuel mixture.

To disassemble Walbro WZ series carburetor, remove air filter cover (36), filter element (35), spring (34) and plate (33). Remove the four screws (1), metal plate (2) and primer bulb (3). Remove screw (4), then separate pump cover (5), gasket (6), plate (7), pump diaphragm (8) and gasket (9) from carburetor body (23). Remove fuel strainer screen from port (44) in carburetor body. Remove the four screws (17) and remove cover (16), diaphragm (15) and gasket (14). Use a small screwdriver to "pop" in (13) from plastic retainers, then remove pin (13), fuel inlet lever (12), fuel needle (10) and spring (11). Remove high speed mixture needle (42) and spring (43). Remove metal sleeve (41) and pull throttle barrel assembly (24) from body as required. Do not disassemble throttle barrel. Clear plastic end cap (40) is bonded to the plastic carburetor body at the factory and should not be removed.

Clean carburetor in a cleaning solution approved for the all plastic body of the carburetor. Inspect all parts for wear or damage. Tip of fuel inlet needle should be smooth and free of grooves. Fuel inlet lever spring (11) free length should be 8.7 mm (0.34 in.). When reassembling carburetor, fuel inlet lever (12) should be adjusted to obtain 1.2-1.5 mm (0.039-0.040 in.) between carburetor body surface and top of lever (D—Fig. KU48).

DPK Series Carburetor. Initial setting of the high speed mixture needle is 1-1/2 turns out from a lightly seated position. Make final adjustments with trimmer line at proper length or blade assembly installed and engine at oper-

Fig. KU47—Exploded view of Walbro WZ variable venturi carburetor used on some models.

1. Screw
2. Plate
3. Primer bulb
4. Screw
5. Cover
6. Gasket
7. Plate
8. Diaphragm
9. Gasket
10. Fuel inlet needle
11. Spring
12. Fuel inlet lever
13. Pin
14. Gasket
15. Diaphragm
16. Cover
17. Screw
18. Bracket
19. Screw
20. Nut
21. Bolt
22. Gasket
23. Body
24. Throttle valve assy.
25. Low speed mixture needle
26. Throttle cable swivel
27. Screw
28. Bracket
29. Spring
30. Idle speed screw
31. "E" ring
32. Metal sleeve support
33. Plate
34. Spring
35. Air filter
36. Cover
37. Wick
38. Gasket
39. Plate
40. Cap
41. Sleeve
42. High speed mixture needle
43. Spring

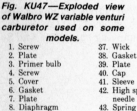

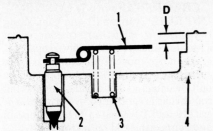

Fig. KU48—View showing correct method for measuring dimension (D). Refer to text.

1. Fuel inlet lever   3. Spring
2. Fuel inlet needle   4. Carburetor body

ating temperature and running. Operate engine at wide open throttle and turn high speed mixture needle in so engine begins to run smoothly, then back out screw 1/8 turn. Normal range of adjustment is 1-2 turns out from a lightly seated position. Adjust idle speed screw so engine idles just below clutch engagement speed. Midrange mixture is determined by the position of clip (7—Fig. KU49) on jet needle (8). There are three grooves located at the upper end of the jet needle (Fig. KU50) and normal position of clip (7—Fig. KU49) is in the middle groove. The mixture will be leaner if clip is installed in the top groove or richer if clip is installed in the bottom groove.

To disassemble carburetor, unscrew throttle cap (4—Fig. KU49) and carefully pull throttle valve assembly out of carburetor body. Remove carburetor from engine. Remove primer lever (3), spring (2) and valve (1). Remove the four screws and separate cover (26) from carburetor body. Remove diaphragm (25) and gasket (24). Remove screw, pin (21), fuel inlet lever (20), fuel inlet needle (19) and spring (23). Remove pump cover (18), diaphragm (17) and gasket (16). Remove fuel mixture needle (12) and needle jet (15).

DPK carburetor is equipped with an integral fuel pump (16, 17 and 18—Fig. KU49).

Inspect all parts carefully. Diaphragms should be flexible. Metal button must be tight on metering diaphragm. When assembling the carburetor the metering diaphragm lever should be 1.4-1.7 mm (0.039-0.040 in.) below the carburetor body (D—Fig. KU48).

IGNITION SYSTEM. All engines are equipped with transistorized ignition system. Ignition system is considered satisfactory if spark will jump across the 3 mm (1/8 in.) gap of a test spark plug. If no spark is produced, check on/off switch, wiring or module air gap.

If switch and wiring are satisfactory, check coil and transistor unit with an ohmmeter. To check coil, set ohmmeter

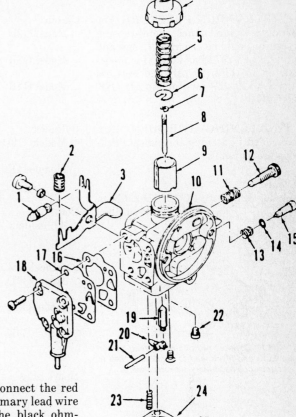

Fig. KU49—Exploded view of DPK diaphragm type carburetor used on some models.

1. Tickler valve
2. Spring
3. Lever
4. Cap
5. Spring
6. Retainer
7. Clip
8. Jet needle
9. Throttle slide
10. Body
11. Spring
12. Idle speed screw
13. Spring
14. "O" ring
15. Mixture screw
16. Pump gasket
17. Pump diaphragm
18. Pump cover
19. Inlet needle valve
20. Metering lever
21. Pin
22. Screw
23. Spring
24. Gasket
25. Diaphragm
26. Cover

to the R x 1 scale and connect the red ohmmeter lead to the primary lead wire (Fig. KU51). Connect the black ohmmeter lead wire to the coil core. Specified resistance of the primary winding is 0.68-0.88 ohms for Models G2K and G4K. Connect the red ohmmeter lead to the spark plug wire and connect the black ohmmeter lead to the coil core (Fig. KU52). Specified resistance of the secondary coil windings is 5525-7475 ohms for Model G2D, 5355-7245 ohms for Model G2K or 5670-6930 ohms for Model G4K.

Transistor unit may be checked using an ohmmeter set at the R x 10K scale. Connect the black ohmmeter lead to the transistor unit case and connect the red ohmmeter lead to the transistor lead wire (Fig. KU53). Ohmmeter should register 60 ohms for Model G2D, 95 ohms for Model G2K or 40 ohms for Model G4K. Connect black ohmmeter lead to and connect the red ohmmeter lead to the transistor unit case. Ohmmeter should register 100 ohms for Model G2D, 40 ohms for Model G2K or 95 ohms for Model G4K.

Air gap between ignition module and flywheel should be 0.2-0.3 mm (0.008-0.012 in.).

LUBRICATION. All models are lubricated by mixing a good quality two-stroke air-cooled engine oil with gasoline. Refer to TRIMMER SERVICE section for correct fuel/oil mixture ratio recommended by trimmer manufacturer.

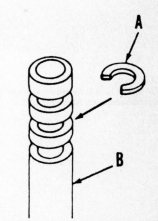

Fig. KU50—Fuel needle clip should be installed in the center groove.

Fig. KU51—Connect red ohmmeter lead to iron laminations and black lead to primary lead to check coil primary side resistance.

REPAIRS

COMPRESSION PRESSURE. For optimum performance, compression pressure should be 490 kPa (71 psi) and not less than 297 kPa (43 psi) for Model G2D or 586 kPa (85 psi) and not less than 393 kPa (57 psi) for Models G2K and G4K.

TIGHTENING TORQUES. Recommended tightening torque specifications are as follows:

Carburetor:
Model G2D . . . . . . 1.9-2.9 N·m
(17-26 in.-lbs.)

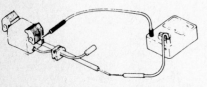

Fig. KU52—Connect red ohmmeter lead to iron laminations and black lead to spark plug lead to check coil secondary side resistance.

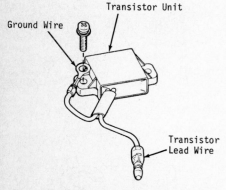

Fig. KU53—Refer to text for procedure and test specifications for transistor unit.

Models G2K & G4K . . 2.9-4.4 N·m
(26-39 in.-lbs.)

Clutch:
Model G2D . . . . . . 4.9-6.6 N·m
(43-52 in.-lbs.)
Model G2K . . . . . . 4.9-7.8 N·m
(43-69 in.-lbs.)
Model G4K . . . . . 10.7-16.6 N·m
(95-147 in.-lbs.)

Cylinder:
Models G2D & G2D . . 3.4-4.4 N·m
(30-39 in.-lbs.)
Model G4K . . . . . . 4.9-7.8 N·m
(43-69 in.-lbs.)

Coil:
All models . . . . . . 1.5-1.9 N·m
(13-17 in.-lbs.)

Flywheel (rotor):
Model G2D . . . . . 15.7-17.6 N·m
(139-156 in.-lbs.)
Model G2K . . . . . 11.7-17.6 N·m
(104-156 in.-lbs.)
Model G4K . . . . . 19.5-29.4 N·m
(173-260 in.-lbs.)

Spark plug:
Model G2D . . . . . 19.5-24.5 N·m
(173-217 in.-lbs.)
Models G2K & G4K . 10.8-21.6 N·m
(130-191 in.-lbs.)

Transistor unit:
Model G2D . . . . . . 1.9-2.5 N·m
(17-26 in.-lbs.)
Models G2K & G4K . . 1.5-2.5 N·m
(13-22 in.-lbs.)

CRANKSHAFT AND CONNECTING ROD. Crankshaft and connecting rod (14—Fig. KU54) are considered an assembly and are not serviced separately. Do not remove connecting rod from crankshaft. Crankshaft is supported by ball bearings at both ends. Connecting rod thrust is controlled by thrust washers (16 and 23) located between piston and connecting rod on piston pin.

To remove crankshaft and connecting rod assembly, remove fuel tank, spark plug, transistor unit, air cleaner, carburetor, muffler guard, muffler, cylinder cover, fan cover and clutch assembly. On G2D models, remove the two bolts retaining clutch shoes and remove clutch shoes and spring as an assembly. Remove clutch plate retaining bolt and use puller (part number 257602) to remove clutch plate. Remove the four bolts and remove clutch case. Use the same puller to remove flywheel. On G2K models, use puller (part number 307604) to remove flywheel. On G4K models, use puller (part number 407605) to remove flywheel. On G2K and G4K models, remove starter pulley using the same puller as used to remove flywheel. On G2D models, remove the three screws and remove ignition coil. On all models, remove the four cylinder screws and carefully separate cylinder from crankcase and off of piston. Pull cylinder straight off, do not twist. Carefully remove piston rings. Remove piston pin retaining rings (15 and 24) and use piston pin puller to remove piston pin. Piston pin puller part number for G2D models is 260410, for G2K models part number is 307606 and for G4K models part number is 400357. Catch thrust washers (16 and 23) as piston is removed. Remove bearing (21) from

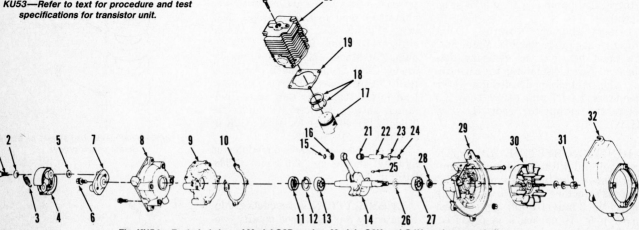

Fig. KU54—Exploded view of Model G2D engine. Models G2K and G4K engines are similar.

1. Clutch bolt
2. Spring washer
3. Spring
4. Clutch shoe
5. Flat washer
6. Bolt
7. Adapter
8. Clutch housing
9. Crankcase half
10. Gasket
11. Seal
12. Snap ring
13. Bearing
14. Crankshaft & connecting rod assy.
15. Retainer
16. Thrust washer
17. Piston
18. Rings
19. Gasket
20. Cylinder
21. Bearing
22. Piston pin
23. Thrust washer
24. Retainer
25. Key
26. Shim
27. Bearing
28. Seal
29. Crankcase half
30. Flywheel
31. Nut
32. Cover

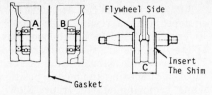

Fig. KU55—Refer to text for formula used to calculate crankshaft end play. Make measurements A, B and C as shown.

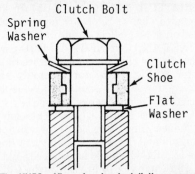

Fig. KU56—View showing installation sequence of clutch bolt, spring washer and flat washer.

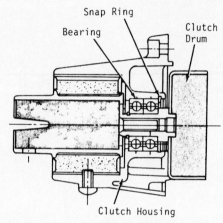

Fig. KU57—View showing installation sequence of clutch drum, bearings and snap ring in clutch housing.

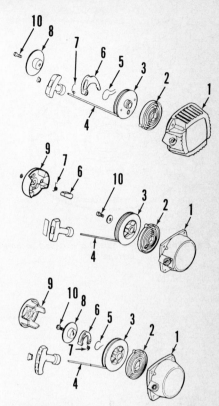

Fig. KU58—Exploded view of rewind starter assemblies. Top assembly is used on G2D engine, center assembly is used on G2K engine and lower assembly is used on G4K engine.

1. Housing		6. Ratchet
2. Rewind spring		7. Spring
3. Pulley		8. Friction plate
4. Rope		9. Starter plate
5. Friction spring		10. Screw

connecting rod. Remove key (25) from crankshaft. Remove the four crankcase bolts and carefully separate crankcase halves. Remove crankshaft and connecting rod assembly. Press bearings from crankshaft as required. Note location of shim (26) used to control crankshaft end play.

Inspect all parts for wear or damage. Crankshaft runout should not exceed 0.07 mm (0.0028 in.). Crankshaft axial play should not exceed 0.4 mm (0.016 in.)

To correctly set crankshaft end play, refer to Fig. KU55. Carefully measure to obtain dimensions A, B and C. Note gasket must be installed on one crankcase half. Note that the letter "S" used in the formula indicates clearance used to determine shim thickness. Use the formula $S = (A + B + 0.3 \text{ mm}) - C$ to determine shim thickness. If clearance "S" calculates to less than 0.3 mm (0.012 in.) no shims are needed. If clearance "S" is 0.3-0.5 mm (0.012-0.020 in.) one shim is required. If clearance "S" is 0.5-0.7 mm (0.020-0.028 in.) two shims are required. Shim or shims must be installed at starter side of crankshaft.

PISTON, PIN AND RINGS. The aluminum piston for all models is equipped with two rings. Rings are prevented from rotating on piston by locating pins installed in each piston ring groove. Make certain ring end gaps are aligned with locating pins prior to installation of piston into cylinder. To remove piston, refer to CRANKSHAFT AND CONNECTING ROD paragraphs. Note location of thrust washers (16 and 23—Fig. KU54) to control connecting rod thrust. Arrow on top of piston must face toward exhaust side of cylinder after piston is installed on connecting rod.

Refer to the following chart for standard piston diameters and wear limits.

Engine	Standard	Limit
Model G2D	32.0 mm	31.9 mm
	(1.280 in.)	(1.276 in.)
Model G2K	34.0 mm	33.86 mm
	(1.360 in.)	(1.374 in.)
Model G4K	40.0 mm	39.86 mm
	(1.600 in.)	(1.594 in.)

Refer to the following chart for standard piston pin diameter and wear limit.

Engine	Standard	Limit
Models G2D		
& G2K	8.0 mm	7.98 mm
	(0.3150 in.)	(0.3140 in.)
Model G4K	11.0 mm	10.98 mm
	(0.4400 in.)	(0.4392 in.)

Refer to the following chart for standard piston pin bore diameter in piston.

Engine	Standard	Limit
Models G2D		
& G2K	8.0 mm	8.04 mm
	(0.3150 in.)	(0.3161 in.)
Model G4K	11.0 mm	11.04 mm
	(0.4400 in.)	(0.4420 in.)

Ring groove width in piston should be 1.5 mm (0.059 in.) and ring end gap should be 1-3 mm (0.004-0.012 in.) and not less than 1.37 mm (0.54 in.) for all models. Piston ring width should be 1.5 mm (0.059 in.) and not less than 1.37 mm (0.054 in.) for all models.

Ring clearance in piston ring groove should be 0.02-0.06 mm (0.0008-0.0024 in.) for all models.

Piston to cylinder clearance for Models G2D and G2K should be 0.025-0.060 mm (0.001-0.0024 in.). Piston to cylinder clearance for Model G4K should be 0.045-0.080 mm (0.0018-0.0030 in.).

CYLINDER. All engines are equipped with a chrome plated cylinder bore. Refer to the following chart for standard cylinder bore diameters and wear limits.

Engine	Standard	Limit
Model G2D	32.0 mm	32.06 mm
	(1.280 in.)	(1.282 in.)
Model G2K	34.0 mm	34.06 mm
	(1.360 in.)	(1.362 in.)
Model G4K	40.0 mm	40.06 mm
	(1.600 in.)	(1.602 in.)

On all engines, if cylinder taper exceeds 0.01 mm (0.0004 in.) or if cylinder out-of-round exceeds 0.03 mm (0.0012 in.), cylinder must be renewed.

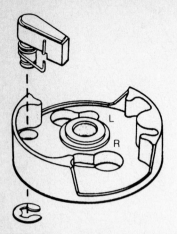

Fig. KU59—Ratchet must be installed in hole marked "R".

CLUTCH. Refer to Fig. KU54 for an exploded view of the centrifugal clutch used on most models. Refer to CRANK-SHAFT AND CONNECTING ROD paragraphs for clutch removal procedure. Refer to Fig. KU57 for assembly sequence for clutch drum and housing parts. To install clutch bolts (1–Fig. KU54), refer to Fig. KU56 for assembly sequence and position for spring washers and flat washers. Clutch spring (3–Fig. KU54) should have a free length of 22.23 mm (0.875 in.) for Model G2D, 23.81 mm (0.938 in.) for Model G2K or 34.93 mm (1.375 in.) for Model G4K. When installing clutch shoes, make certain side of clutch shoes marked with arrow faces out.

RECOIL STARTER. All models are equipped with a rewind type starter. Refer to Fig. KU58 for an exploded view of the rewind starter assemblies used. To disassemble starter, pull starter rope out of housing and hold in position while removing starter rope. Slowly allow rope to rewind on starter pulley. Turn pulley a few turns clockwise to disengage from inner end of rewind spring. Remove center screw and carefully lift pulley out of housing. Use pliers if rewind spring has to be removed. Use care as rewind spring may still be under tension. Rewind spring should be preloaded 2-3 turns during installation of pulley and starter rope. On Model G2K, ratchet (6) is installed in the hole marked "R" (Fig. KU59).

McCULLOCH

ENGINE SERVICE

Model	Bore	Stroke	Displacement
McCulloch	32.2 mm	25.4 mm	21.2 cc
	(1.27 in.)	(1.02 in.)	(1.29 cu. in.)

ENGINE INFORMATION

McCulloch two-stroke air-cooled gasoline engine is used on McCulloch string trimmers and brush cutters.

MAINTENANCE

SPARK PLUG. Recommended spark plug is a Champion CJ8, or equivalent. Specified electrode gap for all models is 0.6-0.7 mm (0.024-0.28 in.).

CARBURETOR. McCulloch engine may be equipped with a Walbro diaphragm type carburetor with a built in fuel pump (Fig. MC50) or a Zama diaphragm type carburetor (Fig. MC52). Refer to appropriate paragraph for model being serviced.

Walbro Diaphragm Type Carburetor. Initial adjustment of fuel mixture needles from a lightly seated position is 1-1/8 turn open for low speed mixture screw (18 – Fig. MC50) and 1-1/4 turn open for high speed mixture needle.

Final adjustments are made with trimmer line at recommended length. Engine should be at operating temperature and running. Turn idle speed screw (31) to obtain 2500-3000 rpm. Trimmer head should not rotate at this speed. Adjust low speed mixture needle (18) to obtain consistent idling and smooth acceleration. Readjust idle speed screw (31) as required. Open throttle fully and adjust high speed mixture needle (17) to obtain highest engine rpm, then turn high speed mixture needle counterclockwise 1/8 turn.

To disassemble carburetor, remove the four screws retaining cover (1) to carburetor body. Remove cover (1), diaphragm (2) and gasket (3). Remove screw (4), pin (5), fuel inlet lever (6), spring (8) and fuel inlet needle (7). Remove screw (9) and remove circuit plate (10), check valve (11) and gasket (12). Remove screw (29), cover (28), gasket (27) and diaphragm (26). Remove inlet screen (24). Remove high and low speed mixture needles and springs. Re-

move throttle plate (13) and shaft (20) as required.

Carefully inspect all parts. Diaphragms should be flexible and free of cracks or tears. When reassembling, fuel inlet lever (6) should be flush with carburetor body (Fig. MC51). Carefully bend fuel inlet lever to obtain correct setting.

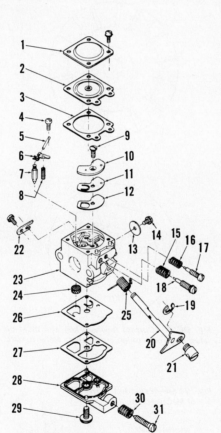

Fig. MC50—Exploded view of Walbro carburetor used on some models.

1. Cover	17. High speed mixture
2. Metering diaphragm	needle
3. Gasket	18. Idle mixture needle
4. Metering lever screw	19. "E" clip
5. Metering lever pin	20. Throttle shaft
6. Metering lever	21. Swivel
7. Fuel inlet valve	22. Throttle shaft clip
8. Metering lever spring	23. Body
9. Circuit plate screw	24. Inlet screen
10. Circuit plate	25. Return spring
11. Check valve	26. Fuel pump diaphragm
12. Gasket	27. Gasket
13. Throttle valve	28. Cover
14. Shutter screw	29. Cover screw
15. Spring	30. Spring
16. Spring	31. Idle speed screw

Zama Diaphragm Type Carburetor. Initial adjustment of low speed (16—Fig. MC52) and high speed (17) mixture needles is one turn open from a lightly seated position.

Final adjustments are made with trimmer line at recommended length. Engine should be at operating temperature and running. Turn idle speed screw (27) to obtain 2500-3000 rpm. Trimmer head should not rotate at this speed. Adjust low speed mixture needle (16) to obtain consistent idling and smooth acceleration. Readjust idle speed screw (27) as required. Open throttle fully and adjust high speed mixture needle (17) to obtain highest engine rpm, then turn high speed mixture needle counterclockwise 1/8 turn.

To disassemble carburetor, remove screw (26), pump cover (25), gasket (24) and diaphragm (23). Remove fuel inlet screen (22). Remove the two screws (1) and remove cover (2), diaphragm (3) and gasket (4). Remove screw (5), pin (7), metering disc (6), fuel inlet lever (8), fuel inlet needle (9) and spring (10). Remve fuel mixture needles and springs. Remove "E" clip (11), throttle plate (13) and throttle shaft (21) as required.

Inspect all parts for wear or damage. Diaphragms should be flexible with no cracks or wrinkles. Fuel inlet lever (8) with metering disc (6) removed, should be flush with carburetor fuel chamber floor (Fig. MC51).

IGNITION SYSTEM. McCulloch engine is equipped with an electronic ignition system manufactured by Wabash (orange module) or Sems (black module). Ignition system is considered satisfactory if spark will jump across the 3 mm (1/8 in.) gap of a test spark plug. If no spark is produced, check on/off switch, wiring and ignition module air gap. Ignition module air gap should be 0.4 mm (0.016 in.). If switch, wiring and module air gap are satisfactory but spark is not present, renew ignition module.

Correct ignition system identification is required to correctly install flywheel. Wabash ignition module is orange in color and Sems ignition module is black. Flywheel on early engine equipped with Wabash ignition system has only one key slot. Wabash ignition must be used on these models unless flywheel is renewed also. Late model and replacement flywheels have two key slots and may be used with either ignition system provided flywheel is

installed correctly. Key slots are identified by the letter (W) for Wabash or (S) for Sems (Fig. MC53). Install flywheel with key in correct slot for ignition system being used.

LUBRICATION. Engine lubrication is obtained by mixing a good quality two-stroke air-cooled engine oil with gasoline. Refer to TRIMMER SERVICE section for correct fuel/oil mixture ratio recommended by trimmer manufacturer.

REPAIRS

COMPRESSION PRESSURE. For optimum performance, compression pressure should be 621 kPa (90 psi). Compression test should be performed with engine cold and throttle and choke plates at wide open positions.

TIGHTENING TORQUES. Recommended tightening torque specifications are as follows:

Spark plug	14-15 N·m (10.4-11.3 ft.-lbs.)
Crankshaft nut	16-20 N·m (11.7-14.6 ft.-lbs.)
Crankcase	.4-4.5 N·m (2.9-3.3 ft.-lbs.)
Cylinder	.5.6-6.2 N·m (4.2-4.6 ft.-lbs.)
Clutch hub	19.7-23.7 N·m (14.6-17.5 ft.-lbs.)
Carburetor	.4.0-4.5 N·m (2.9-3.3 ft.-lbs.)

CRANKSHAFT AND CONNECTING ROD. The crankshaft and connecting rod are serviced as an assembly, individual parts are not available separately.

To remove crankshaft and connecting rod assembly remove fan housing and clutch assembly. Remove carburetor, muffler and fuel tank. Remove starter assembly, flywheel and ignition module. Carefully remove cylinder (27—Fig. MC54). Remove retaining rings (22) and use a suitable piston pin puller to remove pin (23). Note thrust washers (19 and 21) will fall when piston pin is removed. Remove thrust washers and piston. Separate crankcase halves and remove crankshaft and connecting rod assembly. Carefully press ball bearings (12 and 14) off crankshaft as required. If bearings remain in crankcase, it may be necessary to heat crankcase halves slightly to remove bearings.

Inspect all parts for wear or damage. Crankcase runout should not exceed 0.05 mm (0.002 in.). Note it may be necessary to slightly heat crankcase halves to easily install ball bearings (12 and 14).

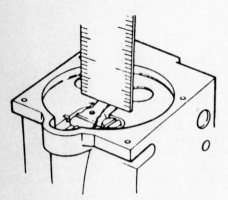

Fig. MC51—Fuel inlet lever should be flush with carburetor body.

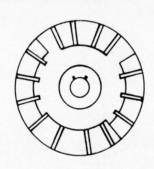

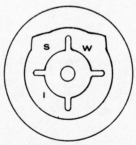

Fig. MC53—Correct flywheel key slot must be used according to ignition system. Refer to text.

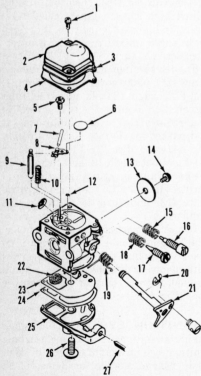

Fig. MC52—Exploded view of Zama diaphragm carburetor used on some models.

1. Screw
2. Cover
3. Diaphragm
4. Gasket
5. Screw
6. Fuel metering lever disc
7. Pin
8. Fuel inlet lever
9. Fuel inlet needle
10. Spring
11. "E" ring
12. Disc
13. Throttle plate
14. Screw
15. Spring
16. Low speed mixture needle
17. High speed mixture needle
18. Spring
19. Spring
20. "E" ring
21. Throttle shaft
22. Screen
23. Diaphragm
24. Gasket
25. Cover
26. Screw
27. Idle speed screw

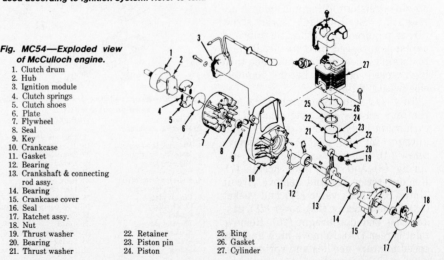

Fig. MC54—Exploded view of McCulloch engine.

1. Clutch drum
2. Hub
3. Ignition module
4. Clutch springs
5. Clutch shoes
6. Plate
7. Flywheel
8. Seal
9. Key
10. Crankcase
11. Gasket
12. Bearing
13. Crankshaft & connecting rod assy.
14. Bearing
15. Crankcase cover
16. Seal
17. Ratchet assy.
18. Nut
19. Thrust washer
20. Bearing
21. Thrust washer
22. Retainer
23. Piston pin
24. Piston
25. Ring
26. Gasket
27. Cylinder

PISTON, PIN AND RINGS. The single ring aluminum piston is equipped with a locating pin in ring groove to prevent ring rotation. Make certain ring end gap is correctly positioned at locating pin before installing piston in cylinder. To remove piston refer to CRANKSHAFT AND CONNECTING ROD paragraphs in this manual.

Standard piston diameter is 32.1 mm (1.268 in.). If piston diameter is 32.08 mm (1.263 in.) or less, renew piston.

Standard piston pin bore diameter is 8.0 mm (0.3049 in.). If piston pin bore diameter is 8.3 mm (0.3161 in.) or more, renew piston.

Standard piston pin diameter is 8.0 mm (0.3049 in.). If piston pin diameter is 7.98 mm (0.3142 in.) or less, renew piston pin.

Standard ring end gap is 0.3 mm (0.012 in.). If ring end gap is 0.5 mm (0.02 in.) or more, renew rings and/or cylinder.

Standard ring side clearance in piston groove is 0.06 mm (0.0024 in.). If ring side clearance is 0.10 mm (0.004 in.) or more, renew ring and/or piston.

CYLINDER. The cylinder bore has a chrome plated surface and must be renewed if plating is worn through or scored excessively. Worn spots will appear dull and may be easily scratched while chrome plating will be bright and much harder.

CLUTCH. Refer to Fig. MC55 for an exploded view of centrifugal clutch assembly. Note snap ring (4) is removed from snap ring bore through opening (O) in clutch drum.

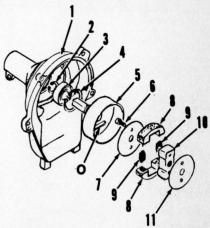

Fig. MC55—Exploded view of clutch assembly.

O. Opening	6. Screw
1. Clutch housing	7. Plate
2. Snap ring	8. Clutch shoes
3. Bearing	9. Clutch springs
4. Snap ring	10. Hub
5. Clutch drum	11. Plate

MITSUBISHI

ENGINE SERVICE

Model	Bore	Stroke	Displacement
T110	30.0 mm	30.0 mm	21.2 cc
	(1.18 in.)	(1.18 in.)	(1.29 cu. in.)
T140	32.0 mm	30.0 mm	24.1 cc
	(1.26 in.)	(1.18 in.)	(1.47 cu. in.)
T180	36.0 mm	32.0 mm	32.5 cc
	(1.42 in.)	(1.26 in.)	(1.98 cu. in.)
T200	39.0 mm	34.0 mm	40.6 cc
	(1.54 in.)	(1.34 in.)	(2.48 cu. in.)

ENGINE INFORMATION

Mitsubishi two-stroke air-cooled gasoline engines are used by several manufacturers of string trimmers and brush cutters. Refer to Fig. MI50 for engine model number interpretation.

MAINTENANCE

SPARK PLUG. Recommended spark plug for all models is a NGK BM6A. Specified electrode gap for all models is 0.6 mm (0.025 in.).

CARBURETOR. All models are equipped with a diaphragm type carburetor (Fig. MI51). Initial adjustment for the high speed mixture needle (4) is 2-1/2 turns open from a lightly seated position.

Final adjustment is made with trimmer line at recommended length or blade assembly installed. Engine should be at operating temperature and running. Operate trimmer at full throttle and adjust high speed mixture needle to obtain maximum engine output with smooth acceleration. Turning mixture needle counterclockwise richens fuel mixture and turning clockwise leans mixture.

Normal setting for fuel needle clip (6—Fig. MI52) is in the center groove in fuel needle (7). When installing fuel inlet lever, adjust lever to obtain 0.5 mm (0.019 in.) clearance between inlet lever end and gasket surface of carburetor.

IGNITION SYSTEM. Models T110, T140 and T180 are equipped with a transistorized ignition system which requires no regular maintenance and Model T200 may be equipped with a magneto ignition system with points and condenser or a transistorized ignition system. Ignition system is considered satisfactory if a spark will jump the 3 mm (1/8 in.) gap of a test spark plug. Air gap for for ignition module is 0.3-0.4 mm (0.012-0.016 in.).

Model T200 is equipped with a magneto ignition system with points and condenser located behind flywheel. Point gap is 0.28-0.38 mm (0.011-0.015 in.). Air gap between ignition coil and flywheel should be 0.41-0.50 mm (0.016-0.020 in.). Points should be adjusted to where points begin to open as match mark on flywheel lines up with "M" or "P" mark cast on crankcase.

LUBRICATION. All models are lubricated by mixing a good quality two-stroke air-cooled engine oil with gasoline. Refer to TRIMMER SERVICE section for correct fuel/oil mixture ratio recommended by trimmer manufacturer.

REPAIRS

CRANKSHAFT AND CONNECTING ROD. Refer to Fig. MI53 for an exploded view of the T200 engine. All other engines are similar in construction. To remove crankshaft, remove all cooling shrouds and rewind starter assembly. Remove muffler and carburetor. Remove ignition module or coil and use suitable puller to remove flywheel. Remove all cylinder retaining bolts, then carefully separate cylinder from crankcase. Cylinder should be pulled straight off piston with no twisting motion. Remove all crankcase retaining bolts, separate crankcase halves and remove crankshaft. If main bearings remain in crankcase half, heat crankcase slightly to aid bearing removal.

Crankshaft and connecting rod are considered an assembly and are not serviced separately. Do not remove connect-

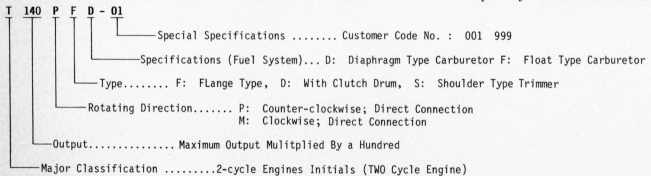

```
T 140 P F D - 01
                      └──── Special Specifications ........ Customer Code No. :  001  999

                  └──────── Specifications (Fuel System)... D:  Diaphragm Type Carburetor  F:  Float Type Carburetor

            └────────────── Type........ F: FLange Type,  D:  With Clutch Drum,  S:  Shoulder Type Trimmer

        └────────────────── Rotating Direction...... P:  Counter-clockwise; Direct Connection
                                                     M:  Clockwise; Direct Connection

    └────────────────────── Output.............. Maximum Output Mulitplied By a Hundred

  └──────────────────────── Major Classification ........2-cycle Engines Initials (TWO Cycle Engine)
```

Fig. MI50—Refer to the chart to interpret engine model number.

ing rod from crankshaft. Standard connecting rod side clearance on crankshaft is 0.16-0.35 mm (0.006-0.014 in.) for all models. Standard crankshaft main bearing journal diameter is 12 mm (0.472 in.) for Models T110, T140

and T180 or 15 mm (0.591 in.) for Model T200. If diameter is 0.05 mm (0.002 in.) less than standard diameter, renew crankshaft.

PISTON, PIN AND RINGS. To remove piston, refer to the CRANKSHAFT AND CONNECTING ROD paragraphs. Rings are pinned in piston groove to prevent ring rotation. Make certain ring end gaps are at locating pins before installing piston in cylinder.

Standard piston diameter is 30 mm (1.18 in.) for Model T110, 32 mm (1.26 in.) for Model T140, 36 mm (1.42 in.) for Model T180 or 39 mm (1.54 in.) for Model T200. If diameter of Models T110, T140 or T180 are 0.06 mm (0.002 in.) less than standard, renew piston. If diameter of Model T200 is 0.10 mm (0.0039 in.) less than standard, renew piston.

Standard ring end gap is 0.1-0.3 mm (0.004-0.012 in.) for all models. If ring end gap exceeds 0.7 mm (0.028 in.), renew rings and/or cylinder.

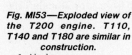

Fig. MI51—View of the diaphragm carburetor used on all models.

1. Throttle cable
2. Choke lever
3. Idle speed screw
4. High speed mixture needle
5. Primer button

Fig. MI53—Exploded view of the T200 engine. T110, T140 and T180 are similar in construction.

1. Air cleaner assy.
2. Carburetor
3. Clutch assy.
4. Ignition coil
5. Nut
6. Flywheel
7. Points & condenser
8. Crankcase
9. Seal
10. Snap ring
11. Bearing
12. Key
13. Retainer
14. Cylinder
15. Gasket
16. Rings
17. Piston
18. Piston pin
19. Bearing
20. Crankshaft & connecting rod assy.
21. Gasket
22. Bearing
23. Shim
24. Crankcase
25. Seal
26. Pulley
27. Nut
28. Housing
29. Screw
30. Friction disc
31. Ratchet
32. Brake spring
33. Pulley
34. Rewind spring

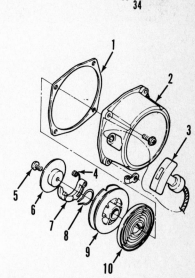

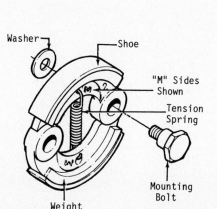

Fig. MI52—Exploded view of fuel needle and related parts.

1. Inner throttle cable
2. Cable adjusting nut
3. Jam nut
4. Housing
5. Cap
6. Clip
7. Fuel needle
8. Spring
9. Spring seat
10. Spring seat retainer
11. Throttle valve

Fig. MI54—Exploded view of clutch shoe assembly used on all models.

Washer — Shoe — "M" Sides Shown — Tension Spring — Mounting Bolt — Weight

Fig. MI55—Exploded view of rewind starter assembly used on Models T110, T140 and T180. Starter used on Model T200 is similar.

1. Gasket
2. Housing
3. Handle
4. Spring
5. Screw
6. Friction disc
7. Ratchet
8. Brake spring
9. Pulley
10. Rewind spring

If clearance between piston and cylinder exceeds 0.10 mm (0.0039 in.) for all models, renew piston and/or cylinder.

Piston is installed on connecting rod so that arrow or circle cast in top of piston is toward carburetor side of engine.

CYLINDER. Cylinder may be unbolted and removed from crankcase after shroud, muffler, carburetor and starter housing are removed.

Renew cylinder if bore is scored, cracked or if piston to cylinder clearance with new piston installed exceeds dimension given in PISTON, PIN AND RINGS paragraphs. Cylinder is chrome plated and must be renewed if chrome is flaking, peeling or worn through.

CLUTCH. Refer to Fig. MI54 for an exploded view of centrifugal clutch used on most models. All models are equipped with two clutch shoes and one clutch spring. Clutch drum is connected to drive shaft in clutch housing. Inside diameter for clutch drum is 54-56 mm (2.13-2.20 in.) for Models T110 and T140, 76-78 mm (2.99-3.07 in.) for Models T180 and T200. Shoes are installed with side marked "M" down.

RECOIL STARTER. All models are equipped with a recoil type starter similar to the one used on Models T110, T140 and T180 (Fig. MI55). To disassemble starter, remove starter housing and assembly from engine. Remove screw (5), friction plate (6), spring (8) and ratchet (7) as an assembly. Remove spring (4). Pull starter rope out and provide enough slack to engage rope in pulley notch and allow pulley to unwind in housing. Carefully remove pulley from housing.

PISTON POWERED PRODUCTS

ENGINE SERVICE

Model	Bore	Stroke	Displacement
31 cc	1.37 in.	1.25 in.	1.9 cu. in.
	(34.8 mm)	(31.8 mm)	(31 cc)

ENGINE INFORMATION

Engine serial number decal is located on aluminum crankcase plate as shown in Fig. P10. Engines are equipped with Walbro diaphragm type carburetor. Cylinder head and cylinder is a single cast unit which may be separated from crankcase.

MAINTENANCE

SPARK PLUG. Recommended spark plug is a Champion DJ8J, or equivalent. Specified electrode gap is 0.025 inch (0.51 mm).

AIR CLEANER. Engine air filter should be cleaned and re-oiled at 10 hour intervals of normal use. If operating in dusty conditions, clean and re-oil more frequently.

To remove air filter, remove the two air filter housing retaining screws (S—Fig. P11) and lift filter housing from engine. Remove foam element (1) and clean housing and carburetor compartment thoroughly. Wash element in mild solution of detergent and water. Rinse thoroughly, wrap element in a dry cloth and squeeze water out. Allow element to air dry. Re-oil element with SAE 30 engine oil and squeeze excess oil out. Install element in housing and install housing on engine.

CARBURETOR. The "all position" Walbro diaphragm type carburetor is equipped with an idle speed adjustment screw and a low speed mixture needle. High speed mixture is controlled by a fixed jet. All adjustment procedures must be performed with trimmer line at proper length or blade installed.

Initial adjustment of low speed mixture needle (21—Fig. P14) is 1-1/2 turns open from a lightly seated position. To initially adjust idle speed screw (4), turn idle speed screw out counterclockwise until throttle lever contacts boss on carburetor, then turn screw in clockwise direction until screw just contacts throttle lever. Turn screw clockwise two full turns from this position.

Final carburetor adjustment is made with engine running and at operating temperature. Operate engine at idle speed (adjust idle speed screw in 1/8 turn increments as necessary) and turn low speed mixture needle slowly clockwise until engine falters. Note this position and turn low speed mixture needle counterclockwise until engine begins to run unevenly. Note this position and set low speed mixture needle halfway between first (lean) and last (rich) positions. Squeeze throttle trigger. If engine falters or hesitates on acceleration, turn low speed mixture needle counterclockwise 1/16 turn and repeat acceleration test. Continue until smooth acceleration is obtained. Adjust idle speed as necessary to maintain idle speed just below clutch engagement speed.

To disassemble carburetor, refer to Fig. P14. Remove the four screws (18) and remove diaphragm cover (17), diaphragm (16) and gasket (15). Remove screw (14) and carefully lift metering valve (12) and pin (13) from carburetor.

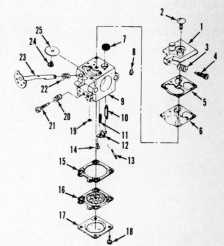

Fig. P14—Exploded view of Walbro diaphragm type carburetor.

1. Cover	14. Screw
2. Screw	15. Gasket
3. Spring	16. Diaphragm
4. Idle speed screw	17. Cover
5. Gasket	18. Screw
6. Diaphragm	19. Welch plug
7. Screen	20. Spring
8. "E" clip	21. Low speed mixture
9. Body	needle
10. Fuel inlet needle	22. Spring
11. Spring	23. Throttle shaft
12. Fuel inlet lever	24. Screw
13. Pin	25. Throttle plate

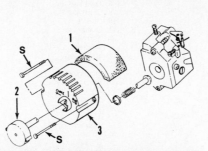

Fig. P11—View showing location of air filter retaining screws (S). Foam pad (1) is used as air filter element. Refer to text for cleaning procedure.

1. Air filter
2. Choke knob   3. Air filter housing

Fig. P10—View showing engine serial number location.

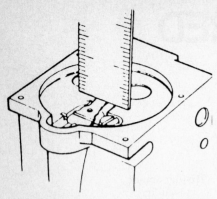

Fig. P15—Metering lever (fuel inlet lever) must be flush with fuel chamber floor as shown. Carefully bend lever to obtain correct adjustment.

Use care not to lose spring (11). Remove screw (2), cover (1), gasket (5), pump diaphragm (6), screen (7), low speed mixture needle (21) and spring (20). Remove screw (24) and throttle plate (25). Remove "E" clip (8) and throttle shaft (23). Welch plugs (19) may be removed as necessary and if new plugs are available.

Clean all metallic parts in a good quality carburetor cleaner. Rinse with clean water and use compressed air to dry. Metering lever should be flush with carburetor body (Fig. P15). Gently bend metering lever to obtain correct adjustment. Diaphragm is installed with rivet head toward metering valve lever.

IGNITION SYSTEM. Ignition module for the solid state ignition system is mounted on cylinder (37—Fig. P17). To service the module, remove the five screws retaining rewind starter

assembly to engine and note location of the single screw with lag type threads. On some models, it will be necessary to remove plastic engine cover and fuel tank. Air gap between module and flywheel is 0.010-0.015 inch (0.25-0.38 mm).

LUBRICATION. Engine is lubricated by mixing gasoline with a good quality two-stroke air-cooled engine oil. Refer to TRIMMER SERVICE section for correct fuel/oil ratio recommended by trimmer manufacturer.

CARBON. Muffler and exhaust ports should be cleaned after every 50 hours of operation if engine is operated continuously at full load. If operated at light or medium load, the cleaning interval can be extended to 100 hours.

REPAIRS

COMPRESSION PRESSURE. For optimum performance cylinder compression pressure should be 90-120 psi (621-828 kPa). Compression pressure should be checked with engine at operating temperature and throttle and choke valves wide open.

TIGHTENING TORQUES. Recommended tightening torque specifications are as follows:

Crankcase plate to
  crankcase . . . . 120 in.-lbs.
                    (13 N·m)
Cylinder to crankcase . . . 120 in.-lbs.
                    (13 N·m)
Carburetor . . . . 40 in.-lbs.
                    (4 N·m)

Reed plate . . . . .15 in.-lbs.
                    (1 N·m)
Flywheel nut . . . . 150 in.-lbs.
                    (17 N·m)
Ignition module . . . . . . .28 in.-lbs.
                    (3 N·m)
Starter housing screws . . .40 in.-lbs.
                    (4 N·m)
Muffler . . . . .56 in.-lbs.
                    (6 N·m)
Air cleaner cover . . . . . .40 in.-lbs.
                    (4 N·m)
Spark plug . . . . 150 in.-lbs.
                    (17 N·m)

CRANKSHAFT. Cantilevered design crankshaft (9—Fig. P17) is supported on flywheel side by two ball bearing type main bearings (13 and 17). Crankshaft must be a press fit in ball bearing type main bearings. Connecting rod is a slip fit on stub crankpin journal. Crankpin journal must be smooth, round and free from scores or damage.

To remove crankshaft, from models equipped with clutch, first remove clutch housing (31—Fig. P18). Unscrew the clutch drum retaining screw (29S) located at bottom of squared drive shaft adapter hole of clutch drum (30) then remove drum. Threads of the slotted head screw are coated with thread locking material and may be difficult to remove. Unscrew clutch hub assembly (28) and shoes from end of crankshaft. On all models, remove the five screws retaining rewind starter housing (26—Fig. P18 or P18A), then remove housing. Note location of the single screw with lag type threads (S). Disconnect spark plug and remove stand assembly (19—Fig. P17). Remove flywheel retaining nut from direct drive models. Remove flywheel (18) and key (33) from all models. Remove air cleaner housing. Remove the two carburetor mounting

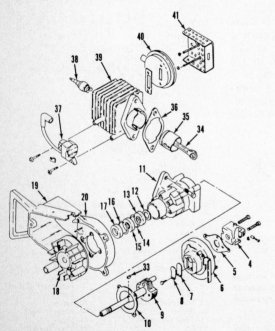

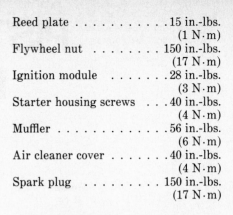

Fig. P17—Exploded view of Piston Powered Product engine.

4. Carburetor
5. Gasket
6. Crankcase plate
7. Reed plate
8. Reed back-up
9. Crankshaft
10. Gasket
11. Crankcase
12. Thrust washer
13. Bearing
14. Snap ring
15. Seal
16. Snap ring
17. Bearing
18. Flywheel
19. Shroud
20. Cover
33. Key
34. Connecting rod
35. Piston
36. Gasket
37. Ignition module
38. Spark plug
39. Cylinder
40. Muffler
41. Muffler guard

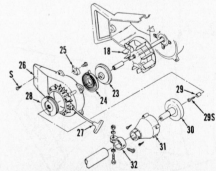

Fig. P18—Exploded view of the clutch, rewind starter and flywheel used on some models. Screw (29S) is trapped in drum (30) by spacer (29).

23. Pulley
24. Rewind spring
25. Retainer
26. Cover
27. Handle
28. Clutch hub assy.
29. Spacer
30. Clutch drum
31. Clutch housing
32. Clamp

screws, carburetor (4) and gasket (5). Remove the four reed plate mounting screws and reed plate assembly (6). Remove fuel tank assembly and fuel line. Remove the three muffler mounting screws and muffler assembly. Remove the two cylinder mounting screws and carefully work cylinder (39) away from piston. Rotate crankshaft until crankpin is at cylinder side of crankcase and slide connecting rod off crankpin to remove connecting rod and piston assembly. Remove the four screws retaining crankcase plate (20) to crankcase and remove plate (Fig. P19). Carefully press crankshaft (9—Fig. P17) out of bearings in crankcase (11). Remove thrust washer (12) from crankshaft. Drive bearings (13 and 17) from crankcase housing, remove snap rings (14 and 16) and drive seal (15) out of crankcase housing.

To reinstall crankshaft, install seal (15) in bearing bore of crankcase 0.875 inch (22.23 mm) from flywheel side of crankcase. Press against flat surface of seal so that cupped side of seal enters crankcase first. Install snap rings (14 and 16). One main bearing (17) has a single shielded side which must be out toward flywheel side of engine after installation. Press bearings (13 and 17) in until seated against snap rings. Install thrust washer (12) on crankshaft main bearing journal and press crankshaft into main bearings. Rotate crankshaft until crankpin is at cylinder side and install connecting rod and piston assembly with cut-out portion of piston skirt toward crankshaft counterweight (Fig. P21). Install gasket (36—Fig. P17) and crankcase plate (20), then tighten screws to specified torque. Make certain ring gap is correctly positioned at ring locating pin and carefully work cylinder (39) over piston until seated against crankcase. Tighten screws to specified torque. Install fuel tank and rubber tank mounts (as equipped). Install reed plate assembly, carburetor, air cleaner and muffler. Install key (33) and flywheel (18), tightening flywheel nut to specified torque. Install rewind starter assembly and clutch (as equipped).

PISTON, RINGS AND CONNECTING ROD. Piston and connecting rod are serviced as an assembly only. Stamped steel connecting rod utilizes caged needle bearings at piston pin and crankpin journal end. Caged bearings are not available separately. Piston ring on single ring piston has a locating pin in ring groove. Piston ring side clearance must not exceed 0.005 inch (0.13 mm). Piston ring width is 0.052 inch (1.32 mm). Piston ring end gap must not exceed 0.085 inch (2.16 mm). Piston standard diameter is 1.375-1.3805 inch (34.93-35.05 mm). Piston skirt is cut-out on crankshaft counterweight side to provide clearance.

CYLINDER. Cylinder must be smooth and free of scratches or flaking. Clean carbon carefully as necessary. Standard cylinder bore diameter is 1.3790-1.3805 inches (35.03-35.05 mm). Check cylinder size by installing a new piston ring squarely in cylinder and measuring ring end gap. If ring end gap exceeds 0.085 inch (2.16 mm), renew cylinder.

CRANKCASE, BEARINGS AND SEAL. Seal (15-Fig. P17) is pressed into crankcase bearing bore 0.875 inch (22.23 mm) from flywheel side. Press seal from flat surface of seal and into bearing bore from flywheel side of crankcase. Install snap rings (14 and 16) and press main bearings in until seated against snap rings. Note one main bearing has a shielded side which must be out toward flywheel side of crankcase.

REED VALVE. Reed plate (6–Fig. P17) utilizes a single reed (7) and reed back-up plate (8) held in position by two screws. Reed and reed back-up plate must be installed as shown in Fig. P20.

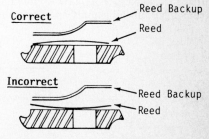

Fig. P20—Reed must be installed as shown.

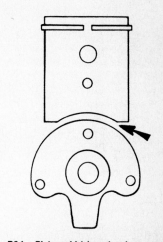

Fig. P21—Piston skirt is cut out on one side to clear crankshaft counterweight.

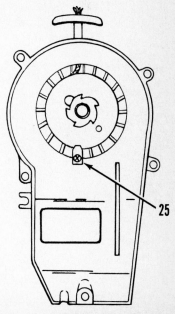

Fig. P22—View showing location of rewind starter pulley retainer (25). Refer to text.

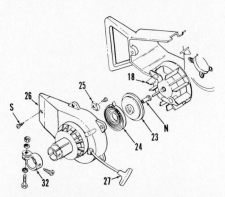

Fig. P18A—Exploded view of rewind starter and drive adapter used on direct drive models. Crankshaft is different than models with clutch and flywheel is retained by nut (N). Refer to Fig. P18 for legend.

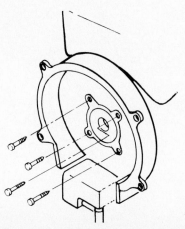

Fig. P19—Tighten screws in crankcase plate in a criss-cross pattern.

REWIND STARTER. Rewind starter dogs and springs are attached to flywheel assembly. To disassemble rewind starter, remove handle (27—Fig. P18 or P18A) and allow rope to wind onto rope pulley until all spring tension is removed. Remove retainer screw and retainer (25—Fig. P22), then carefully lift out pulley. CAUTION: Rewind spring will uncoil rapidly and come out of rewind housing. Use care during this procedure. Before reassembly, lightly coat rewind spring and inner side of pulley with grease. Wind rope entirely onto pulley. Maximum length of rope is 33 inches (89 cm). Hook outer hook on spring to spring retainer in rewind housing and carefully begin coiling spring inside housing using housing and thumb to trap spring coils. With spring wound in housing, place pulley on top of spring and use a hooked wire to work spring into position so pulley will slip all the way down into housing and engage spring. Wind spring just tight enough to provide tension to hold handle against rewind housing and push rope through rope hole in housing. Install handle and tie knot to retain rope in handle.

POULAN

ENGINE SERVICE

Model	Bore	Stroke	Displacement
Poulan	. . . . .	. . . . .	26.2 cc (1.60 cu. in.)

ENGINE INFORMATION

Poulan two-stroke air-cooled gasoline engine is used by several manufacturers of string trimmers and brush cutters.

MAINTENANCE

SPARK PLUG. Recommended spark plug is a Champion CJ8, or equivalent.

Fig. PN50—Exploded view of Walbro carburetor.

1. Cover
2. Metering diaphragm
3. Gasket
4. Metering lever screw
5. Metering lever pin
6. Metering lever
7. Fuel inlet valve
8. Metering lever spring
9. Circuit plate screw
10. Circuit plate
11. Check valve
12. Gasket
13. Throttle valve
14. Shutter screw
15. Spring
16. Spring
17. High speed mixture needle
18. Idle mixture needle
19. "E" clip
20. Throttle shaft
21. Swivel
22. Throttle shaft clip
23. Body
24. Inlet screen
25. Return spring
26. Fuel pump diaphragm
27. Gasket
28. Cover
29. Cover screw
30. Spring
31. Idle speed screw

Specified electrode gap for all models is 0.6-0.7 mm (0.024-0.028 in.).

CARBURETOR. Poulan engine is equipped with a Walbro diaphragm type carburetor with a built in fuel pump (Fig. PN50). Initial adjustment of fuel mixture needle from a lightly seated position is 1-1/8 turn open for low speed mixture needle (18) and 1¼ turn open for high speed mixture needle.

Final adjustments are made with trimmer line at recommended length. Engine should be at operating temperature and running. Turn idle speed screw (31) to obtain 2500-3000 rpm, or just below clutch engagement speed. Adjust low speed mixture needle (18) to obtain consistent idling and smooth acceleration. Readjust idle speed screw (31) as required. Open throttle fully and adjust high speed mixture needle (17) to obtain highest engine rpm, then turn high speed mixture needle counterclockwise 1/8 turn.

To disassemble carburetor, remove the four screws retaining cover (1) to carburetor body. Remove cover (1), diaphragm (2) and gasket (3). Remove screw (4), pin (5), fuel inlet lever (6), spring (8) and fuel inlet needle (7). Remove screw (9) and remove circuit plate (10), check valve (11) and gasket (12). Remove screw (29), cover (28), gasket (27) and diaphragm (26). Remove inlet screen (24). Remove high and low speed mixture needles and springs. Remove throttle plate (13) and shaft (20) as required.

Carefully inspect all parts. Diaphragms should be flexible and free of all cracks or tears. When reassembling, fuel inlet lever (6) should be flush with carburetor body (Fig. PN51). Carefully bend fuel inlet lever to obtain correct setting.

IGNITION SYSTEM. A solid state ignition system with ignition module mounted on cylinder outside of flywheel is used. Ignition system is considered satisfactory if a spark jumps the 3 mm (1/8 in.) gap of a test spark plug. Correct gap between flywheel and ignition module is 0.25-0.36 mm (0.010-0.014 in.).

CARBON. Muffler and cylinder exhaust ports should be cleaned periodical-

ly to prevent loss of power due to carbon build-up. Remove muffler cover and baffle plate and scrape muffler free of carbon. With muffler cover removed, position engine so piston is at top dead center and carefully remove carbon from exhaust ports with wooden scraper. Be careful not to damage the edges of exhaust ports or to scratch piston. Do not attempt to run engine without muffler baffle plate or cover.

LUBRICATION. Engine lubrication is obtained by mixing a good quality two-stroke air-cooled engine oil with gasoline. Refer to TRIMMER SERVICE section for fuel/oil mixture ratio recommended by trimmer manufacturer.

REPAIRS

COMPRESSION PRESSURE. For optimum performance, minimum compression pressure should be 621 kPa (90 psi). Compression test should be performed with engine cold and throttle and choke plates at wide open positions.

TIGHTENING TORQUES. Recommended tightening torque specifications are as follows:

Spark plug . . . . .14-15 N·m
(124-134 in.-lbs.)
Cylinder . . . . .7.0-7.3 N·m
(60-65 in.-lbs.)
Crankcase . . . . .4.5-5.7 N·m
(40-50 in.-lbs.)
Flywheel nut . . . . .18-20 N·m
(156-180 in.-lbs.)

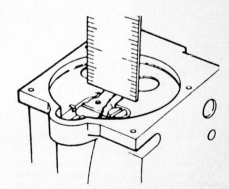

Fig. PN51—Fuel inlet lever should be flush with carburetor body.

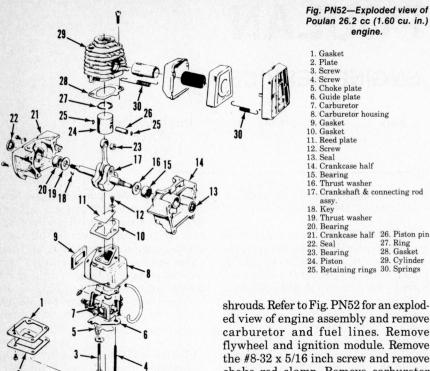

1. Gasket	
2. Plate	
3. Screw	
4. Screw	
5. Choke plate	
6. Guide plate	
7. Carburetor	
8. Carburetor housing	
9. Gasket	
10. Gasket	
11. Reed plate	
12. Screw	
13. Seal	
14. Crankcase half	
15. Bearing	
16. Thrust washer	
17. Crankshaft & connecting rod assy.	
18. Key	
19. Thrust washer	
20. Bearing	
21. Crankcase half	26. Piston pin
22. Seal	27. Ring
23. Bearing	28. Gasket
24. Piston	29. Cylinder
25. Retaining rings	30. Springs

Ignition module . . . . 3.4-4.0 N·m
(30-35 in.-lbs.)
Clutch drum . . . . 3.4-4.0 N·m
(30-35 in.-lbs.)
Clutch assembly . . . . 18-20 N·m
(156-180 in.-lbs.)

CRANKSHAFT AND CONNECTING ROD. The crankshaft and connecting rod are serviced as an assembly only and individual parts are not available.

To remove crankshaft and connecting rod assembly separate engine assembly from engine covers, fuel tank and cooling

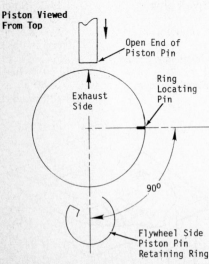

Fig. PN53—Piston is installed on connecting rod with ring locating pin to the right when looking toward exhaust side of engine. Closed end of piston pin must be toward exhaust side after installation.

shrouds. Refer to Fig. PN52 for an exploded view of engine assembly and remove carburetor and fuel lines. Remove flywheel and ignition module. Remove the #8-32 x 5/16 inch screw and remove choke rod clamp. Remove carburetor housing assembly by lifting housing from crankcase and guiding throttle rod from guide on cylinder. Note position of foam throttle and choke rod boots during removal. Remove screw (12) and reed plate (11) as required. Use service tool (31084) to prevent clutch drum rotation and use a 9/64 inch Allen wrench to remove clutch drum. Use service tool (31085) to remove clutch hub assembly. Clutch hub is turned counterclockwise to remove. Remove springs (30) and muffler assembly. Use service tool (31046) to remove the two cylinder retaining screws and remove cylinder. Remove piston pin retainers (25) and use piston pin puller (31069) to remove piston pin. Remove piston pin bushing from connecting rod as required using service tools (31069, 31077 and 31092). Remove the four #10-24 x 5/8 inch screws and carefully separate crankcase halves. Remove crankshaft and connecting rod assembly

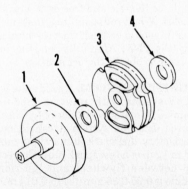

Fig. PN54—Exploded view of clutch assembly showing thrust washer installation.
1. Clutch drum
2. Thrust washer (15381)
3. Clutch hub & spring assy.
4. Thrust washer (15377)

(17) and thrust washers (16 and 19). Use service tools (31033 and 31087) to remove bearings and seals.

Inspect all parts for wear or damage. Service tools (31033 and 31088) should be used to install main bearings (15 and 20) and service tools (31033 and 31087) should be used to install seals (13 and 22). Thrust washers (16 and 19) must be installed so that the side of the washers with the shoulder is toward crankcase. Apply a thin coat of silicon sealer to crankcase halves during reassembly.

PISTON, PIN AND RINGS. The single ring piston is equipped with a ring locating pin in ring groove to prevent ring rotation.

Standard ring end gap is 0.3 mm (0.012 in.). If ring end gap is 0.5 mm (0.02 in.) or more, renew ring and/or cylinder.

Standard ring side clearance in piston groove is 0.06 mm (0.0024 in.). If ring side clearance is 0.10 mm (0.004 in.) or more, renew ring and/or piston.

When installing piston, ring must be correctly positioned over locating pin in ring groove. Install piston on connecting rod so that piston ring locating pin will be positioned as shown in Fig. PN53. Closed end of piston pin must be toward exhaust side of engine. Make certain piston pin retaining rings are correctly seated in piston pin bore of piston. Use care when installing piston into cylinder that cylinder does not rotate.

CYLINDER. The cylinder bore has a chrome plated surface and must be renewed if plating is worn through or scored excessively. Worn spots will appear dull and may be easily scratched while chrome plating will be bright and much harder.

CLUTCH. Refer to CRANKSHAFT AND CONNECTING ROD paragraphs for clutch removal procedure. Refer to Fig. PN54 for an exploded view of clutch assembly. During installation, thrust washer with part number 15377 is installed between clutch hub and crankcase and thrust washer with part number 15381 is installed between clutch hub and drum.

REWIND STARTER. To remove starter pulley, pull rope out to provide slack and install rope in rope slot in pulley. Allow pulley to slowly turn in a clockwise direction to remove rewind spring tension. Remove the #10-24 x ½ inch screw from center pulley post and remove pulley and rope assembly. Rope is wound on pulley in a counterclockwise direction during installation and rewind spring should be preloaded by turning pulley in a counterclockwise direction three full turns.

SACHS-DOLMAR

ENGINE SERVICE

Model	Bore	Stroke	Displacement
Sachs-Dolmar	37.0 mm (1.46 in.)	31.0 mm (1.22 in.)	33.0 cc (2.01 cu. in.)
Sachs-Dolmar	40.0 mm (1.57 in.)	31.0 mm (1.22 in.)	40.0 cc (2.44 cu. in.)

ENGINE INFORMATION

Sachs-Dolmar two-stroke air-cooled gasoline engines are used on Sachs-Dolmar string trimmers and brush cutters.

MAINTENANCE

SPARK PLUG. Recommended spark plug is a NGK BM7 A, or equivalent. Specified electrode gap for all models is 0.6-0.7 mm (0.024-0.028 in.).

CARBURETOR. All models are equipped with a Walbro WT series diaphragm type carburetor with a built in fuel pump (Fig. SD50).

Initial setting of low (26) and high (25) speed mixture needles is two turns open from a lightly seated position.

Final adjustments are made with trimmer line at recommended length or blade assembly installed. Engine should be at operating temperature and running. Adjust low speed mixture needle (26) so that engine idles and accelerates smoothly. Adjust idle speed screw (1) to obtain 2900-3000 engine rpm, or just below idle speed. Use an accurate digital tachometer and adjust high speed mixture needle (25) to obtain 10,800-11,000 engine rpm. Recheck engine idle speed and acceleration.

IGNITION SYSTEM. All models are equipped with an electronic ignition system. Ignition system is considered satisfactory if spark will jump across the 3 mm (1/8 in.) gap of a test spark plug. If no spark is produced, check on/off switch and wiring. If switch and wiring are satisfactory and spark is not present, renew ignition module.

Air gap between ignition module and flywheel should be 0.2-0.3 mm (0.008-0.010 in.).

LUBRICATION. All models are lubricated by mixing gasoline with a good quality two-stroke air-cooled gasoline engine oil. Refer to TRIMMER SERVICE section for correct fuel/oil mixture ratio recommended by trimmer manufacturer.

REPAIRS

TIGHTENING TORQUES. Recommended tightening torque specifications are as follows:

Carburetor . . . . 10 N·m
(7.0 ft.-lbs.)

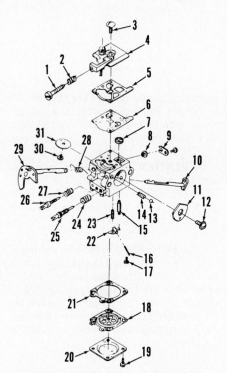

Fig. SD50—Exploded view of Walbro WT diaphragm type carburetor used on all models.

1. Idle speed screw
2. Spring
3. Screw
4. Pump cover
5. Gasket
6. Diaphragm
7. Screen
8. "E" ring
9. Clip
10. Choke shaft
11. Choke plate
12. Screw
13. Ball
14. Spring
15. Fuel inlet needle
16. Pin
17. Screw
18. Diaphragm
19. Screw
20. Cover
21. Gasket
22. Fuel inlet lever
23. Spring
24. Spring
25. High speed mixture needle
26. Low speed mixture needle
27. Spring
28. Spring
29. Throttle shaft
30. Screw
31. Throttle plate

Clutch nut . . . . 25 N·m
(18.5 ft.-lbs.)

Flywheel . . . . 20 N·m
(15.0 ft.-lbs.)

Spark plug . . . . 15 N·m
(11.0 ft.-lbs.)

Cylinder bolts . . . . .6 N·m
(4.5 ft.-lbs.)

Crankcase bolts . . . . .6 N·m
(4.5 ft.-lbs.)

Muffler bolts . . . . 10 N·m
(7.0 ft.-lbs.)

CRANKSHAFT AND CONNECTING ROD. To remove crankshaft, remove all covers and shrouds. Remove clutch, ignition system, fuel tank, clutch flange and cylinder. Use care when separating cylinder from crankcase and pull cylinder straight off piston. Remove crankcase retaining screws and carefully separate crankcase halves. The manufacturer does not recommend separating connecting rod (12 – Fig. SD52) from crankshaft (14) or removing the 12 connecting rod needle bearings (13). Remove seals (7 and 19) and snap rings (8 and 18). Heat crankcase until needle bearings (9 and 17) can be easily removed.

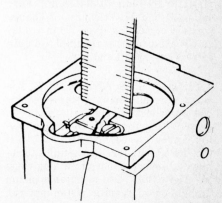

Fig. SD51—Fuel inlet lever must be flush with carburetor body. Carefully bend fuel inlet lever to adjust.

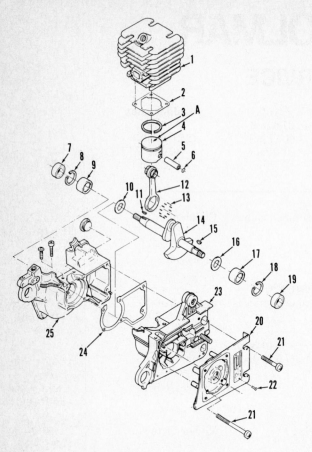

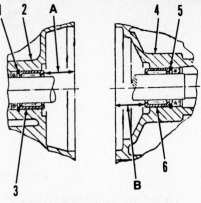

Fig. SD52—Exploded view of engine crankcase, crankshaft and cylinder assembly.

- A. Arrow
- 1. Cylinder
- 2. Gasket
- 3. Ring
- 4. Piston
- 5. Piston pin
- 6. Retaining ring
- 7. Seal
- 8. Snap ring
- 9. Main bearing
- 10. Shim
- 11. Key
- 12. Connecting rod
- 13. Needle bearings
- 14. Crankshaft
- 15. Key
- 16. Shim
- 17. Main bearing
- 18. Snap ring
- 19. Seal
- 20. Clutch flange
- 21. Bolts
- 22. Rivet
- 23. Crankcase half
- 24. Gasket
- 25. Crankcase

Fig. SD53—Cross-section view of main bearings installed in crankcase. Refer to text.

- A. 16 mm (0.63 in.)
- B. 15.7 mm (0.62 in.)
- 1. Snap ring
- 2. Crankcase half (clutch side)
- 3. Main bearing
- 4. Crankcase half
- 5. Snap ring
- 6. Main bearing

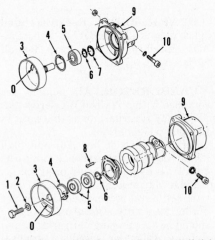

Fig. SD54—Exploded view of the centrifugal clutch assemblies.

- 0. Opening
- 1. Bolt
- 2. Washer
- 3. Clutch drum
- 4. Snap ring
- 5. Bearings
- 6. Snap ring
- 7. Snap ring
- 8. Screw
- 9. Clutch housing
- 10. Clamp bolt

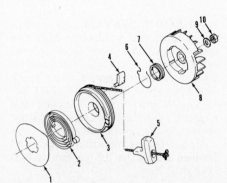

Fig. SD55—Exploded view of the rewind starter assembly.

- 1. Disc
- 2. Rewind spring
- 3. Pulley
- 4. Ratchet
- 5. Rope & handle assy.
- 6. Brake spring
- 7. Snap ring
- 8. Flywheel
- 9. Washer
- 10. Nut

To install needle bearings, heat crankcase until bearings can be installed in crankcase housings. Bearing cage is hardened on one side marked "xxx". If bearing cage edge is not marked, test with a file. Hardened side of bearing is installed toward crankshaft counterweight. Note that bearing (3—Fig. SD53) is installed 16 mm (0.63 in.) from gasket surface and bearing (6) is installed 15.7 mm (0.62 in.) from gasket surface. Bearing cages should not contact snap rings (1 and 5). Depth of main bearings and thickness of shims (10 and 16—Fig. SD52) control crankshaft end play. Correct crankshaft end play is 0.2-0.6 mm (0.79-2.36 in.). Vary shim (10 and 16) thickness or change position of bearing (9 or 17) in crankcase bearing bores as required to obtain correct crankshaft end play.

PISTON, PIN AND RINGS. The single ring aluminum piston is equipped with a locating pin in ring groove to prevent ring rotation. To remove piston, refer to CRANKSHAFT AND CONNECTING ROD paragraphs to remove cylinder. Remove retaining rings (6—Fig. SD52). Use a suitable piston pin puller to remove piston pin (5). Remove piston (4).

Make certain ring end gap is correctly positioned at locating pin before installing piston in cylinder. Arrow (A) on piston top must point toward exhaust side of engine after installation on connecting rod.

CYLINDER. To remove cylinder assembly refer to the CRANKSHAFT AND CONNECTING ROD paragraphs. Inspect cylinder for scoring or excessive wear and renew if damaged.

CLUTCH. Engines may be equipped with one of the clutch assemblies shown in Fig. SD54. To disassemble, remove snap ring (4) through opening (O) in clutch drum. Press drum assembly from clutch housing. Remove all necessary snap rings and remove bearings as required.

REWIND STARTER. Rewind starter assembly shown in Fig. SD55 is used on all models. To disassemble, remove fan housing and flywheel (8). Carefully remove brake spring (6) and snap ring (7). Remove starter pawl ratchet (4). Remove pulley (3), starter rope and handle (5), rewind spring (2) and disc (1) as an assembly keeping disc (1) and pulley (3) tight together during removal to prevent rewind spring from unwinding. Carefully allow tension of rewind spring to be released.

SHINDAIWA

ENGINE SERVICE

Model	Bore	Stroke	Displacement
Shindaiwa	30.0 mm	28.0 mm	19.8 cc
	(1.18 in.)	(1.10 in.)	(1.21 cu. in.)
Shindaiwa	31.0 mm	28.0 mm	21.1 cc
	(1.22 in.)	(1.10 in.)	(1.29 cu. in.)
Shindaiwa	32.0 mm	30.0 mm	24.1 cc
	(1.26 in.)	(1.18 in.)	(1.47 cu. in.)
Shindaiwa	36.0 mm	33.0 mm	33.6 cc
	(1.42 in.)	(1.30 in.)	(2.05 cu. in.)
Shindaiwa	39.0 mm	33.0 mm	39.4 cc
	(1.54 in.)	(1.30 in.)	(2.40 cu. in.)

ENGINE INFORMATION

Shindaiwa two-stroke air-cooled gasoline engines are used by several manufacturers of string trimmers and brush cutters.

MAINTENANCE

SPARK PLUG. Recommended spark plug for all engines is a Champion CJ 8, or equivalent. Specified electrode gap for all engines is 0.6 mm (0.025 in.).

CARBURETOR. Shindaiwa 19.8 cc (1.21 cu. in.) displacement engine is equipped with a Walbro WA series diaphragm type carburetor (Fig. SH45), 21.1 cc (1.29 cu. in.) engine is equipped with a Walbro WZ series variable venturi carburetor (Fig. SH47) and all other engines are equipped with diaphragm type carburetors with a piston type throttle valve manufactured by TK (Fig. SH50). Refer to the appropriate paragraph for model being serviced.

Walbro WA Series Carburetor. Refer to Fig. SH45 for an exploded view of the Walbro WA series carburetor. Initial adjustment of low speed mixture needle (12) is 1-1/4 turns open from a lightly seated position. Initial adjust-

ment of high speed mixture needle (13) is 1-1/16 turns open from a lightly seated position.

Final carburetor adjustment is made with trimmer line at recommended length, engine at operating temperature and running. Turn low speed mixture needle (12) clockwise until engine falters. Note this position and turn low speed mixture screw counterclockwise until engine begins to falters. Note this position and turn low speed mixture needle screw until it is halfway between first (lean) and last (rich) positions. Adjust idle speed screw (3) so that engine idles at 2500-3000 rpm. Operate engine at full rpm and adjust high speed mixture needle (13) using the same procedure outlined for low speed mixture needle. Turn high speed mixture needle in 1/8 turn increments. A properly adjusted carburetor will give high rpm with some unburned residue from muffler.

To disassemble carburetor, remove pump cover retaining screw (1), pump cover (2), diaphragm (5) and gasket (4). Remove inlet screen (6). Remove the four metering cover screws (27), metering cover (26), diaphragm (25) and gasket (24). Remove screw (20), pin (19), fuel lever (18), spring (17) and fuel inlet needle (16). Remove screw (23), circuit plate (22) and gasket (21). Remove high and low speed mixture needles and

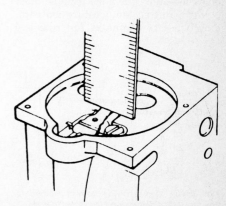

Fig. SH46—Fuel inlet lever should be flush with carburetor body.

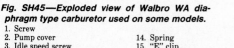

Fig. SH45—Exploded view of Walbro WA diaphragm type carburetor used on some models.

1. Screw		14. Spring
2. Pump cover		15. "E" clip
3. Idle speed screw		16. Fuel inlet needle
4. Gasket		17. Spring
5. Pump diaphragm		18. Fuel inlet lever
6. Screen		19. Pin
7. Body		20. Screw
8. Throttle plate		21. Gasket
9. Throttle shaft		22. Circuit plate
10. Spring		23. Screw
11. Spring		24. Gasket
12. Low speed mixture		25. Diaphragm
needle		26. Cover
13. High speed mixture		27. Screw
needle		

Fig. SH47—Exploded view of Walbro WZ variable venturi carburetor used on some models.

1. Screw
2. Plate
3. Primer bulb
4. Screw
5. Cover
6. Gasket
7. Plate
8. Diaphragm
9. Gasket
10. Fuel inlet needle
11. Spring
12. Fuel inlet lever
13. Pin
14. Gasket
15. Diaphragm
16. Cover
17. Screw
18. Bracket
19. Screw
20. Nut
21. Bolt
22. Gasket
23. Body
24. Throttle valve assy.
25. Low speed mixture needle
26. Throttle cable swivel
27. Screw
28. Bracket
29. Spring
30. Idle speed screw
31. "E" ring
32. Metal sleeve support
33. Plate
34. Spring
35. Air filter
36. Cover
37. Wick
38. Gasket
39. Plate
40. Cap
41. Sleeve
42. High speed mixture needle
43. Spring

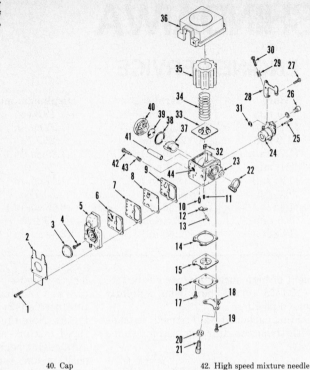

springs. Remove throttle plate (8) and throttle shaft (9) as required.

Clean parts thoroughly and inspect all diaphragms for wrinkles, cracks or tears. Diaphragms should be flexible and soft. Fuel inlet lever (18) should be flush with carburetor body (Fig. SH46).

Walbro WZ Series Carburetor. Refer to Fig. SH47 for an exploded view of the Walbro WZ series carburetor. Initial setting for low speed adjustment screw (25) is at the middle of the five notches. Initial setting for the high speed mixture needle (42) is 1-1/2 turns open from a lightly seated position.

Final adjustment is made with string trimmer line at recommended length or blade assembly installed. Engine must be at operating temperature and running. Operate engine at full rpm and adjust high speed mixture needle to obtain approximately 11000 rpm. Release throttle and allow engine to idle. Adjust idle speed screw (30) to obtain 3000-3300 rpm. If idle rpm cannot be obtained at idle speed screw, turn low speed mixture needle one notch at a time to obtain 3000-3300 rpm. Turning low speed mixture needle counterclockwise richens fuel mixture and turning low speed mixture needle clockwise leans fuel mixture.

To disassemble Walbro WZ series carburetor, remove air filter cover (36), filter element (35), spring (34) and plate (33). Remove the four screws (1), metal plate (2) and primer bulb (3). Remove screw (4) and separate pump cover (5), gasket (6), plate (7), pump diaphragm (8) and gasket (9) from carburetor body (23). Remove fuel strainer screen from port (44) in carburetor body. Remove the four screws (17), cover (16), diaphragm (15) and gasket (14). Use a small screwdriver to "pop" pin (13) from plastic retainers, then remove pin, fuel inlet lever (12), fuel needle (10) and spring (11). Remove high speed mixture needle (42) and spring (43). Remove metal sleeve (41) and pull throttle valve assembly (24) from body as required. Do not disassemble throttle valve. Clear plastic end cap (40) is bonded to the plastic carburetor body at the factory and should not be removed.

Clean carburetor in a cleaning solution approved for the all plastic carburetor body. Inspect all parts for wear or damage. Tip of fuel inlet needle should be smooth and free of grooves. Fuel inlet lever spring (11) free length should be 8.7 mm (0.34 in.). When reassembling carburetor, fuel inlet lever (12) should be adjusted to obtain 1.65 mm (0.059 in.) between carburetor body surface and top of lever (D—Fig. SH48).

TK Series Carburetor. Refer to Fig. SH50 for an exploded view of the TK diaphragm type carburetor. Initial setting for the low speed mixture needle

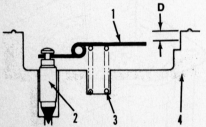

Fig. SH48—View showing correct method for measuring dimension (D). Refer to text.

1. Fuel inlet lever
2. Fuel inlet needle
3. Spring
4. Carburetor body

Fig. SH50—Exploded view of TK diaphragm type carburetor used on some models.

1. Air filter cover
2. Gasket
3. Screen
4. Bracket
5. Filter
6. Screen
7. Housing
8. Throttle valve
9. Fuel needle
10. Clip
11. Spring seat
12. Spring
13. Cap
14. Nut
15. Throttle cable adjuster
16. Spring
17. Idle speed screw
18. Low speed mixture needle
19. Spring
20. Spring
21. High speed mixture needle
22. "O" ring
23. Tube
24. Body
25. Spring
26. Fuel inlet needle
27. Fuel inlet lever
28. Pin
29. Screw
30. Gasket
31. Diaphragm
32. Cover
33. Screw
34. Sealing rings
35. Fuel pump plate
36. Gasket
37. Diaphragm
38. Fuel pump cover
39. Screws
40. Stud
41. Choke lever
42. Choke plate
43. Washer
44. Nut

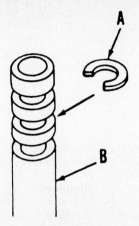

Fig. SH51—Fuel needle clip should be installed in the center groove.

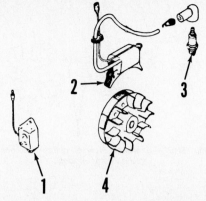

Fig. SH52—Exploded view of ignition system component parts.

1. Igniter
2. Coil
3. Spark plug
4. Flywheel (rotor)

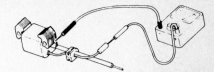

Fig. SH53—Connect red ohmmeter lead to iron laminations and black lead to primary lead to check coil primary side resistance.

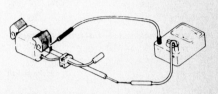

Fig. SH54—Connect red ohmmeter lead to iron laminations and black lead to spark plug lead to check coil secondary side resistance.

(18) is 3/4 turn open from a lightly seated position. Initial setting for the high speed mixture needle (21) is 2 turns open from a lightly seated position.

Final adjustments are made with trimmer head line at recommended length or blade assembly installed. Engine should be at operating temperature and running. Idle speed screw (17) should be adjusted to obtain 2500-3000 engine rpm. Trimmer head or blade should not rotate at this speed. Adjust low speed mixture needle to obtain maximum rpm at idle, then turn screw to richen mixture slightly. Readjust idle speed screw (17) to obtain 2500-3000 engine rpm at idle. Operate engine at full throttle and adjust high speed mixture needle to obtain maximum engine rpm, then turn screw counterclockwise 1/6 turn to richen fuel mixture slightly.

To disassemble carburetor, unscrew cap (13) and remove throttle valve assembly. Remove carburetor from engine. Remove fuel pump retaining screws (39) and separate pump cover (38), diaphragm (37) and gasket (36) from pump plate (35). Remove sealing rings (34). Remove the four metering cover screws (33). Remove metering cover (32), diaphragm (31) and gasket (30). Remove screw (29), pin (28), fuel inlet lever (27), fuel inlet needle (26) and spring (25). Remove low speed mixture needle (18) and high speed mixture needle (21).

Clean and inspect all parts for wear or damage. Inspect fuel inlet needle and renew if needle tip is worn, grooved or damaged. Fuel inlet lever spring (25) should have a free length of 9.5 mm (0.35 in.). Diaphragms should be soft and flexible. Install fuel inlet lever (27) and carefully bend lever to obtain 2.1 mm (0.08 in.) distance (D—Fig. SH48) between carburetor body surface and fuel inlet lever. Clip (10—Fig. SH50)

should be installed in middle groove of fuel needle (Fig. SH51).

IGNITION SYSTEM. All engines are equipped with transistorized ignition system. Ignition system is considered satisfactory if spark will jump across the 3 mm (1/8 in.) gap of a test spark plug. If no spark is produced, check on/off switch and wiring. If switch and wiring are satisfactory, remove coil assembly (2—Fig. SH52). Connect ohmmeter as shown in Fig. SH53 and check coil primary side resistance. Ohmmeter should register approximately 0.830 ohms. Connect ohmmeter as shown in Fig. SH54 and check coil secondary side resistance. Ohmmeter should register approximately 5600 ohms. If coil appears satisfactory, install a new igniter unit (1). Clearance between coil and flywheel (rotor) should be 0.30-0.35 mm (0.12-0.14 in.).

LUBRICATION. All models are lubricated by mixing gasoline with a good quality two-stroke air-cooled engine oil. Refer to TRIMMER SERVICE section for correct fuel/oil mixture ratio recommended by trimmer manufacturer.

REPAIRS

COMPRESSION PRESSURE. For optimum performance, compression pressure for all 19.8, 21.1 and 24.1 cc (1.21, 1.29 and 1.47 cu. in.) engines should be 897-1276 kPa (130-185 psi) or 966-1310 kPa (140-190 psi) for all 33.6 and 39.4 cc (2.05 and 2.40 cu. in.) engines. Compression test should be performed with engine at operating temperature and throttle and choke wide open. A compression reading of 379 kPa (55 psi) or lower for engines with 24.1 cc (1.47 cu. in.) or smaller displacement or a compression reading of 517 kPa (75 psi) for 33.6 cc (2.05 cu. in.)

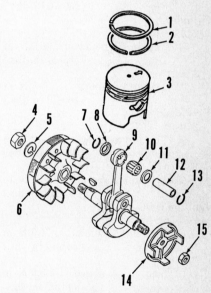

Fig. SH55—Exploded view of crankshaft and connecting rod assembly.

1. Ring
2. Ring
3. Piston
4. Nut
5. Washer
6. Flywheel
7. Retainer
8. Thrust washer
9. Connecting rod & crankshaft assy.
10. Bearing
11. Thrust washer
12. Piston pin
13. Retainer
14. Rewind pulley
15. Nut

or larger engines indicates a need for repair.

TIGHTENING TORQUES. Recommended tightening torque specifications are as follows:

Clutch pin to flywheel:
24.1 cc
(1.47 cu. in.) & below . . 7-10 N·m
(60-90 in.-lbs.)
33.6 cc
(2.05 cu. in.) & above . . 12-14 N·m
(113-130 in.-lbs.)

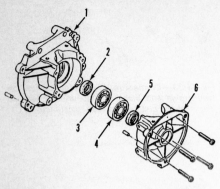

Fig. SH56—Exploded view of crankcase assembly.

1. Crankcase half   4. Bearing
2. Seal   5. Seal
3. Bearing   6. Crankcase half

Crankcase:

24.1 cc
(1.47 cu. in.) & below . . 4-5 N·m
(35-44 in.-lbs.)

33.6 cc
(2.05 cu. in.) & above . . 7-8 N·m
(60-70 in.-lbs.)

Cylinder:

24.1 cc
(1.47 cu. in.) & below . . 4-5 N·m
(35-44 in.-lbs.)

33.6 cc
(2.05 cu. in.) & above . . 7-8 N·m
(60-70 in.-lbs.)

Flywheel:

24.1 cc
(1.47 cu. in.) & below . . 11-13 N·m
(104-122 in.-lbs.)

33.6 cc
(2.05 cu. in.) & above . . .19-24 N·m
(170-218 in.-lbs.)

Ignition coil:

24.1 cc
(1.47 cu. in.) & below . . 4-5 N·m
(35-44 in.-lbs.)

33.6 cc
(2.05 cu. in.) & above . . 5-5.5 N·m
(44-52 in.-lbs.)

Spark plug:

All models . . . . 19-22 N·m
(170-190 in.-lbs.)

CRANKSHAFT AND CONNECT-ING ROD. Refer to Fig. SH55 for an exploded view of crankshaft and connecting rod assembly. Refer also to Fig. SH56 for an exploded view of crankcase showing ball bearing main bearings and crankshaft seals. Crankshaft and connecting rod are considered an assembly and are not serviced separately. Do not remove connecting rod from crankshaft.

To remove crankshaft, remove all cooling shrouds, recoil starter assembly, fuel tank, carburetor, muffler, ignition module and clutch assembly. Remove bolts retaining cylinder to crankcase and carefully work cylinder off of crankcase and piston. Use care not to

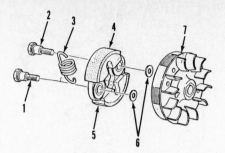

Fig. SH57—Exploded view of clutch assembly used on some models.

1. Clutch bolt   5. Clutch shoe
2. Clutch bolt   6. Washers
3. Clutch spring   7. Flywheel (rotor)
4. Clutch shoe

damage piston or connecting rod. Remove all crankcase bolts and carefully separate crankcase halves.

Do not use any type of tool inserted in crankcase split to separate crankcase.

If necessary, heat crankcase at main bearing areas to allow easier separation. Remove retaining rings and use a piston pin puller to remove piston pin. Remove piston and thrust washers. Note thrust washers are installed between piston and connecting rod at piston pin to control connecting rod thrust. Thrust washers must be installed. Remove piston pin bearing from connecting rod piston pin bore. Press bearings from crankshaft as required.

To reassemble, coat crankcase halves with a silicon type sealer and heat crankcase halves slightly to aid reassembly. Piston is installed so arrow stamped on top of piston will be toward exhaust side of cylinder.

PISTON, PIN AND RINGS. Piston for all models is equipped with two rings which are prevented from rotating on piston by a locating pin installed in each piston ring groove. Make certain ring end gaps are aligned with locating pins prior to installation of piston into cylinder. To remove piston, refer to CRANKSHAFT AND CONNECTING ROD paragraphs. Note location of thrust washers (8 and 11—Fig. SH55) to control connecting rod thrust.

Refer to the following chart for standard piston diameters and wear limits.

Engine	Standard	Limit
19.8 cc	29.975 mm	29.90 mm
(1.21 cu. in.)	(1.180 in.)	(1.177 in.)
21.1 cc	30.970 mm	30.90 mm
(1.29 cu. in.)	(1.219 in.)	(1.217 in.)
24.1 cc	31.970 mm	31.90 mm
(1.47 cu. in.)	(1.259 in.)	(1.256 in.)
33.6 cc	35.970 mm	35.90 mm
(2.05 cu. in.)	(1.416 in.)	(1.413 in.)
39.4 cc	38.950 mm	38.88 mm
(2.40 cu. in.)	(1.534 in.)	(1.531 in.)

Refer to the following chart for standard piston pin bore diameter in piston.

Engine	Standard	Limit
19.8 cc	8.0 mm	8.03 mm
(1.21 cu. in.)	(0.3150 in.)	(0.3161 in.)
21.1 cc	8.0 mm	8.03 mm
(1.29 cu. in.)	(0.3150 in.)	(0.3161 in.)
24.1 cc	9.0 mm	9.03 mm
(1.47 cu. in.)	(0.3540 in.)	(0.3555 in.)
33.6 cc	10.0 mm	10.03 mm
(2.05 cu. in.)	(0.3937 in.)	(0.3949 in.)
39.4 cc	10.0 mm	10.03 mm
(2.40 cu. in.)	(0.3937 in.)	(0.3949 in.)

Ring end gap for all engines should be 1-3 mm (0.004-0.012 in.). Minimum ring end gap is 0.6 mm (0.24 in.).

Piston ring width should be 1.5 mm (0.059 in.) and not less than 1.37 mm (0.054 in.) for all models.

Piston ring thickness for 19.8 and 21.1 cc (1.21 and 1.47 cu. in.) engines should be 1.3 mm (0.051 in.) and not less than 1.1 mm (0.043 in.). Piston ring thickness for 24.1 and 33.6 cc (1.47 and 2.05 cu. in.) engines should be 1.5 mm (0.059 in.) and not less than 1.3 mm (0.051 in.). Piston ring thickness for 39.4 cc (2.40 cu. in.) engine should be 1.7 mm (0.067 in.) and not less than 1.5 mm (0.059 in.).

Ring clearance in piston ring groove for 19.8, 21.1 and 24.1 cc (1.21, 1.29 and 1.47 cu. in.) engines should be 0.04-0.08 mm (0.0016-0.0031 in.) and not more than 0.20 mm (0.008 in.). Ring clearance in piston ring groove for 33.6 and 39.4 cc (2.05 and 2.40 in.) engines should be 0.02-0.06 mm (0.0008-0.0024 in.).

Piston to cylinder clearance for 19.8, 21.1, 24.1 and 33.6 cc (1.21, 1.29, 1.47 and 2.05 cu. in.) engines should be 0.025-0.060 mm (0.001-0.0024 in.). Piston to cylinder clearance for 39.4 cc (2.40 in.) engine should be 0.045-0.080 mm (0.0018-0.0030 in.).

Piston pin diameter for 19.8 and 21.1 cc (1.21 and 1.29 cu. in.) engines should be 8.0 mm (0.3150 in.) and not less than 7.98 mm (0.3142 in.). Piston pin diameter for 24.1 cc (1.47 cu. in.) engine should be 9.0 mm (0.3543 in.) and not less than 8.98 mm (0.3535 in.). Piston pin diameter for 33.6 and 39.4 cc (2.05 and 2.40 cu. in.) engines should be 10.0 mm (0.3937 in.) and not less than 9.98 mm (0.3929 in.).

CYLINDER. All engines are equipped with a chrome plated cylinder bore. Refer to the following chart for standard cylinder bore diameters and wear limits.

Engine	Standard	Limit
19.8 cc	30.0 mm	30.1 mm
(1.21 cu. in.)	(1.181 in.)	(1.185 in.)
21.1 cc	31.0 mm	31.1 mm
(1.29 cu. in.)	(1.220 in.)	(1.224 in.)
24.1 cc	32.0 mm	32.1 mm
(1.47 cu. in.)	(1.260 in.)	(1.264 in.)
33.6 cc	36.0 mm	36.1 mm
(2.05 cu. in.)	(1.417 in.)	(1.421 in.)
39.4 cc	39.0 mm	39.1 mm
(2.40 cu. in.)	(1.535 in.)	(1.539 in.)

On all engines, renew cylinder if taper exceeds 0.01 mm (0.0004 in.) or if cylinder out-of-round exceeds 0.03 mm (0.0012 in.).

CLUTCH. Refer to Fig. SH57 for an exploded view of clutch assembly used on all engines except 33.6 and 39.4 cc (2.05 and 2.40 cu. in.) engines. Clutch assembly for the 33.6 and 39.4 cc (2.05 and 2.40 cu. in.) engines is similar except that four clutch shoes are used instead of two.

To remove clutch assembly, remove fan cover and bolts. Remove bolts (1 and 2) and remove clutch shoe assembly. New clutch shoe lining thickness is 2.0 mm (0.079 in.). Renew shoes if lining thickness is less than 0.08 mm (0.003 in.).

Clutch drum is retained in clutch housing by a snap ring. Remove snap ring and press drum out of the clutch housing bearings. It may be necessary to heat housing slightly to remove clutch drum and bearings as an assembly.

RECOIL STARTER. All models are equipped with a recoil type starter. To disassemble starter, remove starter assembly from crankcase. Remove starter handle and allow rope to rewind onto pulley. Remove retaining screw and friction plate. Remove friction spring and ratchet return spring. Make certain rewind spring tension has been fully released and carefully separate pulley from starter case. Use pliers to remove rewind spring as required. Lubricate spring prior to reassembly. Preload rewind spring 2-3 turns to make sure handle will be returned to the housing.

STIHL

ENGINE SERVICE

Model	Bore	Stroke	Displacement
O15	38.0 mm	28.0 mm	32.0 cc
	(1.50 in.)	(1.10 in.)	(1.96 cu. in.)

ENGINE INFORMATION

Stihl O15 series engines are used on Stihl string trimmers and brushcutters. Refer to following sections for other Stihl engine models.

MAINTENANCE

SPARK PLUG. Recommended spark plug for O15 series engine is a Bosch WKA175T6, or equivalent. Specified electrode gap should be 0.5 mm (0.020 in.).

CARBURETOR. A Walbro Model HDC diaphragm carburetor is used on O15 series engine. Initial adjustment of idle and high speed mixture needles from a lightly seated position is 3/4 turn open. Adjust idle speed screw until engine idles just below clutch engagement speed. Final adjustment should be made with engine at operating temperature and running. Adjust high speed mixture needle to obtain optimum performance with trimmer line at recommended length or blade assembly installed. Adjust idle mixture needle to obtain smooth idle and good acceleration.

Refer to Fig. SL50 for an exploded view of Walbro Model HDC carburetor. Use caution when disassembling carburetor not to lose ball (13) and spring (14) as choke shaft is removed.

Clean and inspect all parts. Inspect diaphragms for defects which may affect operation. Examine fuel inlet needle and seat. The needle is renewable, but carburetor body must be renewed if needle seat is excessively worn or damaged. Sharp objects should not be used to clean orifices or passages as fuel flow may be altered. Compressed air should not be used to clean main nozzle as check valve may be damaged. A check valve repair kit is available to renew a damaged valve. Fuel mixture needles must be renewed if grooved or broken. Inspect mixture needle seats in carburetor body and renew body if seats are damaged or excessively worn. Screens should be clean.

To reassemble carburetor, reverse disassembly procedure. Fuel metering lever should be flush with a straight-edge laid across carburetor body as shown in Fig. SL51. Make certain lever spring correctly contacts locating dimple on lever before measuring lever height. Carefully bend lever to obtain correct height.

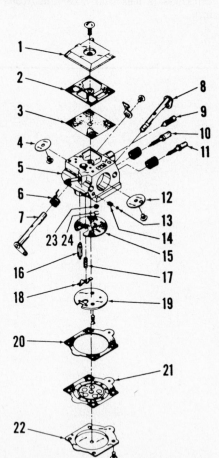

Fig. SL50—Exploded view of Walbro Model HDC diaphragm type carburetor.

1. Pump cover
2. Gasket
3. Fuel pump diaphragm & valves
4. Throttle plate
5. Body
6. Return spring
7. Throttle shaft
8. Choke shaft
9. Idle speed screw
10. Idle mixture needle
11. High speed mixture needle
12. Choke plate
13. Choke friction ball
14. Spring
15. Gasket
16. Fuel inlet valve
17. Spring
18. Diaphragm lever
19. Circuit plate
20. Gasket
21. Metering diaphragm
22. Cover
23. Check valve screen
24. Retainer

IGNITION SYSTEM. Model O15 engine may be equipped with a conventional flywheel magneto ignition system or a breakerless transistor ignition system. Refer to the appropriate paragraph for model being serviced.

Flywheel Magneto Ignition. Ignition breaker point gap should be 3.5-4.0 mm (0.014-0.016 in.). Ignition timing is not adjustable except by adjusting breaker point gap. Ignition timing should occur when piston is 2.2 mm (0.09 in.) BTDC. Magneto edge gap ("E" gap) shown in Fig. SL52 should be 3.0-7.5 mm (0.12-0.29 in.). Magneto edge gap may be adjusted slightly by loosening flywheel nut and rotating flywheel on crankshaft as there is a small clearance between flywheel groove and crankshaft key.

Air gap between ignition coil and flywheel should be 0.5 mm (0.020 in.). Ignition coil windings may be checked using an ohmmeter. Primary winding should have 0.8-1.3 ohms resistance and secondary winding should have 7200-8800 ohms.

Transistor Ignition System. Some models are equipped with a Bosch breakerless transistor ignition system. Ignition should occur when piston is 2.2 mm (0.087 in.) BTDC. Ignition timing may be adjusted slightly by loosening

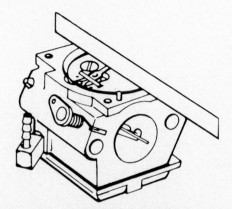

Fig. SL51—Diaphragm lever should just touch a straightedge placed across carburetor body as shown.

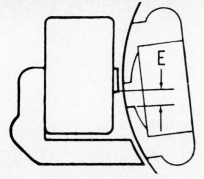

Fig. SL52—Magneto edge gap (E) on should be 3.0-7.5 mm (0.12-0.29 in.).

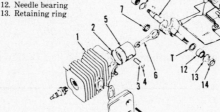

Fig. SL53—Exploded view of engine. Thrust washers (T) are used on late models.

T. Thrust washer
1. Cylinder
2. Piston ring
3. Piston pin
4. Pin retainer
5. Piston
6. Connecting rod
7. Bearing rollers (12)
8. Oil seal
9. Retaining ring
10. Needle bearing
11. Crankshaft
12. Needle bearing
13. Retaining ring
14. Oil seal
15. Crankcase
16. Gasket
17. Handle assy.
18. Oil pick-up

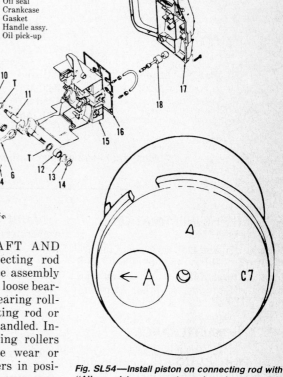

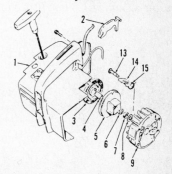

Fig. SL54—Install piston on connecting rod with "A" on piston crown towards exhaust port in cylinder.

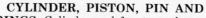

flywheel nut and rotating flywheel on crankshaft as there is a small clearance between flywheel groove and crankshaft key.

Recommended air gap between ignition coil armature legs and flywheel is 0.15-0.2 mm (0.006-0.008 in.). Loosen ignition coil mounting screws and move ignition coil to adjust air gap.

LUBRICATION. The engine is lubricated by mixing gasoline with a good quality two-stroke air-cooled engine oil. Refer to TRIMMER SERVICE section for correct fuel/oil mixture ratio recommended by trimmer manufacturer.

REPAIRS

CRANKSHAFT AND SEALS. The crankshaft is supported in needle bearings (10 and 12—Fig. SL53) held between the cylinder and front crankcase half. Care should be taken when removing cylinder as crankshaft will be loose in crankcase and connecting rod may slide off bearing rollers (7) allowing them to fall into crankcase.

Large diameter needle bearing (10), retaining ring (9) and seal (8) on later models must be installed on flywheel end of crankshaft while smaller diameter bearing retaining ring and seal must be installed on clutch end. Some models are also equipped with thrust washers (T) located between crankshaft bearings and crankshaft. Bearings, retaining rings and seals on early models have the same outer diameter and may be installed on either end of crankshaft. Retaining rings (9 and 13) must fit in ring grooves of crankcase and cylinder. Tighten cylinder-to-crankcase screws to 7 N·m (60 in.-lbs.).

Before reassembling crankcase halves, apply a light coat of nonhardening sealant to crankcase mating surfaces.

CONNECTING ROD. To remove connecting rod, remove crankshaft as

outlined in CRANKSHAFT AND SEALS paragraphs. Connecting rod (6—Fig. SL53) is a one-piece assembly supported on crankpin by 12 loose bearing rollers. Make certain bearing rollers are not lost as connecting rod or crankshaft is removed or handled. Inspect connecting rod, bearing rollers and crankpin for excessive wear or damage. Hold bearing rollers in position with heavy grease during reassembly. Make certain all twelve bearing rollers are in position before assembling crankcase.

CYLINDER, PISTON, PIN AND RINGS. Cylinder and front crankcase are one-piece. Crankshaft and bearings are loose when the cylinder is removed. Care must be taken not to damage mating surfaces of crankcase halves during disassembly.

Cylinder head is integral with cylinder. Piston is equipped with a single piston ring and the piston pin rides directly in the piston and small end of connecting rod. Cylinder bore is chrome plated and should be inspected for damage or excessive wear. Cylinder (1—Fig. SL53) and front crankcase half (15) are available only as a complete assembly.

Piston pin (3) must be installed with closed end of pin toward "A" side of piston crown shown in Fig. SL54 and piston must be installed with "A" side toward exhaust port in cylinder. Piston and piston pin are available in standard sizes only.

Refer to CRANKSHAFT AND SEALS paragraphs for assembly of crankcase and cylinder.

REWIND STARTER. Refer to Fig. SL55 for exploded view of pawl type rewind starter used on all models. Care should be taken if it is necessary to remove rewind spring (3) to prevent spring from uncoiling uncontrolled.

Fig. SL55—Exploded view of rewind starter.

1. Rear housing
2. Trigger interlock
3. Rewind spring
4. Bushing
5. Rope pulley
6. "E" ring
7. Flywheel nut
8. Washer
9. Flywheel
13. Stud
14. Pawl
15. Spring

Rewind spring must be wound in clockwise direction in housing. Wind starter rope in clockwise direction around rope pulley (5) as viewed with pulley installed in starter housing. Turn rope pulley 3-4 turns in clockwise direction before passing rope through rope outlet to place tension on rewind spring. To check spring tension, pull starter rope to full length. It should be possible to rotate rope pulley in clockwise direction with rope fully extended.

Starter pawl studs (13) are driven into flywheel. To renew pawl stud or spring, remove flywheel, then drive stud out of flywheel. Apply "Loctite" to stud before installation.

STIHL

ENGINE SERVICE

Model	Bore	Stroke	Displacement
O20*	38.0 mm	28.0 mm	32.0 cc
	(1.50 in.)	(1.10 in.)	(1.96 cu. in.)
O41	44.0 mm	40.0 mm	61.0 cc
	(1.73 in.)	(1.57 in.)	(3.72 cu. in.)

* Some O20 engines have a displacement of 35.0 cc (2.13 cu. in.).

ENGINE INFORMATION

Stihl O20 and O41 series engines are used on Stihl string trimmers and brushcutters. Refer to preceding and following sections for other Stihl engine models.

MAINTENANCE

SPARK PLUG. Recommended spark plug for all models is a Bosch WSR6F, or equivalent. Specified electrode gap should be 0.5 mm (0.020 in.).

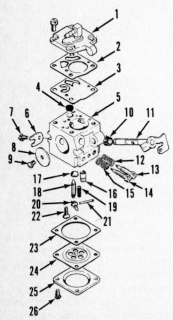

Fig. SL60—Exploded view of diaphragm type carburetor used on all models.

1. Pump cover
2. Gasket
3. Diaphragm
4. Screen
5. Body
6. Clip
7. Screw
8. Throttle plate
9. Screw
10. Spring
11. Throttle shaft
12. Spring
13. High speed mixture needle
14. Low speed mixture needle
15. Spring
16. Check valve
17. Welch plug
18. Fuel inlet needle
19. Spring
20. Fuel inlet lever
21. Pin
22. Screw
23. Gasket
24. Diaphragm
25. Cover
26. Screw

CARBURETOR. A diaphragm type carburetor is used on all models (Fig. SL60). Initial adjustment of low and high speed mixture needles for O20 engine is 1-1/4 turns open from a lightly seated position. Initial adjustment of O41 engine low and high speed mixture needles from a lightly seated position is 1-1/4 turns open for low speed mixture needle and 7/8 turn open for the high speed mixture needle.

To disassemble carburetor, refer to Fig. SL60. Clean filter screen (4). Welch plugs (18 and 24—Fig. SL61) may be removed by drilling plug with a suitable size drill bit, then pry out as shown in Fig. SL62. Care must be taken not to drill into carburetor body.

Inspect inlet lever spring (19—Fig. SL60) and renew if stretched or damaged. Inspect diaphragms for tears, cracks or other damage. Renew low and high speed mixture needles if needle points are grooved or broken. Carburetor body must be renewed if needle seats are damaged. Fuel inlet needle has a rubber tip which seats directly on a machined orifice in carburetor body. Inlet needle or carburetor body should be renewed if worn excessively.

Adjust position of inlet control lever so lever is flush with diaphragm chamber floor as shown in Fig. SL63. Bend lever adjacent to spring to obtain correct position.

IGNITION SYSTEM. Engine may be equipped with a conventional magneto type ignition system, a Bosch capacitor discharge ignition system or a Sems transistorized ignition system. Refer to the appropriate paragraph for model being serviced.

Magneto Ignition System. Ignition breaker point gap should be set at 3.5-4.0 mm (0.014-0.016 in.). Ignition timing is adjusted by loosening stator mounting screws and rotating stator plate. Ignition timing should occur when piston is 2.0-2.3 mm (0.08-0.087 in.) BTDC for O20 engine or 2.4-2.6 mm (0.095-0.102 in.) BTDC for O41 engine.

Ignition coil air gap should be 4-6 mm (0.16-0.24 in.) for O20 engine or 0.2-0.3 mm (0.008-0.012 in.) for O41 engine.

Ignition coil primary and secondary windings may be checked using an ohmmeter. Primary winding resistance should register 1.5-1.9 ohms for O20 engine, 1.9-2.5 ohms for O41 engine with Bosch date code 523 or 1.2-1.7

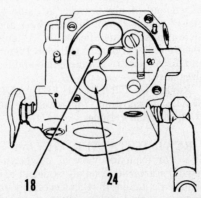

Fig. SL61—View showing location of Welch plugs (18 and 24).

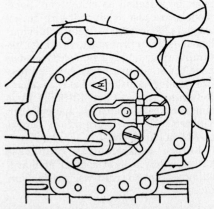

Fig. SL62—A punch can be used to remove Welch plugs after drilling a hole in plug. Refer to text.

ohms for O41 engine with Bosch date code 524.

Bosch Breakerless Ignition System. Ignition module air gap should be 0.2-0.3 mm (0.008-0.012 in.). Ignition should occur when piston is 2.5 mm (0.098 in.) BTDC.

Sems Breakerless Ignition System. Ignition module air gap should be 0.2-0.3 mm (0.008-0.012 in.). Ignition should occur when piston is 2.5 mm (0.098 in.) BTDC.

Ignition module primary and secondary windings may be checked using an ohmmeter. Primary winding resistance should be 0.4-0.5 ohms. Secondary winding resistance should be 2.7-3.3k ohms.

LUBRICATION. All Models are lubricated by mixing gasoline with a good quality two-stroke air-cooled engine oil. Refer to TRIMMER SERVICE section for correct fuel/oil mixture ratio recommended by trimmer manufacturer.

REPAIRS

TIGHTENING TORQUES. Recommended tightening torque specifications are as follows:

Clutch nut . . . . 39 N·m
(29 ft.-lbs.)
Clutch hub . . . . 34 N·m
(25.3 ft.-lbs.)
Clutch hub carrier (O20) . . . 28 N·m
(21 ft.-lbs.)
Flywheel nut:
O20 . . . . 24 N·m
(18 ft.-lbs.)
O41 . . . . 35 N·m
(26 ft.-lbs.)

CRANKSHAFT AND SEALS. All models are equipped with a split type crankcase from which cylinder may be removed separately (Fig. SL64 and SL65). It may be necessary to heat crankcase halves slightly to remove main bearings if they remain in crankcase during disassembly.

CONNECTING ROD. The connecting rod and crankshaft are considered an assembly and individual parts are not available separately. Do not remove connecting rod from crankshaft.

Connecting rod big end rides on a roller bearing and should be inspected for excessive wear or damage. If rod, bearing or crankshaft is damaged, complete crankshaft and connecting rod assembly must be renewed.

CYLINDER, PISTON, PIN AND RINGS. The aluminum alloy piston is equipped with two piston rings. The floating piston pin is retained in the piston with a snap ring at each end. The

pin bore of the piston is unbushed; the connecting rod has a caged needle roller piston pin bearing.

Cylinder bore and cylinder head are cast as one-piece. The cylinder assembly is available only with a fitted piston. Pistons and cylinders are grouped into different size ranges with approximately 0.0005 mm (0.0002 in.) difference between each range. Each group is marked with letters "A" to "E". Letter "A" denotes smallest size with "E" being largest. The code letter is stamped on the top of the piston and on the top of the cylinder. The code letter of the piston and the cylinder must be the same for proper fit of a new piston

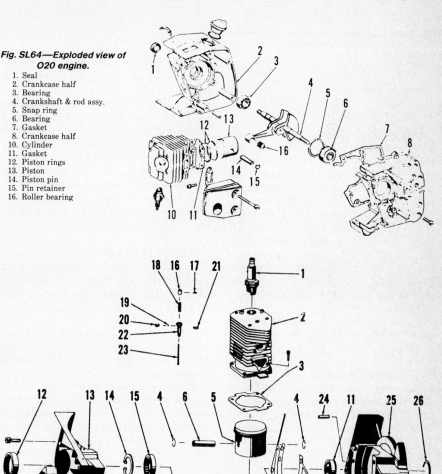

Fig. SL64—Exploded view of O20 engine.

1. Seal
2. Crankcase half
3. Bearing
4. Crankshaft & rod assy.
5. Snap ring
6. Bearing
7. Gasket
8. Crankcase half
10. Cylinder
11. Gasket
12. Piston rings
13. Piston
14. Piston pin
15. Pin retainer
16. Roller bearing

Fig. SL65—Exploded view of O41 engine.

1. Spark plug	8. Crankshaft & rod assy.
2. Cylinder	9. Snap ring
3. Head gasket	10. Knob
4. Snap ring	11. Bearing
5. Piston	12. Seal
6. Piston pin	13. Crankcase half
7. Bearing	14. Snap ring
15. Bearing	21. Tab washer
16. Knob	22. Housing
17. Pin	23. Plunger
18. Spring	24. Pin
19. Pin	25. Crankcase half
20. Spring	26. Snap ring

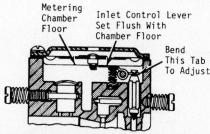

Fig. SL63—Diaphragm lever should be flush with fuel chamber floor as shown.

Metering Chamber Floor

Inlet Control Lever Set Flush With Chamber Floor

Bend This Tab To Adjust

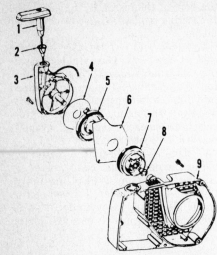

*Fig. SL67—Exploded view of
typical rewind starter used
on O41 engine.*

1. Fuel tank
2. Nut
3. Rope handle
4. Fuel pick-up
5. Filter
6. Gasket
7. Fan cover
8. Felt ring
9. Spring washer
10. Pulley shaft
11. Cover
12. Rewind spring
13. Washer
14. Rope pulley
15. Spring
16. Spring retainer
17. Friction shoe
18. Slotted washer
19. Brake lever
20. Slotted washer
21. Washer
22. Spring
23. Washer
24. "E" ring

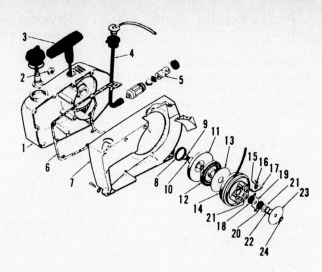

*Fig. SL66—Exploded view of pawl type starter
used on O20 engine.*

1. Rope handle
2. Bushing
3. Housing
4. Washer
5. Rewind spring
6. Cover
7. Rope pulley
8. "E" ring
9. Fan housing

in a new cylinder. However, new pistons are available for installation in used cylinders. Used cylinders with code letters "A" or "B" may use piston with code letter "A". Used cylinder with code letters "A", "B" or "C" may use piston with code letter "B". Used cylinder with code letters "B", "C" or "D" may use piston with code letter "C". Used cylinder with code letters "C", "D" or "E" may use piston with code letter "D". Used cylinder with code letters "D" or "E" may use piston with code letter "E".

Cylinder bore on all models is chrome plated. Cylinder should be renewed if chrome plating is flaking, scored or worn away.

To reinstall piston on connecting rod, install one snap ring in piston. Lubricate the piston pin needle bearing with motor oil, then slide bearing into pin bore of connecting rod. Install piston on rod so that arrow on piston crown points toward exhaust port. Push piston in far enough to install second snap ring.

After piston and rod assembly is attached to crankshaft, rotate crankshaft to top dead center and support piston with a wood block that will fit between piston skirt and crankcase when cylinder gasket is in place. A notch should be cut in the wood block so that it will fit around the connecting rod. Lubricate piston and rings with motor oil, then compress rings with compressor that can be removed after cylinder is pushed down over piston. On some models it may be necessary to remove the cylinder and install an additional gasket between the cylinder and crankcase if piston strikes top of cylinder.

REWIND STARTER. Friction shoe type and pawl type starters have been used. Refer to Fig. SL66 for an exploded view of starter assembly used on O20 engine and to Fig. SL67 for an exploded view of starter assembly used on O41 engine. Refer to Fig. SL68 for proper method of assembly of friction shoe plates to starter brake lever on O41 engine starter.

To place tension on rope of starter shown in Fig. SL66 for O20 engine, pull starter rope, then hold rope pulley to prevent spring from rewinding rope on pulley. Pull rope back through rope outlet and wrap two additional turns of rope on pulley without moving pulley. Release pulley and allow rope to rewind. Rope handle should be pulled against housing, but spring should not be completely wound when rope is pulled to greatest length.

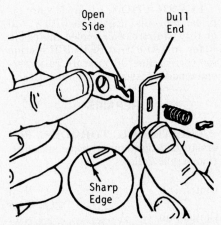

*Fig. SL68—Illustration showing proper method
of assembly of friction shoe plates to starter
brake lever.*

To place tension on O41 engine starter rope, pull rope out of handle until notch in pulley is adjacent to rope outlet, then hold pulley to prevent rope from rewinding. Pull rope back through outlet and out of notch in pulley. Turn rope pulley two turns clockwise and release rope back through notch. Check starter operation. Rope handle should be held against housing by spring tension, but spring should not be completely wound when rope is pulled to greatest length.

STIHL

ENGINE SERVICE

Model	Bore	Stroke	Displacement
O8S	47.0 mm	32.0	56.0 cc
	(1.85 in.)	(1.26 in.)	(3.39 cu. in.)

ENGINE INFORMATION

Stihl O8S series engines are used on Stihl string trimmers and brushcutters. Refer to preceding sections for other Stihl engine models.

MAINTENANCE

SPARK PLUG. Recommended spark plug for O8S engine is a Bosch W175T7, or equivalent. Specified electrode gap should be 0.5 mm (0.020 in.).

CARBURETOR. O8S engine is equipped with a Tillotson diaphragm type carburetor. Initial adjustment of idle and high speed mixture needles is one turn open from a lightly seated position.

Final adjustments are made with trimmer line at recommended length or blade assembly installed. Engine should be at operating temperature and running. Adjust low speed mixture needle and idle speed screw until engine idles just below clutch engagement speed. Adjust high speed mixture needle to obtain optimum performance under load. Do not adjust high speed mixture needle too lean as engine may be damaged.

To disassemble carburetor, refer to Fig. SL70. Remove and clean filter screen (4). Welch plugs (18 and 24—Fig. SL71) can be removed by drilling plug with a suitable size drill bit, then pry out as shown in Fig. SL72. Care must be taken not to drill into carburetor body.

Inspect inlet lever spring (19—Fig. SL70) and renew if stretched or damaged. Inspect diaphragms for tears, cracks or other damage. Renew idle and high speed mixture needles if needle points are grooved or broken. Carburetor body must be renewed if needle seats are damaged. Fuel inlet needle has a rubber tip which seats directly on a machined orifice in carburetor body. Inlet needle or carburetor body should be renewed if worn excessively.

Inlet control lever should be adjusted so that control lever is flush with fuel chamber floor as shown in Fig. SL73. Carefully bend lever adjacent to spring to obtain correct position.

GOVERNOR. Model O8S is equipped with an air vane type governor. The governor linkage is attached to the carburetor choke shaft lever. Maximum speed is controlled by the air vane governor closing the choke plate.

Governed speed is adjusted by changing the tension of the governor spring. The adjusting plate is mounted to the engine behind the starter housing as shown in Fig. SL74. After maximum governed speed is adjusted at factory, position of spring is secured by a lead seal. If necessary to readjust governor, new position of governor spring should be sealed or wired securely. Maximum no-load governed speed is 8000 rpm.

IGNITION SYSTEM. OS8 engine is equipped with a conventional magneto type igntion system.

Coil air gap should be 0.5 mm (0.020 in.). Ignition breaker point gap should be 3.5-4.0 mm (0.014-0.016 in.). Ignition timing is adjusted by loosening stator mounting screws and rotating stator plate. Ignition should occur when piston is 1.9-2.1 mm (0.075-0.083 in.) BTDC.

Coil primary and secondary windings may be checked using an ohmmeter. Primary winding resistance should be 1.9-2.5 ohms for Bosch coil with date code 523 or 1.2-1.7 ohms for Bosch coil with date code 524. Secondary winding resistance should be 5.0-6.7k ohms for

Fig. SL70—Exploded view of diaphragm type carburetor.

1. Pump cover
2. Gasket
3. Diaphragm
4. Screen
5. Body
6. Clip
7. Screw
8. Throttle plate
9. Screw
10. Spring
11. Throttle shaft
12. Spring
13. High speed mixture needle
14. Low speed mixture needle
15. Spring
16. Check valve
17. Welch plug
18. Fuel inlet needle
19. Spring
20. Fuel inlet lever
21. Pin
22. Screw
23. Gasket
24. Diaphragm
25. Cover
26. Screw

Fig. SL71—View showing location of Welch plugs (18 and 24).

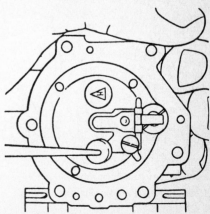

Fig. SL72—A punch can be used to remove Welch plugs after drilling a hole in plug. Refer to text.

Bosch coil with date code 523 or 5.0-6.7k ohms for Bosch coil with date code 524.

LUBRICATION. All Models are lubricated by mixing gasoline with a good quality two-stroke air-cooled engine oil. Refer to TRIMMER SERVICE section for correct fuel/oil mixture ratio recommended by trimmer manufacturer.

REPAIRS

TIGHTENING TORQUES. Recommended tightening torque specifications are as follows:

Clutch nut . . . . .34 N·m
(25 ft.-lbs.)
Flywheel nut . . . . .29 N·m
(21.7 ft.-lbs.)
Spark plug . . . . .24 N·m
(18 ft.-lbs.)
Cylinder screws . . . . .10 N·m
(7.2 ft.-lbs.)

CRANKSHAFT AND SEALS. All models are equipped with a split type crankcase from which cylinder may be removed separately (Fig. SL75). Crankshaft is supported at both ends in ball type main bearings and crankshaft end play is controlled by shims (11) installed between the bearing (10) and shoulders on the crankshaft on early models, or between bearing and crankcase on later models. Shims are available in a variety of thicknesses. Correct crankshaft end play is 0.2-0.3 mm (0.0008-0.012 in.). It may be necessary to heat crankcase halves slightly to remove main bearings if they remain in crankcase during disassembly.

CONNECTING ROD. The connecting rod and crankshaft are considered an assembly and individual parts are not available separately. Do not remove connecting rod from crankshaft.

Connecting rod big end rides on a roller bearing and should be inspected for excessive wear or damage. If rod, bearing or crankshaft is damaged, complete crankshaft and connecting rod assembly must be renewed.

CYLINDER, PISTON, PIN AND RINGS. The aluminum alloy piston is equipped with two piston rings. The floating piston pin is retained in the piston with a snap ring at each end. The pin bore of the piston is unbushed; the connecting rod has a caged needle roller piston pin bearing.

Cylinder bore and cylinder head are cast as one-piece. The cylinder is available only with a fitted piston. Pistons and cylinders are grouped into different size ranges with approximately 0.0005 mm (0.0002 in.) difference between each range. Each group is marked with letters "A" to "E". Letter "A" denotes smallest size with "E" being largest. The code letter is stamped on the top of the piston and on the top of the cylinder on all models. The code letter of the piston and the cylinder must be the same for proper fit of a new piston in a new cylinder. However, new pistons are available for installation in used cylinders. Used cylinders with code letters "A" or "B" may use piston with code letter "A". Used cylinder with code letters "A", "B" or "C" may use piston with code letter "B". Used cylinder with code letters "B", "C" or "D" may use piston with code letter "C". Used cylinder with code letters "C", "D" or "E" may use piston with code letter "D". Used cylinder with code letters "D" or "E" may use piston with code letter "E".

Cylinder bore on all models is chrome plated. Cylinder should be renewed if chrome plating is flaking, scored or worn away.

To reinstall piston on connecting rod, install one snap ring in piston. Lubricate the piston pin needle bearing with motor oil, then slide bearing into pin bore of connecting rod. Install piston on rod so that arrow on piston crown points toward exhaust port. Push piston in far enough to install second snap ring.

After piston and rod assembly is attached to crankshaft, rotate crankshaft to top dead center and support piston with a wood block that will fit between piston

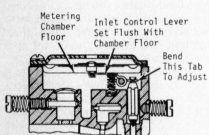

Fig. SL73—Diaphragm lever should be flush with fuel chamber floor as shown.

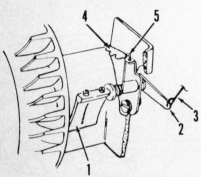

Fig. SL74—View of air vane type governor.

1. Air vane
2. Lever
3. Throttle link
4. Notched plate
5. Governor spring

Fig. SL75—Exploded view of O8S engine.

1. Spark plug
2. Cylinder
3. Head gasket
4. Snap ring
5. Piston pin
6. Piston
7. Crankcase half
8. Seal
9. Snap ring
10. Ball bearing
11. Shim
12. Gasket
13. Dowel pin
14. Crankcase half
15. Washer
16. Bearing
17. Crankshaft & rod assy.

Fig. SL76—Exploded view of pawl type starter.

1. Fuel tank
2. Nut
3. Rope handle
4. Fuel pick-up
5. Filter
6. Gasket
7. Fan cover
8. Felt ring
9. Spring washer
10. Pulley shaft
11. Cover
12. Rewind spring
13. Washer
14. Rope pulley
15. Spring
16. Spring retainer
17. Friction shoe
18. Slotted washer
19. Brake lever
20. Slotted washer
21. Washer
22. Spring
23. Washer
24. "E" ring

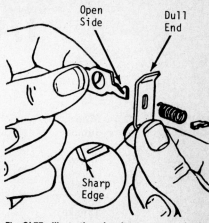

Fig. SL77—Illustration showing proper method of assembly of friction shoe plates to starter brake lever.

skirt and crankcase when cylinder gasket is in place. A notch should be cut in the wood block so that it will fit around the connecting rod. Lubricate piston and rings with motor oil, then compress rings with compressor that can be removed after cylinder is pushed down over piston. On some models it may be necessary to remove the cylinder and install an additional gasket between the cylinder and crankcase if piston strikes top of cylinder.

REWIND STARTER. O8S engine is equipped with a pawl type rewind starter assembly similar to Fig. SL76.

To place tension on engine starter rope, pull rope out of handle until notch in pulley is adjacent to rope outlet, then hold pulley to prevent rope from rewinding. Pull rope back through outlet and out of notch in pulley. Turn rope pulley two turns clockwise and release rope back through notch. Check starter operation.

Rope handle should be held against housing by spring tension, but spring should not be completely wound when rope is pulled to greatest length.

Refer to Fig. SL77 for correct assembly of starter shoes on brake lever. Make certain assembly is installed as shown in exploded views and leading edges of friction shoes are sharp or shoes may not properly engage drum.

TANAKA (TAS)

ENGINE SERVICE

Model	Bore	Stroke	Displacement
Tanaka	27.0 mm (1.06 in.)	28.0 mm (1.10 in.)	16.0 cc (0.94 cu. in.)
Tanaka	30.0 mm (1.18 in.)	28.0 mm (1.10 in.)	20.0 cc (1.22 cu. in.)
Tanaka	31.0 mm (1.22 in.)	30.0 mm (1.18 in.)	22.6 cc (1.38 cu. in.)
Tanaka	36.0 mm (1.42 in.)	30.0 mm (1.18 in.)	30.5 cc (1.86 cu. in.)
Tanaka	38.0 mm (1.50 in.)	33.0 mm (1.30 in.)	37.4 cc (2.28 cu. in.)
Tanaka	41.0 mm (1.61 in.)	38.0 mm (1.50 in.)	50.2 cc (3.06 cu. in.)

ENGINE INFORMATION

Tanaka (Tas) two-stroke air-cooled gasoline engines are used on Tanaka string trimmers and brushcutters and by some other manufacturers of string trimmers and brush cutters.

MAINTENANCE

SPARK PLUG. Recommended spark plug for all models is a NGK BM-6A, or equivalent. Specified electrode gap is 0.6 mm (0.024 in.).

CARBURETOR.

Tanaka (Tas) engines may be equipped a diaphragm type carburetor (Fig. TA18), a float type carburetor (Fig. TA19 or TA20) or a rotary type carburetor (Fig. TA21). Refer to appropriate paragraphs for model being serviced.

Diaphragm Carburetor. To disassemble diaphragm type carburetor, remove screw (9—Fig. TA18) and pump cover (10). Remove gasket (8) and diaphragm (7). Remove fuel inlet screen (12). Remove cover (1), diaphragm (2) and gasket (3). Remove screw (18), circuit plate (19), circuit plate diaphragm valve (20) and gasket (21). Remove screw (17), pin (16), inlet lever (15), fuel inlet needle (14) and spring (13). Remove fuel mixture needles (5 and 4) and springs. Clean and inspect all parts. When reassembling, fuel inlet lever must be flush with fuel chamber floor. Bend lever carefully to obtain correct adjustment.

Float Type Carburetor. Two different float type carburetors have been used (Fig. TA19 or TA20). Service procedure for both carburetors is similar. To disassemble carburetor shown in Fig. TA19, carefully remove cap (1) and withdraw throttle valve assembly. Note location of clip (4) on fuel needle (5) if throttle valve is disassembled. Remove carburetor from engine. Remove float bowl (13), pin (16), float lever (11) and fuel inlet needle (10). Remove main jet (9) and mixture needle (17).

Clean and inspect all parts. Fuel inlet needle tip must not be grooved or damaged. Renew parts as necessary.

Rotary Type Carburetor. Refer to Fig. TA21 for an exploded view of the rotary type carburetor used on some models.

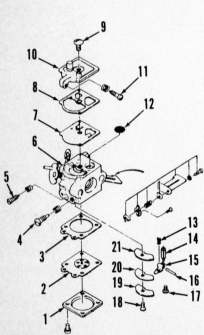

Fig. TA18—Exploded view of the diaphragm type carburetor used on some models.

1. Cover	12. Screen
2. Diaphragm	13. Spring
3. Gasket	14. Fuel inlet needle
4. Mixture needle	15. Fuel inlet lever
5. Mixture needle	16. Pin
6. Body	17. Screw
7. Diaphragm	18. Screw
8. Gasket	19. Circuit plate
9. Screw	20. Circuit plate
10. Cover	diaphragm valve
11. Idle speed screw	21. Gasket

Fig. TA19—Exploded view of one of the float type carburetors used on some models.

1. Cap	11. Float lever
2. Spring	12. Float
3. Seat	13. Float bowl
4. Clip	14. Gasket
5. Fuel needle	15. Screw
6. Throttle valve	16. Pin
7. Body	17. Mixture needle
8. Gasket	18. Gasket
9. Main jet	19. Clamp
10. Fuel needle	

To disassemble carburetor, remove cap (1) and carefully withdraw throttle assembly. Note location of clip (4) on fuel needle. Remove carburetor from engine. Remove reservoir (13), clip (14) and rubber cap (15). Pull check valve (12) out of reservoir. Remove check valve cap (10) and "O" ring (11). Remove fuel mixture needle (8) and main jet (9).

IGNITION SYSTEM. Tanaka engines may be equipped with breaker point type ignition or electronic ignition system. Refer to appropriate paragraphs for models being serviced.

Breaker Point Type Ignition. Ignition condenser and contact set are located behind the flywheel. To adjust, remove flywheel and rotate crankshaft so that contact set is at widest open position. Adjust gap to 0.35 mm (0.014 in.).

Timing should be set so that points are just beginning to open when the "M" mark on flywheel magneto is aligned with mark on crankcase on 16.0 and 30.5 cc (0.84 and 1.86 cu. in.) engines (Fig. TA22) or with outer edge of magneto stator (Fig. TA23). Air gap between flywheel and ignition coil should be 0.35 mm (0.014 in.).

Transistorized Ignition System. Transistorized ignition system is operating satisfactorily if spark will jump across the 3 mm (1/8 in.) gap of a test spark plug. If no spark is produced, check on/off switch, wiring and module air gap. If switch and wiring are determined to be satisfactory and magneto air gap is 0.2 mm (0.008 in.), renew ignition module.

LUBRICATION. All models are lubricated by mixing gasoline with a good quality two-stroke air-cooled engine oil. Refer to TRIMMER SERVICE section for correct fuel/oil mixture ratio recommended by trimmer manufacturer.

REPAIRS

TIGHTENING TORQUES. Recommended tightening torque specifications are as follows:

Clutch . . . . .24-29 N·m
(18-21.6 ft.-lbs.)
Flywheel nut . . . . .19-22 N·m
(14.4-16.6 ft.-lbs.)
Cylinder bolts. . . . . .3.2-3.6 N·m
(4-5 ft.-lbs.)

Crankcase bolts . . . . .3.2-3.6 N·m
(4-5 ft.-lbs.)

CRANKSHAFT AND CONNECTING ROD. Crankshaft and connecting rod are considered an assembly and individual parts are not available separately. Do not remove connecting rod from crankshaft.

To remove crankshaft and connecting rod assembly, remove fuel tank, fuel pump (as equipped) and starter housing assembly. Remove cylinder, muffler and fan shrouds. Remove clutch assembly and clutch housing. Use suitable puller to remove flywheel. Remove muffler and cylinder retaining bolts. Carefully remove cylinder. Remove all crankshaft keys and crankcase retaining bolts. Carefully separate crankcase halves, then remove crankshaft and connecting rod assembly from case.

Inspect all parts for wear or damage.

If main bearings remain in crankcase, heat crankcase slightly to aid bearing removal.

If connecting rod side clearance exceeds 0.05 mm (0.002 in.), renew crankshaft and connecting rod assembly. If crankshaft end play exceeds 0.03 mm (0.001 in.), adjust shim number or thickness at main bearings.

PISTON, PIN AND RINGS. To remove piston refer to CRANKSHAFT AND CONNECTING ROD paragraphs. After removing crankshaft and connec-

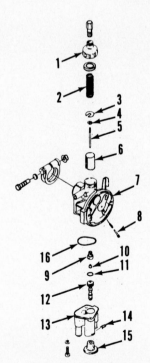

Fig. TA20—Exploded view of one of the float type carburetors used on some models.

1. Spring
2. Seat
3. Clip
4. Fuel needle
5. Throttle valve
6. Body
7. Fuel inlet needle
8. Mixture needle
9. Float lever
10. Pin
11. Main jet holder
12. Main jet
13. Float
14. Gasket
15. Float bowl

Fig. TA21—Exploded view of the rotary type carburetor used on some models.

1. Cap
2. Spring
3. Seat
4. Clip
5. Fuel needle
6. Throttle valve
7. Body
8. Mixture needle
9. Main jet
10. Cap
11. "O" ring
12. Check valve
13. Reservoir
14. Clip
15. Rubber cap
16. Gasket

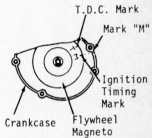

Fig. TA22—Align "M" mark on flywheel magneto with mark on crankcase as shown.

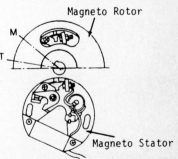

Fig. TA23—Align outer edge of magneto stator with the metal core of ignition coil.

ting rod assembly, use a suitable piston pin puller to remove piston pin, then separate piston from connecting rod.

When assembling piston to connecting rod, arrow on top of piston should point to carburetor side on 30.5 cc (1.86 cu. in.) engines or toward exhaust port side on all other engines.

Refer to the following chart for standard piston skirt diameters and wear limits.

Engine	Standard	Limit
16.0 cc	26.96 mm	26.81 mm
(0.94 cu. in.)	(1.061 in.)	(1.056 in.)
20.0 cc	29.95 mm	29.80 mm
(1.22 cu. in.)	(1.179 in.)	(1.173 in.)
22.6 cc	30.94 mm	30.89 mm
(1.38 cu. in.)	(1.220 in.)	(1.217 in.)
30.5 cc	35.98 mm	35.80 mm
(1.86 cu. in.)	(1.417 in.)	(1.409 in.)
37.4 cc	37.97 mm	37.80 mm
(2.28 cu. in.)	(1.495 in.)	(1.488 in.)
50.2 cc	40.90 mm	40.70 mm
(3.06 cu. in.)	(1.610 in.)	(1.602 in.)

Piston ring end gap should not exceed 0.8 mm (0.03 in.). Clearance between piston groove and ring should not exceed 0.2 mm (0.008 in.).

Standard piston pin diameter and diameter of piston pin bore in piston is 7 mm (0.276 in.) for 16 and 20 cc (0.94 and 1.22 cu. in.) engines, 8 mm (0.315 in.) for 22.6 cc (1.38 cu. in.) engine, 9 mm (0.354 in.) for 30.5 cc (1.86 cu. in.) engine or 10 mm (0.394 in.) for 37.5 and 50.2 cc (2.28 and 3.06 cu. in.) engine.

CYLINDER. To remove cylinder, refer to the CRANKSHAFT AND CONNECT-ING ROD paragraphs. Inspect cylinder for wear or damage. Refer to the following chart for standard cylinder bore diameters and wear limits.

Engine	Standard	Limit
16.0 cc	27.00 mm	27.10 mm
(0.94 cu. in.)	(1.063 in.)	(1.067 in.)
20.0 cc	30.00 mm	30.10 mm
(1.22 cu. in.)	(1.181 in.)	(1.185 in.)
22.6 cc	31.00 mm	31.10 mm
(1.38 cu. in.)	(1.220 in.)	(1.224 in.)
30.5 cc	36.00 mm	36.10 mm
(1.86 cu. in.)	(1.417 in.)	(1.421 in.)
37.4 cc	38.00 mm	38.10 mm
(2.28 cu. in.)	(1.496 in.)	(1.500 in.)
50.2 cc	41.00 mm	41.10 mm
(3.06 cu. in.)	(1.614 in.)	(1.618 in.)

If cylinder bore diameter exceeds wear limit, renew cylinder.

TECUMSEH

ENGINE SERVICE

Model	Bore	Stroke	Displacement
TC200	1.4375 in.	2.250 in.	2.0 cu. in.
	(36.51 mm)	(57.15 mm)	(32.8 cc)

ENGINE INFORMATION

Engine type and model numbers are stamped into blower housing base as indicated in Fig. T9. Always furnish engine model and type number when ordering parts. Tecumseh TC200 engine is used by several manufacturers of string trimmers and brushcutters.

MAINTENANCE

SPARK PLUG. Recommended spark plug is a Champion RCJ-8Y, or equivalent. Specified electrode gap is 0.030 inch (0.76 mm).

AIR CLEANER. Air cleaner element should be removed and cleaned at eight hour intervals of use. Polyurethane element may be washed in a mild detergent and water solution and squeezed until all dirt is removed. Rinse thoroughly. Wrap in clean dry cloth and squeeze until completely dry. Apply engine oil to element and squeeze out excess. Clean air cleaner body and cover and dry thoroughly.

CARBURETOR. Tecumseh TC200 engines used on string trimmers are equipped with diaphragm type carburetor with a single idle mixture needle. Initial adjustment of idle mixture needle is one turn open from a lightly seated position.

Final carburetor adjustment is made with engine at operating temperature and running. Operate engine at idle speed and turn idle mixture needle slowly clockwise until engine falters. Note this position and turn idle mixture needle counterclockwise until engine begins to run unevenly. Note this position and turn adjustment screw until it is halfway between first (lean) and last (rich) positions.

To disassemble carburetor, refer to Fig. T11. Remove idle speed stop screw (9) and spring. Remove pump cover (10), gasket (11) and diaphragm (12). Remove cover (1), diaphragm (2) and gasket (3). Carefully remove pin (15), metering lever (4), inlet needle valve (5) and spring (6). Remove screws retaining throttle plate to throttle shaft (8). Remove screws retaining choke plate to choke shaft (14). Remove "E" clip from throttle shaft and choke shaft and remove shafts. Remove all nonmetallic parts, idle mixture needle, fuel inlet screen and fuel inlet (13). Remove all Welch plugs.

Clean and inspect all parts. Do not allow parts to soak in cleaning solvent longer than 30 minutes.

To reassemble, install fuel inlet needle, metering lever spring and pin. Metering lever hooks onto the inlet needle and rests on the metering spring. Entire assembly is held in place by metering lever pin screw. Tip of metering lever must be 0.060-0.070 inch (1.52-1.78 mm) from the face of carburetor body (Fig. T12).

Install diaphragm gasket so tabs of gaskets align with the bosses on the carburetor body. After gasket is in place, install the diaphragm again aligning tabs to bosses. The head of the rivet in the diaphragm must be toward the carburetor body. Check the atmospheric vent hole in the diaphragm cover to make certain it is clean. Install cover on carburetor.

Install pump diaphragm with the corner holes aligning with the same holes in the carburetor body. Align pump gasket in the same manner and place pump cover onto carburetor.

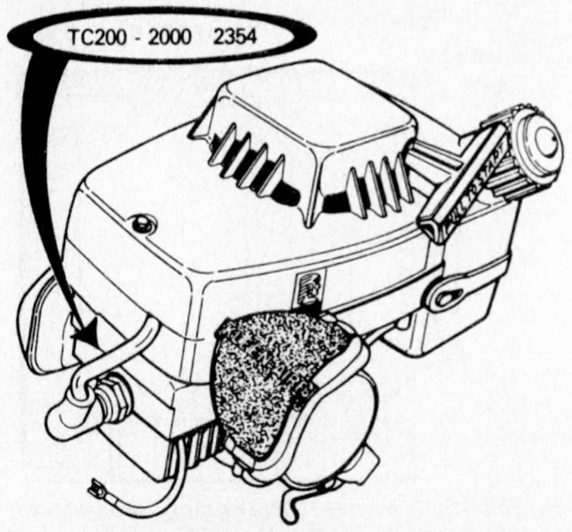

Fig. T9—Engine model and type number is stamped into blower housing base.

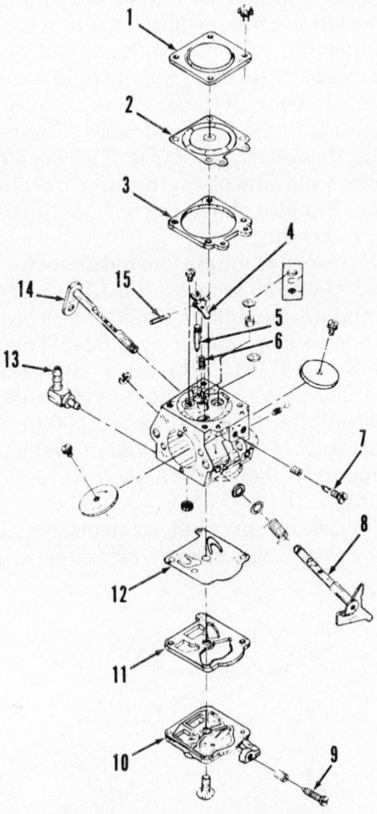

Fig. T11—Exploded view of diaphragm type carburetor used on TC200 engine.

1. Cover	9. Idle speed screw
2. Diaphragm	10. Cover
3. Gasket	11. Gasket
4. Metering lever	12. Diaphragm
5. Inlet needle valve	13. Fuel inlet
6. Spring	14. Choke shaft
7. Idle mixture needle	15. Pin
8. Throttle shaft	

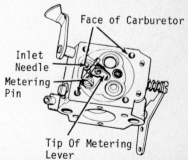

Fig. T12—Tip of metering valve lever should be 0.060-0.070 inch (1.52-1.78 mm) from the face of carburetor body.

Numbers on throttle plate should face to the outside when throttle is closed. Apply a small amount of Loctite grade "A" to fuel inlet before installation.

IGNITION SYSTEM. All Model TC200 engines are equipped with a solid state ignition module located outside the flywheel. Correct air gap between laminations of module and magnets of flywheel is 0.012 inch (0.30 mm). Use Tecumseh gage part number 670297.

GOVERNOR ADJUSTMENT. Model TC200 engine is equipped with an air vane type governor. Refer to ENGINE REASSEMBLY paragraphs for adjustment procedure.

LUBRICATION. Engine is lubricated by mixing gasoline with a good quality two-stroke air-cooled engine oil. Refer to TRIMMER SERVICE section for correct fuel/oil mixture ratio recommended by trimmer manufacturer.

CARBON. Muffler and exhaust ports should be cleaned after every 50 hours of operation if engine is operated continuously at full load. If operated at light or medium load, the cleaning interval can be extended to 100 hours.

REPAIRS

TIGHTENING TORQUES. Recommended tightening torque specifications are as follows:

Crankcase cover
to crankcase . . . . 70-100 in.-lbs.
(8-11 N·m)
Cylinder to crankcase . . 60-75 in.-lbs.
(7-8 N·m)
Carburetor . . . . 20-32 in.-lbs.
(2.3-3.6 N·m)
Flywheel nut . . . . 180-240 in.-lbs.
(20-27 N·m)
Ignition module . . . . 30-40 in.-lbs.
(3.4-4.5 N·m)
Starter retainer screw . . . . 45-55 in.-lbs.
(5.1-6.2 N·m)

CRANKSHAFT. To remove crankshaft, drain fuel tank, remove tank strap and disconnect fuel line at carburetor. Disconnect and remove spark plug. Remove the three screws retaining blower housing and rewind starter assembly and remove housing. Remove the two screws retaining ignition module. Use strap wrench to hold flywheel. Use flywheel puller (670299) to remove flywheel. Remove air cleaner assembly with carburetor, spacer, gaskets and screen. Mark and remove governor link from carburetor throttle lever. Remove the three 5/16 inch cap screws, then separate blower housing base from crankcase. Attach engine holder tool (670300) with the three blower housing base screws. Place tool in a bench vise. Remove muffler springs using tool fabricated from a 12 inch piece of heavy wire with a ¼ inch hook made on one end. Remove the four cylinder retaining nuts, then pull cylinder off squarely and in line with piston. Use caution so rod does not bend. Install seal protector (670206) at magneto end of crankshaft and seal protector (670263) at pto end of crankshaft. Remove crankcase cover screws, then carefully separate crankcase cover from crankcase. Rotate crankshaft to top dead center and withdraw crankshaft through crankcase cover opening while sliding connecting rod off crankpin and over crankshaft. Refer to Fig. T18. Use care not to lose any of the 23 crankpin needle bearings which will be loose. Flanged side of connecting rod (Fig. T19) must be toward pto side of engine after installation. Handle connecting rod carefully to avoid bending.

Standard crankpin journal diameter is 0.5985-0.5990 inch (15.202-15.215 mm). Standard crankshaft pto side main bearing journal diameter is 0.6248-0.6253 inch (15.870-15.880 mm). Standard crankshaft magneto side main bearing journal diameter is 0.4998-0.5003 inch (12.69-12.71 mm). Crankshaft end play should be 0.004-0.012 inch (0.10-0.30 mm).

To install crankshaft, clean mating surfaces of crankcase, cylinder and

crankcase cover. Avoid scarring or burring mating surfaces.

Crankshaft main bearing in crankcase of early model engines did not have a retaining ring as shown in Fig. T20. Retaining ring was installed as a running change in late model engines. To install new caged bearing in crankcase, place bearing on installation tool (670302) with the numbered side of bearing away from tool. Press bearing into crankcase until tool is flush with crankcase housing. Install retaining ring (as equipped). Place seal for magneto side onto seal installation tool (670301) so metal case of seal enters tool first. Press seal in until tool is flush with crankcase. Use the same procedure to install bearing and seal in crankcase cover using bearing installation tool (670304) and seal installation tool (670303).

New crankpin needle bearings are on bearing strips. Heavy grease may be used to retain old bearings on crankpin journal as required. During reassembly, connecting rod must not be forced onto crankpin journal as rod failure or bending will result. Apply Loctite 515 to mating surfaces of crankcase during reassembly and use seal protectors when installing lip seals over ends of crankshaft. When installing cylinder over piston, install a wooden block with a slot cut out for connecting rod under piston to provide support and prevent connecting rod damage. Exhaust ports in cylinder are on the same side of engine as muffler resting boss. Make certain cylinder is correctly positioned, stagger ring end gaps and compress rings using a suitable ring compressor which can be removed after cylinder is installed over piston. Install cylinder and push cylinder onto crankcase studs to expose 1-2 threads of studs. Install the four nuts onto exposed threads of studs, then push cylinder further down to capture nuts on studs. Tighten nuts in a criss-cross pattern to secified torque.

Install muffler using fabricated tool to install springs. Install blower housing

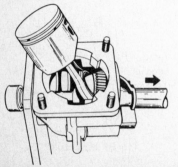

Fig. T18—Connecting rod must be carefully worked over crankpin during crankshaft removal. Do not lose the 23 loose crankpin needle bearings.

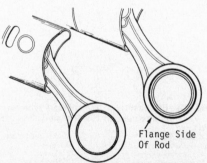

Fig. T19—Flanged side of connecting rod must face pto side of engine after installation.

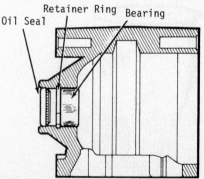

Fig. T20—Early Model TC200 engines did not have retaining ring shown. Retaining ring was installed as a running change in late model engines.

base and tighten the three screws to specified torque.

Refer to Fig. T26 to install governor air vane assembly. Speed adjustment lever is held in place by inserting screw into the blower housing base. Long end of governor spring hooks into the notch on neck of air vane. Short end hooks into the hole in speed adjustment lever. To decrease governed speed of engine, bend speed adjusting lever towards spark plug end of engine. To increase governed speed of engine, bend lever in the opposite direction. Throttle link is inserted into hole in the neck of the air vane and the hole closest to the throttle shaft in throttle plate.

Install carburetor, spacer, gaskets, screen and air cleaner body on engine. Tighten screws to specified torque. Install and adjust ignition module. Install blower housing/rewind starter assembly and tighten screws to specified torque. Install fuel tank.

PISTON, RINGS AND CONNECTING ROD. Standard piston diameter is 1.4327-1.4340 inch (36.39-36.42 mm). Standard width of both ring grooves is 0.050-0.051 inch (1.27-1.29 mm). Standard piston ring width is 0.46-0.47 inch (11.7-11.9 mm). Standard ring end gap is 0.004-0.014 inch (0.10-0.36 mm).

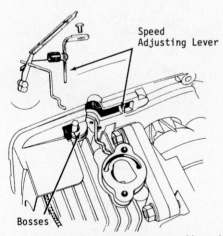

Fig. T26—View of air vane governor assembly used on Model TC200 engines. Refer to text.

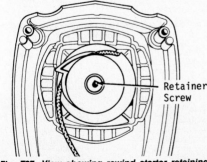

Fig. T27—View showing rewind starter retaining screw.

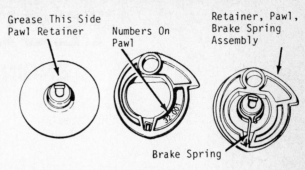

Fig. T28—View of rewind starter pawl and retainer. Refer to text.

CYLINDER. Cylinder must be smooth and free of scratches or flaking. Clean carbon carefully as necessary. Standard bore size is 1.4375 inches (36.513 mm).

TECUMSEH SPECIAL TOOLS. Tecumseh special tools are available to aid in engine disassembly and reassembly are listed by use and tool part number.

FLYWHEEL PULLER 670299
AIR GAP GAGE 670297
ENGINE HOLDER 670300
SEAL PROTECTOR
  (MAG. END) 670206
SEAL PROTECTOR
  (PTO END) 670263
SEAL INSTALLER
  (MAG END) 670301
SEAL INSTALLER
  (PTO END) 670303
BEARING INSTALLER
  (MAG END) 670302
BEARING INSTALLER
  (PTO END) 670304

REWIND STARTER. The rewind starter assembly is incorporated into blower housing. Blower housing design varies according to engine model and specification number. To release rewind spring tension, remove staple in starter handle and slowly let spring tension release by winding rope onto rope sheave. Remove the 5/16 inch retainer screw (Fig. T27). Remove pawl retainer and pawl (Fig. T28) and extract starter pulley. Use caution not to pull rewind spring out of housing at this time. Uncoiling spring can be very dangerous. If rewind spring is damaged or weak, use caution when removing spring from housing.

To reassemble, grease center post of housing and portion of housing where rewind spring will rest. Grip rewind spring firmly with needlenose pliers ahead of spring tail. Insert spring and hook tail into housing as shown in Fig. T29. Make certain spring is seated in housing before removing needlenose pliers from spring. Grease top of spring. Insert starter rope into starter pulley and tie a left handed knot in end of rope. With neck of starter pulley up, wind starter rope in a counterclockwise rotation. Place end of

rope in notch of pulley and place pulley in housing. Press down on pulley and rotate until pulley attaches to rewind spring. Refer to Fig. T30. Lubricate pawl retainer with grease and place the pawl, numbers up, onto retainer. Place brake spring on center of retainer with tab locating into pawl (Fig. T28). Tab on pawl retainer must align with notch in center post of housing and locating hole in pawl must mesh with boss on starter pulley (Fig. T31). Install retainer screw (Fig. T27) and torque to specified torque. Use starter rope to wind spring a minimum of 2 turns counterclockwise and a maximum of 3 turns. Feed starter rope through starter grommet and secure starter handle using a left hand knot.

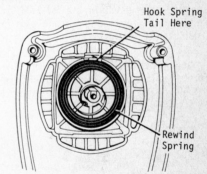

Fig. T29—View of rewind spring and housing.

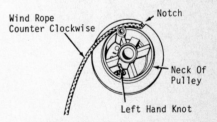

Fig. T30—View showing rewind starter rope as shown and as outlined in text.

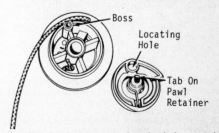

Fig. T31—Boss must engage locating hole on pawl retainer. Refer to text.

TECUMSEH
ENGINE SERVICE

Model	Bore	Stroke	Displacement
AV520	2.09 in.	1.50 in.	5.2 cu. in.
	(53 mm)	(38 mm)	(85 cc)

ENGINE INFORMATION

Engine type and model number tags will be at one of a number of locations. Refer to Fig. T50. Always furnish engine model and type number when ordering parts. Model AV520 engines used on string trimmers and brushcutters are equipped with a diaphragm type carburetor and utilize a ball bearing type main bearing at magneto side and a needle type main bearing at pto side.

MAINTENANCE

SPARK PLUG. Recommended spark plug is a Champion RJ-17M, or equivalent. Specified electrode gap is 0.030 inch (0.76 mm).

AIR CLEANER. Refer to Fig. T51 for an exploded view of air cleaner used

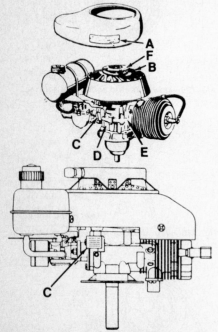

Fig. T50—The engine serial number and type number may be found at one of the locations indicated above.

A. Nameplate on air shroud
B. Model & type number plate
C. Metal tab on crankcase
D. Stamped on crankcase
E. Stamped on cylinder flange
F. Stamped on starter pulley

on most models. Polyurethane element may be washed in a mild detergent and water solution and squeezed until all dirt is removed. Rinse thoroughly. Wrap in clean dry cloth, then squeeze until completely dry. Apply engine oil to element and squeeze out excess. Clean air cleaner body and cover and dry thoroughly.

CARBURETOR. Tecumseh Model AV520 engine is equipped with a diaphragm type carburetor shown in Fig. T52. Most models are equipped with carburetor shown utilizing fixed high speed metering and adjustable low speed mixture needle; however, some models may be equipped with both low speed and high speed mixture needles. Carburetor model number is stamped on carburetor flange (Fig. T53).

Initial adjustment of low speed and high speed (as equipped) mixture needles is one turn open from a lightly seated position.

Final carburetor adjustment is made with engine at operating temperature and running. Operate engine at idle speed and turn low speed mixture needle slowly clockwise until engine falters. Note this position and turn low speed mixture needle counterclockwise until engine begins to falter. Note this position and turn mixture needle until it is halfway between first (lean) and last (rich) positions. Operate engine at rated governed speed with trimmer line at correct length or brush blade installed and use the same procedure to

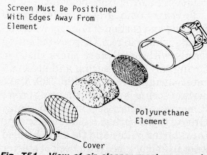

Screen Must Be Positioned With Edges Away From Element

Polyurethane Element

Cover

Fig. T51—View of air cleaner most commonly used on these engines. Refer to text for service procedures.

adjust the high speed mixture needle (as equipped) as used for the low speed mixture needle. Make adjustments on high speed mixture needle in 1/8 turn increments.

To disassemble carburetor, refer to Fig. T52. Remove throttle (29) and choke (8) plates and shafts. Remove low

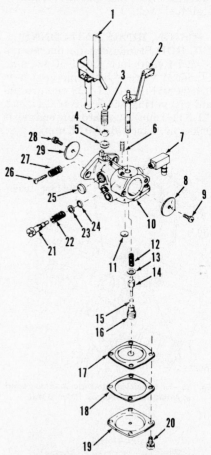

Fig. T52—Exploded view of diaphragm type carburetor used on Model AV520.

1. Throttle shaft
2. Choke shaft
3. Return spring
4. Steel washer
5. Felt washer
6. Choke positioning spring
7. Fuel fitting
8. Choke plate
9. Screw
10. Carburetor body
11. Welch plug
12. Valve spring
13. Gasket
14. Inlet needle
15. Neoprene seat
15. Neoprene seat
16. Seat fitting
17. Diaphragm
18. Gasket
19. Cover
20. Screw
21. Idle mixture needle
22. Spring
23. Washer
24. "O" ring
25. Welch plug
26. Idle speed screw
27. Spring
28. Screw
29. Throttle plate

speed mixture needle, remove "O" ring on mixture needle and note design of screw. If equipped with high speed mixture needle, remove needle and discard "O" ring. Drill an off center hole in idle fuel chamber Welch plug (25), then pry out with suitable tool. Remove the four screws (20) retaining diaphragm cover (19) and remove cover, gasket (18) and diaphragm (17). Early type inlet needle seat fitting (16) is slotted and may be removed using a screwdriver. Late style inlet needle seat fitting (16) must be removed using a thin wall 9/32 inch socket. Inlet needle is spring loaded. Use care when removing not to lose spring (12). Remove and discard neoprene needle seat (15) located in inlet needle seat fitting (16). Remove fuel inlet fitting (7). Note presence of filter screen in fuel inlet fitting. Drill off center hole in Welch plug (11) and remove plug.

Make certain all "O" rings and non-metallic parts are removed, then soak carburetor parts in clean carburetor cleaner for 30 minutes. Rinse in clean water and use compressed air to dry. To reassemble, make certain fuel inlet fitting filter screen is clear and press fitting partially in, apply Loctite 512 to exposed portion of fitting and press fitting in until seated. Refer to Fig. T54 and install new Welch plugs (11 and 25—Fig. T52). Install spring (12), needle (14), gasket (13), seat (15) and fitting (16). Make certain new diaphragm is the same style as the old diaphragm which was removed. Diaphragm rivet head

must always be toward inlet needle valve (Fig. T55). Refer to Fig. T56 to determine installation location of diaphragm and gasket, then install in proper sequence. Install cover (19—Fig. T52). Place new "O" rings on fuel mixture needles and install needles until they are lightly seated, then back out one turn. Install choke shaft (2) and install choke plate (8) with flat of choke plate toward fuel inlet side of carburetor and mark on face of choke plate parallel with choke shaft. Install throttle shaft (1) and install throttle plate with short line stamped in plate to top of carburetor, parallel with throttle shaft, and facing out when throttle is closed.

IGNITION SYSTEM. Model AV520 engines may be equipped with a magneto type ignition system or a solid state ignition system. Refer to appropriate paragraph for model being serviced.

Magneto Ignition. Coil (12—Fig. T57), condenser (15) and breaker point assembly (6) are located behind flywheel (1). To renew breaker points and condenser, remove rewind starter assembly (1—Fig. T60) and blower housing (6). Remove nut (2), washer (3), starter cup (4) and screen (5). Use flywheel puller set (670215) to remove flywheel. DO NOT use knock off tool as main bearing damage will occur. Remove clip retainer (2—Fig. T57), cover (3) and gasket (4). Disconnect wiring from breaker point assembly (6), remove screw (7) and lift out breaker point assembly. Remove screw (14) and lift out condenser. Install new condenser and breaker point assembly. Place one drop of engine oil on lubricating felt (9). Rotate engine until breaker point cam (5) opens breaker point set to maximum opening. Adjust breaker point plate until point gap is 0.020 inch

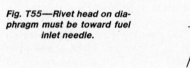

Fig. T55—Rivet head on diaphragm must be toward fuel inlet needle.

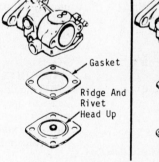

Fig. T56—Gasket and diaphragm installation sequence is determined by letter "F" stamped on carburetor flange.

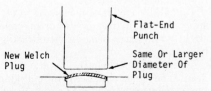

Fig. T53—View showing location of carburetor identification number on Tecumseh diaphragm type carburetor.

Flat-End Punch

New Welch Plug

Same Or Larger Diameter Of Plug

Fig. T54—Use a flat punch the same diameter or larger to install new Welch plugs.

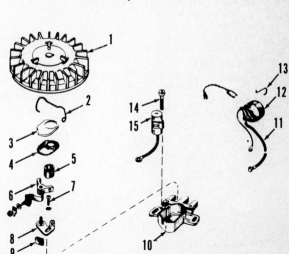

Fig. T57—Exploded view of magneto ignition system used on Model AV520 engine.

1. Flywheel
2. Retainer
3. Cover
4. Gasket
5. Cam
6. Breaker points
7. Screw
8. Breaker point plate
9. Lubricating felt
10. Stator assy.
11. Spark plug lead
12. Coil
13. Coil locking clip
14. Screw
15. Condenser

(0.51 mm). Tighten screw (7) to maintain setting. Stator assembly should be positioned so ignition breaker points just open when piston top is 0.070 inch (1.78 mm) before top dead center with points correctly gapped. Correct air gap between coil and flywheel is 0.015 inch (0.38 mm).

Solid State Ignition. The Tecumseh solid state ignition system does not use ignition points. The only moving part of the system is the rotating flywheel with the charging magnets. As the flywheel magnet passes position (1A—Fig. T58), a low voltage AC current is induced into input coil (2). The current passes through rectifier (3) converting this current to DC current. It then travels to the capacitor (4) where it is stored. The flywheel rotates approximately 180 to position (1B). As it passes trigger coil (5), it induces a very small electric charge into coil. This charge passes through resistor (6) and turns on the SCR (silicon controlled rectifier) switch (7). With SCR switch closed, the low voltage current stored in capacitor (4)

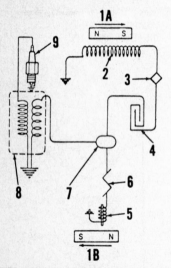

Fig. T58—Diagram of Tecumseh solid state ignition system. Items (3, 4, 5, 6 and 7) are encased in magneto assembly.

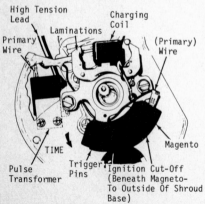

Fig. T59—View showing location of solid state ignition system component parts.

travels to the pulse transformer (8). The voltage is stepped up instantaneously and the current is discharged across the electrodes of spark plug (9), producing a spark.

If system fails to produce a spark at spark plug, first make certain coil air gap between coil and flywheel is 0.005-0.008 inch (0.13-0.20 mm). Check the high tension lead (Fig. T59). If condition of the high tension lead is questionable, renew the pulse transformer and high tension lead assembly. Check the condition of primary wire. Renew primary wire if insulation is faulty. The ignition charging coil (magneto), electronic triggering system and mounting plate are available only as an assembly. If necessary to renew this assembly, place the unit in position on the engine. Start the retaining screws, turn the mounting plate counterclockwise as far as possible, then tighten retaining screws to 5-7 ft.-lbs. (7-10 N·m).

GOVERNOR ADJUSTMENT. Model AV520 engine is equipped with an air vane type governor located on throttle shaft. Idle speed stop screw (26 Fig. T52) should be set to allow engine to idle at 2600 rpm. High speed stop screw (47—Fig. T60) should be set to limit engine maximum rpm to 4600-4800 rpm.

LUBRICATION. Engine is lubricated by mixing gasoline with a good quality two-stroke air-cooled engine oil. Refer to TRIMMER SERVICE section for correct mixture ratio recommended by trimmer manufacturer.

CARBON. Muffler and exhaust ports should be cleaned after every 50 hours of operation if engine is operated continuously at full load. If operated at light or medium load, the cleaning interval can be extended to 100 hours.

REPAIRS

TIGHTENING TORQUES. Recommended tightening torque specifications are as follows:

Crankcase base to
  crankcase . . . . 70-80 in.-lbs.
  (8-10 N·m)
Cylinder head . . . . . . 80-100 in.-lbs.
  (10-11 N·m)
Connecting rod . . . . . 70-80 in.-lbs.
  (8-10 N·m)
Flywheel nut . . . . .264-324 in.-lbs.
  (30-37 N·m)
Ignition module . . . . .30-40 in.-lbs.
  (3.4-4.5 N·m)
Reed valve plate . . . . . 50-60 in.-lbs.
  (6-7 N·m)

Rewind retainer screw . 65-75 in.-lbs.
  (7-8 N·m)

CRANKSHAFT AND BEARINGS. To remove crankshaft and main bearings, remove rewind starter assembly (1—Fig. T60), blower housing (6) and fuel tank. Remove muffler, nut (2), washer (3), starter cup (4) and screen (5). Note location and condition of air vane governor. Use flywheel puller set (670215) to remove flywheel. DO NOT use knock off tool to remove flywheel. Remove ignition system component parts. Remove carburetor assembly (40) and reed plate assembly (38). Remove cylinder head (30) and gasket (29). Remove the two connecting rod cap screws and carefully remove connecting rod cap (19). Use care not to lose the connecting rod needle bearings (18). Push connecting rod and piston assembly out of cylinder. Remove piston pin retaining ring (24). Heat piston top slowly until piston pin (23) can be easily pushed out. Caged bearing (21) can be pressed out. Remove the four cap screws retaining base (13) plate to block and tap base plate to break gasket bond. Remove base plate/crankshaft assembly as a unit. If ball bearing main is noisy or damaged, slowly heat bearing area of base plate until ball bearing can be easily removed. Press bearing off of crankshaft. Insert tip of ice pick or similar tool into location shown in Fig. T61, then remove the wire retainer (10—Fig. T60). Remove retainer plate (11) and seal (12). Repeat procedure to remove wire retainer (34), retainer plate (35) and seal (36) in block. Press caged needle bearing (27) out of block.

Standard crankpin journal diameter is 0.8442-0.8450 inch (21.443-21.463 mm). Standard crankshaft pto side main bearing journal diameter is 0.9998-1.0003 inch (25.395-25.407 mm). Standard crankshaft magneto side main bearing journal diameter is 0.6691-0.6695 inch (16.995-17.005 mm). There should be zero crankshaft end play.

When installing ball bearing on magneto end of crankshaft, place a 1/4 inch (6.35 mm) dot of Loctite 601 in two places 180° apart on crankshaft main bearing journal and press ball bearing into position. It may be necessary to heat base slightly when installing crankshaft so that ball bearing will slip into bearing bore easily.

To install caged needle bearing in pto side of crankcase, heat crankcase slightly and press bearing into bearing bore.

To install crankshaft, install caged needle bearing and seal in cylinder block/crankcase assembly as outlined. Install ball bearing on crankshaft. In-

Fig. T60—Exploded view of Model AV520 engine.

1. Rewind starter assy.
2. Nut
3. Washer
4. Starter cup
5. Screen
6. Blower housing
7. Flywheel
8. Cam
9. Coil & stator assy.
10. Retainer
11. Retainer plate
12. Seal
13. Base
14. Ball bearing
15. Gasket
16. Key
17. Crankshaft
18. Needle bearings & liner
19. Connecting rod cap
20. Connecting rod
21. Bearing
22. Piston
23. Piston pin
24. Retainer
25. Ring
26. Ring
27. Bearing
28. Cylinder & block
29. Gasket
30. Cylinder head
31. Spark plug
32. Gasket
33. Muffler
34. Retainer
35. Retainer plate
36. Seal
37. Gasket
38. Reed plate assy.
39. Gasket
40. Carburetor
41. Gasket
42. Housing
43. Screen
44. Element
45. Screen
46. Cover
47. Governor high speed stop screw
48. Lever adjuster
49. Spacer
50. Spring
51. Lever
52. Spring

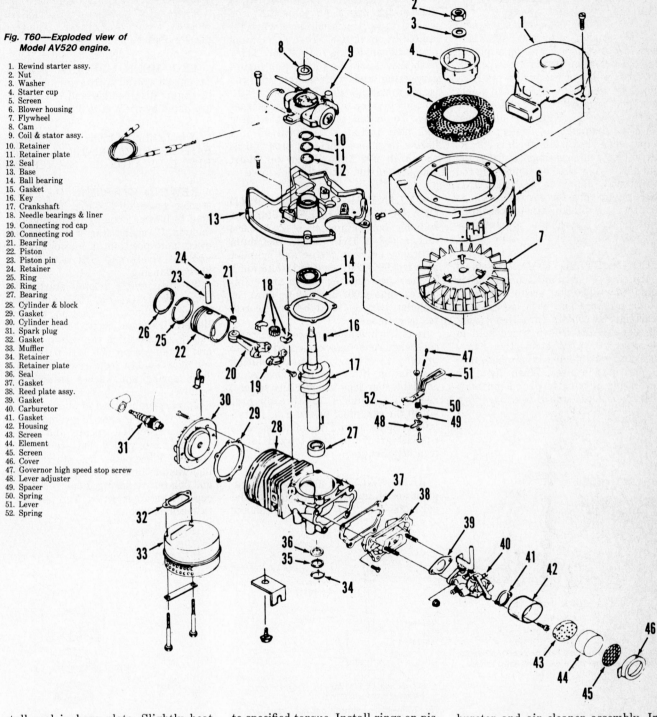

stall seal in base plate. Slightly heat base plate (13—Fig. T60) and install crankshaft and ball bearing assembly in base plate. Make certain to use seal protectors or tape to prevent seal damage. Place a thin bead of silicon type sealer to base plate gasket. Install crankshaft through caged needle bearing in cylinder block/crankcase assembly and carefully work crankshaft through seal and bearing until base plate contacts cylinder block/crankcase assembly. Use seal protector or tape to prevent seal damage. Install the four base plate retaining screws and tighten

to specified torque. Install rings on piston and connecting rod assembly, stagger ring end gaps. Install needle bearing connecting rod bearings on crankshaft journal and remove paper backing on new bearings or use heavy grease on used bearings to retain in position. Compress rings and carefully install piston and connecting rod assembly into cylinder and crankcase. Install connecting rod cap and tighten screws to specified torque. Place a thin bead of silicon sealer to reed plate gasket and install gasket and reed plate. Tighten screws to specified torque. Install car-

buretor and air cleaner assembly. Install ignition system components and adjust as required. Continue to reverse disassembly procedure for reassembly.

PISTON, PIN AND RINGS. Standard piston diameter is 2.0870-2.0880 inch (53.010-53.035 mm). Upper and lower ring groove width is 0.0645-0.0655 inch (1.638-1.763 mm). Standard piston ring width is 0.0615-0.0625 inch (1.562-1.587 mm). Standard ring end gap is 0.006-0.016 inch (0.15-0.40 mm). If rings are beveled on inner edge, beveled edge is installed toward top of piston (Fig.

T64). Stagger ring end gaps around circumference of piston.

An offset piston is used on some models and is identified by a "V" or "1111" hash marks stamped into top of piston. The older version piston arrowhead is 90° from a line of the piston pin bore. Newer version piston arrowhead points in a line parallel to the piston bore. Refer to Fig. T62. Newer version wrist pin bore diameter is smaller at the arrowhead side. Piston which is not offset will have no markings on piston top and may be installed on connecting rod either way. Refer to CONNECTING ROD paragraphs for correct piston to connecting rod installation procedure.

Standard piston pin diameter is 0.4997-0.4999 inch (12.692-12.697 mm).

CONNECTING ROD. The steel connecting rod used on Model AV520 is equipped with a caged needle bearing at piston pin bore and with loose needle bearings at crankpin bore. New crankpin bore needle bearings are held in place by a waxed strip. Use heavy grease to retain old crankpin bore needle bearings in place. When installing new caged bearing in piston pin bore, press on lettered side of bearing. Offset

piston is installed on connecting rod so that match marks on connecting rod will be toward magneto side when installed in crankcase. When assembling piston to connecting rod, "V" or "1111" hash marks will be to the left side of connecting rod with connecting rod match marks up (Fig. T62). Piston with no marks on top may be installed either way. To install piston on connecting rod, heat piston in oil until oil just begins to smoke. Install piston pin as shown in Fig. T63. Piston pin must slide into piston easily. Do not force.

CYLINDER, BLOCK AND CRANKSHAFT SEALS. Standard cylinder bore diameter is 2.093-2.094 inches (53.16-53.18 mm). Maximum clearance between piston and cylinder bore is 0.005-0.007 inch (0.13-0.18 mm). If clearance between piston and cylinder exceeds 0.007 inch (0.18 mm), or cylinder bore is scratched or scored, renew cylinder.

It is important to exercise extreme care when renewing crankshaft seals to prevent their being damaged during installation. If a protector sleeve is not available, use tape to cover any splines, keyways, shoulders or threads over which the seal must pass during installation. Seals should be installed with channel groove of seal toward inside (center) of engine.

REED VALVES. Model AV520 engines are equipped with reed type inlet valve (38—Fig. T60). Reed petals should

not stand out more than 0.010 inch (0.25 mm) from the reed plate and must not be bent, distorted or cracked. The reed plate must be smooth and flat.

TECUMSEH SPECIAL TOOLS. Tecumseh special tools available to aid in engine disassembly and reassembly are listed by use and tool part number.

FLYWHEEL PULLER 670215
BALL BEARING DRIVER . . .670258
DIAL INDICATOR 670241

REWIND STARTER. The rewind starter assembly (1—Fig. T60) is riveted to blower housing (6) during production. If rewind starter must be renewed, note position on blower housing and cut rivets and bolt new unit to blower housing.

To disassemble rewind starter, remove handle (1—Fig. T65) and allow spring to slowly unwind in housing. Remove retainer screw (10), retainer cup (9), starter dog (8), dog spring (6) and brake spring (7). Lift pulley and spring assembly from rewind housing. Turn spring and keeper assembly to remove.

To reassemble rewind starter, apply a light coat of grease to rewind spring and place rewind spring and keeper assembly into pulley. Turn to lock into position. Place pulley into starter housing. Install brake spring, starter dog and dog return spring. Replace retainer cup and retainer screw. Tighten screw to specified torque.

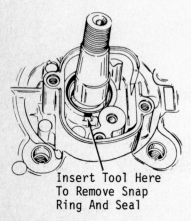

Insert Tool Here To Remove Snap Ring And Seal

Fig. T61—Wire retainer ring must be removed to remove retainer plate and seal. Refer to text.

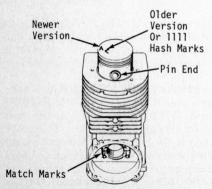

Fig. T62—View showing correct installation of connecting rod and piston assembly.

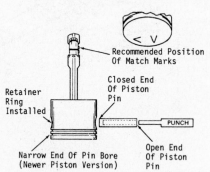

Fig. T63—View showing correct procedure for piston pin installation. Refer to text.

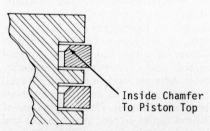

Inside Chamfer To Piston Top

Fig. T64—If inner ring edge is beveled, beveled side is installed toward top of piston.

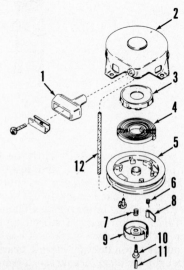

Fig. T65—Exploded view of rewind starter assembly.

1. Handle	7. Brake spring
2. Housing	8. Dog
3. Keeper	9. Retainer
4. Spring	10. Screw
5. Pulley	11. Centering pin
6. Dog spring	12. Rope

TML (TRAIL)

ENGINE SERVICE

Model	Bore	Stroke	Displacement
150528	1.44 in.	1.28 in.	2.1 cu. in.
	(36.5 mm)	(32.5 mm)	(35 cc)

ENGINE INFORMATION

TML (Trail) two-stroke air-cooled gasoline engine is used on TML trimmers and brush cutters. The die cast aluminum cylinder is an integral part of one crankcase half. The crankshaft is supported in caged roller bearings at each end. Engine is equipped with a one piece connecting rod which rides on roller bearings.

MAINTENANCE

SPARK PLUG. Recommended spark plug is a Champion CJ6, or equivalent. Specified electrode gap is 0.025 inch (0.6 mm).

CARBURETOR. TML engine is equipped with a Walbro diaphragm type carburetor (Fig. TL1). Initial adjustment of low speed mixture needle (12) is 1-1/4 turns open from a lightly seated position. Initial adjustment of high speed mixture needle (13) is 1-1/16 turns open from a lightly seated position.

Final carburetor adjustment is made with trimmer line at recommended length, engine at operating temperature and running. Turn low speed mixture needle (12) clockwise until engine falters. Note this position and turn low speed mixture needle counterclockwise until engine falters. Note this position and turn low speed mixture needle until it is halfway between first (lean) and last (rich) positions. Adjust idle speed screw (3) until engine idles at 2500-3000 rpm, or just below clutch engagement speed. Operate engine at full rpm and adjust high speed mixture needle (13) using the same procedure outlined for low speed mixture needle. Turn high speed mixture needle in 1/8 turn increments. A properly adjusted carburetor will give high rpm with some unburned residue from muffler.

To disassemble carburetor, remove pump cover retaining screw (1), pump cover (2), diaphragm (5) and gasket (4). Remove inlet screen (6). Remove the four metering cover screws (27), me-

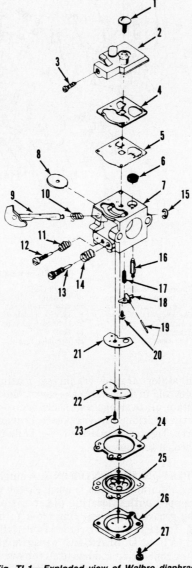

Fig. TL1—Exploded view of Walbro diaphragm type carburetor.

1. Screw
2. Pump cover
3. Idle screw
4. Gasket
5. Pump diaphragm
6. Inlet screen
7. Body
8. Throttle plate
9. Throttle shaft
10. Spring
11. Spring
12. Low speed mixture needle
13. High speed mixture needle
14. Spring
15. "E" clip
16. Fuel inlet needle
17. Spring
18. Fuel inlet lever
19. Pin
20. Screw
21. Gasket
22. Circuit plate
23. Screw
24. Gasket
25. Metering diaphragm
26. Cover
27. Screw

tering cover (26), diaphragm (25) and gasket (24). Remove screw (20), pin (19), fuel lever (18), spring (17) and fuel inlet needle (16). Remove screw (23), circuit plate (22) and gasket (21). Remove high and low speed mixture needles and springs. Remove throttle plate (8) and throttle shaft (9) as required.

Clean parts thoroughly and inspect all diaphragms for wrinkles, cracks or tears. Diaphragms should be flexible and soft. Fuel inlet lever (18) should be flush with carburetor body (Fig. TL2).

IGNITION SYSTEM. Engine is equipped with a solid state ignition system. Ignition system is considered satisfactory if spark will jump across the 3 mm (1/8 in.) gap of a test spark plug. If no spark is produced, check on/off switch, wiring and air gap. If switch, wiring and air gap are satisfactory, install a new ignition module (11—Fig. TL3).

Correct air gap for ignition module is 0.015 inch (0.38 mm). If ignition module screws are loosened or removed, apply Loctite 242 thread locking compound to screw threads prior to installation. Timing is not adjustable.

LUBRICATION. Manufacturer recommends mixing gasoline with a good quality two-stroke, air-cooled engine oil. Refer to TRIMMER SERVICE section for correct fuel/oil mixture ratio recommended by trimmer manufacturer.

CARBON. Muffler and exhaust ports should be cleaned after every 50 hours of operation if engine is operated continuously at full load. If operated at light or medium load, the cleaning interval can be extended to 100 hours.

REPAIRS

COMPRESSION PRESSURE. For optimum performance, compression pressure for a cold engine with throttle and choke wide open should be 120-140 psi (827-965 kPa). Minimum acceptable

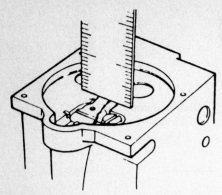

Fig. TL2—Fuel inlet valve lever should be flush with carburetor surface.

compression pressure for a cold engine is 90 psi (620 kPa).

TIGHTENING TORQUES. Recommended tightening torque specifications are as follows:

Crankcase cover . . . . 70 in.-lbs.
                          (8 N·m)
Flywheel nut . . . . 175 in.-lbs.
                         (20 N·m)
Ignition module . . . . . . 25 in.-lbs.
                         (3 N·m)
Carburetor . . . . 30 in.-lbs.
                         (3.4 N·m)

CRANKSHAFT AND BEARINGS. Crankshaft (17—Fig. TL3) is supported at each end in a caged needle bearings clamped in bearing bores at crankcase split. To remove crankshaft, remove all cooling shrouds, recoil starter assembly, fuel tank, muffler and carburetor. Remove nut, flywheel and clutch. Remove the crankcase retaining bolts (20), then remove crankcase cover (19). Carefully remove crankshaft, pulling piston out of cylinder as crankshaft is removed. When handling crankshaft, hold connecting rod toward counterweight side to prevent the 11 connecting rod needle bearings from falling out. Remove all seals, bearings and thrust washers. Work connecting rod off small end of crankshaft using care to catch the 11 connecting rod needle bearings (18).

To reassemble, coat connecting rod needle bearings with heavy grease and install all 11 bearings on crankshaft connecting rod journal. Work connecting rod over small end of crankshaft and over bearings. Thrust washers are installed with chamfered side toward crankshaft web. Seals are installed with spring side toward the inner side of crankcase. Apply a thin coat of sili-

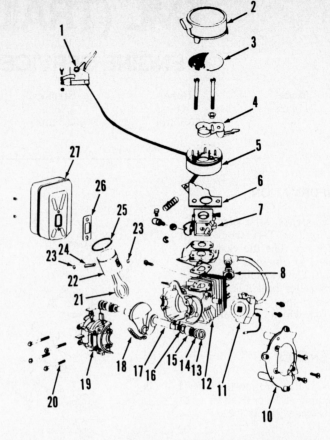

Fig. TL3—Exploded view of 150528 engine.

1. Throttle cable assy.	8. Spark plug	15. Bearing	22. Piston
2. Air cleaner cover	9. Flywheel	16. Thrust washer	23. Retaining ring
3. Filter	10. Base plate	17. Crankshaft	24. Piston pin
4. Choke	11. Ignition module	18. Needle bearings (11)	25. Ring
5. Housing	12. Cylinder/crankcase	19. Crankcase cover	26. Gasket
6. Bracket	13. Seal	20. Crankcase cover bolts	27. Muffler
7. Carburetor	14. Retaining ring	21. Connecting rod	

con sealer around crankcase mating edges and install crankcase cover. Make certain all bearings and seals are correctly positioned in crankcase bearing bores. Tighten crankcase cover bolts to specified torque.

PISTON, PIN AND RING. A single ring aluminum piston is used. Piston is equipped with a locating pin in piston ring groove to prevent ring from turning. To remove piston, refer to CRANKSHAFT AND BEARING paragraphs. After connecting rod has been removed, remove retaining rings (23-Fig. TL3) and press piston pin from piston. Remove piston.

Inspect piston for scratches, scoring or excessive wear. Renew piston as required.

CONNECTING ROD. The one piece connecting rod rides on 11 needle bearings at crankshaft journal. Piston pin rides directly in connecting rod piston pin bore. To remove connecting rod, refer to CRANKSHAFT AND BEARINGS paragraphs.

CYLINDER. The die-cast aluminum cylinder has a chrome plated bore and is an integral part of one crankcase half. To remove cylinder, refer to CRANKSHAFT AND BEARINGS paragraphs. Cylinder should be renewed if it is scored, chrome is flaking off or aluminum is showing. If in doubt as to whether a spot is where aluminum is showing, try to scratch the area carefully. Aluminum will scratch easily and chrome plating will not.

TWO-STROKE ENGINES

MIXING GASOLINE AND OIL

Most two-stroke engines are lubricated by oil mixed with the gasoline. The manufacturers carefully determine which type of oil and how much oil should be mixed with the gasoline to provide the most desirable operation, then list these mixing instructions. Often two or more gasoline to oil ratios will be listed depending upon type of oil or severity of service. You should always follow the manufacturer's recommended mixing instructions, because mixing the wrong amount of oil or using the wrong type of oil can cause extensive engine damage. Too much oil can cause lower power, spark plug fouling and excessive carbon buildup. Not enough oil will cause inadequate lubrication and will probably result in scuffing, seizure or other forms of engine damage. Only use gasoline type and octane rating recommended by manufacturer. Never use gasoline which has been stored for a long period of time.

Accurate measurement of gasoline and oil is necessary to assure correct lubrication. Proper quantities of gasoline and oil for some of the more common mixture ratios are shown in the accompanying chart.

When mixing, use a separate approved safety container which is large enough to hold the desired amount of fuel with additional space for mixing. Pour about one-half of the required amount of gasoline into container, add the required amount of oil, then shake vigorously until completely mix-ed. Pour remaining amount of gasoline into container, then complete mixing by shaking. Serious engine damage can be caused by incomplete mixing. Never attempt to mix gasoline and oil in the unit's fuel tank.

Always observe safe handling practices when working with gasoline. Gasoline is extremely flammable. Do not smoke or allow sparks or open flame around fuel or in the presence of fuel vapors. Be sure area is well-ventilated. Observe fire prevention rules.

Ratio	Gasoline	Oil
10:1	.63 Gallon	½ Pint (237mL)
14:1	.88 Gallon	½ Pint (237mL)
16:1	1.00 Gallon	½ Pint (237mL)
20:1	1.25 Gallons	½ Pint (237mL)
30:1	1.88 Gallons	½ Pint (237mL)
32:1	2.00 Gallons	½ Pint (237mL)
50:1	3.13 Gallons	½ Pint (237mL)

Ratio	Gasoline	Oil
10:1	1 Gallon	.79 Pint (379mL)
14:1	1 Gallon	.57 Pint (270mL)
16:1	1 Gallon	.50 Pint (237mL)
20:1	1 Gallon	.40 Pint (189mL)
30:1	1 Gallon	.27 Pint (126mL)
32:1	1 Gallon	.25 Pint (118mL)
50:1	1 Gallon	.16 Pint (76mL)

METRIC CONVERSION

Cubic meters	= .02832	x Cubic Feet	Metric tons (1,000 kilograms)	x 1.1023	= Tons (2,000 Pounds)
Cubic meters	x 1.308	= Cubic Yards			
Cubic meters	= .765	x Cubic Yards			
Liters	x 61.023	= Cubic Inches	Metric tons (1,000 kilograms)	= .9072	x Tons (2,000 Pounds)
Liters	= .01639	x Cubic Inches			
Liters	x .26418	= U.S. Gallons			
Liters	= 3.7854	x U.S. Gallons	Kilowatts	= 1.3405	x Horsepower
Grams	x 15.4324	= Grains	Kilowatts	x .746	= Horsepower
Grams	= .0648	x Grains			
Grams	x .03527	= Ounces, avoirdupois	Millimeters	x .03937	= Inches
			Millimeters	= 25.400	x Inches
Grams	= 28.3495	x Ounces, avoirdupois	Meters	x 3.2809	= Feet
			Meters	= .3048	x Feet
Kilograms	x 2.2046	= Pounds	Kilometers	x .621377	= Miles
Kilograms	= .4536	x Pounds	Kilometers	= 1.6093	x Miles
Kilograms per square centimeter	x 14.2231	= Pounds per square Inch	Square centimeters	x .15500	= Square Inches
Kilograms per square centimeter	= .0703	x Pounds per square Inch	Square centimeters	= 6.4515	x Square Inches
			Square meters	x 10.76410	= Square Feet
Kilograms per cubic meter	x .06243	= Pounds per cubic Foot	Square meters	= .09290	x Square Feet
			Cubic centimeters	x .061025	= Cubic Inches
Kilograms per cubic meter	= 16.01890	x Pounds per cubic Foot	Cubic centimeters	= 16.3866	x Cubic Inches
			Cubic meters	x 35.3156	= Cubic Feet

Conversion table — Millimeters to Inches (decimal and fractional equivalents)

MM.	INCHES			MM.	INCHES			MM.	INCHES			MM.	INCHES			MM.	INCHES			MM.	INCHES		
1	0.0394	1/32	+	51	2.0079	2.0	+	101	3.9764	3 31/32	+	151	5.9449	5 15/16	+	201	7.9134	7 29/32	+	251	9.8819	9 7/8	+
2	0.0787	3/32	−	52	2.0472	2 1/16	+	102	4.0157	4 1/32	−	152	5.9842	5 31/32	+	202	7.9527	7 15/16	+	252	9.9212	9 29/32	+
3	0.1181	1/8	−	53	2.0866	2 3/32	−	103	4.0551	4 1/16	−	153	6.0236	6 1/32	−	203	7.9921	8.0	−	253	9.9606	9 31/32	
4	0.1575	5/32	+	54	2.1260	2 1/8	+	104	4.0945	4 3/32	+	154	6.0630	6 1/16	+	204	8.0315	8 1/32	+	254	10.0000	10.0	
5	0.1969	3/16	+	55	2.1654	2 5/32	+	105	4.1339	4 1/8	+	155	6.1024	6 3/32	+	205	8.0709	8 1/16	+	255	10.0393	10 1/32	+
6	0.2362	1/4	−	56	2.2047	2 7/32	−	106	4.1732	4 3/16	−	156	6.1417	6 5/32	−	206	8.1102	8 1/8	−	256	10.0787	10 5/64	−
7	0.2756	9/32	−	57	2.2441	2 1/4	−	107	4.2126	4 7/32	−	157	6.1811	6 3/16	−	207	8.1496	8 5/32	−	257	10.1181	10 1/8	−
8	0.3150	5/16	+	58	2.2835	2 9/32	+	108	4.2520	4 1/4	−	158	6.2205	6 7/32	−	208	8.1890	8 3/16	+	258	10.1575	10 5/32	+
9	0.3543	11/32	+	59	2.3228	2 5/16	+	109	4.2913	4 9/32	+	159	6.2598	6 1/4	+	209	8.2283	8 7/32	+	259	10.1968	10 3/16	+
10	0.3937	13/32	−	60	2.3622	2 3/8	−	110	4.3307	4 11/32	−	160	6.2992	6 5/16	−	210	8.2677	8 1/4	−	260	10.2362	10 1/4	−
11	0.4331	7/16	−	61	2.4016	2 13/32	−	111	4.3701	4 3/8	−	161	6.3386	6 11/32	−	211	8.3071	8 5/16	−	261	10.2756	10 9/32	−
12	0.4724	15/32	+	62	2.4409	2 7/16	+	112	4.4094	4 13/32	+	162	6.3779	6 3/8	+	212	8.3464	8 11/32	+	262	10.3149	10 5/16	+
13	0.5118	1/2	+	63	2.4803	2 15/32	+	113	4.4488	4 7/16	+	163	6.4173	6 13/32	+	213	8.3858	8 3/8	+	263	10.3543	10 11/32	+
14	0.5512	9/16	−	64	2.5197	2 17/32	−	114	4.4882	4 1/2	−	164	6.4567	6 15/32	−	214	8.4252	8 7/16	−	264	10.3937	10 13/32	−
15	0.5906	19/32	−	65	2.5591	2 9/16	−	115	4.5276	4 17/32	−	165	6.4961	6 1/2	−	215	8.4646	8 15/32	−	265	10.4330	10 7/16	−
16	0.6299	5/8	+	66	2.5984	2 19/32	+	116	4.5669	4 9/16	+	166	6.5354	6 17/32	+	216	8.5039	8 1/2	+	266	10.4724	10 15/32	+
17	0.6693	21/32	+	67	2.6378	2 5/8	+	117	4.6063	4 19/32	+	167	6.5748	6 9/16	+	217	8.5433	8 17/32	+	267	10.5118	10 1/2	+
18	0.7087	23/32	−	68	2.6772	2 11/16	−	118	4.6457	4 21/32	+	168	6.6142	6 5/8	−	218	8.5827	8 19/32	−	268	10.5512	10 9/16	−
19	0.7480	3/4	−	69	2.7165	2 23/32	−	119	4.6850	4 11/16	−	169	6.6535	6 21/32	−	219	8.6220	8 5/8	−	269	10.5905	10 19/32	−
20	0.7874	25/32	+	70	2.7559	2 3/4	+	120	4.7244	4 23/32	+	170	6.6929	6 11/16	+	220	8.6614	8 21/32	+	270	10.6299	10 5/8	+
21	0.8268	13/16	+	71	2.7953	2 25/32	+	121	4.7638	4 3/4	+	171	6.7323	6 23/32	+	221	8.7008	8 11/16	+	271	10.6693	10 21/32	+
22	0.8661	7/8	−	72	2.8346	2 27/32	−	122	4.8031	4 13/16	−	172	6.7716	6 25/32	−	222	8.7401	8 3/4	−	272	10.7086	10 23/32	−
23	0.9055	29/32	−	73	2.8740	2 7/8	−	123	4.8425	4 27/32	−	173	6.8110	6 13/16	+	223	8.7795	8 25/32	−	273	10.7480	10 3/4	−
24	0.9449	15/16	+	74	2.9134	2 29/32	+	124	4.8819	4 7/8	+	174	6.8504	6 27/32	+	224	8.8189	8 13/16	+	274	10.7874	10 25/32	+
25	0.9843	31/32	+	75	2.9528	2 15/16	+	125	4.9213	4 29/32	+	175	6.8898	6 7/8	+	225	8.8583	8 27/32	+	275	10.8268	10 13/16	+
26	1.0236	1 1/32	−	76	2.9921	3.0	−	126	4.9606	4 31/32	−	176	6.9291	6 15/16	−	226	8.8976	8 29/32	−	276	10.8661	10 7/8	−
27	1.0630	1 1/16	+	77	3.0315	3 1/32	+	127	5.0000	5.0		177	6.9685	6 31/32	−	227	8.9370	8 15/16	−	277	10.9055	10 29/32	−
28	1.1024	1 3/32	+	78	3.0709	3 1/16	+	128	5.0394	5 1/32	+	178	7.0079	7.0	+	228	8.9764	8 31/32	+	278	10.9449	10 15/16	+
29	1.1417	1 9/64	−	79	3.1102	3 1/8	−	129	5.0787	5 1/16	−	179	7.0472	7 1/16	−	229	9.0157	9 1/64	−	279	10.9842	10 31/32	+
30	1.1811	1 3/16	−	80	3.1496	3 5/32	−	130	5.1181	5 1/8	−	180	7.0866	7 3/32	−	230	9.0551	9 1/16	−	280	11.0236	11 1/32	−
31	1.2205	1 7/32	+	81	3.1890	3 3/16	+	131	5.1575	5 5/32	+	181	7.1260	7 1/8	+	231	9.0945	9 3/32	+	281	11.0630	11 1/16	+
32	1.2598	1 1/4	+	82	3.2283	3 7/32	+	132	5.1968	5 3/16	+	182	7.1653	7 5/32	+	232	9.1338	9 1/8	+	282	11.1023	11 1/8	+
33	1.2992	1 5/16	−	83	3.2677	3 9/32	−	133	5.2362	5 1/4	−	183	7.2047	7 7/32	−	233	9.1732	9 3/16	−	283	11.1417	11 5/32	−
34	1.3386	1 11/32	−	84	3.3071	3 5/16	−	134	5.2756	5 9/32	−	184	7.2441	7 1/4	−	234	9.2126	9 7/32	−	284	11.1811	11 3/16	−
35	1.3780	1 3/8	−	85	3.3465	3 11/32	+	135	5.3150	5 5/16	+	185	7.2835	7 9/32	+	235	9.2520	9 1/4	+	285	11.2204	11 7/32	+
36	1.4173	1 13/32	+	86	3.3858	3 3/8	+	136	5.3543	5 11/32	+	186	7.3228	7 5/16	+	236	9.2913	9 9/32	+	286	11.2598	11 1/4	+
37	1.4567	1 15/32	−	87	3.4252	3 7/16	−	137	5.3937	5 13/32	−	187	7.3622	7 3/8	−	237	9.3307	9 11/32	−	287	11.2992	11 5/16	−
38	1.4961	1 1/2	−	88	3.4646	3 15/32	−	138	5.4331	5 7/16	−	188	7.4016	7 13/32	−	238	9.3701	9 3/8	−	288	11.3386	11 11/32	−
39	1.5354	1 17/32	+	89	3.5039	3 1/2	+	139	5.4724	5 15/32	+	189	7.4409	7 7/16	+	239	9.4094	9 13/32	+	289	11.3779	11 3/8	+
40	1.5748	1 9/16	+	90	3.5433	3 17/32	+	140	5.5118	5 1/2	+	190	7.4803	7 15/32	+	240	9.4488	9 7/16	+	290	11.4173	11 13/32	+
41	1.6142	1 5/8	−	91	3.5827	3 19/32	−	141	5.5512	5 9/16	−	191	7.5197	7 17/32	−	241	9.4882	9 1/2	−	291	11.4567	11 15/32	−
42	1.6535	1 21/32	−	92	3.6220	3 5/8	−	142	5.5905	5 19/32	−	192	7.5590	7 9/16	−	242	9.5275	9 17/32	−	292	11.4960	11 1/2	−
43	1.6929	1 11/16	+	93	3.6614	3 21/32	+	143	5.6299	5 5/8	+	193	7.5984	7 19/32	+	243	9.5669	9 9/16	+	293	11.5354	11 17/32	+
44	1.7323	1 23/32	+	94	3.7008	3 11/16	+	144	5.6693	5 21/32	+	194	7.6378	7 5/8	−	244	9.6063	9 19/32	+	294	11.5748	11 9/16	+
45	1.7717	1 25/32	−	95	3.7402	3 3/4	−	145	5.7087	5 23/32	−	195	7.6772	7 11/16	−	245	9.6457	9 21/32	−	295	11.6142	11 5/8	−
46	1.8110	1 13/16	−	96	3.7795	3 25/32	−	146	5.7480	5 3/4	−	196	7.7165	7 23/32	+	246	9.6850	9 11/16	+	296	11.6535	11 21/32	+
47	1.8504	1 27/32	+	97	3.8189	3 13/16	+	147	5.7874	5 25/32	+	197	7.7559	7 3/4	−	247	9.7244	9 23/32	+	297	11.6929	11 11/16	+
48	1.8898	1 7/8	+	98	3.8583	3 27/32	+	148	5.8268	5 13/16	+	198	7.7953	7 25/32	+	248	9.7638	9 3/4	+	298	11.7323	11 23/32	+
49	1.9291	1 15/16	−	99	3.8976	3 29/32	−	149	5.8661	5 7/8	−	199	7.8346	7 27/32	−	249	9.8031	9 13/16	−	299	11.7716	11 25/32	−
50	1.9685	1 31/32	−	100	3.9370	3 15/16	−	150	5.9055	5 29/32	−	200	7.8740	7 7/8	−	250	9.8425	9 27/32	−	300	11.8110	11 13/16	−

NOTE. The + or − sign indicates that the decimal equivalent is larger or smaller than the fractional equivalent.

MANUFACTURER'S ADDRESSES

ALPINA
Alpina North America
Box 112
Northport, WA 99157
(604) 367-9202

BLACK & DECKER
Black & Decker (U.S.) Inc.
10 North Park Drive
Hunt Valley, MD 21030
(301) 683-7975

BUNTON
Bunton Company
P.O. Box 33247
4303 Poplar Level Road
Louisville, KY 40232
(502) 966-0550

JOHN DEERE
Deere & Company
John Deere Road
Moline, IL 61265
(309) 752-4613

ECHO
Echo, Inc.
400 Oakwood Rd.
Lake Zurich, IL 60047
(312) 540-8400

GREEN MACHINE
HMC
20710 S. Alameda
Long Beach, CA 90810
(213) 603-9888

HOFFCO
Hoffco, Inc.
358 N.W. F. Street
Richmond, IN 47374
(317) 966-8161

HOMELITE
Homelite Corporation
P.O. Box 7047
Charlotte, NC 28217
(704) 588-3200

HUSQVARNA
Husqvarna Power Products
907 West Irving Park Rd.
Itasca, IL 60143
(312) 773-2777

KAAZ
Kaaz America Corporation
10035 S. Pioneer Blvd.
Santa Fe Springs, CA 90670
(213) 949-9454

LAWN BOY
Lawn Boy Product Group
5846 Distribution Dr.
Memphis, TN 38181
(901) 795-9204

MARUYAMA
Maruyama U.S., Inc.
15436 NE 95th Street
Redmond, WA 98052
(206) 885-0811

McCULLOCH
McCulloch Corporation
P.O. Box 92180
Los Angeles, CA 90009
(213) 827-7111

PIONEER/PARTNER
Pioneer Partner Company
909 West Irving Park Rd.
Itasca, IL 60143
(312) 773-2824

POULAN/WEED EATER/YARD PRO
Poulan/Weed Eater, Div.
WCI, Inc.
5020 Flournoy-Lucas Rd.
Shreveport, LA 71129
(318) 687-0100

ROBIN
Robin Products Group
U.S. Importer - Carswell Import &
Marketing Assoc.
3750 N. Liberty St.
Winston Salem, NC 27115
(919) 767-9432

ROPER/RALLY
Roper Corporation
12052 Middleground Rd.
Savannah, GA 31419
(912) 925-8010

RYAN
Ryan Product Group
5846 Distribution Dr.
Memphis, TN 38181
(901) 795-9204

SACHS-DOLMAR
Sachs Dolmar Division
P.O. Box 78526
Shreveport, LA 71137
(318) 226-0081

SEARS
Sears, Roebuck & Co.
Sears Tower
Chicago, IL 60684

SHINDAIWA
Shindaiwa, Inc.
11975 S.W. Herman Rd.
Sherwood, OR 97140
(503) 692-3070

SNAPPER
Snapper Power Equipment
Macon Highway
McDonough, GA 30253
(404) 957-9141

STIHL
Stihl, Inc.
536 Viking Drive
Virginia Beach, VA 23452
(804) 486-8444

TANAKA
Tanaka Kogyo (USA) Co.
22121 Crystal Creek Blvd. S.E.
Bothell, WA 98012
(206) 481-2000

TML
Trinden Marketing
575 Clarke Rd.
London, Ont.
Canada N5V 2E1

TORO
The Toro Company
8111 Lyndale Ave. South
Minneapolis, MN 54420
(612) 887-8801

WARDS
Montgomery Ward
Montgomery Ward Plaza
Chicago, IL 60671
(312) 467-2624

WESTERN AUTO
Western Auto
2107 Grand
Kansas City, MO 64108
(816) 346-4000

YAZOO
Yazoo Mfg. Co. Inc.
3650 Bay Street
Jackson, MS 39216
(601) 366-6421

MAINTENANCE LOG

MAINTENANCE LOG

MAINTENANCE LOG

NOTES

NOTES

NOTES